에듀윌과 함께 시작하면,
당신도 합격할 수 있습니다!

편입 합격 후 대학에 진학했으나 학과 전공이 맞지 않아
휴학 후 다시 편입을 결심하여 서강대에 합격한 3학년 대학생

직장생활을 하며 2년간 편입공부를 해
인서울 대학에 당당히 합격한 30대 직장인

대학진학을 포기하고 20살 때 학점은행제 독학사를 통해 전문학사를 취득하고
편입을 준비하여 합격한 21살 전문학사 수험생

군복무 중 취업에 대해 고민하다 공대계열 학과로 편입을 결심하여
1년 만에 한양대에 합격한 복학생

누구나 합격할 수 있습니다.
시작하겠다는 '다짐' 하나면 충분합니다.

마지막 페이지를 덮으면,

**에듀윌과 함께
편입 합격이 시작됩니다.**

업계 최고! 완벽한 교수 라인업
스타 교수진 대규모 입성

3년 연속 서성한반 100% 합격자 배출 에듀윌 교수진에
과목별 1타 교수진 대규모 입성

기본이론부터 문제풀이까지 6개월 핵심압축 커리큘럼

기본이론 완성	핵심유형 완성	기출심화 완성	적중실전 완성	파이널
기본이론 압축 정리	핵심포인트 집중 이해	기출문제 실전훈련	출제유력 예상문제 풀이	대학별 예상 모의고사

* 서성한반(P사) 교수진 전격입성 | 2019~2021년 서성한반(P사) 수강생 합격자 서울소재 20개 대학 기준 3년 연속 100% 합격자 배출
  (서울소재 20개 대학: 연세, 고려, 서강, 성균관, 한양, 중앙, 이화, 한국외, 경희, 서울시립, 건국, 국민, 동국, 숭실, 홍익, 숙명, 세종, 명지, 광운, 서울여)
* 1타 교수진 : W사 2022년 프리패스 수강 데이터 산출 (저스틴, 권윤아, 고하늬, 홍석기 2022.01~2022.12)

에듀윌 편입 시리즈
전격 출간

3년 연속 100% 합격자 배출 교수진이 만든 교재로
합격의 차이를 직접 경험해 보세요.

* 본 교재 이미지는 변동될 수 있습니다.
* 여러분의 합격을 도와줄 편입 시리즈 정보는 에듀윌 홈페이지(www.eduwill.net)에서 확인하세요.

노베이스 수험생을 위한
쌩기초 풀-패키지 무료배포

클라쓰가 남다른 1타 교수진으로 새롭게 탄생!
한 달이면 기초 탈출! 신규회원이면 누구나 신청 가능!

신규강의
업데이트
40만원
상당

24만원
상당

1타 교수진의 쉽고 알찬 쌩기초 입문 강의

· 1타 교수진 노하우 총 집합
· 기초 지식부터 입문 이론까지
· 초단기 쌩 노베이스 완벽 탈출

토익 베이직 RC/LC 강의

· 첫 토익부터 700+ 한 달이면 끝
· 편입 공인영어 성적 준비를 위한 토익 기초 지원
· 쉬운 토익 공식! 에듀윌 토익 강의

합격비법 가이드

· 대학별 최신 편입 전형 제공
· 최신 편입 관련 정보 모음
· 합격전략 및 합격자 수기 제공

기출어휘 체크북

· 편입생이 꼭 알아야 할 편입 어휘의 모든 것
· 최신 기출 어휘를 빈도순으로 구성
· 3,000개의 어휘를 한 권으로 압축

편입 합격!
에듀윌과 함께하면 현실이 됩니다.

쌩기초 풀패키지
무료 이벤트

* 1타 교수진 : W사 2022년 프리패스 수강 데이터 산출 (저스틴, 권윤아, 고하늬, 홍석기 2022.01~2022.12)
* 본 혜택과 경로는 예고 없이 변경되거나 대체될 수 있습니다.

에듀윌 편입 솔루션

문법 BASIC

편저자 에듀윌 편입 LAB

GRAMMAR BASIC

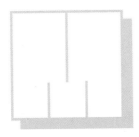
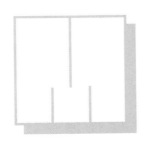

문법이 어려워?

이 책을 봐!

편입 최초
프리미엄 해설 수록

eduwill

Preface 이 책의 **머리말**

안녕하세요. 에듀윌 편입 LAB입니다.

에듀윌 편입 솔루션 문법 Basic을 쓰며 가장 많이 했던 생각은 한 가지였습니다.
그것은 바로 문법을 어려워하고 싫어하는 학생들에게 어떻게 하면 흥미를 잃지 않고
눈에 보이는 실력 향상을 이끌어 낼 수 있냐 하는 것이었습니다.
'내가 영어를 못했을 때 이렇게 도움을 받았더라면 ....'
이와 같은 고민을 토대로 수정에 수정을 거치다 보니 예상했던 것보다 훨씬 더 오랜
시간이 걸렸습니다.
그 결과 세상에 나온 이 책은 편입 문법 문제집의 패러다임을 바꿀 수 있는 책이라고
자신 있게 말씀드릴 수 있습니다.

에듀윌 편입 솔루션 문법 Basic은 최근 10년 내에 출제된 기출문제를 각 파트별로
구성해 놓았습니다.
또한 영어를 잘하는 사람이 아닌 영어를 못하는 사람의 기준으로 혼자서도 문제를
풀고 궁금증을 해결할 수 있도록 시중에는 존재하지 않는 형태의 해설이 제공되어
있습니다.

부디 **에듀윌 편입 솔루션 문법 Basic**을 통하여 학생들 개개인의 실력이 향상되어 그
렇게 약했던 문법에서 고득점을 받아 합격의 기쁨을 누리시길 기원합니다.

감사합니다.

Foreword 이 책의 구성

문제

문제편은 크게 〈❶ 파트별 문제〉, 〈❷ Review Test〉의 형태로 구성되어 있습니다.

같은 문제를 Review Test라는 이름으로 반복하여 수록해 놓은 이유는 Guide(이 책의 활용법)에 서술해 놓았으니 최대한의 실력 향상을 위해 반드시 읽어 보기를 권장합니다.

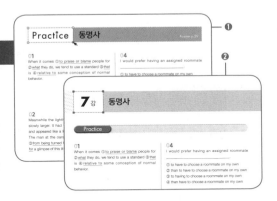

정답과 해설

정답과 해설편의 모든 문제는 예시와 같이 〈❶ 정답의 단서(형광펜)〉, 〈❷ 문장의 구조 분석〉, 〈❸ 각 보기 설명〉의 형태로 구성되어 있습니다.

<구조 분석 표시의 예>

영어는 그 어떤 언어보다 수식어구가 발달한 언어입니다. 뼈대와 수식어구만 잘 구분할 줄 알아도 글의 구조가 보입니다. 그래서 구조 분석은 영어 공부의 최우선 순위입니다. 해설에서 표기된 구조 분석의 약속은 이렇습니다.

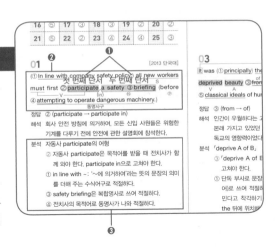

- 문장의 뼈대를 구성하는 성분: S(주어), V(동사), O(목적어), I.O(간접목적어), D.O(직접목적어), C(보어), O.C(목적보어)
- 품사 구분: Ⓝ(명사), ⓐ(형용사), ⓓ(부사), Ⓟ(전치사), 삼각형(접속사)
- 네모 괄호: [명사구/ 명사절]
  영어는 여러 개의 단어를 합쳐 하나의 명사로 쓸 수 있습니다. 문장에서 여러 단어가 합쳐져 길어진 형태의 명사를 [네모 괄호]로 표시해 놓았으니, 만약 [네모 괄호]가 있다면 아무리 길어도 그 자체를 하나의 명사로 보시면 됩니다.
- 둥근 괄호: (수식어구)
  영어는 수식어구가 발달한 언어이기 때문에 문장의 뼈대와 수식어구를 구분할 수 있어야 합니다. 구조 분석에서 (둥근 괄호)가 있다면 문장의 의미를 돕기 위한 수식 성분의 역할입니다.

Guide 이 책의 **활용법**

1. 예습법

1-1 각 파트별 이론을 공부한 후, 해당 파트의 문제를 풀어 봅니다.

1-2 시간을 정해 놓지 않고 배운 이론을 최대한 떠올리며 풀어 봅니다.
많이 틀려도 좋습니다. 파트별 문제 풀이는 당장의 점수를 올리는 것이 목적이 아니라, 문제를 풀며 그동안 배운 이론을 익히는 것이 주된 목적입니다.

1-3 문제를 풀 때, 자세히 구조 분석을 하며 정답의 단서라고 생각되는 것을 표시합니다.

2. 복습법

2-1 채점을 합니다. 본인이 표시한 단서와 해설지에 표시된 정답의 단서가 같은지 확인합니다.
모든 문법 문제에는 정답으로 향하는 단서가 존재합니다. 단, 하나의 단서만 가지고 정답을 찾을 수 있는 문제도 있는 반면에, 두 개 이상의 단서를 통해 정답을 찾아야 하는 문제도 있습니다. 정답 단서 표시는 이 책의 구성(p.3)에 설명되어 있습니다.

2-2 구조 분석을 확인합니다.
해설편의 구조 분석과 내가 했던 구조 분석이 어느 정도 일치되는지 확인합니다. 영어는 구조가 보여야 문법 문제를 풀어낼 수 있고, 독해와 문장 완성에서 글을 읽을 수 있습니다.

2-3 <Review Test> 다시 풀기
이 책은 기존 문법 문제집들과 다르게 후반부(p.134)에 앞에서 풀어 본 문제와 동일한 〈Review Test〉가 수록되어 있습니다. 〈Review Test〉는 해당 파트의 문제를 풀고 풀이까지 완벽하게 하고 난 뒤에 적어도 3~5일 이상의 기간이 지나고 다시 그 파트의 문제를 풀어 보라는 용도입니다. 문제를 한 번 풀어 봤다고 혹은 열심히 풀이했다고 그 지식이 온전히 머릿속에 들어갈 수 없습니다. 풀이를 했음에도 불구하고 〈Review Test〉를 풀 때 여전히 똑같은 문제를 틀릴 수 있습니다. 그때 포기하는 것이 아니라 오히려 '이 게 나의 부족한 부분이라는 것'을 깨닫고 다시 복습하는 시간을 가진다면 경쟁자들보다 한발 앞서 나갈 수 있으니 귀찮더라도 꼭 〈Review Test〉도 풀어 보기를 권장합니다.

Contents 이 책의 **차례**

1강 동사

동사의 어형이란?

동사의 어형은 각 동사가 가지고 있는 쓰임새를 말한다. 한국어는 동사에서 문장이 끝나지만, 영어는 동사에서 문장이 시작되는 언어라는 것을 명심해야 한다. 그러다 보니 영어의 동사는 각각의 어형(쓰임새)을 가지고 있는데 문제에서 바로 이 부분을 주로 묻게 된다. 그래서 문제로 묻는 각 동사의 어형을 익힌다는 생각으로 문제를 풀어야 한다.

동사 주요 포인트

01 1형식 자동사 뒤 전치사를 지우고 묻는 유형
ex. He *complained* me. (×) / He **complained to** me. (○)

02 1형식 자동사 뒤 전치사의 선택을 묻는 유형
ex. The family *consists with* two people. (×) / The family **consists of** two people. (○)

03 2형식 오감동사 뒤 형용사와 부사의 선택을 묻는 유형
ex. Mary *looks happily*. (×) / Mary **looks happy**. (○)

04 3형식 타동사 뒤 전치사를 쓰고 묻는 유형
ex. She *discussed about* the matter. (×) / She **discussed** the matter. (○)

05 3형식 타동사의 목적어 뒤 전치사의 선택을 묻는 유형
ex. He *prevented* me *to go* out. (×) / He **prevented** me **from going** out. (○)

06 3형식 타동사의 목적어 자리에 준동사(to R ~/R-ing)의 선택을 묻는 유형
ex. Tom *enjoys to watch* movies. (×) / Tom **enjoys watching** movies. (○)

07 5형식 타동사의 목적보어 앞 to be, as의 유무를 묻는 유형
ex. She *regards* him *to be* stupid. (×) / She **regards** him **as** stupid. (○)

08 5형식 타동사의 목적보어 자리에서 준동사(to R ~/R ~/R-ing)의 선택을 묻는 유형
ex. He *made* me *to wash* the car. (×) / He **made** me **wash** the car. (○)

09 5형식 타동사의 '가목적어–진목적어'를 묻는 유형
ex. She found *easy to get* up early. (×) / She found **it** easy **to get** up early. (○)

10 헷갈리기 쉬운 자동사와 타동사의 구분을 묻는 유형
ex. The sun *raises* on the east. (×) / The sun **rises** on the east. (○)

Practice **01** 동사

01

① In line with company safety policy, all new workers must first ② participate a safety ③ briefing before ④ attempting to operate dangerous machinery.

02

Men who ① enter into ② female-dominated fields easily ③ move up to supervisory positions, a phenomenon ④ known as the glass escalator.

03

It was ① principally the influence of Christianity ② that deprived beauty ③ from the central place it ④ had in ⑤ classical ideals of human excellence.

04

Wall Street analysts _____ optimistic about the performance of value stocks.

① reached   ② resulted

③ remained   ④ revealed

05

The sun ① was ② raising ③ over the mountain when I ④ rose out of bed and ⑤ sat at the table.

06

The committee didn't really _____ meeting a lot of opposition to the new plan for traffic control.

① anticipate   ② predict
③ expect   ④ prepare

07

Visitors to the zoo are requested to refrain _____ feeding the animals in their cages.

① from   ② with
③ to   ④ of

08

① Unbeknown to my parents, I took several college courses in creative writing and was ② excelling. After reading one of my short stories, my first creative writing teacher decided that I was ③ to be a writer. I decided ④ following my passion instead of obeying my family's decree.

09

My father believed that family members should help each other and made us _____ some chores every Saturdays.

① to do   ② does
③ do   ④ did

10

It's ① very hard to get people ② examine their life unless you ③ remind them it's not going to ④ last forever.

11

The most underrated ① of the major senses, smell has direct access ② at the more primitive, or basic, parts of the brain. Brain imaging techniques ③ have shown that smell can activate mood, emotion, and memory without ④ being consciously perceived.

12

Because the rain ① fell ② all night, the ③ clogged drain pipe ④ bursted and ⑤ flooded the house.

13

We ① decided to go on a trip to the mountains but forgot ② taking the map, ③ so we stopped ④ to buy ⑤ one at a gas station.

14

A ① proposed law ② would make the illegal consumption or sale of dog meat ③ punishing by ④ a fine of up to 5,000 euros.

15

In ① the 1880s, the public's ② well-justified skepticism about doctors encouraged ③ leading medical professors, many of whom ④ had studied in France and Germany, ⑤ began restructuring American medical education.

16

① As more and more teenagers socialize ② online, middle school and high school teachers are increasingly seeing a ③ breezy form of ④ Internet English ⑤ to jump from e-mail into schoolwork.

17

① Anticipating a future ② in which millions of Americans will prefer to ③ shopping in the security of their living rooms, the mall industry is experiencing a ④ full-blown mid-life crisis.

18

People ① with strong personal relationships are 50% ② more likely to outlive ③ than those ④ without.

19

The study ① concerned itself mainly with ② the affects of ③ anxiety on decision making ④ in high-risk situations.

20

While most American architects in the early 1900s looked to Europe for ideas, Frank Lloyd Wright found Japanese design and art _____.

① inspire
② more inspiring
③ is more inspiring
④ are more inspiring

21

One ① third to ② nearly half of the people in the majority of countries ③ surveyed admitted they wanted ④ their spouse ⑤ losing weight.

22

Physicists often find _____ to separate a beam of particles into a spectrum according to their energy.

① it is used   ② it useful

③ useful   ④ its use

23

The company's attorney _____ to them that we should use caution in deciding what information to release to the public.

① notified   ② informed

③ told   ④ said

24

Based on an analysis of the most successful ① executives' schedules and activities, I discovered ② seven practices you ③ should seriously consider ④ to adopt in order to make the most of your morning.

25

The book fair ① outdoors was ② to be opened yesterday, but they were obliged ③ to postponing it ④ on account of the sudden blizzard.

01

Nowadays some might find emotional renewal in pleasant parks and natural lands, but the disadvantaged _____.

① cannot afford reaching to them
② cannot afford to reach them
③ could not afford to reach to them
④ could not afford to reaching them

02

① Using specialized cells, plants can sense gravity ② and redistribute hormones, ③ called auxins, to stimulate growth and allow vital features of the plant ④ develop. However, a big puzzle is ⑤ how this transport process occurs at a cellular level.

03

In ① what appears to be a hallway, a hooded detainee seems ② be handcuffed ③ in an awkward position ④ atop two boxes.

04

① In the draft, ② obtained by the Associated Press, the Security Council demands that all parties in Syria immediately ③ to stop any violence irrespective ④ of where it comes from.

05

① Having failed ② creating a consensus, the boss asked ③ that the decision ④ be put off.

06

① In addition the founding fathers of America ② opposed a strong government ③ because it might ④ interfere people's freedom.

07

William H. Johnson's ① artistic debt to Scandinavia is evident in paintings that ② range from sensitive portraits of citizens in his wife's Danish home, Kerteminde, ③ and ④ awe-inspiring views of fjords and mountain peaks ⑤ in the western and northern regions of Norway.

08

More efforts should be made to attract ① highly skilled foreign workers to help keep the country's growth engine ② to move. A serious consideration ③ should be given to a proposal to permit foreigners ④ who have stayed here for more than 10 years.

09

"The evolutionary biologist," Huxley says, "is tempted to ask ① whether the aim should not be ② to let the mammal ③ die within us, so as the more effectually to permit the man ④ live."

10

The superintendent of the jail, who was standing ① apart from the rest of warders, ② moodily ③ prodding the gravel with his stick, ④ rose his head ⑤ at the sound.

11

Yesterday I had to have my car ＿＿＿＿＿＿ away by the police, since it suddenly stopped on a highway.

① towing   ② tow
③ towed   ④ town

12

① Although a multinational investigation team blamed the North ② to sink the South Korean warship Cheonan ③ in a torpedo attack, North Korea denies ④ its involvement.

13

Although you must get off while the bus is ① being cleaned, you may ② leave your suitcases and ③ other belongings ④ laying on your seats.

14

Yet these truths are ① no solace against the kind of alienation that comes of ② being ever the suspect, a fearsome entity ③ with whom pedestrians avoid ④ to make eye contact.

15

① A knowledgeable and open-minded ② evaluation of your current lifestyle might ③ lead to decide to make ④ a few fundamental changes.

16

The exact cause of ① aging is unknown, ② but genetic factors ③ are known to ④ influence on longevity.

17

The president's declaration of an emergency was a procedural maneuver to make it easier for hospitals, should they be swamped with sick people, _____ them to alternate sites for triage and treatment.

① transfer   ② to transfer
③ will transfer   ④ transferring

18

The psychologist William James ① believed that ② facial expressions not only ③ provide a visible sign of an emotion ④ but also actually ⑤ contribute the feeling itself.

19

They admitted nearly 200 people, all of whom sat on simple chairs and ① who could easily hear the accompanying music ② playing on piano by a local girl, who ③ would attempt to match the music ④ to the tone of the particular scene.

20

Students dislike _____ to fill an hour or two hours each night with meaningless homework.

① have been　　　　② having
③ to have　　　　　④ to have been

21

However prepared or well-meaning parents may be, it is difficult for them to acknowledge that their children have grown up, but it is extremely important for them to let the children _____ their own mind.

① to make up
② to making up
③ making them up
④ make up

22

You ① can't just close your eyes and wish us ② back in Kansas among kindly folk who obligingly ③ conform outdated expectations ④ of age.

23

Maria Callas was a woman for whom the term prima donna could have been invented. She was an American-born Greek soprano and made her professional debut in 1942, and since then she _____ to be a singer-actress.

① long considered herself
② was long herself considered
③ long considering herself
④ herself long considering

24

Microfinance ① enables village people in ② developing countries ③ borrow ④ small amounts of money from Microfinance Institutions ⑤ in order to set up small community businesses.

25

As more ① is understood about the genetics and the brains of people who ② stutter, researchers hope that medication aimed directly ③ by the disorder eventually will ④ become available.

2강 시제

시제란?

행위가 있었던 시점을 동사에 나타내는 표현이다. 따라서 동사에 밑줄이 있다면 시제를 따져봐야 한다. 단, 시제 문제를 풀 때 학생들이 빠지는 가장 큰 함정은 바로 한국어의 해석이다. 엄밀히 말하자면, 한국어의 해석과 영어의 시제는 전혀 상관이 없다. 그렇기 때문에 한국어로 해석을 하여 영어의 시제를 따진다는 생각 자체를 버려야 하는 것이 시제를 풀어내는 요령 중 가장 중요하다.

시제 주요 포인트

01 한국어의 해석으로 영어의 시제를 파악하지 않는다.

02 시점부사와 동사의 시제 일치를 묻는 유형

   ex. Jane *missed* him *since* she graduated. (×) / Jane **has missed** him **since** she graduated. (○)

03 진행 절대 불가능 동사를 묻는 유형

   ex. The pen *is belonging* to me. (×) / The pen **belongs** to me. (○)

04 시간·조건의 뜻을 가진 부사절에서 현재시제가 미래를 대신하는 유형

   ex. When he *will come*, I will go out. (×) / When he **comes**, I will go out. (○)

05 주절 동사와 종속절의 시제 비교를 묻는 유형

   ex. He *said* that she *has joined* the team. (×) / He **said** that she **had joined** the team. (○)

01

Tim Morrison, ① who tried to hang ② himself after years of ③ being bullied, ④ has died last Monday.

02

There _____ several attempts to define morality since Middle Ages.

① has been   ② have been
③ was   ④ were

03

The instructor had gone ① over the problems ② many times ③ before the students ④ will take the final examination.

04

The Greeks began to ① write from left to right around the fifth century B.C. because they ② increasingly believe that right was "good" and left was "bad." This belief ③ is still common in many countries today, and ④ left-handed people suffer because of it.

05

By the end of the 1800s, the ① output of ② European artists, writers and scientists ③ have accelerated to the point where ④ it dwarfed the ⑤ productiveness of the 1700s.

06

What causes plants to bloom? Although you may think that plants _____ based on the amount of sunlight they receive, they actually bloom according to the amount of uninterrupted darkness.

① flower   ② flowered

③ flowering   ④ to flower

07

Mr. Kim will already _____ his presentation by the time you reach the convention center.

① have finished   ② finished

③ finish   ④ have been finished

08

He could remember ①driving along the road just ②before the accident ③happens, but he couldn't ④remember the accident itself.

09

I ①worked with Peter ②for the past five years and I always found him ③to be a lawyer of ④the highest caliber.

10

When the Supreme Court ①rules in 1896 ②in favor of the South's "separate but equal" racial doctrine, the federal government ③put its stamp of approval ④on state laws requiring cradle-to-grave segregation of the races.

11

Harrisburg, ①a transportation center in the ②days of riverboat ③traffic, has been Pennsylvania's capital ④in 1812.

12

Most historians ①agree that the English alphabet descended ②from ancient Egyptian hieroglyphics that were first recorded ③more than 5,000 years ④before.

13

A research report from the Ministry of Knowledge Economy also showed that ①prolonged global recession caused the nation's exports ②to slow and ③dampened consumer sentiment, which also negatively ④affect labor productivity.

14

①By the time Ryan graduates, he ②has spent fours years in college and ③a total of sixteen years of his life in school. Like many students, Ryan believes that the time and money ④spent on his education ⑤will pay off.

15

When you ①will realize your bullies will be offended ②no matter what you do, you'll ③stop trying to please ④them.

16

This enrichment process was ①what determined the composition of the Solar System 4.5 billion years ago, and ultimately ②makes possible the chemistry of life ③on Earth ④as per the "Big Bang" theory.

17

Such Bohemianism could ①be construed as affectation, and it's possible that early in life Katherine Mathilda Winton ②has deliberately cultivated a style that would ③signal her disregard for ④a world she found stultifying.

18

In the eight hundred years ①since his death, people ②sought in vain for the grave of Genghis Khan, the 13th-century conqueror and imperial ruler who, at the time of his death, ③occupied the largest contiguous empire, ④stretching from the Caspian Sea to the Pacific.

19

I met Kerry years ago when he first ①became an assistant professor. We both taught biology, but Kerry ②liked to use a lot of mathematics in his teaching. This ③upset his students, who ④believe that they would escape math by studying biology.

20

①Once marine biologists had determined the precise migratory route of the California whale, they ②are finding that the distance covered was ③much greater than ④had been thought.

21

Our superior location, just next to the Jackson Wildlife Preserve, _____ a beautiful natural environment that will help you achieve total well-being.

① ensures
② would ensure
③ had ensured
④ did ensure

22

①In the coming years, the Internet will have ②an even greater impact on the way we shop, get our news, ③entertained, conduct financial affairs, and ④talk with friends and family.

23

He ①was ultimately ②known to millions ③who had no clear idea of what he ④has done.

24

In an attempt to prevent students from concentrating ①only on school tests, the Seoul Office of Education said that ②it was ③considering abolishing exams and ④replace them with essays to encourage creativity.

25

After a couple of environmental researchers had drawn diagrams in ①their notebooks and ②wrote explanations of the formations ③which they had observed, they returned to their campsite ④to compare notes.

3강 수동태

능동태와 수동태란?

태의 종류에는 능동태와 수동태가 있다. 이 둘의 차이는 바로 주어가 기준점이 된다. 주어가 동사의 행위를 하는 주체라면 능동태로 표현하고, 주어가 동사의 행위를 당하는 대상이라면 수동태로 표현한다. 다만 '태'라는 것은 동사에만 표현할 수 있다는 것을 기억해야 한다.

ex. Tom made the desk. (톰이 그 책상을 만든 주체이므로 능동태 동사로 표현한다.)

= The desk was made by Tom. (책상이 톰에 의해 만들어진 대상이므로 수동태로 표현한다.)

결국 수동태의 출제 포인트는 단순하다. 바로 능동태와 수동태의 선택을 묻는다. 동사에 밑줄이 있다면 반드시 태를 따져 보고 넘어가야 한다는 것을 명심하고 접근해야 한다.

수동태 주요 포인트

01 3형식 동사의 능동태와 수동태의 구분을 묻는 유형

ex. The matter *discussed* in detail. (×) / The matter **was discussed** in detail. (○)

02 5형식 동사의 능동태와 수동태의 구분을 묻는 유형

ex. The subject *calls* physics. (×) / The subject **is called** physics. (○)

He *was asked play* the game. (×) / He **was asked to play** the game. (○)

03 수동태가 불가능한 자동사를 묻는 유형

ex. We *was arrived* here. (×) / We **arrived** here. (○)

04 자·타동사와 상관없이 수동태 절대 불가능 동사를 묻는 유형

ex. Water *is consisted* of oxygen and hydrogen. (×)

Water **consists** of oxygen and hydrogen. (○)

05 타동사구(자동사+전치사)의 수동태를 묻는 유형

ex. He *was laughed* by her. (×) / He **was laughed at** by her. (○)

01

① Because gorillas have often been killed ② to permit the capture of their young for zoos and humans have recently been ③ occupied more and more of their habitat, gorillas are now threatened ④ with extinction.

02

Professor Bueno de Mesquita adds that authoritarian governments around the world, ① including China's, ② are shown that they can reap the benefits of economic development while ③ resisting any pressure ④ to relax their power.

03

Art has not always been what we think ① it is today. An object regarded as Art today may not ② have perceived as such when it was first made, ③ nor was the person who ④ made it necessarily regarded as an artist.

04

Typically, ① more trade fairs ② are holding in the fall than in ③ any other month ④ because of the weather in this region.

05

The researchers are developing sensors that ① could be placed on vehicles that regularly cross a bridge, ② such as city buses and police cars. These ③ could be measured how the bridge ④ responds to the vehicle ⑤ moving across it, and report any suspicious changes.

06

Deviance is any non-conformist behavior which ① disapproved of by society or a social group, ② whether it is ③ illegal or not. It is ④ norm-breaking behavior, and can range from being ⑤ eccentric to criminal activity.

07

In 1999, an eighteen-year-old participant died in a gene therapy experiment. His death showed that the researchers _____ the risks of their procedure.

① have not adequately assessed
② have not been adequately assessed
③ had not adequately assessed
④ had not been adequately assessed

08

In Borneo, ① where I was born and ② grown up, I have worked ③ in tropical conditions cutting survey lines through a forest that was ④ like a jungle.

09

A total eclipse can ① be lasted up to 7 minutes, ② during ③ which time the moon's shadow moves across Earth at a rate of about 0.6 kilometers ④ per second.

10

We ① take ethical investment very seriously. Recently we ② were involved in a project to build a large dam in the Asian country of Paradiso. We discovered that ③ large numbers of farming people ④ would force to leave the area flooded by the dam.

11

The right hemisphere of the human brain is less ① crucial to language production and ② appears to be ③ more concerned the ④ creation of images.

12

① About three hundred years before Caesar, human geography ② treated ③ only in conjunction ④ with description of particular areas.

13

It is a fact ① that pesticides ② considered unsuitable in rich countries ③ are remained in use in many poor ④ ones.

14

The attack ① was occurred ② while they were customers at a ③ convenience store ④ in March 2012.

15

So far from being a misfortune, poverty may, by vigorous self-help, _____ into a blessing.

① be converted
② have converted
③ is converted
④ have been converting

16

A strange ① coincidence ② was happened when ③ the news ④ was ⑤ announced this morning.

17

The association of Europe with political freedom _____ in ancient Greece.

① had first been made
② which was first made
③ was first made
④ first made
⑤ was first making

18

① As historical databases ② relatively impoverish, we might expect the ③ newer discipline of quantitative sociolinguistics to ④ cast some light on the matter.

19

Fifty-six people, ① including two ② retired generals, ③ were went on trial in Turkey's second case against a clandestine group ④ accused of ⑤ plotting to overthrow the government of Prime Minister Recep Erdogan.

20

Hundreds of civilians were ① reporting killed in ② shelling, as the army struggled ③ to root out Tamil rebels from ④ the last few square kilometers of land ⑤ under their control.

21

Scientists now know that all objects ① compose of many molecules and the ② force of gravity ③ pulls on ④ each of them.

22

By ① the time when the attack ② was arrived, the defenders ③ could be ④ disconcerted, wavering, worried, hesitant, vacillating.

23

The bodily processes behind taste _____ unclear to date.

① are remained
② remain
③ have been remained
④ remaining

24

The public ① was brought to the realization that ② if Superman could ③ be paralyzed, it could ④ be happened to anybody.

25

The orphans living in the rural village _____ to the amusement park.

① considered took
② considered to take
③ were considered to be taken
④ were considered being taken

01

Because of his stupid behavior, Max was _____ by everybody.

① laughed at   ② laughing at

③ laughed   ④ laughing

02

When private property ①came into existence, and when private property ②could inherit by one of their sons, fathers began ③to look for the son ④to whom they could leave their property.

03

After careful deliberation, the proposed merger _____ by the CEO.

① assent   ② is assented

③ is assenting   ④ assents

04

Although these procedures are ①most commonly used to detect the most common genetic ②disorders — Down syndrome, for example — ③they could, in principle, ④use to detect more minor genetic abnormalities.

05

Pope Francis on Sunday ①was offered a Christmas hope for peace in a world ②lacerated by war and terrorism, urging people ③to remember migrants, refugees and those ④hit by economic instability ⑤caused by "idolatry of money."

06

To our surprise, Erik Dickinson fell ①short of his parents' expectations, ②disappointing them who kept the faith in their son's potential for success, when he ③was proved to be ④a failure as a statesman.

07

A distinction between two kinds of intelligence — crystallized and fluid intelligence — ① has been widely studied by researchers studying adult learning. Crystallized intelligence ② is heavily dependent on education and experience. It ③ is consisted of the set of skills and knowledge that we each learn as part of growing up in any culture. Fluid intelligence, in contrast, ④ is thought to be a more basic set of abilities, not so dependent on specific education.

08

① It seems almost certain that the 60 years after penicillin ② came to market ③ will eventually view ④ as just an interlude in the eternal war between us and them.

09

Today it emerged that about 500 red-winged blackbirds and starlings _____ in Louisiana. Their tiny corpses littered a short stretch of highway near the city of Labarre after apparently falling dead from the sky.

① have found dead
② found dead
③ had found dead
④ had been found dead

10

If we don't get a ① satisfying solution to the problem, we'll ② be forcing to ③ take action ④ against your company.

11

The ① renovated business center, ② which has several restaurants, boutiques and Internet cafes, ③ can be accommodated ④ as many as 1,000 guests.

12

Columbia ① has suffered the heaviest rain in decades ② due to the La Nina weather phenomenon, which ③ is caused water temperature in the Pacific Ocean ④ to drop.

13

① At the meeting held in December, ② it was announced that the choice of recipients ③ had finally limited ④ to Dr. Evert, Professor Applebaum, or her.

14

The injury ①was occurred when the ②25-year-old man ③was running through stunts ④at England's Leavesden Studios.

15

The ①lens and cornea are ②supply with ③nutrients and oxygen by the ④aqueous fluid.

16

To ①ring in the Year of the Rabbit, ②three major museums ③are held exhibitions ④to introduce visitors to the mythology of the rabbit in Korean culture.

17

We have ①been endured the ②successively ③higher levels of unemployment during ④the past three recessions.

18

In 1963 Maria Mayer ①awarded the Nobel Prize ②in physics for her ③findings on the ④constituents of the atomic ⑤nucleus.

19

The event ①is proved to be a great chance ②for us to meet high school ③alumni and other friends ④all at once.

20

A Hong Kong journalist who _____ in mainland China for nearly 16 months for spying charges will face trial this week.

① detains
② is detaining
③ has detained
④ has been detained

21

The world is ①made up with objects. They have properties ②independent of any people or other beings who experience them. For example, ③take a rock, It's a separate object and it's hard. Even if no people or other beings ④existed in the universe, it would still be a separate object and it would still be hard.

22

In most of our practical activities, we ①rely upon our senses and develop intuitions we can ②trust. When important issues ③raise, regardless of what others may say, our own senses and intuitions are our best ④guides for action.

23

Although the media were ①largely denied access ②with the battlefields, the Gulf War ③nevertheless gained the reputation of the first real-time television war, and the images ④projected into American homes ⑤helped to incite the most passionate war fever since World War II.

24

A natural harbor ①is preferred to an artificial one, for ②the latter is expensive to construct and tends to depreciate rapidly. Hence it is recommended that available capital and manpower ③expend in improving natural harbors. ④No error

25

We conclude that brown bears, and perhaps other large mammals, have continuously _____ the archipelago for at least 40,000 years.

① stayed   ② dwelled
③ been dwelled   ④ been lived
⑤ inhabited

조동사

조동사란?

말 그대로 동사를 도와주기 위해 나오는 단어이다. 조동사는 물어볼 수 있는 지식의 범위가 좁은 편이라 다른 파트에 비해서 출제 빈도가 월등히 떨어진다. 몇 가지의 정해진 지식만 익히면 문제에 접근하는 것은 어렵지 않을 것이다. 조동사는 주조동사와 서법 조동사로 나뉘지만 문법 문제로 묻는 것은 서법 조동사의 용법을 주로 묻는다.

조동사 주요 포인트

01 「need, dare」 부정문에서 조동사의 용법을 묻는 유형
ex. You *need not to play* the piano. (×) / You **need not play** the piano. (○)

02 「may/might as well A as B = would rather A than B」
ex. You *may as well go* at once *as staying* at home. (×)
You **may as well go** at once **as stay** at home. (○)

03 cannot but+R ~ = cannot help+R-ing ~ = have no choice but+to R ~
ex. I **cannot** (choose/help) but **play**/~~playing~~/~~to play~~ soccer.
= I **can't help**(= avoid) **playing**/~~play~~/~~to play~~ soccer.
= I **have no** (other) **choice**(= alternative) but to **play**/~~play~~/~~playing~~ soccer.

04 used to+R ~
ex. He *used to going* swimming. (×) / He **used to go** swimming. (○)

05 명령형 단어+that+S+(should)+R ~
ex. I *ordered that she went* to school. (×) / I **ordered that she go** to school. (○)

01

① One of the central and most difficult moral questions of our age is: Do the terminally ill ② has the right to ③ take their own lives before they suffer great pain or become ④ a burden to others?

02

One of the ① chief things in science ② is careful observation, for things that ③ look rather alike may actually ④ very different when we come ⑤ to look closely.

03

① Keen on green policies, David Cameron used to ② cycling to work in a variety of ③ fetching helmets with his brief case following ④ by car.

04

When there is no alternative for a drug, patients and insurance companies have no choice _____ price a drug-maker set.

① but to pay
② but to pay whatever
③ other than pay whatever
④ other than paying

05

U.S. marines ① on a recent trip to Afghanistan ② offered medical care to local women in the village of Lakari, but ③ some of these women said they would rather die ④ than being touched by a male doctor.

06

If there are any barriers to further progress, then science _____ at unprecedented speed just before it crashes into them.

① well may to move
② well may be move
③ may well be moving
④ may well to move

07

① Sensing the imminent arrival of his infant son, Dr. Frankenstein demanded that his maid ② disinfected his house ③ in order to make sure that the baby is well ④ taken care of.

08

Rey, ① who asked that neither his last name ② nor his given name ③ was used to protect his and his family's privacy, ④ grew up in Chappaqua, the rich Westchester suburb.

09

The yen is weakening. But Tokyo _____ its interest rates again.

① dares not raise
② dare not raise
③ does not dare raise
④ dare not to raise

10

He suggested that all applicants _____ the forms at the front desk and submit them.

① filled out
② be filling out
③ should have filled out
④ fill out

11

① The mayor disparaged our efforts ② to beautify the town square by saying that the flower bed we had planted ③ looked somewhat worse than the weeds ④ it had replacing.

12

Only ① after the agreement was ② made did the CEO ③ decided to forgo having his workers ④ do mandatory overtime work.

13

① Never did I dream that he made ② such a surprising suggestion that the government ③ gives up the bribery tradition which ④ has remained for a long period of time.

14

The ① irritable sergeant ② was insistent that nothing ③ supersedes the drilling of ④ the forty new men.

15

They planned to sell luxury T-shirts and shoes to coincide with the movie's release, but Sarah demanded that the merchandise _____ sold only through her Bitten line.

① should   ② were
③ be   ④ being
⑤ are

16

I _____ to be a practicing doctor, but now I'm more interested in research.

① was used to want
② used to want
③ used to wanting
④ was used to wanting

17

A: Did you criticize his mistake?
B: Yes, but _____ it.

① I'd not rather do
② I'd rather not to do
③ I'd rather not doing
④ I'd rather not have done

18

The professor requested that the student _____ his paper as soon as possible.

① should finish to write
② should finish the writing
③ finish writing
④ finishes writing
⑤ finished writing

19

They couldn't but _____ at the funny scene.

① laughing
② laugh
③ laughed
④ to laugh

20

① It is mandatory ② that a registered student ③ maintains his or her GPA ④ of B⁺ in the major field.

21

She worked very hard so that she _____ pass the entrance exam.

① will   ② shall
③ may   ④ could

22

Some students moved that Kim _____ elected the next chair.

① will be   ② was
③ be   ④ had been

23

The scientists could not ①help ②but talking about the success ③of the Voyager missions ④among themselves.

24

If the universe is expanding, then in the past it _____ now.

① would have been smaller than it is
② would be smaller than it is
③ must have been smaller than it is
④ must be smaller than it is

25

A: I am surprised that John didn't return your call.
B: He _____ not have gotten my message.

① must   ② could
③ should   ④ ought

5강 가정법

가정법이란?

가정법은 말 그대로 이미 지난 사실을 가정하거나, 앞으로의 일을 가정하는 것을 말한다. 가정법에서 물어보는 포인트는 딱 하나, 바로 시제이다. 결국 가정법은 시제 그 이상도 이하도 아닌, 시제 그 하나만을 묻기 때문에 문제를 접하며 반복적 숙달이 중요하다.

가정법 주요 포인트

01 가정법 과거에서 if절의 동사와 주절 동사의 시제를 묻는 유형
ex. If+S+Ved / were ~, S+would/could/should/might+R ...

02 가정법 과거완료에서 if절의 동사와 주절 동사의 시제를 묻는 유형
ex. If+S+had p.p. ~, S+would/should/could/might+have p.p. ...

03 가정법 혼합에서 if절의 동사와 주절 동사의 시제를 묻는 유형
ex. If+S+had p.p. ~, S+would/should/could/might+R ...(현재 시점부사)

04 도치된 형태에서 도치된 문장의 동사와 주절 동사의 시제를 묻는 유형
ex. Were+S ~, S+would/should/could/might+R ...

Had+S+p.p. ~, S+would/should/could/might+have p.p. ...

Should+S+R ~, S+will/would+R ...

Should+S+R ~, R ...(명령문)

05 I wish/as if/It is time 절 속의 동사의 시제를 묻는 유형
ex. I wish+(that)+S+Ved, were/had p.p. ~

S+Vs/Ved+as if+S+Ved, were/had p.p. ~

It is time+(that)+S+Ved/should R ~

06 가정법과 직설법이 혼용된 문장에서 동사의 시제를 묻는 유형
ex. S+Vs ~(현재)/Ved ~(과거) otherwise+S+would R ~/would have p.p. ~

S+would R ~/would have p.p. ~ but+(that)+S+Vs ~(현재)/Ved ~(과거)

01

If the convenience store provided more various products, the residents _____ shopping more often.

① will go   ② would go
③ went   ④ would have gone

02

①In the mid-19th century, if you ②wanted to have a scientific fight, you could have ③picked no better subject ④than paleontology.

03

If I ①was in his place, I ②would be very much ③concerned about the future and would certainly be ④taking steps to improve my situation.

04

Had the former President not endorsed him during the last campaign, the first-time presidential candidate _____ lost the election by a narrow margin.

① could not have
② might have
③ shall have
④ ought to have

05

If my boss _____ while I'm out, please tell her that I'll be back as soon as I finish interviewing the candidates.

① call   ② should call
③ will call   ④ called

06

If today I lived in a Communist country where certain principles dear to the Christian faith are suppressed, _____ that country's antireligious laws.

① I will openly advocate disobeying
② I would openly advocate disobeying
③ I will have openly advocated disobeying
④ I would have openly advocated disobeying

07

If qualitatively diverse products were to be offered on one-dimensional consumers, incapable of absorbing the diversity, consumption _____ be limited.

① will   ② can
③ would   ④ shall

08

The author _____ her article was so controversial had it not been for the spate of correspondence.

① would never think
② have never thought
③ have never been thought
④ would never have thought

09

If you _____ English harder when you were young, now you could speak English better.

① had been studying
② studied
③ should have studied
④ had studied

10

_____ empirical evidence to support his views and to finding ways to test them statistically, his influence on economics would have been greater.

① If he devoted much effort to gather
② Did he devoted more effort to gather
③ Had he devoted more effort to gathering
④ If he had devoted much effort gathering

11

_____, I would take them on a night cruise on the river.

① If I have been asked to take visitors on a tour of my city
② If I would be asked to take visitors on a tour of my city
③ If I had asked to take visitors on a tour of my city
④ If I were asked to take visitors on a tour of my city

12

_____, my sister would not have been able to live out her dream as a prominent fashion designer today.

① If it was not an open admission policy
② If there has not been for an open admission policy
③ If it would not have been for an open admission policy
④ If it had not been for an open admission policy

13

I felt _____ I were living two people's lives.

① although   ② even though
③ even if   ④ as if

14

The French philosopher Pascal remarks ① that seemingly trivial occurrences we might not even be aware ② of ③ affect geopolitical event. He famously wrote, "Cleopatra's nose, ④ were it been shorter, the whole face of the world would have been changed."

15

If I had been the CEO, I _____ the company and hired more staff.

① restructured
② would restructure
③ would have restructured
④ would have been restructured

16

The security of England depends on gentlemen being allowed to live peaceably in their homes as decent landlords and masters. _____ the aristocrats of France followed our example, they would not have found themselves severed at the neck.

① If   ② Unless
③ Had   ④ With

17

If sales had not improved, we _____ to consider selling the company last year.

① have
② will have
③ will have had
④ would have had
⑤ would have been had

18

The travels of Marco Polo in the twelfth century would not have been so well known _____ for the book he wrote while in jail.

① had it not been
② it had not been
③ were it not
④ it were not

19

It seems that few businessmen participated in the charity ball for the street children; otherwise, more money _____.

① would have been raised
② was being raised
③ had been raised
④ might have been raising

20

Years later, she said, had her father told me the truth, I _____ a much better girl.

① could have been
② can have been
③ will have been
④ had been

21

I ①would buy this fancy ②furniture yesterday, ③had I had enough cash ④on hand.

22

I often found myself regretting my own existence, and wishing myself dead; and _____ the hope of being free, I have no doubt but that I should have killed myself.

① but for
② unless
③ concerning
④ no less than

23

_____ I visited the company earlier, I could have obtained enormous help from lots of different sectors of its management.

① Since   ② If
③ Unless   ④ Had

24

On Sunday afternoon, John planted flowers in his garden by himself. He might _____ $350 if he had hired someone to do the job.

① paying   ② be paid
③ have paid   ④ have been paid

25

An insurance company might send investigators to determine the cause of a mysterious fire. If the investigators sent back a report that the fire was caused by the presence of oxygen in the atmosphere, they would not keep their jobs very long. And yet they would be right. Had there been no oxygen present, there _____ no fire.

① has been   ② is
③ will be   ④ would be
⑤ would have been

6강 부정사

부정사란?
준동사의 범주에 들어가는 표현을 말한다. 준동사란 동사가 아니라는 뜻이기 때문에 동사 앞에 **to**를 붙여 주게 되었는데, 이 형태(**to R**)를 문법에서 '부정사'라고 부르게 된 것이다. 영어를 배울 때 절대 빠질 수 없는 것이 바로 부정사다. 하지만 의외로 문법 문제의 출제 비중은 낮은 편에 속한다.

부정사 주요 포인트

01 부정사(to R ~)의 의미상 주어를 묻는 유형
  ex. It is *easy of you* to study English. (×) / It is **easy for you** to study English. (○)
  It is *stupid for you* to talk to him. (×) / It is **stupid of you** to talk to him. (○)

02 부정사의 태(능동태, 수동태)를 묻는 유형
  ex. The news is *to hear* in the class. (×) / The news is **to be heard** in the class. (○)

03 부정사 앞에 부정어(not)의 위치
  ex. She promised *to not go* there. (×) / She promised **not to go** there. (○)

04 「enough to R ~」 to R와 R-ing의 구분을 묻는 유형
  ex. He is rich *enough buying* the tool. (×) / He is rich **enough to buy** the tool. (○)

05 「too ~ to R ...」 상관관계를 묻는 유형
  ex. She is *too poor buying* the book. (×) / She is **too poor to buy** the book. (○)

06 부정사 to와 전치사 to의 구분을 통해 동사원형(R)과 동명사(R-ing)를 묻는 유형
  ex. He is asked *to playing* soccer. (×) / He is asked **to play** the soccer. (○)

01

Cellphones, ①which are usually ②used to helping people keep track of each other, are ③starting to take on quite a different function — helping users ④hide their whereabouts.

02

George _____ improve his test score, but he did not have enough time to study.

① knew   ② knew how that
③ knew how   ④ knew how to

03

When ①it comes to the economic expansion, the 1990s ②was a very special period ③that is unlikely ④to repeat for a while in recorded American history.

04

You may ①well have misunderstandings about forgiveness ②that ③lead you to ④rejecting it out of hand.

05

By 1901 there were enough automobiles on New York's roadways _____ the state to rule that they had to be registered.

① caused   ② would cause
③ causing   ④ to cause

06

① In order ② to be not late for the flight and ③ have ④ enough time for breakfast, I suggest ⑤ getting up at five in the morning.

07

Some people say it's asking too little of Rio _____ man-made structures to represent the city's aspirations.

① expects
② has expected
③ is expected
④ to expect

08

Medical bills in the United States have risen outrageously since the beginning of the 1960's and steps need _____ to reverse this trend or the average American will not be able to afford medical care.

① to take
② to be taken
③ to being taken
④ being taken

09

The US government had been ① preparing for a hurricane in New Orleans for ② a number of years and had ③ already decided on a plan ④ getting people out of the city.

10

Constantinople ① could win the battle ② but not the war, ③ for there were ④ very many Bulgarians for Greeks ⑤ to rule.

11

Many researchers have strived ①toward a theory that is ②enough eclectic to encompass all of ③their insights in ④some form.

12

While I wished to obtain ①a sound knowledge of ②all aspects of zoology, I planned ③to devote especially ④to insects.

13

In 1798 the circulation of the journal was 3,000 copies and that number is estimated to _____ by 1809.

① double
② be doubling
③ have doubled
④ have had doubled

14

London restaurants use old newspapers _____ "fish and chips," a traditional Britain dish.

① wrap   ② wraps
③ wrapped   ④ to wrap

15

The city is _____ by one man.

① small enough to be run
② too small for being running
③ too small to run
④ small enough to have run

16

_____ that years ago, the quality and styling of many GM vehicles fell away behind Toyota.

① Sufficiently is it to say
② Suffice it to say
③ Suffice this to say
④ Sufficient this is to say

17

It remains _____ whether a respected economist will have the necessary clout to stick to the reform path.

① to see   ② for seeing
③ to be seen   ④ for being seen

18

Unfortunately, ① the differences in the range of roles that languages play frequently ② lead some people to believe that some languages which do not fulfill ③ a wide range of functions are in fact ④ incapable to do so.

19

It would be like ① drinking whisky simply ② to get drunk, which ③ is likely in the long run ④ diminishing your pleasure in the stuff.

20

The magnitude 9.0 Tohoku earthquake ① on March 11, 2011, ② which occurred near the northeast coast of Honshu, Japan, ③ was estimated ④ to be caused between 30,000 and 40,000 deaths.

21

In 1991, in the aftermath of Anita Hill's testimony against Supreme Court nominee Clarence Thomas, President George Bush ① signed a law ② granting sexual-harassment plaintiffs the right to ③ trial by jury and ④ claiming to financial damages.

22

Sisyphus's continuous pushing of the stone up the hill only _____ it roll down again served as the literary model for the third of Zeno's paradoxes.

① having
② having been
③ have
④ to have

23

Around ① the globe, temperatures ② are said ③ to climb about ④ 1.1 degrees in the 20th century.

24

His customers are too worried about ① affording the necessities of life, like food and health care, ② splurging on games, and those who ③ do make a purchase tend to ④ look for the cheapest items on the shelves.

25

① Repairs to the Washington Monument will require massive scaffolding ② to build around the obelisk and may keep it ③ closed into 2014 after ④ it was damaged by an earthquake last year.

7강 동명사

동명사란?

준동사의 범주에 들어가는 표현을 말한다. 준동사란 동사가 아니라는 뜻이기 때문에 동사 뒤에 -ing를 붙여 주게 되었는데, 이 형태(R-ing)를 문법에서 '동명사'라고 부르게 된 것이다. 동명사라는 것은 R-ing 형태가 통째로 하나의 명사 역할로 쓰이는 것을 말한다.

동명사 주요 포인트

01 동명사(R-ing)의 의미상 주어를 묻는 유형

ex. She admits *him stealing* money. (×) / She admits **his stealing** money. (○)

02 동명사의 태(능동태, 수동태)를 묻는 유형

ex. The meeting risks *canceling*. (×) / The meeting risks **being canceled**. (○)

03 동명사의 관용적 표현을 묻는 유형

ex. He *spent money to buy* the car. (×) / He **spent money buying** the car. (○)

04 전치사의 목적어 자리를 묻는 유형

ex. I accused him *of steal* money. (×) / I accused him **of stealing** money. (○)

05 전치사 to와 부정사 to의 구분을 통해 동명사(R-ing)와 동사원형(R)을 묻는 유형

ex. We *looked forward to see* you again. (×) / We **looked forward to seeing** you again. (○)

01

When it comes ① to praise or blame people for ② what they do, we tend to use a standard ③ that is ④ relative to some conception of normal behavior.

02

Meanwhile the lighthouse ① had been growing slowly larger. It had now almost assumed color, and appeared like a little gray shadow on the sky. The man at the oars ② could not be prevented ③ from being turned his head rather often ④ to try for a glimpse of this little gray shadow.

03

Neighborhoods are very clearly ① demarcated according to income level, and there is not much overlap. Poor people live in poor neighborhoods that are characterized by ② dilapidated buildings, broken glass, graffiti, and a general state of disrepair. People are not dedicated to ③ create an aesthetically ④ pleasing environment.

04

I would prefer having an assigned roommate _____.

① to have to choose a roommate on my own
② than to have to choose a roommate on my own
③ to having to choose a roommate on my own
④ than have to choose a roommate on my own

05

She still has nightmares from _____ in a small dark cupboard for hours.

① locking up
② having locked up
③ having been locked up
④ locked up

06

Instead of _____ formal and well rehearsed, the performance was spontaneous, contradictory and mutually respectful.

① that   ② being

③ its   ④ such

07

We are all looking forward with eager anticipation _____ what James and Bradley will say.

① hear   ② to hear

③ hearing   ④ to hearing

08

From researches ① conducted by biologists, ② it is known that ants are guided by a secretion ③ paid onto the soil through the sting, in the manner of ink ④ drawing out of a pen.

09

① With the help of modern mass communication, an ② increasing number of governments in the developing world ③ are committed to ④ support family-planning programs.

10

A recidivist is a person who keeps ① going back to a life of crime ② even ③ after punished; in other words, an ④ incurable criminal.

11

① While many museums are strictly no-go zones for ② photography, for one "museum" in the Philippines taking happy snaps ③ are an ④ essential part of the visitor's experience.

12

There is ① no objection his joining the party ② provided he is willing to ③ fit in with the plans of the group and is ready and able to ④ do his share of the work.

13

The patrollers got used ① to see Alice ② wander about and she became just another fixture in the patrollers' night, worthy of no more attention ③ than a hooting owl or a rabbit ④ hopping across the road.

14

① Examining the link between nationality and prosperity in the age of globalism, Milanovic has concluded that ② a human being's place and culture ③ have become the dominant factor ④ in determination standard of living.

15

Women tend to spend as much time as they can _____ those they love.

① support, help, and nurture

② to support, to help, and to nurture

③ supporting, helping, and nurturing

④ supported, helped, and nurtured

16

In spite of some earlier ① confuse ② concerning the opening date of the new plant, we are ③ confident that we will be ready ④ by September 1.

17

Some galleries obtain money through sponsorship. Works of art are often expensive and galleries _____.

① can buy rarely them without organize a public appeal

② can buy rarely them without organized a public appeal

③ can rarely buy them without a public appeal organizing

④ can rarely buy them without organizing a public appeal

18

I appreciate ① you helping me ② to do the dishes, but I wish you would ③ lay them down on the table more ④ carefully.

19

① Instead of ② sticking to one study location, ③ simply change the room ④ where a person studies improves retention.

20

The Belts zoo spend ① a lot of time on ② educating children about the ③ importance of ④ rare species ⑤ in their homeland.

21

Samuel Walton ① pioneered the first ② mail-order business by ③ pay cash for merchandise ④ directly from manufacturers.

22

In Monmouth County, New Jersey, snow drifts of up to five feet contributed to ① stall a passenger bus on the Garden State Parkway, where snow plows were having a difficult time ② clearing because there were so many ③ stranded cars ④ cluttering the ramps, state police spokesman Steve Jones said.

23

① Once you become accustomed to ② use this new system, you'll find it ③ much easier ④ to operate than the previous one.

24

Governor Hester sees small business as the best hope for _____ the state's economy.

① revitalize   ② revitalized

③ revitalizing   ④ revitalization

25

Far from ① be ② of no consequence, this confusion ③ plays a positive role ④ in his theoretical edifice.

8강 분사

분사란?

분사의 형태는 현재분사(R-ing)와 과거분사(p.p.)로 나뉜다. 다만 반드시 학생들이 알아야 할 점은 분사는 결국 형용사일 뿐이라는 것이다. 영어에서 형용사는 명사를 수식하는 역할 그 이상, 그 이하도 아니기 때문에 수식어를 구분하며 분사(형용사)라는 것을 파악해야 문제에 접근할 수 있다. 결국 물어보는 것은 현재분사(R-ing)와 과거분사(p.p.)의 구분이다.

분사 주요 포인트

01 명사 앞에서 수식하는 R-ing(현재분사)와 p.p.(과거분사)의 선택을 묻는 유형
ex. the *breaking* window (×) / the **broken** window (○)

02 명사 뒤에서 수식하는 R-ing(현재분사)와 p.p.(과거분사)의 선택을 묻는 유형
ex. The man (*written* the book) is Tom. (×) / The man (**writing** the book) is Tom. (○)

03 문장의 구조 분석을 통해 쓸데없는 동사를 분사(형용사)로 고쳐야 하는 유형
ex. The dog *barks* at me is named Dubu. (×) / The dog **barking** at me is named Dubu. (○)

01

Kansas farmers ①used the weed killer 2, 4-D had a ②higher-than-average risk ③of ④contracting malignant ⑤lymphoma.

02

The ①absence of organic materials, some scientists ②speculated, was the result of intense ultraviolet ③radiation penetrating the atmosphere of Mars and ④destroyed organic compounds in the soil.

03

Another interesting application of ultrasound is the ultrasonic ranging unit ①using in some cameras ②to provide an ③almost instantaneous measurement of the distance between the camera and the objects ④to be photographed.

04

_____ as an opera singer, John McCormack made his Covent Garden debut in 1907, at age 23. Later he expanded his singing style to include elements of Irish ballads and traditional folk songs.

① Was trained   ② To train
③ Trained   ④ Training

05

A few years ago Canadian lottery officials ①learned the importance of careful ②counting the hard way when they ③decided to give back some ④unclaiming prize money that had ⑤accumulated.

06

I finally ①reached Tom ②in his office, and he said he ③would ship the ④redesigning brochures ⑤by express mail.

07

①Consisted of 93 percent water, ②the banana tree, ③which is the largest plant ④on Earth without a woody stem, is a very fragile plant.

08

Luis Chiappe, an expert on early birds at the Natural History Museum of Los Angeles County, suggests that flight ①likely occurred as a by-product of arm flapping ②in ground-dwelled dinosaurs, as the predecessors of birds used their ③feathered arms to increase their running speed or balance themselves ④as they made fast turns.

09

Brazil's economy performed ①much worse than ②expected in the third quarter, ③grown by less than 1% ④compared with the same period a year ⑤earlier.

10

①Buoyed by the winter sports season, consumption of instant noodles ②has spiked, with the monthly sales for last December ③exceeded 40 billion won ④for the first time.

11

The Kyoto Protocol is an ambitious effort to reduce the man-made emissions _____ responsible for global warming.

① believed   ② believing
③ to believe   ④ have believed

12

Law enforcement officials say that ①in theory the bureau could take a lead role ②in reducing gun crime, ③but that it is hindered by ④politically driving laws.

13

Some snorers who have a condition ①calling sleep apnea stop breathing ②up to thirty or forty times ③an hour because the throat muscles relax ④too much and block the airway.

14

China's first emperor was buried _____ 7,000 life-sized clay figures of soldiers standing in battle formation along by life-sized ceramic chariots.

① surrounded   ② surrounding
③ surrounded by   ④ surround with
⑤ surrounding with

15

When Spielberg was a teenager, his parents divorced, and the ①hurtful impact of that event would become a ②recurred theme in his movies— children ③uprooted and ④traumatized by parents' divorce.

16

Holmes compares himself to Dupin and Lecoq, _____ them as really existing historical figures.

① treated ② being treated
③ treating ④ having been treated

17

The integral connection between vassal ①and serf ②depicting in conventional accounts ③was destined to come ④under intense scrutiny among a new ⑤breed of analyst.

18

Political and economic relations between countries ①are to ②be based upon complete equality ③of the parties ④concern.

19

Every successful ①advertisement uses a creative strategy ②based on an idea that will attract the attention of the ③targeting consumer ④audience.

20

I had a really interesting conversation ①with a fellow working in the industry ②who claims that a lot of movies ③making these days are modeled conceptually after ④amusement park rides.

21

The fear that animals feel is carved ① deeply in the amygdaloid portion of the brain. When a rat spots a cat, its sympathetic nerve ② tenses because its amygdaloid body is stimulated, ③ caused the rat to stiffen and ④ let out deep breaths.

22

People ① sign up through the Affordable Care Act's marketplaces tend to be older, officials said Monday, a demographic mix that ② could cause premiums ③ to rise in the future if the pattern ④ persists.

23

It had been startling and ① disappointed to me to find out that story books ② had been written by people, that books ③ were not natural wonders, ④ coming up ⑤ of themselves like grass.

24

_____ for many years, this house will not withstand the cold weather this winter.

① Not having painted
② Having not painted
③ Not having been painted
④ Having not been painted

25

Songs were passed among musicians orally, although the works of trouveres in northern France were sometimes documented by literary groups. _____ their mostly oral tradition, the songs were typically not documented.

① Give   ② To give
③ Giving   ④ Given

01

It believes it is time ①to reconsider our ②long-holding belief that animals ③should be kept out of hospitals and ④away from ⑤sick people.

02

The Good-People Charity Foundation, _____ about a decade ago, is now the world's largest complex of museums, art galleries and research facilities.

① found   ② founded
③ being found   ④ was founded

03

①For those ②wanted a luxury stay at the heart of Seoul's business and tourist districts, many people ③say that ABC Hotel Seoul is the best ④option.

04

The Thinker, a famous bronze and marble sculpture by August Rodin, depicts a pensive man, that is, one _____ in deep thought.

① captured
② captures
③ capturing
④ has been captured

05

The result of a lack of clarity ①on questions of poetics ②has been the astonishing helplessness of ③most scholars when ④confronting with the task of actually analysing and evaluating a work of art.

06

_____ high school, the job applicant was not considered for the position.

① Not finished
② Not having finished
③ Having not finished
④ Having not been finished

07

① Buffered by oceans to the east and west, and ② peaceful neighbors to the north and south, America enjoys a degree of security ③ unmatching by world powers ④ in earlier ages.

08

All passengers ① travel on commercial jets ② are advised ③ to allow an hour ④ for boarding.

09

Any executive _____ how to keep workers healthy is invited to a seminar to be held on July 5, at the Seoul Center.

① concerning about
② concerning
③ who concerned about
④ concerned about

10

① Within developed countries, there are ② well-documenting differences ③ in mortality rates ④ by race, income, or education.

11

SBL Group, ① a Colorado-based company, said Mr. Sam Butler will ② resign as CEO ③ due to a long health problem ④ followed a stroke three years ago.

12

All construction contractors are required to adhere to the legal guidelines in the building code when _____ existing structures.

① to renovate   ② renovated
③ renovating   ④ renovation

13

① Though ② knowing as a soybean tycoon, Maggi ③ has helped ④ make that nation the world's No.1 beef exporter.

14

Bolivia today is undergoing ① profound change, and those ② bring it about are the very people ③ that have been kept in a state of paralyzed submission ④ for centuries.

15

Those most recently _____ in the insurance program will have to pay higher premiums for the same coverage.

① enroll   ② enrolling
③ enrolled   ④ enrollment

16

What happened was that in my ① forties, back in the Dublin of my birth, I began ② working for the most ③ respecting newspaper in the country — *The Irish Times* — ④ as an opinion columnist.

17

We ① were terrified by sounds; ② the screaming of the wind; the ③ restless rustle of leaves in the trees; and the sudden, ④ overwhelmed ⑤ explosions of thunder.

18

① A series of recalls ② involved contaminated foods this year, including an outbreak of salmonella from tainted peanuts ③ that killed at least eight people and sickened 600, has consumers ④ rightly worried about the safety of their meals.

19

In 1066, a bright comet _____ in the sky attracted much attention.

① appears   ② appearing
③ it appeared   ④ was appearing

20

While the cold air is expected to leak out of the region, it could be a mightly slow leak, _____ the duration of the cold and the snow cover.

① give   ② given

③ giving   ④ to give

21

According to a recent study, ①depressed patients are ②more likely to stand with ③their necks bent forward, shoulders collapsed, and ④arms drew in toward the body.

22

French authorities are still hunting for suspects ①linked to ②planned terrorist attacks, including an ③alleged suicide bomb plot ④targeted New Year celebrations in Paris.

23

The desire to help ①correct the worst injustices of the economic system in our own countries also leads us to reach out to help ②impoverishing people in other lands. What makes ③such an effort feasible today is the fact that so much of what people suffer from ④is preventable with science and technology.

24

Korea has long ①lost any claim to ②being a land of clean air and clear water, but the ongoing controversy ③surrounded the safety of ④drinking water is another wake-up call against possible contamination of this most basic resource.

25

Functionalists generally maintain that sex differentiation ①contributes to overall social stability, but conflict theorists charge that the relationship ②between females and males is ③one of unequal power, with ④men dominate women.

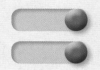

에듀윌 편입
솔루션 문법 Basic

9강 접속사

접속사란?

접속사는 단어, 구(두 단어 이상), 절(문장)을 이어 주는 역할을 한다. 접속사는 크게 등위접속사와 종속접속사로 나뉘고, 종속접속사는 세부적으로 명사절, 형용사절(관계사절), 부사절의 역할을 한다. 접속사에서 문제로 출제되는 대부분은 종속 접속사의 명사절과 부사절이다. 접속사는 문법 문제로 묻는 유형이 너무 많아 포인트만 정리하고 예문은 문제에서 접하도 록 하자!!

접속사 주요 포인트

01 부사절을 줄여 놓은 분사구문에서 R-ing(능동태)와 p.p.(수동태)의 구분을 묻는 유형

02 명사절 접속사 what의 용법을 묻는 유형

03 how(ever) 뒤 어순을 묻는 유형

04 명사절(간접의문문)의 어순을 묻는 유형

05 명사절 접속사 whether과 if의 구분을 묻는 유형

06 「S+had no sooner(scarcely/hardly)+p.p. ~ than[(when/before)]+S+Ved ...: ~하자마자 …하다 부정부사와 접속사의 상관관계, 부정어 문두강조 도치, 시제를 묻는 유형

07 「It is/was ~ that ...」의 강조구문에서 접속사 that의 선택을 묻는 유형

08 같은 뜻을 가진 접속사와 전치사의 구분을 묻는 유형

09 양보 부사절의 어순을 묻는 유형

10 「The reason is that+S+V ~」의 구문에서 that과 because의 구분을 묻는 유형

11 결과의 「so/such ~ that+S+V ...」 용법을 묻는 유형

12 등위접속사의 병치 형태를 묻는 유형

13 등위상관접속사의 상관관계와 품사의 일치를 묻는 유형

14 although와 but의 공존 불가능을 묻는 유형

01

Dom _____ you'll live forever but live
each day _____ you'll die tomorrow.

① even though　　② unless
③ in case　　④ as though

02

_____ unavoidable the Civil War may
have been, it was more devastating and exhausting
than any European war between 1815 and 1914.

① Whatever　　② Whether
③ However　　④ Otherwise

03

No sooner ① had Mr. Obama abandoned U.S. plans
for the missile defense system ② then Moscow
announced it was dropping ③ its plans ④ to deploy
the interceptors.

04

_____ of heights, that roller coaster is
one ride I'll never go on.

① Terrified
② Being terrified
③ Since I'm terrified
④ It was the terror

05

I ① look upon myself as very fortunate in that I
② have found men so interesting ③ whom I am
almost incapable ④ of being bored by them.

06

It was due to his lateness _____ such a thing plunged him into the disaster, which eventually changed his whole life.

① when   ② that

③ as   ④ what

07

A fairly good income is very important; however, it is still more important that a man should follow the vocation for which he is best fitted, _____ it happens to be well paid.

① what   ② whether

③ where   ④ how

08

If freshly ① squeezing, the orange juice in a one-cup ② serving provides ③ twice the minimum daily requirement ④ for vitamin C.

09

While we sleep, research indicates, the brain replays the patterns of activity ① it experienced during waking hours, ② allowing us to ③ enter what one psychologist calls ④ it a neural virtual reality.

10

It always seems to taste ① wonderful no matter ② how ③ sloppy I measure ④ things.

11

① That most students need above all else is practice ② in writing, and particularly in writing about things that ③ matter to them, so that they will begin to feel the satisfaction that comes from getting important thoughts ④ down in words.

12

The ① debate over if language is natural, I.e., do we call ② a table a table because that's the way it is?, or conventional, ie., do we call it a table because that's what we decided to call it? in Plato's Cratylus is ③ the very question that everyone ④ agrees opens Saussure's teachings and ties them together.

13

① Mating done, the female yucca moth ② climbs atop one of the flower's six stamens and gathers ③ a cache of pollen, ④ used tentacles for the tusk.

14

The ① long-suffering smartphone maker reported a surprise bump in operating profits, ② provided some hope that ③ its turnaround efforts are starting ④ to gain traction.

15

① Saying that the Miss World pageant should be focused more on ② that a woman could ③ do with a title like Miss World, the organization announced that ④ future pageants will not include a swimsuit round.

16

Only after Al Gore left politics ① did he ② find a formula for accomplishing his life's work, ③ created a global media brand around the PowerPoint presentation that became his aptly ④ titled book and documentary *An Inconvenient Truth*.

17

In *As You Like It*, Rosalind began a journey, ① disguising herself as a man when she earned the wrath of her uncle and was ② driven out of the house. The common point here is ③ that the love affair got entangled ④ because women who mistook heroines in men's attire as men.

18

You do not educate a person's palate by ① telling him that ② what he ③ has been in the habit of eating is disgusting, but ④ persuaded him to try a dish of properly cooked food.

19

_____ to be comprehended today, America Online started out in 1985 as simply one of many service firms providing customers with a new way to connect to the Internet.

① Difficult is
② It is difficult
③ Though is it difficult
④ Difficult as it may be

20

① Convicting for stealing a loaf of ② bread for his sister's ③ starving children, Jean Valjean ④ was sentenced to five years of hard labor and ⑤ another fourteen years for attempting to escape.

21

The most fundamental questions of ① what humans came to be the kind of animal ② we are can only be answered by a theory ③ in which culture has its proper role and ④ in which it is intimately ⑤ intertwined with other aspects of biology.

22

The zookeeper must make sure the bear is completely off the ground _____.

① as is it weighed
② as to weigh up
③ as it is weighed
④ as it weighs itself

23

But _____ the other's desire and the subject's possession are fantasies of the subject.

① both   ② alike
③ not   ④ not only

24

In the Disney version at least, it is Geppetto's wish, not Pinocchio's, _____ the puppet become real.

① what   ② which
③ that   ④ as

25

Compared to Korea and Japan, controversy over globalization began a little later in Taiwan. There are a couple of reasons to explain _____.

① why was this the case
② why this was the case
③ the case was why this
④ the case why was this

정답과 해설 p.88

01

She wondered if children loved pink and blue out of instinct, _____ a social compulsion that they are not aware of.

① because ② because of
③ or because ④ or because of

02

The Fed is raising rates and the dollar is rising, but the rest of the world is still moving in the opposite direction, _____ a "Great Divergence" in monetary policy.

① creating ② creates
③ is creating ④ created

03

① Defining in a limited sense, a tale is a story, usually short, that ② sets forth strange and wonderful events in more or less ③ bare summary, without ④ detailed character-drawing.

04

It is assumed ① what *Homo erectus* ② must have had a communication system ③ more complex than ④ any of today's living primates.

05

Exactly _____ we can replace our soil disappearing through erosion is not known.

① unless ② since
③ how ④ what

06

_____, the 정답과 해설 to many kinds of pain, from sore joints and back pain to headaches and stomachaches, may be in the kitchen rather than in the medicine cabinet.

① As may it sound surprising
② Surprising as it may sound
③ Sound surprising as it may
④ May sound surprising as it
⑤ It may sound surprising as

07

Despite the freedom of the press, in the U.S. there are limits on _____.

① what can the press publish
② can the press publish what
③ what the press can publish
④ the press what can publish

08

While touring the deserts of Argentina and Chile ①which many travellers found ②spectacular, ③it was found that Dr. Smith ④contracted malaria.

09

Such house chores, _____ important for home management, may not be favorite job for anyone.

① they are   ② as
③ though   ④ despite

10

Researchers have discovered that body fat produces proteins that trigger inflammation, thus _____ to the development of heart disease, stroke, and diabetes.

① contributes   ② has contributed
③ being contributed   ④ contributing

11

①I am still undecided ②whether I should insist upon complete performance of the contract ③or to forgive the obligation ④in anticipation of concessions in later negotiating sessions.

12

Timothy J. McVeigh was convicted of bombing a federal office building in Oklahoma city, _____ the deaths of 168 people.

① causing
② and caused
③ it caused
④ which it caused

13

Planets are ① probably formed as a ② result of both gases ③ or particles drawn ④ together in space by gravity.

14

_____ you can't talk right.

① The reason you can't get a job is because
② The reason for you can't get a job is because
③ The reason for you can't get a job is that
④ The reason you can't get a job is that

15

Historically, ① the most dangerous part of a lawmaker's job ② has been ③ not violence, but ④ to travel.

16

Historians have long been reluctant ① to recognize that Queen Victoria was not just a monarch ② and one of the most prominent working mothers in history — ③ one who was both deeply in love with her husband ④ and resentful of the demands on her as a mother and a wife.

17

Bone is one of the hardest materials in the body and, _____, it has a remarkable ability to resist tension and other forces acting on it.

① although relatively light in weight
② having been relatively light in weight
③ that it is relatively light in weight
④ to be relatively light in weight

18

It may be worth ① noting that the hijackers ② themselves correctly foresaw ③ what the threat to their mission would come from the passengers and not from a military source external ④ to the plane.

19

I ① used to work ② as a salesman, and I know how important ③ is image in ④ any job.

20

Just as Napoleon faced defeat in Russia, _____ Hitler saw his dreams of conquest evaporate at the siege of Leningrad.

① so   ② and
③ as   ④ yet
⑤ but

21

Although he ①has worked in other ②media and other forms, ③but Bean gained considerable success with his ④pit-fired earthenware ⑤bowls.

22

The most general charge ①brought by its contemporaries ②against the schoolroom of the seventeenth century was that ③its failure to adapt its ideals to the profound changes which were becoming ④manifest in social life.

23

Chicken pox and measles, ①despite common and rarely fatal among Europeans, often ②proved lethal ③to Native Americans, and more dangerous diseases such as small pox ④were especially deadly.

24

In the past, inexperienced young adults, when _____ with crucial life decisions, tended to accept the judgement of parents and other authority figures.

① be faced   ② facing
③ faced   ④ to face

25

The cost of college education ①has risen ②too rapidly ③during the past several years that it is now ④beyond the reach of many people.

에듀윌 편입
솔루션 문법 Basic

10강 관계사

관계사란?

관계사는 형용사절을 다르게 부르는 이름이다. 즉, 관계사절(관계대명사, 관계형용사, 관계부사)은 통째로 하나의 형용사로 쓰여 뒤에서 앞에 있는 명사를 수식하는 역할 그 이상도 이하도 아니다. 관계사절에서 문법 문제로 가장 많이 묻는 것은 단연코 관계대명사이다.

관계사 주요 포인트

01 관계대명사 who와 whom의 구분을 묻는 유형

02 관계대명사 who(m)와 which의 구분을 묻는 유형

03 관계대명사(which, that)와 명사절 접속사 what의 구분을 묻는 유형

04 관계대명사절 이하 성분(명사)의 불완전성을 묻는 유형

05 관계대명사와 「전치사+관계대명사」의 구분을 묻는 유형

06 관계부사(when, where, why, how)의 구분을 묻는 유형

07 주격 관계대명사절 이하 동사의 수 일치를 묻는 유형

08 콤마(,) 뒤 관계대명사 that의 불가능을 묻는 유형

09 「전치사+that+S+V ~」의 불가능을 묻는 유형

10 관계형용사(소유격 관계대명사)의 용법을 묻는 유형

11 유사관계대명사의 구분을 묻는 유형

12 복합관계대명사 whoever와 whomever의 구분을 묻는 유형

01

Virginia Woolf, ① which developed new literary ideas ② for effecting social change, ③ led the intellectual movement for ④ freedom from the British government.

02

As women have ① moved away from the traditional status of ② homemaker, notions of ③ that a marriage ④ should be have changed to accommodate the new reality.

03

The closer you get to an election, ① the harder it can be to tell ② where the candidates stand ③ on the issues ④ what matter ⑤ most.

04

There is something ① uncanny about the clarity with which he ② recognized his hopeless position, and the calm ③ which he accepted ④ the inevitable ⑤ was superhuman in its aspect: "I am absent-minded and could not direct my own life now."

05

① Feminist theory has assumed that there is some ② existing identity, understood ③ through the category of women, who not only initiates feminist interests and goals within discourse, but constitutes the subject ④ whom political representation is pursued.

06

Insulin is a substance ① for which enables muscles ② to absorb sugar from the blood, and ③ to break it up ④ for the purpose of obtaining energy.

07

Mark had been ① an excellent student at the college, but he found that the abstract concepts ② what he had learned in the classroom left him ③ ill-equipped to deal with ④ the concrete circumstances of life.

08

① That she said seems to be not ② so much an opinion ③ as a criticism about ④ the way the company has been operated.

09

Reports nationwide indicate that DWI (driving while intoxicated) is a factor in one-fourth of all reported auto crashes _____.

① called by the police
② calling the police
③ when the police are called
④ in which the police are called

10

Farmers sold their ① crops to a trader, ② when sold them to another trader and ③ so on until ④ they ended up in a shop.

11

There are ①a lot of ②times ③how we need to talk to people ④who come from other countries.

12

Language is a tool for saying as well as possible _____ we intend to say.

① which   ② when
③ where   ④ what

13

Textrix, the company ①for which Alex works part-time, ②tends to employ people who are ③highly motivated and ④who has at least ⑤10 years of experience in the field.

14

The Centuriate assembly, ①what only an official ②with imperium could summon, was organized like the army with the ③presiding official acting ④as a commander and the voters as soldiers.

15

Some studies have ①called into question whether ②high and variable pitch and exaggerated stress ③are the crucial elements in the baby talk ④which infants respond.

16

Governments are paying ①increasing attention to international ②comparisons as they search ③for effective policies ④whose enhance individuals' social and economic prospects.

17

Advances ①in technology now allow us to prolong life ②in ways that were unimaginable decades ago. But should people be forced or expected to prolong lives that ③are unbearably painful, or that ④is in effect "lifeless"?

18

The plastic waste in the ocean breaks down into tiny pieces known as microplastics, _____ or even toxic to sea creatures who ingest it.

① which scientists believe can harm
② which scientists believe can be harmful
③ in which scientists believe can harm
④ in which scientists believe can be harmful

19

These experiences, and others which can't all be ①enumerated here, ②help us ③to find a place of fullness, ④which we orient ourselves morally or spiritually.

20

Many germs have had to devise tricks to let them spread between potential victims, and many of those tricks are _____ we experience as "symptoms of disease."

① what   ② that
③ while   ④ which

21

Knowledge of the rate ①which a ship is traveling through ②the water is important if the navigator ③needs to estimate the time ④of arrival.

22

Pending folder is ①which you put messages ②that you do not need to respond to immediately but ③that you need to keep 'active' for the time being — for example, ④if someone promised to get back to you and you need a reminder to follow up.

23

The new e-ticketing system, _____ was installed last month, is working well.

① what   ② whom
③ where   ④ that
⑤ which

24

There are two other bodies ①orbiting near Earth ②that is sometimes ③referred to as moons, though they are not strictly ④worthy of the title.

25

The physicians favored a program ①guaranteed to save two hundred ②lives over one ③who had a one-third probability of saving everyone and a ④two-thirds probability of saving no one.

01

Early studies ① have also shown an increase in physical ailments — sore backs, dry eyes, painful necks — among kids who ② are asked to work most of the day on computers ③ which using desks ④ designed for pencil and paper.

02

① To Warren Buffet, his father's library ② must have been like a recommended booklist. When he was eight years old, Buffet started ③ reading the books in the library. His reading habit might have been ④ that turned him into the Oracle of Omaha.

03

The city is struggling with a $26.5 million budget gap, the result of a long decline in Camden's property tax base and Gov. Christie's decision to cut state aid, _____ made up more than 80 percent of Camden's budget last year.

① who   ② that
③ what   ④ which

04

The city fathers allocated ① a substantial sum for the ② restoration of the train station ③ but which was soon ④ dissipated in research and planning.

05

You ① don't seem to understand ② that ③ I'm trying to do ④ with the new pricing system.

06

The regional manager has been looking for an applicant _____ language skills include Korean and Chinese.

① who   ② which
③ whom   ④ whose

07

The passive in the English language ①is very useful ②when you want to emphasize the object ③which the action is happening rather than the person ④carrying out the action.

08

①When going out to hunt, Brazilian Indians from the Xavante tribe ②follow a complex hierarchy, ③that specifies the tasks the old and young should do ④when capturing animals.

09

In this book, Mary Evans explores _____ social theory has engaged with and illuminated the question of relations between genders and the social world.

① the extent to which
② the extent to what
③ the extent which
④ the extent to those
⑤ the extent that it

10

Despite the current oil glut, ①the world's known reserves of both petroleum and natural gas ②are expected to be declining ③by the end of the century, and ④it would be folly to burn ⑤which remains to generate electricity.

11

Although English ①is widely accepted today as being the universal language of business, most multinational companies will expect you ②to speak the language of one of the countries ③which they do business, ④in addition to English.

12

①Careful measurements reveal that the reaction rate is ②too slow to account for ③the ozone concentrations observed, i.e. the process predicts higher peak ozone concentrations ④that are observed.

13

Korea ① successfully hosted the Group of 20 ② summit in Seoul on November 11–12, ③ what is believed to have helped ④ boost the nation's diplomatic clout and international reputation.

14

Another area ① which bits and bytes are ② used is ③ measuring computer memory ④ storage capacity.

15

Did you know that ① most flight attendants fly with their own food? It is because the meals airlines ② give them to passengers ③ have gotten smaller ④ over the year and leave them still hungry. So it is not unusual for flight attendants ⑤ to bring their own snacks like fruit, protein bars and sandwiches.

16

As older people have accumulated their own know-how in their careers, they have many resources and skills _____.

① teach and guide younger people
② with which to teach and guide younger people
③ which they might teach and guide younger people
④ what might teach and guide younger people

17

_____ cannot be an extremist.

① Whoever is doing such activities
② Who is doing such activities
③ No matter how is doing such activities
④ How is doing such activities

18

Frog skin allows both water and oxygen ① to pass through, ② which mean if the air or water ③ is contaminated, the contaminant ④ can easily enter and damage the frog's body.

19

A satellite is composed of 30 modular units, _____ equipped with a set of sensors.

① each of which is
② each of which are
③ some of which is
④ which of them are

20

The strike ①for increased wages ②consisted of hundreds of immigrants, most of ③them ④were earning less than minimum wages.

21

Morgan Stanley, the financial firm ①who shares ②have declined 45 percent this year, ③plans to cut about 1,600 jobs amid an industrywide ④drop in revenue from investment banking and trading.

22

①One college professor developed the idea ②which rats might perform better on the detection test ③if they lived in a rich environment ④than in a small barren cage.

23

①The period in American history ②during when the ③sale of alcohol ④was banned was called Prohibition.

24

This study does not attempt a fully-fledged account of these concerns, but simply points to their importance when considering _____ state theories are constructed.

① way in which
② the way how
③ way which
④ way that
⑤ the way in which

25

In 1921, a movement started in several parts of the world, _____ was to make table tennis a serious sport.

① which goal
② its goal
③ the goal of which
④ which of the goal

11강 명사와 관사

명사란?

명사는 문장의 주요 성분으로 주어, 목적어, 보어, 전치사의 목적어 역할을 하는 품사이다. 영어라는 언어에서 명사라는 품사는 문장에서 필수 역할을 하지만 문법 문제에서 명사는 그 비중이 굉장히 낮은 편에 속한다.

관사란?

관사는 명사 앞에 쓰는 단어로 부정관사(a/an)와 정관사(the)로 나뉜다. 관사는 명사와 따로 떼서 생각할 수 없기 때문에 합쳐서 생각하는 것이 좋다. 명사와 관사를 합쳐도 전체 문법 문제의 2% 미만의 비중을 차지하기에 몇 가지의 지식만 기억하면 된다.

명사와 관사 주요 포인트

01 절대 불가산 명사(집합적 물질 명사)를 묻는 유형
ex. I bought *a furniture*. (×) / I bought **furniture**. (○)

02 「by+교통·통신 명사」 앞 관사 불가를 묻는 유형
ex. She went there *by a bus*. (×) / She went there **by bus**. (○)

03 「one of+the 복수명사」를 묻는 유형
ex. *One of the apple* is sold. (×) / **One of the apples** is sold. (○)

04 복수형 불가 percent를 묻는 유형
ex. *85 percents* of people are women. (×) / **85 percent** of people are women. (○)

05 정관사 the를 써야 하는 명사(태양, 달, 악기명) 앞 관사를 빼고 묻는 유형
ex. He played *guitar*. (×) / He played *the guitar*. (○)

06 the를 쓰지 못하는 연도 / the를 써야 하는 연대
ex. I was born *in the 1992*. (×) / I was born **in 1992**. (○)
　　 Korea was a poor country *in 1960s*. (×) / Korea was a poor country **in the 1960s**. (○)

07 the same+N, the only+N, the third(서수)+N, the -est/most ~(최상급)+N
ex. *First chapter* is Verb. (×) / **The first chapter** is Verb. (○)

01

Many of the mammals that dwell in the desert are active only at _____ as the intense heat of a desert day can be fatal to warm-blooded animals.

① a night   ② night
③ the night   ④ nights

02

The number of Americans who are obese ① continues to increase ② at alarming rate while in Italy ③ the percentage of obese people is half of ④ what it is in the United States.

03

In the United States, ① having chosen ② to purchase ③ same item created an immediate affinity ④ among Americans.

04

The story you hear all the time — of ① a stagnant economy in which high taxes and generous social benefits have undermined incentives, ② stalling growth and innovation — bears ③ few resemblance to ④ the surprisingly positive facts.

05

It might appear to ① any casual visitor who may have taken a few rides ② about town ③ by a taxicab that all New Yorkers are filled with a ④ loud-mouthed ill will toward each other.

06

Most people ① are accustomed to thinking of lie detectors ② as foolproof — as machines that can, without error, ③ separate the guilty from ④ the innocence.

07

Football, often ① confused with soccer in some countries, is a ② fast-moving ③ team sports ④ played mainly in the U.S. and Canada.

08

According to a Washington Post poll ① taken in 1999, eighty-seven ② percents of Americans ③ want the U.S. and China ④ to sign an ⑤ arms agreement.

09

① In popular terminology, ② any long snowstorm with ③ large amount of wind is ④ called a blizzard.

10

Language, in all aspects, ① consists of abstract units of ② informations that are ③ organized and combined ④ following specific computational procedures.

11

One of the best-known ① kind of predictably irrational behavior ② has been called the endowment effect — the idea that once something is ③ in your possession, it becomes more valuable ④ to you because it's yours and you don't want to lose it.

12

There are concerns for the safety of ① scores of people after a ship carrying 118 passengers and ② crews lost power in rough ③ waters off an Indonesian island ④ on Saturday.

13

Ebola, a ① highly infectious virus ② that can kill up to 90 ③ percent of the people who catch it, is one of the ④ world most deadly diseases, ⑤ causing terror among infected communities.

14

_____, Sasha rarely misses three-point shots.

① Her excellent basketball play
② Excellent basketball player
③ An excellent basketball player is
④ An excellent basketball player

15

The ① evidences show that children of women ② who work are not more ③ likely to have lower school ④ achievement than children of stay-at-home moms.

16

In order to arrest a person, the police ①has to be reasonably sure that a crime ② has been committed. The police must give the suspect the reasons why he ③is being arrested and ④tell him his rights under the law.

17

①The housekeeping problems of living in a shelter begin ②as soon as the shelter is occupied. ③Medical supplies, utensils, and equipments, as well as food, if not already stored in the shelter, ④must be quickly gathered up and carried inside.

18

Though the term *individualism* did not appear ①until late 1820s, when market societies were well established, the principles ②it encompasses ③were already instated ④by the mid-eighteenth century.

19

①The constellation Orion includes ②the all stars in the familiar pattern of the hunter, ③along with the region of the sky ④in which these stars are found.

20

①The post office has promised ②to resume ③first class mail delivery to ④area on Friday.

21

In 2009 Brazil, ①long the world's worst offender, saw its pace of jungle clearing plummet to ②the third of its historical rate. That's ③due in part to the recession, as falling commodity prices made clearcutting for farms ④less profitable.

22

Over the course of his career he designed over _____ for homes, offices and hotels.

① one thousand furnitures
② one thousand furniture
③ one thousand pieces of furnitures
④ one thousand pieces of furniture

23

①As job hunts became tough after the financial crisis, ②an anecdotal evidence suggested that ③more young people ④considered public service.

24

Air Force One was ①due to land in Washington ②in Tuesday morning after an overnight flight from the island of Oahu. The president is returning from vacation ③the same day Republican presidential candidates square off in the Iowa caucuses, the first ④nominating contest of the 2012 campaign.

25

These four major corporations ①have tasked their troops ②to employ all ③means necessary to explore ④moon for rubium deposits, ⑤then establish and secure rubium refineries.

12강 대명사

대명사란?

영어는 똑같은 단어를 반복하여 쓰는 것을 꺼린다. 그렇게 발달하게 된 품사가 바로 대명사이다. 결국 대명사는 앞에 있는 명사 중 하나를 대신 받는 '명사'라는 것을 기억해야 한다.

대명사 주요 포인트

01 대신 받는 명사를 찾아 대명사의 수 일치와 성을 묻는 유형

02 대명사의 격(주격, 소유격, 목적격)을 묻는 유형
  ex. This is between you and *I*. (×) / This is between you and **me**. (○)

03 후치 수식을 받는 대명사 that과 those의 구분을 묻는 유형

04 most와 almost의 구분을 묻는 유형
  ex. *Almost* people are poor. (×) / **Most** people are poor. (○)

05 one, another, the other / some, others, the others의 구분을 묻는 유형

06 all, most, some of 뒤 관사의 유무를 묻는 유형
  ex. *Some of books* are interesting. (×) / **Some of the books** are interesting. (○)

07 대명사 many와 much의 수 일치를 묻는 유형
  ex. *Many* of the students *is* present. (×) / **Many** of the students **are** present. (○)
    Much of the money *are* spent. (×) / **Much** of the money **is** spent. (○)

08 대명사 none과 형용사 no의 구분을 묻는 유형
  ex. There is *none* wind. (×) / There is **no** wind. (○)

01

The duties of the priest ① towards the secrecy of the ② confessional seemed so grave to me that I wondered ③ how anybody had ever found in himself the courage to undertake ④ it.

02

Martin Luther King Jr.'s assassination ironically ① resulted in a series of violent ② riots across nearly every major city in America, though ③ it always ④ advocated the use of nonviolent protest.

03

Researchers at the university ① are investigating a series of ② indicators that ③ could help ④ themselves ⑤ predict earthquakes.

04

Government authorities will focus their attention ① on the expansion of the nation's railway facilities, ② as ③ it is emerging ④ as the most environmentally-friendly method of transportation.

05

For the last two weeks I ① have had to ② stay up ③ the most of the night to observe star configurations ④ for a project for my astronomy class.

06

I should like to see children ① taught that they should not say they like things ② which they do not like ③ merely because certain other people say they like ④ it.

07

_____ the writers who have produced important work since our last edition have been updated.

① The most of   ② Almost all
③ The almost   ④ Almost some

08

The conflict over the past decade ① has cost more than 100,000 lives in Groznyy, the capital of Chechnya. ② Much of the city ③ remain in ruins and ④ Chechen-led terrorists are spreading the conflict to ⑤ neighboring republics.

09

Science has obviously multiplied the power of the warmakers. The weapons of the moment can kill more people more secretly and more unpleasantly than _____ of the past.

① these   ② those
③ that   ④ this

10

Two ① bus-crashes in separate locations in Morocco ② have claimed 27 lives, including ③ that of a German and a ④ Dutch tourist.

11

Every year, ① hundreds of people leave important jobs in the government to take more lucrative positions in private industry. ② Some go to work as lobbyists, ③ another as consultants to business, ④ still others as key executives in corporations, foundations and universities.

12

① Almost orders ship within 3 to 5 business days of purchase. Shipping times may ② vary due to availability of merchandise. ③ Should you change or cancel your order, please contact us immediately. ④ Once the parcel was sent to the post office, we will be unable to make ⑤ any changes.

13

Some former White House residents have remained ① in the public eye ② for life, while ③ the others have slipped ④ into obscurity.

14

① Most of critics agrees that the gothic has been ② an important presence in America beginning with Charles Brockden Brown and that ③ it continues to influence the nation's culture and to ④ permeate the nation's literature at every level.

15

In science one experiment, ① whether it ② succeeds or fails, is ③ logically followed by ④ other in a ⑤ theoretically infinite progression.

16

Although sleep disorder is ① associated with heart disease in both men and women, ② they may negatively ③ affect the heart rates of women more than ④ those of men.

17

In ① the La Sierra region you'll find the temperate weather ② patterns that give Ecuador ③ it's status ④ as the Land of Eternal Spring.

18

Acute stress is ① the most common form of stress. It ② comes from demands and pressures of ③ the recent past and ④ anticipated demands and pressures of the near future. Acute stress is thrilling and exciting in small doses, but ⑤ too many is exhausting.

19

Artificial intelligence (AI) is part of our global culture, and ① their impact on our everyday lives ② is growing. Searching for news ③ about AI presents a deluge of information. Why not ④ use a little AI of our own ⑤ to better handle the task?

20

① By the time Ralph Rogers completes his testimony, every major executive of our company but Mark Jamieson ② and I ③ will have been accused of complicity in the stock swindle. ④ No error

21

① Most of the water at the bottom of the North Pacific Ocean ② has not been exposed to sunlight in at least 800 years and ③ some of them has been down there ④ for two millennia.

22

Those who distrust science ① as a guide to conduct, ② whether individual or social, ③ seem to overlook ④ their pragmatic nature, or perhaps they scorn it for that very reason.

23

① Spending money on tablet computers may ② seem an extravagance, but some ③ of educators say they are more than ④ just a cool toy.

24

Why a person has ① none friendship is ② something that cannot ③ be adequately ④ determined by ⑤ a survey.

25

In this movie, a young woman working as a sales associate at a department store takes a mannequin that resembles _____ to the rooftop of the building and drops it to the ground, morbidly curious to know what it feels like to jump off there.

① him   ② himself
③ her   ④ herself

13강 형용사

형용사란?

형용사는 명사를 수식하는 단어이다. 단, 명사 앞에 위치할 수도 있고, 명사 뒤에 위치할 수도 있다. 어느 위치이건 형용사는 명사를 수식하는 역할 그 이상도 이하도 아니라는 것을 명심하고 몇 가지의 문제 포인트만 기억하면 된다.

형용사 주요 포인트

01 가산명사를 수식하는 many, a few, few / 불가산명사를 수식하는 much, a little, little
ex. There is *few* hope. (×) / There is **little** hope. (○)
　　I had *little* opportunities. (×) / I had **few** opportunities. (○)

02 명사 뒤에만 위치해야 하는 alike, alive, alone, asleep, afraid를 묻는 유형
ex. Asleep baby just woke up. (×) / A **sleeping** baby just woke up. (○)

03 「숫자-(하이픈) 연결명사」를 묻는 유형
ex. She is ten-*years*-old girl. (×) / She is ten-**year**-old girl. (○)

04 every+기수(two, three 등)+Ns(복수명사) / every+서수(second, third 등)+N(단수명사)
ex. Olympic games are held *every four year*. (×) / Olympic games are held **every four years**. (○)
　　Olympic games are held *every fourth years*. (×)
　　Olympic games are held **every fourth year**. (○)

05 (n)either의 형용사 용법을 묻는 유형
ex. Neither sisters attended class. (×) / **Neither sister** attended class. (○)

06 수단위 명사의 단수형과 복수형을 묻는 유형
ex. Hundred of students are absent. (×) / **Hundreds of** students are absent. (○)

01

① Those who pass their lives in foreign travel find they contract ② much ties of hospitality, but ③ form no ④ friendships.

02

The prime minister ① held to his long-standing goal ② of a balanced budget and, ③ alike his predecessor, ④ called for considerable ⑤ increase in public expenditure.

03

The fertility rate of women with ① higher incomes ② is higher while women who ③ pursue careers tend to have ④ less babies.

04

When I mailed ① the 200-pages manuscript ② to my editor, I didn't ③ realize that the pages were ④ completely ⑤ out of order.

05

The number of work permits ① issued to Hong Kong ② nationals during the ③ twelve-months period ④ was ⑤ eight hundred.

06

A distinction ① between 'fact' and 'fiction' seems ② unlike to get us very far, not least because ③ the distinction itself ④ is often a questionable one.

07

Although the unique circumstances of every life ① result in ② each of us having an individual way ③ of speaking, we generally tend to ④ sound alike others who share similar educational backgrounds with us.

08

It was July 10, 2012, and I was an ordinary ① 17-years-old girl, who'd been ② feeling unwell. ③ With my mother by my side, I now sat in Dr. Mahbob's office and ④ awaited my diagnosis.

09

① Many evidence ② indicates that ③ the number of gorillas ④ in the wild is decreasing ⑤ drastically.

10

Today's young people have very adult worries about the uncertainty of the future and the lack of jobs in particular, far _____.

① different to what their parents' generation
② from different their parents' generation
③ different what their parents' generation
④ different from their parents' generation

11

When a fluid is ① in motion, its flow can be characterized in one of two ways. The flow ② is said to be streamline, or laminar, if every particle that ③ passes a particular point moves along exactly ④ smooth the same path followed by previous particles passing that point.

12

The World Conference Against Racism is supposed to put ① on the table such sensitive issues ② that reparation for slavery and the question of ③ whether Zionism is racism ④ or not.

13

① None direct flights are ② currently scheduled from New York to Seoul, ③ but an airline agent can recommend ④ an alternative travel route.

14

The Olympic Games, which take place once every four ① year, are ② considered the most competitive ③ of athletic ④ competitions.

15

Recent presidents have made ① a great deal of pledges they didn't keep. You may not like everything I tell you tonight, but you ② deserve to hear the truth. On the economy we've made ③ a little progress, but we still have ④ a great deal of work to do.

16

If you want ① to be happy, here are ② a little tips ③ for overcoming six common ④ barriers to happiness.

17

Nearly ① two-thirds of Americans ② choose higher payroll taxes for Medicare and Social Security over ③ reduced benefits in either ④ programs.

18

CPRSS, the ① official news organization of China, ② disseminates information ③ to domestic ④ and internationally newspapers.

19

The company is _____, flying to 80 destinations in 55 countries.

① a world second profitable airline
② the world secondly profitable airline
③ the world's second most profitable airline
④ a world's secondly most profitable airline

20

During the past decade _____ have cobwebbed across the continent, putting cheap flights within the reach of every vocationer or jobseeker.

① the score of new routes
② scores of new route
③ scores of new routes
④ the score of new route

21

Credit insurance against default on corporate bonds costs _____ default insurance for the government debt.

① nine time as many as
② nine times as much as
③ nine times as many as
④ nine time as much as

22

_____ here is that these situations tend to repeat themselves and things seem to roughly continue the same.

① What interesting
② What an interesting
③ Being interested
④ Of interest
⑤ Having been interested

23

Government economists are taking a _____ view of the country's IT market this year, citing a recent pattern of slowing growth.

① conserved
② conserving
③ conservation
④ conservative

24

Robinson ① desired a happy marriage and hoped ② to be a great man ③ in politics; he achieved ④ neither goals.

25

United Nations ① is accusing the militia ② of blocking emergency food supplies to ③ tens of ④ thousand of people in the suburban area.

14강 부사

부사란?

명사를 제외한 나머지 모든 품사(형용사, 부사, 동사)와 문장 전체의 의미를 돕기 위해 나오는 수식어(구, 절)이다. 부사 역시 문법 문제로 묻는 포인트가 많다고 할 수는 없다. 하지만 그 중 형용사와 부사의 구분을 묻는 문제는 문법의 전체 파트를 통틀어 보아도 엄청난 비중을 차지한다. 그리고 형용사와 부사의 구분은 자리만이 아닌 해석이 필요하다는 것 역시 주의해야 한다.

부사 주요 포인트

01 명사를 수식하는 형용사 / 명사 외에 모든 품사를 수식하는 부사의 구분을 묻는 유형

ex. These are *basically* predictions. (×) / These are **basic** predictions. (○)

02 how, too, as, so 뒤 「형용사+a/an+명사」의 어순을 묻는 유형

ex. It is *too a good deal* to lose. (×) / It is **too good a deal** to lose. (○)

03 such, quite, rather 뒤 「a/an+형용사+명사」의 어순을 묻는 유형

ex. This is *a quite small city*. (×) / This is **quite a small city**. (○)

04 how(ever) 뒤 형용사와 부사가 있을 때 그 구분을 묻는 유형

ex. I know how *easily* the exam is. (×) / I know how **easy** the exam is. (○)

I know how *heavy* she depends on me. (×) / I know how **heavily** she depends on me. (○)

05 more ~ than 사이에서 형용사/부사의 구분을 묻는 유형

ex. Sue is more *beautifully* than Jane. (×) / Sue is more **beautiful** than Jane. (○)

06 「the more 형용사/부사」의 구분을 묻는 유형

ex. The more *precisely* his words are, the more effective the communication is. (×)

The more **precise** his words are, the more effective the communication is. (○)

07 be R-ing(진행), be p.p.(수동), have p.p.(완료) 사이에서 형용사/부사의 구분을 묻는 유형

ex. He is *current* learning the skill. (×) / He is **currently** learning the skill. (○)

08 자동사와 전치사 사이에서 형용사/부사의 구분을 묻는 유형

ex. She depended *heavy* on him. (×) / She depended **heavily** on him. (○)

01

The son ① of Italian immigrants grows up ② poorly in San Francisco and becomes the greatest baseball player ③ of his day, marries an American goddess and never ④ in word or deed befouls his legend and greatness.

02

① At issue is whether Treasury Inflation-Protected Securities, commonly ② known as TIPS, are ③ too a good deal for investors: Opponents say the government ④ has been losing money on them while defenders question ⑤ the accounting.

03

It would ① thus be futile to argue that industrialization destroyed the great ② extended family of ③ the past, since such a family type ④ rare existed.

04

① Most people think ② of deserts as dry, flat areas with little vegetation and little ③ or no rainfall, but this is ④ hard true.

05

① Although mankind has ② undergone no general improvement in intelligence or ③ morality, it has made ④ extraordinarily progress in the accumulation of knowledge.

06

Photoperiodism is the ① functional or behavioral ② response of an organism to ③ changes in duration of daily, ④ seasonally, or yearly periods of light and darkness.

07

She has ① so a ② good memory ③ that she can remember ④ a person's exact words ⑤ even a week later.

08

A scandal last month at the University of Virginia, where 122 students are ① being investigated for ② possible plagiarism of term papers, ③ revealed ④ how easily cheating has become.

09

Tomatoes, ① actual a fruit that is used as ② a vegetable, began ③ gaining wide acceptance as ④ a food plant in the United States ⑤ between 1820 and 1850.

10

① A jet stream is a flat and narrow tube ② of air that moves more ③ rapid than the ④ surrounding air.

11

When I spoke English, people nodded ① at me, smiled ② sweet, said encouraging words. ③ Even the people in my culture ④ would say that I'd do well in ⑤ life.

12

Bone is one of ① the hardest materials in the body and, although ② relative light in weight, it has a remarkable ability ③ to resist tension and other forces ④ acting on it.

13

① In spite of a tremendous amount of ② electronic gadgetry, ③ air traffic control still depends ④ heavy on people.

14

① Environmental conscious and ② socially minded travelers ③ should try to determine ④ how much of an opportunity they will have to ⑤ make a contribution at their destinations.

15

① Humans leave their ② nuclear families when they ③ get married. ④ Similar, chimpanzees often join a new group to ⑤ mate and reproduce.

16

The terrain of Antarctica, ① near one and a half ② times as big ③ as the United States, ④ is amazingly varied.

17

We think and talk _____ to have conscious awareness of and control over everything we think and say.

① at too fast a rate
② in too fast a rate
③ at a too fast rate
④ in a too fast rate

18

Due to our ① overwhelmingly growth of nearly 1,000% ② over the last three years, we have an immediate need and ③ are willing to train even ④ non-experienced individuals in local markets.

19

① The actual causes for international conflicts may differ ② substantial ③ from the reasons ④ provided in public statements.

20

① The question of ② whether computers can have ③ minds is ④ rapid becoming ⑤ a significant issue.

21

With electronic health records ① seen ② widely as a way to make medical care better, it is ③ disturbing ④ how slow they are being adopted by doctors.

22

The internet now plays _____ in many people's lives that it is essential for us to try to decide whether it is good or bad.

① such important a part
② such a part important
③ so important a part
④ a part so important

23

Barbara McLintock was a creative thinker among scientists, one for whom intuition played _____ formal experimentation and analysis.

① as an important role as
② as important a role as
③ as a role important as
④ as important as a role

24

While ① being big is still an advantage — size offers ② a better survival cushion if food ③ proves hard to find — there are other factors that limit ④ how easy that trait is passed down.

25

After the Grimm Brothers ① had ② collected "housewives' tales" ③ from around the country, they ④ edited them into stories ⑤ appropriately for children.

에듀윌 편입
솔루션 문법 Basic

15강 비교

비교란?

비교의 종류에는 원급 비교(as ~ as ...), 우등 비교(-er/more ~ than ...), 최상급(the -est/most ~)이 있다. 이 셋의 비교 형태는 각각 전혀 다른 의미를 지니지만 비교 파트의 문법 문제는 보통 해석이 수반되지 않고 분석으로 접근하는 경우가 대부분이니 문제로 묻는 몇 가지의 포인트에 주의한다면 어렵지 않을 것이다.

비교 주요 포인트

01 원급 비교(as ~ as ...), 우등 비교(-er/more ~ than ...), 최상급 비교(the -est/most ~)의 어울림을 묻는 유형

02 문장에 than이 있을 때 앞에 비교(-er/more ~) 표현의 유무를 묻는 유형
ex. He acquired *high* grade *than* Mary. (×) / He acquired **higher** grade **than** Mary. (○)

03 비교(-er/more ~) 앞에 예외적으로 정관사 the를 쓰는 경우를 묻는 유형

04 「the more+형용사/부사+S+V ~, the more+형용사/부사+S+V ...」 형태의 점진 비교 구문의 어순을 묻는 유형
ex. The more *his words are precise*, the more effective the communication is. (×)
The more **precise his words are**, the more effective the communication is. (○)

05 배수사의 위치를 묻는 유형
ex. The river is *longer two times than* the stream. (×)
The river is **two times longer than** the stream. (○)

06 twice 뒤 -er/more ~ than의 불가능을 묻는 유형
ex. I earned *twice more* money *than* you. (×) / I earned **twice as** much money **as** you. (○)

07 최상급 앞 정관사 the의 유무를 묻는 유형
ex. She is *most beautiful* of the girls. (×) / She is **the most beautiful** of the girls. (○)

08 -ior로 끝나는 형용사 뒤 전치사 to와 비교의 than의 선택을 묻는 유형
ex. She is three years *senior than* me. (×) / She is three years **senior to** me. (○)

09 비교 대상의 일치를 묻는 유형
ex. *The climate* of Korea is like *Japan*. (×) / **The climate** of Korea is like **that** of Japan. (○)

01

In a study of local brain activity in people ① performing a language task, people with ② stroke-related aphasia showed ③ high activity levels in the right half of the brain than ④ people who did not have aphasia.

02

The students whose parents let them see R-rated movies sometimes or all the time were _____ have tried smoking during the study period as those who never saw the movies.

① almost five times as likely to
② almost as five times likely to
③ as almost five times likely to
④ almost five times more likely to

03

The more I learned about the current trend in intellectual property law, _____ that novel forms of cultural copyright come with substantial risks.

① the more became it obvious
② it became the more obvious
③ the more obvious it became
④ the more it obvious became

04

Of several word processors that are ① being used these days, most of Americans and Europeans think that MS Word is ② the better since it is ③ easier to learn than other ④ ones.

05

She finally became even ① very violent in her disposition than her husband himself. She was not satisfied ② with simply doing ③ as well as he had commanded; she seemed anxious ④ to do better.

06

① Hurricane Charley is one of ② most destructive hurricanes ③ ever to hit ④ the United States. More than 20 people died ⑤ because of Charley's effects.

07

① Although ② most of the wild horses in the western range have already been ③ rounded up, the more remote the area, ④ the greatest the possibility that ⑤ they can still be found.

08

Mortgage ① approvals in Britain were more than ② a third higher in November ③ as a year earlier as government subsidies for homebuyers helped the property recovery ④ gather pace.

09

I can tell you that the new director of our department is _____ man I have ever met.

① the most quite stupid
② most the quite stupid
③ the quite most stupid
④ quite the most stupid

10

Young adults who live with their parents are ① nearly as ② likely to say they are satisfied with their housing situation ③ like those who live ④ on their own.

11

In some countries, ① higher levels of enrollment for young adult women ② are linked to improved access ③ to education, but they can also imply a later insertion into the labor market ④ then for men.

12

New York City commuters spend ① little time ② annually delayed by traffic congestion ③ than the average ④ for very large cities.

13

① Of the three main forms of fossil fuels — coal, petroleum, and natural gas — petroleum is ② the more common, providing approximately 40 percent of ③ the world's energy, ④ with coal and natural gas each providing nearly 25 percent.

14

① Many believe that people in Asian countries ② tend to be ③ more reserved than ④ the western countries.

15

Researchers have found ① in a review of studies that the density of billboards advertising tobacco products ② is ③ more than twice as high in black neighborhoods ④ than in white.

16

Babies' intelligence, ① the research shows, is very ② different from adults and ③ from the kind of intelligence we usually ④ cultivate in school.

17

The longer the treatment for snakebite is delayed, _____.

① one risks losing a limb is greater
② the greater one risks losing a limb
③ the greatest one risks losing a limb
④ the greater one risks to lose a limb
⑤ one risks to lose a limb is greater

18

My ① going to such a place was part of my mother's not so secret plan ② to change my character, which she worried ③ was becoming too much like ④ her.

19

We are as much delighted ① by benevolence ② than we are gratified by the scent ③ of perfume ④ or nauseated by a foul stench.

20

① One big advantage writing ② offers over speaking is that we can refine our message, making ③ it as ④ succinctly as possible.

21

The institutions of science mean ①that the theories and ideas that scientists have developed are far superior ②than the ③ones that we human ④beings had before the growth of modern science.

22

We really ①do perceive the sun ②as ③close to us ④than it actually is.

23

The problem of school education that John ①is experiencing is similar to ②you ③in that they both ④stem from the lack of interaction between students and teachers.

24

The placement of ①the sun at the center of the universe by Galileo was ②certainly more important than ③the principle of buoyancy and may be more important than ④any scientific discovery in the history of the world.

25

She makes ①much high grades than her sisters; however, ②they are a great deal ③more sociable than ④she is.

16강 일치와 도치

일치란?

문법 문제에서 일치라고 하면 크게 주어와 동사의 수 일치와 대명사의 수 일치를 말한다. 대명사의 수 일치는 대명사에서 이미 다루고 왔으니 여기서는 주어와 동사의 수 일치만 따지면 된다.

도치란?

도치란 영어의 원래 어순인 「주어+동사」를 뒤집어 「동사+주어」로 쓰는 것을 말한다. 결국 도치를 해야만 하는 형태를 익혀야 문제를 풀어낼 수 있다. 도치를 해야만 하는 형태가 나오면 반드시 어순을 묻는다는 것을 명심해야 한다.

일치와 도치 주요 포인트

01 다양한 수식어구를 통해 멀어진 주어와 동사의 수 일치를 묻는 유형

02 여러 가지 대명사가 주어로 나왔을 때 동사와 수 일치를 묻는 유형

03 부정대명사가 주어로 나왔을 때 of 뒤 명사와 동사의 수 일치를 묻는 유형

04 「a number of+Ns」, 「the number of+Ns」가 주어로 나왔을 때 동사의 수 일치를 묻는 유형
ex. A number of students *is* rich. (×) / A number of students **are** rich. (○)
The number of boys *are* increasing. (×) The number of boys **is** increasing. (○)

05 도치된 상태에서 뒤에 나온 주어와 동사의 수 일치를 묻는 유형
ex. Among sea creatures *are the tuna*. (×) / Among sea creatures **is the tuna**.

06 등위상관접속사가 주어로 나왔을 때 동사와 수 일치를 묻는 유형
ex. *They* as well as he *is* present. (×) / **They** as well as he **are** present. (○)

07 부정어를 문두로 이동하여 강조했을 때 주어, 동사의 도치를 묻는 유형
ex. Never *I have* seen him. (×) / Never **have I** seen him. (○)

08 「only 부사/only 전명구/only 부사절」을 문두로 이동시켜 강조했을 때 주어, 동사의 도치를 묻는 유형
ex. Only yesterday *I knew* the fact. (×) / Only yesterday **did I know** the fact. (○)

09 보어를 강조하여 문두로 이동했을 때 주어, 동사의 도치를 묻는 유형

10 장소, 시간, 방향의 전명구를 강조하여 문두로 이동했을 때 주어, 동사의 도치를 묻는 유형

01

A computerized map of the freeways using information gathered by sensors embedded in the pavement _____ on a local cable channel during rush hours.

① to air   ② airing
③ air   ④ airs

02

Beijing's decision to require that all new personal computers ① sold in China ② contain software that ③ bars access to certain Internet content ④ seem self-destructive and foolish.

03

One study found ① that those who consistently felt impatient and pressed for time ② was more than twice as likely ③ as laid-back types ④ to develop high blood pressure over ⑤ a 13-year period.

04

Writers ① intent on informing their readers often, ② without realizing it, ③ includes a word or phrase that ④ expresses their ⑤ personal point of view.

05

① Seldom we have these types of arguments, but if we're ② concerned about our friendship, we need to ③ talk about it more and try to ④ cooperate with each other.

06

① Since the end of World War II, the dynamic growth of communication systems of all types ② have provided a unique opportunity for the development of new methods ③ to influence public opinion ④ on a wide range of activities and behaviors.

07

The series ① of natural phenomena ② could be described in ③ their entirety without mentioning the value of things, and our scale of valuation remains meaningful, whether or not one of its objects ④ appear frequently or at all in reality.

08

Throughout the ① developed world, we are at a point ② in our evolution ③ at which famine, ④ which essentially governed the rise and fall of civilizations throughout history, ⑤ are no longer an acute threat.

09

Paying for union services ① only when you need ② them ③ are like paying taxes for police and fire services only if you use ④ them.

10

Only occasionally _____ reading Tom's newspaper, over his shoulder, as she sat in the station waiting room.

① found she herself
② she finds herself
③ did herself she find
④ did she find herself

11

The takeover of the New York Stock Exchange's owner illustrates ① starkly how trading in commodities and derivatives ② have become ③ much more lucrative than ④ trading in corporate shares.

12

_____ scholars who regularly publish their professional works has doubled since 2002.

① As many as
② As most of
③ The quantity of
④ The number of

13

Those who favor the new administrative law say that the present law does not set spending limits on lobbyists' gifts to politicians, _____ statewide funds.

① nor it limits
② nor does it limit
③ nor they limit
④ nor do they limit
⑤ nor they are limited

14

The religion of the Hopi Indians ① include ② several different ceremonies ③ intended to influence or ④ pay respect to nature.

15

Every non-Western society is searching for a path to modernity that it can feel _____ in some way local, authentic and, in that sense, non-Western.

① is   ② are
③ being   ④ be

16

From that act of civil disobedience _____ spawned the New Power Party, which allied with the DDP and won five legislative seats of its own.

① had   ② were

③ has   ④ was

17

It is true that ① much of the Korean Art as it ② developed through the early years ③ were influenced by ④ the Chinese.

18

Just as the early 20th century had the great master Pablo Casals, ① the latter part of the last century had Rostropovich. Despite ② being regarded as the best in his era, he was modest and humble. ③ That he recorded the entire Bach Cello Suites when he was over 60 ④ prove his modesty.

19

① Like baseball parks and basketball-hockey arenas, football stadiums have ② for decades ③ been evolving into places ④ where an increasing amount of the real estate ⑤ are devoted to premium-priced seating.

20

Each year the number of students who ① are unable to find ② a dorm room for the semester and forced to live ③ off campus without meal plans ④ are soaring.

21

_____ that everyone left the auditorium.

① So monotonously did he speak
② He so did speak monotonously
③ Monotonously did he speak so
④ So did he monotonously speak

22

Wages and the cost of living _____ in virtually equal proportions through the generations.

① have grown   ② having grown
③ growing   ④ grows

23

It ① is often remarked that the advent of the movies and the ② ever faster pace of modern life ③ has conspired to make description a ④ less essential part of prose narrative in our ⑤ own times.

24

People in a growth mindset do not just seek challenge, they ① thrive on it. The bigger the challenge, ② the more they stretch. And nowhere ③ it can be seen more clearly than in the world of sport. You can just watch people ④ stretch and grow.

25

Good parents wouldn't jump to conclusions, _____ assume that every problem was a catastrophe they needed to fix.

① never they would
② or would they
③ neither they would
④ nor would they

01

Companies ① taking a longer term view of profit with the idea of being ② socially responsible through sustainable development ③ is being rewarded both with government support and by consumers ④ as they make their purchases.

02

The danger of eating ① too much pepper, ② not to speak of drinking only soft drinks and beers, ③ do not seem to worry ④ either Susan or John.

03

Somewhere between the business newsletter, the consumer magazine, and a hobby _____ zines (pronounced "zeens").

① are periodicals called
② are called periodicals
③ periodicals are called
④ called periodicals are

04

Some scientists propose that thumb ① sucking in children ② are a habit which is ③ developed at random, but recent theory suggests that is neurologically and genetically ④ based.

05

The truth is that ① the commonest response to violence is ② one of repugnance, and ③ that a significant number of people everywhere ④ tries to oppose it ⑤ in whatever ways they can.

06

The point ① at which physical decline ② with age ③ begins adversely to affect ④ a driver's capability ⑤ have not yet been studied.

07

The lowest stockpiles in ① decades mean there ② are less grain to buffer the impact of drought, ③ floods, and crop failures, ④ making prices ⑤ more volatile.

08

① As is usual in such cases, she was the apple of his father's eye. Among his courtiers ② were young man of that fineness of blood and lowness of station common to the heroes of romance who love royal maidens. This royal maiden was well content with her lover, ③ for he was handsome and brave to a degree ④ unsurpassed in all this kingdom.

09

① Neither the Bronte sisters nor their brother Branwell ② are remembered ③ as healthy or happy. ④ No error

10

① Neither of my parents, ② who was born in Eastern Europe, ③ understands the full implications of ④ a democratic electoral system.

11

The number of countries ① capable of developing nuclear weapons ② have increased to more ③ than 20 ④ in recent years.

12

In April, Steve Jobs launched his iPad. And it was good. The iPad was not the first eReader or Tablet on the market, nor _____ as multi-functional as the iPhone. You can't make phone calls with an iPad.

① it was not   ② it was

③ was it   ④ it was so

13

Only ①with recent advances in genetic science ②has physicians been able to begin ③curing genetic diseases. Doctors can now treat ④a number of genetic diseases that individuals may inherit from their parents.

14

Research in ①learning ②suggests that ③getting good grades ④depend more on effective study skills than on a high IQ.

15

I say ①with confidence that neither of my children ②have ③ever before bothered to read ④a single word of this book.

16

That the committee members could not agree with each other about solving those problems _____ caused more serious problems.

① is   ② was
③ has   ④ have

17

The prominence of names like Rockefeller, Carnegie, Hill and Armour ①indicate that business ②was still thought of as a field of personal competition, ③of heroic endeavor, and ④not of corporate manipulation.

18

Only when the skill is repeated with consistently correct outcomes _____.

① has it truly been learned
② has been it truly learned
③ it has truly been learned
④ has it truly been learning
⑤ it has been truly learning

19

①At least part of their great secret ②is that ③they both live in the same country. White and black have shared that secret for a long time now, and ④has done an efficient job of keeping ⑤it from each other.

20

The ①varied classes of organic compounds with their basically common pattern as well as ②with their peculiarities and reactions ③serves as groundwork for this course. ④No error

21

Beneath the epidermal cells _____ the body-wall muscle, which is relatively thick in some species under certain circumstances.

① exist   ② exists
③ exist where   ④ where it existed
⑤ where exist

22

Avery's most recent works, ①in addition to television shows, ②has been several popular movies and cable broadcast comedy programs. He also frequently ③donates his time to charity events ④to help raise money for children in need.

23

The grand, ①leading principle, ②toward which every ③argument unfolded in these pages directly converges, ④are the absolute and essential importance of human development in its richest diversity.

24

But ①what genuinely recommends the service is the public playlist facility, allowing individual users ②to curate and publish groupings of songs ③based on whatever criteria ④takes their fancy.

25

Mistinguett was not highly talented as a dancer, _____ a good voice, but she had vitality and conviction, and even in old age she was able to play young parts.

① neither had she
② nor she have
③ neither did she have
④ nor did she have

에듀윌 편입
솔루션 문법 Basic

17강 문의구성

문의구성이란?

문의구성은 문장의 구성을 줄인 표현이다. 즉, 문의구성은 문장에서 각각의 품사 혹은 단어들이 가진 역할을 제대로 하는지, 문장을 구성하는 데 있어 오류는 없는지에 대한 부분을 묻는다. 평소에 구조 분석하는 것을 습관화한다면 쉽게 풀어낼 수 있다. 하지만 구조 분석은 기본적인 품사 개념과 접속사, 준동사의 지식이 필수적으로 수반되어야 하기 때문에 2~3달 정도의 연습 시간이 필요하다.

문의구성 주요 포인트

01 문장을 구성하는 주어의 자리를 묻는 유형

02 문장을 구성하는 동사의 자리를 묻는 유형

03 동격을 나타낼 수 있는 「콤마(,)+명사」의 구조를 묻는 유형

04 수식어구가 필요한 자리를 묻는 유형

05 「A, B, and/or C」 병치에서 연결되는 품사를 묻는 유형

01

There ①is inscribed on the walls the ②follow proverb: "Do unto others ③as you would have ④them unto you."

02

He cannot find a suitable job despite _____.

① has been trained thoroughly in repairing and maintaining computers
② his thorough training in the repair and maintenance of computers
③ being trained thoroughly in how to repair and maintaining computers
④ the fact of receiving a thorough computer training in their repair and their maintenance

03

Controversial matters ①involving the whole sections ②were discussed; nevertheless, ③most of the representatives ④remaining calm.

04

Our appetite for food, _____ many modern humans, is a natural drive for survival.

① a problem for
② is a problem for
③ being a problem
④ its problem is

05

When ①the final story has been written for that final newspaper ②sometime in the future, you can be sure ③that it's substance will be some ④violent act that has occurred.

06

Socrates was _____ searches for the truth and the meaning of life.

① a philosopher, a person who

② a philosopher, a person

③ a philosopher and a person who

④ a philosopher and person

07

_____ small specimen of the embryonic fluid is removed from a fetus, it will be possible to determine whether the baby will be born with birth defects.

① If a   ② That a

③ A   ④ After it is a

08

Now mobile chatting is a widely accepted phenomenon, but _____ a novelty in the telecommunications industry.

① once it being

② it was once

③ once there being

④ there was once

09

In November 1989, ① amid the tide of revolt that was sweeping Eastern Europe, ② protesters' seizing the moment and ③ demand new elections ④ led to the resignation of the communist leadership and ⑤ to the end of communism in Czechoslovakia.

10

Chloroplasts evolved ① about 1.6 billion years ago ② then one cell, incapable of using the ③ sun's energy, engulfed ④ another cell that could.

11

So profuse and ①vary is our use of these words that ②it is not easy to define just ③what we mean ④by them.

12

Trucks routinely need fuel, oil, and _____ to remove road grime from the chassis and windows.

① thorough washed
② a thorough washing
③ thoroughly washed
④ a thoroughly washing
⑤ are thoroughly washed

13

Frederick Law Olmsted, who ① designed Manhattan's Central Park, ②wanting the park ③to be a "democratic playground" ④where everyone ⑤was equal.

14

Our teacher ①expects us to be on time, ②to do ③all our homework, and ④sitting quietly ⑤in class.

15

①Undoubtedly, Cathy was taking ②a social science class when her father went to ③the school to see her. Anyone ④has taken the course was not ⑤allowed to use a mobile phone.

16

Detroit was the birthplace of ①both the industrial age and the ②nation's middle class, and the ③city's rise and fall ④being a window into the challenges ⑤facing all of modern America.

17

Multinational companies _____ it increasingly important to employ internationally acceptable brand names.

① finding   ② are finding
③ they are finding   ④ that find

18

The notes are ①by Robert, who is a Dante scholar and a professor emeritus ②at Princeton, ③where he taught the Divine Comedy ④during forty-two years.

19

When he ①was a little boy, Mark Twain ②would walk along the piers, ③watch the river boats, ④swimming and fish in the Mississippi, ⑤much like his famous character, Tom Sawyer.

20

Classroom routines are ①an important factor in keeping children ②constructively busy, in ③encouraging self-discipline, and above all, ④to facilitate learning.

21

Rory, a ranger in an African National Park, ①believes that people should ②do their bit to stop poaching, "whether it's putting some coins ③in a tin, writing an article, or ④just spread the word."

22

Only now are questions such as how a material was produced, how much energy will be used to take care of it, and what happens to it at the end of its life _____ to echo through the industry.

① begin
② begins
③ beginning
④ has begun

23

Emerson ①himself, however, writing at the dawn of ②the industrial ③age, observing ④with interest the proliferation of railways, ware houses, canals and factories, ⑤wishing to make room for the possibility of alternative forms of beauty.

24

More than two-thirds of about 20,680 Olympic athletes _____ for a recent report had caffeine in their urine.

① studied
② study
③ to study
④ studying

25

①Talks with North Korea ②which may create a situation favorable ③to the emergence of ④a middle class that will push for ⑤democratization.

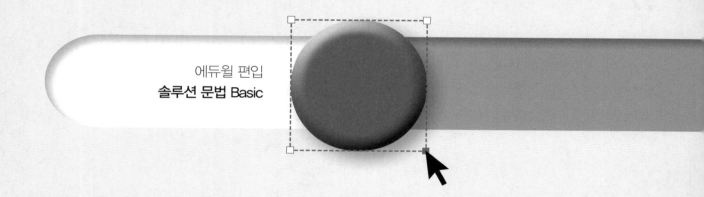

에듀윌 편입
솔루션 문법 Basic

Grammar

Review Test

Practice 01

정답과 해설 p.167

01

① In line with company safety policy, all new workers must first ② participate a safety ③ briefing before ④ attempting to operate dangerous machinery.

02

Men who ① enter into ② female-dominated fields easily ③ move up to supervisory positions, a phenomenon ④ known as the glass escalator.

03

It was ① principally the influence of Christianity ② that deprived beauty ③ from the central place it ④ had in ⑤ classical ideals of human excellence.

04

Wall Street analysts _____ optimistic about the performance of value stocks.

① reached   ② resulted
③ remained   ④ revealed

05

The sun ① was ② raising ③ over the mountain when I ④ rose out of bed and ⑤ sat at the table.

06

The committee didn't really _____ meeting a lot of opposition to the new plan for traffic control.

① anticipate   ② predict
③ expect   ④ prepare

07

Visitors to the zoo are requested to refrain _____ feeding the animals in their cages.

① from   ② with
③ to   ④ of

08

① Unbeknown to my parents, I took several college courses in creative writing and was ② excelling. After reading one of my short stories, my first creative writing teacher decided that I was ③ to be a writer. I decided ④ following my passion instead of obeying my family's decree.

09

My father believed that family members should help each other and made us _____ some chores every Saturdays.

① to do   ② does
③ do   ④ did

10

It's ① very hard to get people ② examine their life unless you ③ remind them it's not going to ④ last forever.

11

The most underrated ① of the major senses, smell has direct access ② at the more primitive, or basic, parts of the brain. Brain imaging techniques ③ have shown that smell can activate mood, emotion, and memory without ④ being consciously perceived.

12

Because the rain ① fell ② all night, the ③ clogged drain pipe ④ bursted and ⑤ flooded the house.

13

We ① decided to go on a trip to the mountains but forgot ② taking the map, ③ so we stopped ④ to buy ⑤ one at a gas station.

14

A ① proposed law ② would make the illegal consumption or sale of dog meat ③ punishing by ④ a fine of up to 5,000 euros.

15

In ① the 1880s, the public's ② well-justified skepticism about doctors encouraged ③ leading medical professors, many of whom ④ had studied in France and Germany, ⑤ began restructuring American medical education.

16

① As more and more teenagers socialize ② online, middle school and high school teachers are increasingly seeing a ③ breezy form of ④ Internet English ⑤ to jump from e-mail into schoolwork.

17

① Anticipating a future ② in which millions of Americans will prefer to ③ shopping in the security of their living rooms, the mall industry is experiencing a ④ full-blown mid-life crisis.

18

People ① with strong personal relationships are 50% ② more likely to outlive ③ than those ④ without.

19

The study ① concerned itself mainly with ② the affects of ③ anxiety on decision making ④ in high-risk situations.

20

While most American architects in the early 1900s looked to Europe for ideas, Frank Lloyd Wright found Japanese design and art _____.

① inspire
② more inspiring
③ is more inspiring
④ are more inspiring

21

One ① third to ② nearly half of the people in the majority of countries ③ surveyed admitted they wanted ④ their spouse ⑤ losing weight.

22

Physicists often find _____ to separate a beam of particles into a spectrum according to their energy.

① it is used   ② it useful
③ useful   ④ its use

23

The company's attorney _____ to them that we should use caution in deciding what information to release to the public.

① notified   ② informed
③ told   ④ said

24

Based on an analysis of the most successful ① executives' schedules and activities, I discovered ② seven practices you ③ should seriously consider ④ to adopt in order to make the most of your morning.

25

The book fair ① outdoors was ② to be opened yesterday, but they were obliged ③ to postponing it ④ on account of the sudden blizzard.

01

Nowadays some might find emotional renewal in pleasant parks and natural lands, but the disadvantaged _____.

① cannot afford reaching to them
② cannot afford to reach them
③ could not afford to reach to them
④ could not afford to reaching them

02

① Using specialized cells, plants can sense gravity ② and redistribute hormones, ③ called auxins, to stimulate growth and allow vital features of the plant ④ develop. However, a big puzzle is ⑤ how this transport process occurs at a cellular level.

03

In ① what appears to be a hallway, a hooded detainee seems ② be handcuffed ③ in an awkward position ④ atop two boxes.

04

① In the draft, ② obtained by the Associated Press, the Security Council demands that all parties in Syria immediately ③ to stop any violence irrespective ④ of where it comes from.

05

① Having failed ② creating a consensus, the boss asked ③ that the decision ④ be put off.

06

① In addition the founding fathers of America ② opposed a strong government ③ because it might ④ interfere people's freedom.

07

William H. Johnson's ①artistic debt to Scandinavia is evident in paintings that ②range from sensitive portraits of citizens in his wife's Danish home, Kerteminde, ③and ④awe-inspiring views of fjords and mountain peaks ⑤in the western and northern regions of Norway.

08

More efforts should be made to attract ①highly skilled foreign workers to help keep the country's growth engine ②to move. A serious consideration ③should be given to a proposal to permit foreigners ④who have stayed here for more than 10 years.

09

"The evolutionary biologist," Huxley says, "is tempted to ask ①whether the aim should not be ②to let the mammal ③die within us, so as the more effectually to permit the man ④live."

10

The superintendent of the jail, who was standing ①apart from the rest of warders, ②moodily ③prodding the gravel with his stick, ④rose his head ⑤at the sound.

11

Yesterday I had to have my car _____ away by the police, since it suddenly stopped on a highway.

① towing ② tow
③ towed ④ town

12

①Although a multinational investigation team blamed the North ②to sink the South Korean warship Cheonan ③in a torpedo attack, North Korea denies ④its involvement.

13

Although you must get off while the bus is ① being cleaned, you may ② leave your suitcases and ③ other belongings ④ laying on your seats.

14

Yet these truths are ① no solace against the kind of alienation that comes of ② being ever the suspect, a fearsome entity ③ with whom pedestrians avoid ④ to make eye contact.

15

① A knowledgeable and open-minded ② evaluation of your current lifestyle might ③ lead to decide to make ④ a few fundamental changes.

16

The exact cause of ① aging is unknown, ② but genetic factors ③ are known to ④ influence on longevity.

17

The president's declaration of an emergency was a procedural maneuver to make it easier for hospitals, should they be swamped with sick people, _____ them to alternate sites for triage and treatment.

① transfer   ② to transfer

③ will transfer   ④ transferring

18

The psychologist William James ① believed that ② facial expressions not only ③ provide a visible sign of an emotion ④ but also actually ⑤ contribute the feeling itself.

19

They admitted nearly 200 people, all of whom sat on simple chairs and ① who could easily hear the accompanying music ② playing on piano by a local girl, who ③ would attempt to match the music ④ to the tone of the particular scene.

20

Students dislike _____ to fill an hour or two hours each night with meaningless homework.

① have been　　　② having

③ to have　　　④ to have been

21

However prepared or well-meaning parents may be, it is difficult for them to acknowledge that their children have grown up, but it is extremely important for them to let the children _____ their own mind.

① to make up

② to making up

③ making them up

④ make up

22

You ① can't just close your eyes and wish us ② back in Kansas among kindly folk who obligingly ③ conform outdated expectations ④ of age.

23

Maria Callas was a woman for whom the term prima donna could have been invented. She was an American-born Greek soprano and made her professional debut in 1942, and since then she _____ to be a singer-actress.

① long considered herself

② was long herself considered

③ long considering herself

④ herself long considering

24

Microfinance ① enables village people in ② developing countries ③ borrow ④ small amounts of money from Microfinance Institutions ⑤ in order to set up small community businesses.

25

As more ① is understood about the genetics and the brains of people who ② stutter, researchers hope that medication aimed directly ③ by the disorder eventually will ④ become available.

Practice

정답과 해설 p.167

01

Tim Morrison, ① who tried to hang ② himself after years of ③ being bullied, ④ has died last Monday.

02

There _____ several attempts to define morality since Middle Ages.

① has been   ② have been
③ was   ④ were

03

The instructor had gone ① over the problems ② many times ③ before the students ④ will take the final examination.

04

The Greeks began to ① write from left to right around the fifth century B.C. because they ② increasingly believe that right was "good" and left was "bad." This belief ③ is still common in many countries today, and ④ left-handed people suffer because of it.

05

By the end of the 1800s, the ① output of ② European artists, writers and scientists ③ have accelerated to the point where ④ it dwarfed the ⑤ productiveness of the 1700s.

06

What causes plants to bloom? Although you may think that plants _____ based on the amount of sunlight they receive, they actually bloom according to the amount of uninterrupted darkness.

① flower   ② flowered
③ flowering   ④ to flower

07

Mr. Kim will already _____ his presentation by the time you reach the convention center.

① have finished   ② finished

③ finish   ④ have been finished

08

He could remember ① driving along the road just ② before the accident ③ happens, but he couldn't ④ remember the accident itself.

09

I ① worked with Peter ② for the past five years and I always found him ③ to be a lawyer of ④ the highest caliber.

10

When the Supreme Court ① rules in 1896 ② in favor of the South's "separate but equal" racial doctrine, the federal government ③ put its stamp of approval ④ on state laws requiring cradle-to-grave segregation of the races.

11

Harrisburg, ① a transportation center in the ② days of riverboat ③ traffic, has been Pennsylvania's capital ④ in 1812.

12

Most historians ① agree that the English alphabet descended ② from ancient Egyptian hieroglyphics that were first recorded ③ more than 5,000 years ④ before.

13

A research report from the Ministry of Knowledge Economy also showed that ① prolonged global recession caused the nation's exports ② to slow and ③ dampened consumer sentiment, which also negatively ④ affect labor productivity.

14

① By the time Ryan graduates, he ② has spent fours years in college and ③ a total of sixteen years of his life in school. Like many students, Ryan believes that the time and money ④ spent on his education ⑤ will pay off.

15

When you ① will realize your bullies will be offended ② no matter what you do, you'll ③ stop trying to please ④ them.

16

This enrichment process was ① what determined the composition of the Solar System 4.5 billion years ago, and ultimately ② makes possible the chemistry of life ③ on Earth ④ as per the "Big Bang" theory.

17

Such Bohemianism could ① be construed as affectation, and it's possible that early in life Katherine Mathilda Winton ② has deliberately cultivated a style that would ③ signal her disregard for ④ a world she found stultifying.

18

In the eight hundred years ① since his death, people ② sought in vain for the grave of Genghis Khan, the 13th-century conqueror and imperial ruler who, at the time of his death, ③ occupied the largest contiguous empire, ④ stretching from the Caspian Sea to the Pacific.

19

I met Kerry years ago when he first ① became an assistant professor. We both taught biology, but Kerry ② liked to use a lot of mathematics in his teaching. This ③ upset his students, who ④ believe that they would escape math by studying biology.

20

① Once marine biologists had determined the precise migratory route of the California whale, they ② are finding that the distance covered was ③ much greater than ④ had been thought.

21

Our superior location, just next to the Jackson Wildlife Preserve, _____ a beautiful natural environment that will help you achieve total well-being.

① ensures
② would ensure
③ had ensured
④ did ensure

22

① In the coming years, the Internet will have ② an even greater impact on the way we shop, get our news, ③ entertained, conduct financial affairs, and ④ talk with friends and family.

23

He ① was ultimately ② known to millions ③ who had no clear idea of what he ④ has done.

24

In an attempt to prevent students from concentrating ① only on school tests, the Seoul Office of Education said that ② it was ③ considering abolishing exams and ④ replace them with essays to encourage creativity.

25

After a couple of environmental researchers had drawn diagrams in ① their notebooks and ② wrote explanations of the formations ③ which they had observed, they returned to their campsite ④ to compare notes.

Practice 01 정답과 해설 p.167

01

① Because gorillas have often been killed ② to permit the capture of their young for zoos and humans have recently been ③ occupied more and more of their habitat, gorillas are now threatened ④ with extinction.

02

Professor Bueno de Mesquita adds that authoritarian governments around the world, ① including China's, ② are shown that they can reap the benefits of economic development while ③ resisting any pressure ④ to relax their power.

03

Art has not always been what we think ① it is today. An object regarded as Art today may not ② have perceived as such when it was first made, ③ nor was the person who ④ made it necessarily regarded as an artist.

04

Typically, ① more trade fairs ② are holding in the fall than in ③ any other month ④ because of the weather in this region.

05

The researchers are developing sensors that ① could be placed on vehicles that regularly cross a bridge, ② such as city buses and police cars. These ③ could be measured how the bridge ④ responds to the vehicle ⑤ moving across it, and report any suspicious changes.

06

Deviance is any non-conformist behavior which ① disapproved of by society or a social group, ② whether it is ③ illegal or not. It is ④ norm-breaking behavior, and can range from being ⑤ eccentric to criminal activity.

07

In 1999, an eighteen-year-old participant died in a gene therapy experiment. His death showed that the researchers _____ the risks of their procedure.

① have not adequately assessed
② have not been adequately assessed
③ had not adequately assessed
④ had not been adequately assessed

08

In Borneo, ①where I was born and ②grown up, I have worked ③in tropical conditions cutting survey lines through a forest that was ④like a jungle.

09

A total eclipse can ①be lasted up to 7 minutes, ②during ③which time the moon's shadow moves across Earth at a rate of about 0.6 kilometers ④per second.

10

We ①take ethical investment very seriously. Recently we ②were involved in a project to build a large dam in the Asian country of Paradiso. We discovered that ③large numbers of farming people ④would force to leave the area flooded by the dam.

11

The right hemisphere of the human brain is less ①crucial to language production and ②appears to be ③more concerned the ④creation of images.

12

①About three hundred years before Caesar, human geography ②treated ③only in conjunction ④with description of particular areas.

13

It is a fact ①that pesticides ②considered unsuitable in rich countries ③are remained in use in many poor ④ones.

14

The attack ① was occurred ② while they were customers at a ③ convenience store ④ in March 2012.

15

So far from being a misfortune, poverty may, by vigorous self-help, _____ into a blessing.

① be converted
② have converted
③ is converted
④ have been converting

16

A strange ① coincidence ② was happened when ③ the news ④ was ⑤ announced this morning.

17

The association of Europe with political freedom _____ in ancient Greece.

① had first been made
② which was first made
③ was first made
④ first made
⑤ was first making

18

① As historical databases ② relatively impoverish, we might expect the ③ newer discipline of quantitative sociolinguistics to ④ cast some light on the matter.

19

Fifty-six people, ① including two ② retired generals, ③ were went on trial in Turkey's second case against a clandestine group ④ accused of ⑤ plotting to overthrow the government of Prime Minister Recep Erdogan.

20

Hundreds of civilians were ① reporting killed in ② shelling, as the army struggled ③ to root out Tamil rebels from ④ the last few square kilometers of land ⑤ under their control.

21

Scientists now know that all objects ① compose of many molecules and the ② force of gravity ③ pulls on ④ each of them.

22

By ① the time when the attack ② was arrived, the defenders ③ could be ④ disconcerted, wavering, worried, hesitant, vacillating.

23

The bodily processes behind taste _____ unclear to date.

① are remained
② remain
③ have been remained
④ remaining

24

The public ① was brought to the realization that ② if Superman could ③ be paralyzed, it could ④ be happened to anybody.

25

The orphans living in the rural village _____ to the amusement park.

① considered took
② considered to take
③ were considered to be taken
④ were considered being taken

01

Because of his stupid behavior, Max was _____ by everybody.

① laughed at   ② laughing at
③ laughed   ④ laughing

02

When private property ① came into existence, and when private property ② could inherit by one of their sons, fathers began ③ to look for the son ④ to whom they could leave their property.

03

After careful deliberation, the proposed merger _____ by the CEO.

① assent   ② is assented
③ is assenting   ④ assents

04

Although these procedures are ① most commonly used to detect the most common genetic ② disorders — Down syndrome, for example — ③ they could, in principle, ④ use to detect more minor genetic abnormalities.

05

Pope Francis on Sunday ① was offered a Christmas hope for peace in a world ② lacerated by war and terrorism, urging people ③ to remember migrants, refugees and those ④ hit by economic instability ⑤ caused by "idolatry of money."

06

To our surprise, Erik Dickinson fell ① short of his parents' expectations, ② disappointing them who kept the faith in their son's potential for success, when he ③ was proved to be ④ a failure as a statesman.

07

A distinction between two kinds of intelligence — crystallized and fluid intelligence — ① has been widely studied by researchers studying adult learning. Crystallized intelligence ② is heavily dependent on education and experience. It ③ is consisted of the set of skills and knowledge that we each learn as part of growing up in any culture. Fluid intelligence, in contrast, ④ is thought to be a more basic set of abilities, not so dependent on specific education.

08

① It seems almost certain that the 60 years after penicillin ② came to market ③ will eventually view ④ as just an interlude in the eternal war between us and them.

09

Today it emerged that about 500 red-winged blackbirds and starlings _____ in Louisiana. Their tiny corpses littered a short stretch of highway near the city of Labarre after apparently falling dead from the sky.

① have found dead
② found dead
③ had found dead
④ had been found dead

10

If we don't get a ① satisfying solution to the problem, we'll ② be forcing to ③ take action ④ against your company.

11

The ① renovated business center, ② which has several restaurants, boutiques and Internet cafes, ③ can be accommodated ④ as many as 1,000 guests.

12

Columbia ① has suffered the heaviest rain in decades ② due to the La Nina weather phenomenon, which ③ is caused water temperature in the Pacific Ocean ④ to drop.

13

① At the meeting held in December, ② it was announced that the choice of recipients ③ had finally limited ④ to Dr. Evert, Professor Applebaum, or her.

14

The injury ①was occurred when the ②25-year-old man ③was running through stunts ④at England's Leavesden Studios.

15

The ①lens and cornea are ②supply with ③nutrients and oxygen by the ④aqueous fluid.

16

To ①ring in the Year of the Rabbit, ②three major museums ③are held exhibitions ④to introduce visitors to the mythology of the rabbit in Korean culture.

17

We have ①been endured the ②successively ③higher levels of unemployment during ④the past three recessions.

18

In 1963 Maria Mayer ①awarded the Nobel Prize ②in physics for her ③findings on the ④constituents of the atomic ⑤nucleus.

19

The event ①is proved to be a great chance ②for us to meet high school ③alumni and other friends ④all at once.

20

A Hong Kong journalist who _____ in mainland China for nearly 16 months for spying charges will face trial this week.

① detains
② is detaining
③ has detained
④ has been detained

21

The world is ① made up with objects. They have properties ② independent of any people or other beings who experience them. For example, ③ take a rock, It's a separate object and it's hard. Even if no people or other beings ④ existed in the universe, it would still be a separate object and it would still be hard.

22

In most of our practical activities, we ① rely upon our senses and develop intuitions we can ② trust. When important issues ③ raise, regardless of what others may say, our own senses and intuitions are our best ④ guides for action.

23

Although the media were ① largely denied access ② with the battlefields, the Gulf War ③ nevertheless gained the reputation of the first real-time television war, and the images ④ projected into American homes ⑤ helped to incite the most passionate war fever since World War II.

24

A natural harbor ① is preferred to an artificial one, for ② the latter is expensive to construct and tends to depreciate rapidly. Hence it is recommended that available capital and manpower ③ expend in improving natural harbors. ④ No error

25

We conclude that brown bears, and perhaps other large mammals, have continuously _____ the archipelago for at least 40,000 years.

① stayed   ② dwelled
③ been dwelled   ④ been lived
⑤ inhabited

Practice
정답과 해설 p.167

01

① One of the central and most difficult moral questions of our age is: Do the terminally ill ② has the right to ③ take their own lives before they suffer great pain or become ④ a burden to others?

02

One of the ① chief things in science ② is careful observation, for things that ③ look rather alike may actually ④ very different when we come ⑤ to look closely.

03

① Keen on green policies, David Cameron used to ② cycling to work in a variety of ③ fetching helmets with his brief case following ④ by car.

04

When there is no alternative for a drug, patients and insurance companies have no choice _____ price a drug-maker set.

① but to pay
② but to pay whatever
③ other than pay whatever
④ other than paying

05

U.S. marines ① on a recent trip to Afghanistan ② offered medical care to local women in the village of Lakari, but ③ some of these women said they would rather die ④ than being touched by a male doctor.

06

If there are any barriers to further progress, then science _____ at unprecedented speed just before it crashes into them.

① well may to move
② well may be move
③ may well be moving
④ may well to move

07

① Sensing the imminent arrival of his infant son, Dr. Frankenstein demanded that his maid ② disinfected his house ③ in order to make sure that the baby is well ④ taken care of.

08

Rey, ① who asked that neither his last name ② nor his given name ③ was used to protect his and his family's privacy, ④ grew up in Chappaqua, the rich Westchester suburb.

09

The yen is weakening. But Tokyo _____ its interest rates again.

① dares not raise

② dare not raise

③ does not dare raise

④ dare not to raise

10

He suggested that all applicants _____ the forms at the front desk and submit them.

① filled out

② be filling out

③ should have filled out

④ fill out

11

① The mayor disparaged our efforts ② to beautify the town square by saying that the flower bed we had planted ③ looked somewhat worse than the weeds ④ it had replacing.

12

Only ① after the agreement was ② made did the CEO ③ decided to forgo having his workers ④ do mandatory overtime work.

13

① Never did I dream that he made ② such a surprising suggestion that the government ③ gives up the bribery tradition which ④ has remained for a long period of time.

14

The ① irritable sergeant ② was insistent that nothing ③ supersedes the drilling of ④ the forty new men.

15

They planned to sell luxury T-shirts and shoes to coincide with the movie's release, but Sarah demanded that the merchandise _____ sold only through her Bitten line.

① should   ② were

③ be   ④ being

⑤ are

16

I _____ to be a practicing doctor, but now I'm more interested in research.

① was used to want

② used to want

③ used to wanting

④ was used to wanting

17

A: Did you criticize his mistake?

B: Yes, but _____ it.

① I'd not rather do

② I'd rather not to do

③ I'd rather not doing

④ I'd rather not have done

18

The professor requested that the student _____ his paper as soon as possible.

① should finish to write

② should finish the writing

③ finish writing

④ finishes writing

⑤ finished writing

19

They couldn't but _____ at the funny scene.

① laughing　　　② laugh

③ laughed　　　④ to laugh

20

① It is mandatory ② that a registered student ③ maintains his or her GPA ④ of B⁺ in the major field.

21

She worked very hard so that she _____ pass the entrance exam.

① will　　　② shall

③ may　　　④ could

22

Some students moved that Kim _____ elected the next chair.

① will be　　　② was

③ be　　　④ had been

23

The scientists could not ① help ② but talking about the success ③ of the Voyager missions ④ among themselves.

24

If the universe is expanding, then in the past it _____ now.

① would have been smaller than it is

② would be smaller than it is

③ must have been smaller than it is

④ must be smaller than it is

25

A: I am surprised that John didn't return your call.

B: He _____ not have gotten my message.

① must　　　② could

③ should　　　④ ought

정답과 해설 p.168

Practice

01

If the convenience store provided more various products, the residents _____ shopping more often.

① will go   ② would go
③ went   ④ would have gone

02

①In the mid-19th century, if you ②wanted to have a scientific fight, you could have ③picked no better subject ④than paleontology.

03

If I ①was in his place, I ②would be very much ③concerned about the future and would certainly be ④taking steps to improve my situation.

04

Had the former President not endorsed him during the last campaign, the first-time presidential candidate _____ lost the election by a narrow margin.

① could not have
② might have
③ shall have
④ ought to have

05

If my boss _____ while I'm out, please tell her that I'll be back as soon as I finish interviewing the candidates.

① call   ② should call
③ will call   ④ called

06

If today I lived in a Communist country where certain principles dear to the Christian faith are suppressed, _____ that country's antireligious laws.

① I will openly advocate disobeying
② I would openly advocate disobeying
③ I will have openly advocated disobeying
④ I would have openly advocated disobeying

07

If qualitatively diverse products were to be offered on one-dimensional consumers, incapable of absorbing the diversity, consumption _____ be limited.

① will   ② can

③ would   ④ shall

08

The author _____ her article was so controversial had it not been for the spate of correspondence.

① would never think

② have never thought

③ have never been thought

④ would never have thought

09

If you _____ English harder when you were young, now you could speak English better.

① had been studying

② studied

③ should have studied

④ had studied

10

_____ empirical evidence to support his views and to finding ways to test them statistically, his influence on economics would have been greater.

① If he devoted much effort to gather

② Did he devoted more effort to gather

③ Had he devoted more effort to gathering

④ If he had devoted much effort gathering

11

_____, I would take them on a night cruise on the river.

① If I have been asked to take visitors on a tour of my city

② If I would be asked to take visitors on a tour of my city

③ If I had asked to take visitors on a tour of my city

④ If I were asked to take visitors on a tour of my city

12

_____, my sister would not have been able to live out her dream as a prominent fashion designer today.

① If it was not an open admission policy

② If there has not been for an open admission policy

③ If it would not have been for an open admission policy

④ If it had not been for an open admission policy

13

I felt _____ I were living two people's lives.

① although   ② even though

③ even if   ④ as if

14

The French philosopher Pascal remarks ① that seemingly trivial occurrences we might not even be aware ② of ③ affect geopolitical event. He famously wrote, "Cleopatra's nose, ④ were it been shorter, the whole face of the world would have been changed."

15

If I had been the CEO, I _____ the company and hired more staff.

① restructured

② would restructure

③ would have restructured

④ would have been restructured

16

The security of England depends on gentlemen being allowed to live peaceably in their homes as decent landlords and masters. _____ the aristocrats of France followed our example, they would not have found themselves severed at the neck.

① If   ② Unless

③ Had   ④ With

17

If sales had not improved, we _____ to consider selling the company last year.

① have

② will have

③ will have had

④ would have had

⑤ would have been had

18

The travels of Marco Polo in the twelfth century would not have been so well known _____ for the book he wrote while in jail.

① had it not been

② it had not been

③ were it not

④ it were not

19

It seems that few businessmen participated in the charity ball for the street children; otherwise, more money _____.

① would have been raised
② was being raised
③ had been raised
④ might have been raising

20

Years later, she said, had her father told me the truth, I _____ a much better girl.

① could have been
② can have been
③ will have been
④ had been

21

I ① would buy this fancy ② furniture yesterday, ③ had I had enough cash ④ on hand.

22

I often found myself regretting my own existence, and wishing myself dead; and _____ the hope of being free, I have no doubt but that I should have killed myself.

① but for
② unless
③ concerning
④ no less than

23

_____ I visited the company earlier, I could have obtained enormous help from lots of different sectors of its management.

① Since   ② If
③ Unless   ④ Had

24

On Sunday afternoon, John planted flowers in his garden by himself. He might _____ $350 if he had hired someone to do the job.

① paying   ② be paid
③ have paid   ④ have been paid

25

An insurance company might send investigators to determine the cause of a mysterious fire. If the investigators sent back a report that the fire was caused by the presence of oxygen in the atmosphere, they would not keep their jobs very long. And yet they would be right. Had there been no oxygen present, there _____ no fire.

① has been   ② is
③ will be   ④ would be
⑤ would have been

정답과 해설 p.168

Practice

01

Cellphones, ① which are usually ② used to helping people keep track of each other, are ③ starting to take on quite a different function — helping users ④ hide their whereabouts.

02

George _____ improve his test score, but he did not have enough time to study.

① knew   ② knew how that
③ knew how   ④ knew how to

03

When ① it comes to the economic expansion, the 1990s ② was a very special period ③ that is unlikely ④ to repeat for a while in recorded American history.

04

You may ① well have misunderstandings about forgiveness ② that ③ lead you to ④ rejecting it out of hand.

05

By 1901 there were enough automobiles on New York's roadways _____ the state to rule that they had to be registered.

① caused   ② would cause
③ causing   ④ to cause

06

① In order ② to be not late for the flight and ③ have ④ enough time for breakfast, I suggest ⑤ getting up at five in the morning.

07

Some people say it's asking too little of Rio
_____ man-made structures to represent
the city's aspirations.

① expects
② has expected
③ is expected
④ to expect

08

Medical bills in the United States have risen
outrageously since the beginning of the 1960's and
steps need _____ to reverse this trend or
the average American will not be able to afford
medical care.

① to take
② to be taken
③ to being taken
④ being taken

09

The US government had been ① preparing for a
hurricane in New Orleans for ② a number of years
and had ③ already decided on a plan ④ getting
people out of the city.

10

Constantinople ① could win the battle ② but not
the war, ③ for there were ④ very many Bulgarians
for Greeks ⑤ to rule.

11

Many researchers have strived ① toward a theory
that is ② enough eclectic to encompass all of
③ their insights in ④ some form.

12

While I wished to obtain ① a sound knowledge of
② all aspects of zoology, I planned ③ to devote
especially ④ to insects.

13

In 1798 the circulation of the journal was 3,000
copies and that number is estimated to _____
by 1809.

① double
② be doubling
③ have doubled
④ have had doubled

14

London restaurants use old newspapers _____ "fish and chips," a traditional Britain dish.

① wrap   ② wraps

③ wrapped   ④ to wrap

15

The city is _____ by one man.

① small enough to be run

② too small for being running

③ too small to run

④ small enough to have run

16

_____ that years ago, the quality and styling of many GM vehicles fell away behind Toyota.

① Sufficiently is it to say

② Suffice it to say

③ Suffice this to say

④ Sufficient this is to say

17

It remains _____ whether a respected economist will have the necessary clout to stick to the reform path.

① to see   ② for seeing

③ to be seen   ④ for being seen

18

Unfortunately, ① the differences in the range of roles that languages play frequently ② lead some people to believe that some languages which do not fulfill ③ a wide range of functions are in fact ④ incapable to do so.

19

It would be like ① drinking whisky simply ② to get drunk, which ③ is likely in the long run ④ diminishing your pleasure in the stuff.

20

The magnitude 9.0 Tohoku earthquake ①on March 11, 2011, ②which occurred near the northeast coast of Honshu, Japan, ③was estimated ④to be caused between 30,000 and 40,000 deaths.

21

In 1991, in the aftermath of Anita Hill's testimony against Supreme Court nominee Clarence Thomas, President George Bush ①signed a law ②granting sexual-harassment plaintiffs the right to ③trial by jury and ④claiming to financial damages.

22

Sisyphus's continuous pushing of the stone up the hill only _____ it roll down again served as the literary model for the third of Zeno's paradoxes.

① having
② having been
③ have
④ to have

23

Around ①the globe, temperatures ②are said ③to climb about ④1.1 degrees in the 20th century.

24

His customers are too worried about ①affording the necessities of life, like food and health care, ②splurging on games, and those who ③do make a purchase tend to ④look for the cheapest items on the shelves.

25

①Repairs to the Washington Monument will require massive scaffolding ②to build around the obelisk and may keep it ③closed into 2014 after ④it was damaged by an earthquake last year.

정답과 해설 p.168

Practice

01

When it comes ① to praise or blame people for ② what they do, we tend to use a standard ③ that is ④ relative to some conception of normal behavior.

02

Meanwhile the lighthouse ① had been growing slowly larger. It had now almost assumed color, and appeared like a little gray shadow on the sky. The man at the oars ② could not be prevented ③ from being turned his head rather often ④ to try for a glimpse of this little gray shadow.

03

Neighborhoods are very clearly ① demarcated according to income level, and there is not much overlap. Poor people live in poor neighborhoods that are characterized by ② dilapidated buildings, broken glass, graffiti, and a general state of disrepair. People are not dedicated to ③ create an aesthetically ④ pleasing environment.

04

I would prefer having an assigned roommate _____.

① to have to choose a roommate on my own
② than to have to choose a roommate on my own
③ to having to choose a roommate on my own
④ than have to choose a roommate on my own

05

She still has nightmares from _____ in a small dark cupboard for hours.

① locking up
② having locked up
③ having been locked up
④ locked up

06

Instead of _____ formal and well rehearsed, the performance was spontaneous, contradictory and mutually respectful.

① that   ② being
③ its   ④ such

07

We are all looking forward with eager anticipation
_____ what James and Bradley will say.

① hear   ② to hear
③ hearing   ④ to hearing

08

From researches ① conducted by biologists, ② it is
known that ants are guided by a secretion ③ paid
onto the soil through the sting, in the manner of ink
④ drawing out of a pen.

09

① With the help of modern mass communication,
an ② increasing number of governments in the
developing world ③ are committed to ④ support
family-planning programs.

10

A recidivist is a person who keeps ① going back to
a life of crime ② even ③ after punished; in other
words, an ④ incurable criminal.

11

① While many museums are strictly no-go zones
for ② photography, for one "museum" in the
Philippines taking happy snaps ③ are an ④ essential
part of the visitor's experience.

12

There is ① no objection his joining the party
② provided he is willing to ③ fit in with the plans of
the group and is ready and able to ④ do his share
of the work.

13

The patrollers got used ① to see Alice ② wander
about and she became just another fixture in the
patrollers' night, worthy of no more attention ③ than
a hooting owl or a rabbit ④ hopping across the
road.

14

① Examining the link between nationality and prosperity in the age of globalism, Milanovic has concluded that ② a human being's place and culture ③ have become the dominant factor ④ in determination standard of living.

15

Women tend to spend as much time as they can _____ those they love.

① support, help, and nurture
② to support, to help, and to nurture
③ supporting, helping, and nurturing
④ supported, helped, and nurtured

16

In spite of some earlier ① confuse ② concerning the opening date of the new plant, we are ③ confident that we will be ready ④ by September 1.

17

Some galleries obtain money through sponsorship. Works of art are often expensive and galleries _____.

① can buy rarely them without organize a public appeal
② can buy rarely them without organized a public appeal
③ can rarely buy them without a public appeal organizing
④ can rarely buy them without organizing a public appeal

18

I appreciate ① you helping me ② to do the dishes, but I wish you would ③ lay them down on the table more ④ carefully.

19

① Instead of ② sticking to one study location, ③ simply change the room ④ where a person studies improves retention.

20

The Belts zoo spend ①a lot of time on ②educating children about the ③importance of ④rare species ⑤in their homeland.

21

Samuel Walton ①pioneered the first ②mail-order business by ③pay cash for merchandise ④directly from manufacturers.

22

In Monmouth County, New Jersey, snow drifts of up to five feet contributed to ①stall a passenger bus on the Garden State Parkway, where snow plows were having a difficult time ②clearing because there were so many ③stranded cars ④cluttering the ramps, state police spokesman Steve Jones said.

23

①Once you become accustomed to ②use this new system, you'll find it ③much easier ④to operate than the previous one.

24

Governor Hester sees small business as the best hope for _____ the state's economy.

① revitalize   ② revitalized
③ revitalizing   ④ revitalization

25

Far from ①be ②of no consequence, this confusion ③plays a positive role ④in his theoretical edifice.

Practice 01   정답과 해설 p.168

01

Kansas farmers ①used the weed killer 2, 4-D had a ②higher-than-average risk ③of ④contracting malignant ⑤lymphoma.

02

The ①absence of organic materials, some scientists ②speculated, was the result of intense ultraviolet ③radiation penetrating the atmosphere of Mars and ④destroyed organic compounds in the soil.

03

Another interesting application of ultrasound is the ultrasonic ranging unit ①using in some cameras ②to provide an ③almost instantaneous measurement of the distance between the camera and the objects ④to be photographed.

04

_____ as an opera singer, John McCormack made his Covent Garden debut in 1907, at age 23. Later he expanded his singing style to include elements of Irish ballads and traditional folk songs.

① Was trained   ② To train
③ Trained   ④ Training

05

A few years ago Canadian lottery officials ①learned the importance of careful ②counting the hard way when they ③decided to give back some ④unclaiming prize money that had ⑤accumulated.

06

I finally ①reached Tom ②in his office, and he said he ③would ship the ④redesigning brochures ⑤by express mail.

07

① Consisted of 93 percent water, ② the banana tree, ③ which is the largest plant ④ on Earth without a woody stem, is a very fragile plant.

08

Luis Chiappe, an expert on early birds at the Natural History Museum of Los Angeles County, suggests that flight ① likely occurred as a by-product of arm flapping ② in ground-dwelled dinosaurs, as the predecessors of birds used their ③ feathered arms to increase their running speed or balance themselves ④ as they made fast turns.

09

Brazil's economy performed ① much worse than ② expected in the third quarter, ③ grown by less than 1% ④ compared with the same period a year ⑤ earlier.

10

① Buoyed by the winter sports season, consumption of instant noodles ② has spiked, with the monthly sales for last December ③ exceeded 40 billion won ④ for the first time.

11

The Kyoto Protocol is an ambitious effort to reduce the man-made emissions _____ responsible for global warming.

① believed   ② believing
③ to believe   ④ have believed

12

Law enforcement officials say that ① in theory the bureau could take a lead role ② in reducing gun crime, ③ but that it is hindered by ④ politically driving laws.

13

Some snorers who have a condition ① calling sleep apnea stop breathing ② up to thirty or forty times ③ an hour because the throat muscles relax ④ too much and block the airway.

14

China's first emperor was buried _____ 7,000 life-sized clay figures of soldiers standing in battle formation along by life-sized ceramic chariots.

① surrounded   ② surrounding
③ surrounded by   ④ surround with
⑤ surrounding with

15

When Spielberg was a teenager, his parents divorced, and the ① hurtful impact of that event would become a ② recurred theme in his movies — children ③ uprooted and ④ traumatized by parents' divorce.

16

Holmes compares himself to Dupin and Lecoq, _____ them as really existing historical figures.

① treated   ② being treated
③ treating   ④ having been treated

17

The integral connection between vassal ① and serf ② depicting in conventional accounts ③ was destined to come ④ under intense scrutiny among a new ⑤ breed of analyst.

18

Political and economic relations between countries ① are to ② be based upon complete equality ③ of the parties ④ concern.

19

Every successful ① advertisement uses a creative strategy ② based on an idea that will attract the attention of the ③ targeting consumer ④ audience.

20

I had a really interesting conversation ① with a fellow working in the industry ② who claims that a lot of movies ③ making these days are modeled conceptually after ④ amusement park rides.

21

The fear that animals feel is carved ① deeply in the amygdaloid portion of the brain. When a rat spots a cat, its sympathetic nerve ② tenses because its amygdaloid body is stimulated, ③ caused the rat to stiffen and ④ let out deep breaths.

22

People ① sign up through the Affordable Care Act's marketplaces tend to be older, officials said Monday, a demographic mix that ② could cause premiums ③ to rise in the future if the pattern ④ persists.

23

It had been startling and ① disappointed to me to find out that story books ② had been written by people, that books ③ were not natural wonders, ④ coming up ⑤ of themselves like grass.

24

_____ for many years, this house will not withstand the cold weather this winter.

① Not having painted
② Having not painted
③ Not having been painted
④ Having not been painted

25

Songs were passed among musicians orally, although the works of trouveres in northern France were sometimes documented by literary groups. _____ their mostly oral tradition, the songs were typically not documented.

① Give   ② To give
③ Giving   ④ Given

01

It believes it is time ① to reconsider our ② long-holding belief that animals ③ should be kept out of hospitals and ④ away from ⑤ sick people.

02

The Good-People Charity Foundation, _____ about a decade ago, is now the world's largest complex of museums, art galleries and research facilities.

① found   ② founded
③ being found   ④ was founded

03

① For those ② wanted a luxury stay at the heart of Seoul's business and tourist districts, many people ③ say that ABC Hotel Seoul is the best ④ option.

04

The Thinker, a famous bronze and marble sculpture by August Rodin, depicts a pensive man, that is, one _____ in deep thought.

① captured
② captures
③ capturing
④ has been captured

05

The result of a lack of clarity ① on questions of poetics ② has been the astonishing helplessness of ③ most scholars when ④ confronting with the task of actually analysing and evaluating a work of art.

06

_____ high school, the job applicant was not considered for the position.

① Not finished
② Not having finished
③ Having not finished
④ Having not been finished

07

① Buffered by oceans to the east and west, and ② peaceful neighbors to the north and south, America enjoys a degree of security ③ unmatching by world powers ④ in earlier ages.

08

All passengers ① travel on commercial jets ② are advised ③ to allow an hour ④ for boarding.

09

Any executive _____ how to keep workers healthy is invited to a seminar to be held on July 5, at the Seoul Center.

① concerning about
② concerning
③ who concerned about
④ concerned about

10

① Within developed countries, there are ② well-documenting differences ③ in mortality rates ④ by race, income, or education.

11

SBL Group, ① a Colorado-based company, said Mr. Sam Butler will ② resign as CEO ③ due to a long health problem ④ followed a stroke three years ago.

12

All construction contractors are required to adhere to the legal guidelines in the building code when _____ existing structures.

① to renovate   ② renovated
③ renovating   ④ renovation

13

① Though ② knowing as a soybean tycoon, Maggi ③ has helped ④ make that nation the world's No.1 beef exporter.

14

Bolivia today is undergoing ① profound change, and those ② bring it about are the very people ③ that have been kept in a state of paralyzed submission ④ for centuries.

15

Those most recently _____ in the insurance program will have to pay higher premiums for the same coverage.

① enroll   ② enrolling

③ enrolled   ④ enrollment

16

What happened was that in my ① forties, back in the Dublin of my birth, I began ② working for the most ③ respecting newspaper in the country — *The Irish Times* — ④ as an opinion columnist.

17

We ① were terrified by sounds; ② the screaming of the wind; the ③ restless rustle of leaves in the trees; and the sudden, ④ overwhelmed ⑤ explosions of thunder.

18

① A series of recalls ② involved contaminated foods this year, including an outbreak of salmonella from tainted peanuts ③ that killed at least eight people and sickened 600, has consumers ④ rightly worried about the safety of their meals.

19

In 1066, a bright comet _____ in the sky attracted much attention.

① appears   ② appearing

③ it appeared   ④ was appearing

20

While the cold air is expected to leak out of the region, it could be a mightly slow leak, _____ the duration of the cold and the snow cover.

① give   ② given
③ giving   ④ to give

21

According to a recent study, ① depressed patients are ② more likely to stand with ③ their necks bent forward, shoulders collapsed, and ④ arms drew in toward the body.

22

French authorities are still hunting for suspects ① linked to ② planned terrorist attacks, including an ③ alleged suicide bomb plot ④ targeted New Year celebrations in Paris.

23

The desire to help ① correct the worst injustices of the economic system in our own countries also leads us to reach out to help ② impoverishing people in other lands. What makes ③ such an effort feasible today is the fact that so much of what people suffer from ④ is preventable with science and technology.

24

Korea has long ① lost any claim to ② being a land of clean air and clear water, but the ongoing controversy ③ surrounded the safety of ④ drinking water is another wake-up call against possible contamination of this most basic resource.

25

Functionalists generally maintain that sex differentiation ① contributes to overall social stability, but conflict theorists charge that the relationship ② between females and males is ③ one of unequal power, with ④ men dominate women.

9강 접속사

Practice 01

01

Dream _____ you'll live forever but live each day _____ you'll die tomorrow.

① even though ② unless
③ in case ④ as though

02

_____ unavoidable the Civil War may have been, it was more devastating and exhausting than any European war between 1815 and 1914.

① Whatever ② Whether
③ However ④ Otherwise

03

No sooner ①had Mr. Obama abandoned U.S. plans for the missile defense system ②then Moscow announced it was dropping ③its plans ④to deploy the interceptors.

04

_____ of heights, that roller coaster is one ride I'll never go on.

① Terrified
② Being terrified
③ Since I'm terrified
④ It was the terror

05

I ①look upon myself as very fortunate in that I ②have found men so interesting ③whom I am almost incapable ④of being bored by them.

06

It was due to his lateness _____ such a thing plunged him into the disaster, which eventually changed his whole life.

① when ② that
③ as ④ what

정답과 해설 p.168

07

A fairly good income is very important; however, it is still more important that a man should follow the vocation for which he is best fitted, _____ it happens to be well paid.

① what   ② whether
③ where   ④ how

08

If freshly ① squeezing, the orange juice in a one-cup ② serving provides ③ twice the minimum daily requirement ④ for vitamin C.

09

While we sleep, research indicates, the brain replays the patterns of activity ① it experienced during waking hours, ② allowing us to ③ enter what one psychologist calls ④ it a neural virtual reality.

10

It always seems to taste ① wonderful no matter ② how ③ sloppy I measure ④ things.

11

① That most students need above all else is practice ② in writing, and particularly in writing about things that ③ matter to them, so that they will begin to feel the satisfaction that comes from getting important thoughts ④ down in words.

12

The ① debate over if language is natural, I.e., do we call ② a table a table because that's the way it is?, or conventional, ie., do we call it a table because that's what we decided to call it? in Plato's Cratylus is ③ the very question that everyone ④ agrees opens Saussure's teachings and ties them together.

13

① Mating done, the female yucca moth ② climbs atop one of the flower's six stamens and gathers ③ a cache of pollen, ④ used tentacles for the tusk.

14

The ① long-suffering smartphone maker reported a surprise bump in operating profits, ② provided some hope that ③ its turnaround efforts are starting ④ to gain traction.

15

① Saying that the Miss World pageant should be focused more on ② that a woman could ③ do with a title like Miss World, the organization announced that ④ future pageants will not include a swimsuit round.

16

Only after Al Gore left politics ① did he ② find a formula for accomplishing his life's work, ③ created a global media brand around the PowerPoint presentation that became his aptly ④ titled book and documentary *An Inconvenient Truth*.

17

In *As You Like It*, Rosalind began a journey, ① disguising herself as a man when she earned the wrath of her uncle and was ② driven out of the house. The common point here is ③ that the love affair got entangled ④ because women who mistook heroines in men's attire as men.

18

You do not educate a person's palate by ① telling him that ② what he ③ has been in the habit of eating is disgusting, but ④ persuaded him to try a dish of properly cooked food.

19

_____ to be comprehended today, America Online started out in 1985 as simply one of many service firms providing customers with a new way to connect to the Internet.

① Difficult is
② It is difficult
③ Though is it difficult
④ Difficult as it may be

20

①Convicting for stealing a loaf of ②bread for his sister's ③starving children, Jean Valjean ④was sentenced to five years of hard labor and ⑤another fourteen years for attempting to escape.

21

The most fundamental questions of ① what humans came to be the kind of animal ②we are can only be answered by a theory ③in which culture has its proper role and ④in which it is intimately ⑤intertwined with other aspects of biology.

22

The zookeeper must make sure the bear is completely off the ground _____.

① as is it weighed
② as to weigh up
③ as it is weighed
④ as it weighs itself

23

But _____ the other's desire and the subject's possession are fantasies of the subject.

① both   ② alike
③ not   ④ not only

24

In the Disney version at least, it is Geppetto's wish, not Pinocchio's, _____ the puppet become real.

① what   ② which
③ that   ④ as

25

Compared to Korea and Japan, controversy over globalization began a little later in Taiwan. There are a couple of reasons to explain _____.

① why was this the case
② why this was the case
③ the case was why this
④ the case why was this

01

She wondered if children loved pink and blue out of instinct, _____ a social compulsion that they are not aware of.

① because
② because of
③ or because
④ or because of

02

The Fed is raising rates and the dollar is rising, but the rest of the world is still moving in the opposite direction, _____ a "Great Divergence" in monetary policy.

① creating
② creates
③ is creating
④ created

03

① Defining in a limited sense, a tale is a story, usually short, that ② sets forth strange and wonderful events in more or less ③ bare summary, without ④ detailed character-drawing.

04

It is assumed ① what *Homo erectus* ② must have had a communication system ③ more complex than ④ any of today's living primates.

05

Exactly _____ we can replace our soil disappearing through erosion is not known.

① unless
② since
③ how
④ what

06

_____, the 정답과 해설 to many kinds of pain, from sore joints and back pain to headaches and stomachaches, may be in the kitchen rather than in the medicine cabinet.

① As may it sound surprising
② Surprising as it may sound
③ Sound surprising as it may
④ May sound surprising as it
⑤ It may sound surprising as

07

Despite the freedom of the press, in the U.S. there are limits on _____.

① what can the press publish
② can the press publish what
③ what the press can publish
④ the press what can publish

08

While touring the deserts of Argentina and Chile ① which many travellers found ② spectacular, ③ it was found that Dr. Smith ④ contracted malaria.

09

Such house chores, _____ important for home management, may not be favorite job for anyone.

① they are   ② as
③ though   ④ despite

10

Researchers have discovered that body fat produces proteins that trigger inflammation, thus _____ to the development of heart disease, stroke, and diabetes.

① contributes   ② has contributed
③ being contributed   ④ contributing

11

① I am still undecided ② whether I should insist upon complete performance of the contract ③ or to forgive the obligation ④ in anticipation of concessions in later negotiating sessions.

12

Timothy J. McVeigh was convicted of bombing a federal office building in Oklahoma city, _____ the deaths of 168 people.

① causing
② and caused
③ it caused
④ which it caused

13

Planets are ① probably formed as a ② result of both gases ③ or particles drawn ④ together in space by gravity.

14

_____ you can't talk right.

① The reason you can't get a job is because
② The reason for you can't get a job is because
③ The reason for you can't get a job is that
④ The reason you can't get a job is that

15

Historically, ① the most dangerous part of a lawmaker's job ② has been ③ not violence, but ④ to travel.

16

Historians have long been reluctant ① to recognize that Queen Victoria was not just a monarch ② and one of the most prominent working mothers in history — ③ one who was both deeply in love with her husband ④ and resentful of the demands on her as a mother and a wife.

17

Bone is one of the hardest materials in the body and, _____, it has a remarkable ability to resist tension and other forces acting on it.

① although relatively light in weight
② having been relatively light in weight
③ that it is relatively light in weight
④ to be relatively light in weight

18

It may be worth ① noting that the hijackers ② themselves correctly foresaw ③ what the threat to their mission would come from the passengers and not from a military source external ④ to the plane.

19

I ① used to work ② as a salesman, and I know how important ③ is image in ④ any job.

20

Just as Napoleon faced defeat in Russia, _____ Hitler saw his dreams of conquest evaporate at the siege of Leningrad.

① so   ② and
③ as   ④ yet
⑤ but

21

Although he ① has worked in other ② media and other forms, ③ but Bean gained considerable success with his ④ pit-fired earthenware ⑤ bowls.

22

The most general charge ① brought by its contemporaries ② against the schoolroom of the seventeenth century was that ③ its failure to adapt its ideals to the profound changes which were becoming ④ manifest in social life.

23

Chicken pox and measles, ① despite common and rarely fatal among Europeans, often ② proved lethal ③ to Native Americans, and more dangerous diseases such as small pox ④ were especially deadly.

24

In the past, inexperienced young adults, when _____ with crucial life decisions, tended to accept the judgement of parents and other authority figures.

① be faced   ② facing
③ faced   ④ to face

25

The cost of college education ① has risen ② too rapidly ③ during the past several years that it is now ④ beyond the reach of many people.

10강 관계사

Practice 01

정답과 해설 p.169

01

Virginia Woolf, ① which developed new literary ideas ② for effecting social change, ③ led the intellectual movement for ④ freedom from the British government.

02

As women have ① moved away from the traditional status of ② homemaker, notions of ③ that a marriage ④ should be have changed to accommodate the new reality.

03

The closer you get to an election, ① the harder it can be to tell ② where the candidates stand ③ on the issues ④ what matter ⑤ most.

04

There is something ① uncanny about the clarity with which he ② recognized his hopeless position, and the calm ③ which he accepted ④ the inevitable ⑤ was superhuman in its aspect: "I am absent-minded and could not direct my own life now."

05

① Feminist theory has assumed that there is some ② existing identity, understood ③ through the category of women, who not only initiates feminist interests and goals within discourse, but constitutes the subject ④ whom political representation is pursued.

06

Insulin is a substance ① for which enables muscles ② to absorb sugar from the blood, and ③ to break it up ④ for the purpose of obtaining energy.

07

Mark had been ① an excellent student at the college, but he found that the abstract concepts ② what he had learned in the classroom left him ③ ill-equipped to deal with ④ the concrete circumstances of life.

08

① That she said seems to be not ② so much an opinion ③ as a criticism about ④ the way the company has been operated.

09

Reports nationwide indicate that DWI (driving while intoxicated) is a factor in one-fourth of all reported auto crashes _____.

① called by the police
② calling the police
③ when the police are called
④ in which the police are called

10

Farmers sold their ① crops to a trader, ② when sold them to another trader and ③ so on until ④ they ended up in a shop.

11

There are ① a lot of ② times ③ how we need to talk to people ④ who come from other countries.

12

Language is a tool for saying as well as possible _____ we intend to say.

① which   ② when
③ where   ④ what

13

Textrix, the company ①for which Alex works part-time, ②tends to employ people who are ③highly motivated and ④who has at least ⑤10 years of experience in the field.

14

The Centuriate assembly, ①what only an official ②with imperium could summon, was organized like the army with the ③presiding official acting ④as a commander and the voters as soldiers.

15

Some studies have ①called into question whether ②high and variable pitch and exaggerated stress ③are the crucial elements in the baby talk ④which infants respond.

16

Governments are paying ①increasing attention to international ②comparisons as they search ③for effective policies ④whose enhance individuals' social and economic prospects.

17

Advances ①in technology now allow us to prolong life ②in ways that were unimaginable decades ago. But should people be forced or expected to prolong lives that ③are unbearably painful, or that ④is in effect "lifeless"?

18

The plastic waste in the ocean breaks down into tiny pieces known as microplastics, _____ or even toxic to sea creatures who ingest it.

① which scientists believe can harm
② which scientists believe can be harmful
③ in which scientists believe can harm
④ in which scientists believe can be harmful

19

These experiences, and others which can't all be ①enumerated here, ②help us ③to find a place of fullness, ④which we orient ourselves morally or spiritually.

20

Many germs have had to devise tricks to let them spread between potential victims, and many of those tricks are _____ we experience as "symptoms of disease."

① what
② that
③ while
④ which

21

Knowledge of the rate ① which a ship is traveling through ② the water is important if the navigator ③ needs to estimate the time ④ of arrival.

22

Pending folder is ① which you put messages ② that you do not need to respond to immediately but ③ that you need to keep 'active' for the time being — for example, ④ if someone promised to get back to you and you need a reminder to follow up.

23

The new e-ticketing system, _____ was installed last month, is working well.

① what
② whom
③ where
④ that
⑤ which

24

There are two other bodies ① orbiting near Earth ② that is sometimes ③ referred to as moons, though they are not strictly ④ worthy of the title.

25

The physicians favored a program ① guaranteed to save two hundred ② lives over one ③ who had a one-third probability of saving everyone and a ④ two-thirds probability of saving no one.

01

Early studies ① have also shown an increase in physical ailments — sore backs, dry eyes, painful necks — among kids who ② are asked to work most of the day on computers ③ which using desks ④ designed for pencil and paper.

02

① To Warren Buffet, his father's library ② must have been like a recommended booklist. When he was eight years old, Buffet started ③ reading the books in the library. His reading habit might have been ④ that turned him into the Oracle of Omaha.

03

The city is struggling with a $26.5 million budget gap, the result of a long decline in Camden's property tax base and Gov. Christie's decision to cut state aid, _____ made up more than 80 percent of Camden's budget last year.

① who   ② that
③ what   ④ which

04

The city fathers allocated ① a substantial sum for the ② restoration of the train station ③ but which was soon ④ dissipated in research and planning.

05

You ① don't seem to understand ② that ③ I'm trying to do ④ with the new pricing system.

06

The regional manager has been looking for an applicant _____ language skills include Korean and Chinese.

① who   ② which
③ whom   ④ whose

07

The passive in the English language ① is very useful ② when you want to emphasize the object ③ which the action is happening rather than the person ④ carrying out the action.

08

① When going out to hunt, Brazilian Indians from the Xavante tribe ② follow a complex hierarchy, ③ that specifies the tasks the old and young should do ④ when capturing animals.

09

In this book, Mary Evans explores _____ social theory has engaged with and illuminated the question of relations between genders and the social world.

① the extent to which
② the extent to what
③ the extent which
④ the extent to those
⑤ the extent that it

10

Despite the current oil glut, ① the world's known reserves of both petroleum and natural gas ② are expected to be declining ③ by the end of the century, and ④ it would be folly to burn ⑤ which remains to generate electricity.

11

Although English ① is widely accepted today as being the universal language of business, most multinational companies will expect you ② to speak the language of one of the countries ③ which they do business, ④ in addition to English.

12

① Careful measurements reveal that the reaction rate is ② too slow to account for ③ the ozone concentrations observed, i.e. the process predicts higher peak ozone concentrations ④ that are observed.

13

Korea ① successfully hosted the Group of 20 ② summit in Seoul on November 11–12, ③ what is believed to have helped ④ boost the nation's diplomatic clout and international reputation.

14

Another area ① which bits and bytes are ② used is ③ measuring computer memory ④ storage capacity.

15

Did you know that ① most flight attendants fly with their own food? It is because the meals airlines ② give them to passengers ③ have gotten smaller ④ over the year and leave them still hungry. So it is not unusual for flight attendants ⑤ to bring their own snacks like fruit, protein bars and sandwiches.

16

As older people have accumulated their own know-how in their careers, they have many resources and skills _____.

① teach and guide younger people

② with which to teach and guide younger people

③ which they might teach and guide younger people

④ what might teach and guide younger people

17

_____ cannot be an extremist.

① Whoever is doing such activities

② Who is doing such activities

③ No matter how is doing such activities

④ How is doing such activities

18

Frog skin allows both water and oxygen ① to pass through, ② which mean if the air or water ③ is contaminated, the contaminant ④ can easily enter and damage the frog's body.

19

A satellite is composed of 30 modular units, _____ equipped with a set of sensors.

① each of which is

② each of which are

③ some of which is

④ which of them are

20

The strike ①for increased wages ②consisted of hundreds of immigrants, most of ③them ④were earning less than minimum wages.

21

Morgan Stanley, the financial firm ①who shares ②have declined 45 percent this year, ③plans to cut about 1,600 jobs amid an industrywide ④drop in revenue from investment banking and trading.

22

①One college professor developed the idea ②which rats might perform better on the detection test ③if they lived in a rich environment ④than in a small barren cage.

23

①The period in American history ②during when the ③sale of alcohol ④was banned was called Prohibition.

24

This study does not attempt a fully-fledged account of these concerns, but simply points to their importance when considering _____ state theories are constructed.

① way in which
② the way how
③ way which
④ way that
⑤ the way in which

25

In 1921, a movement started in several parts of the world, _____ was to make table tennis a serious sport.

① which goal
② its goal
③ the goal of which
④ which of the goal

Practice

정답과 해설 p.169

01

Many of the mammals that dwell in the desert are active only at _____ as the intense heat of a desert day can be fatal to warm-blooded animals.

① a night
② night
③ the night
④ nights

02

The number of Americans who are obese ①continues to increase ②at alarming rate while in Italy ③the percentage of obese people is half of ④what it is in the United States.

03

In the United States, ①having chosen ②to purchase ③same item created an immediate affinity ④among Americans.

04

The story you hear all the time — of ①a stagnant economy in which high taxes and generous social benefits have undermined incentives, ②stalling growth and innovation — bears ③few resemblance to ④the surprisingly positive facts.

05

It might appear to ①any casual visitor who may have taken a few rides ②about town ③by a taxicab that all New Yorkers are filled with a ④loud-mouthed ill will toward each other.

06

Most people ①are accustomed to thinking of lie detectors ②as foolproof — as machines that can, without error, ③separate the guilty from ④the innocence.

07

Football, often ① confused with soccer in some countries, is a ② fast-moving ③ team sports ④ played mainly in the U.S. and Canada.

08

According to a Washington Post poll ① taken in 1999, eighty-seven ② percents of Americans ③ want the U.S. and China ④ to sign an ⑤ arms agreement.

09

① In popular terminology, ② any long snowstorm with ③ large amount of wind is ④ called a blizzard.

10

Language, in all aspects, ① consists of abstract units of ② informations that are ③ organized and combined ④ following specific computational procedures.

11

One of the best-known ① kind of predictably irrational behavior ② has been called the endowment effect — the idea that once something is ③ in your possession, it becomes more valuable ④ to you because it's yours and you don't want to lose it.

12

There are concerns for the safety of ① scores of people after a ship carrying 118 passengers and ② crews lost power in rough ③ waters off an Indonesian island ④ on Saturday.

13

Ebola, a ① highly infectious virus ② that can kill up to 90 ③ percent of the people who catch it, is one of the ④ world most deadly diseases, ⑤ causing terror among infected communities.

14

_____, Sasha rarely misses three-point shots.

① Her excellent basketball play
② Excellent basketball player
③ An excellent basketball player is
④ An excellent basketball player

15

The ① evidences show that children of women ② who work are not more ③ likely to have lower school ④ achievement than children of stay-at-home moms.

16

In order to arrest a person, the police ① has to be reasonably sure that a crime ② has been committed. The police must give the suspect the reasons why he ③ is being arrested and ④ tell him his rights under the law.

17

① The housekeeping problems of living in a shelter begin ② as soon as the shelter is occupied. ③ Medical supplies, utensils, and equipments, as well as food, if not already stored in the shelter, ④ must be quickly gathered up and carried inside.

18

Though the term *individualism* did not appear ① until late 1820s, when market societies were well established, the principles ② it encompasses ③ were already instated ④ by the mid-eighteenth century.

19

① The constellation Orion includes ② the all stars in the familiar pattern of the hunter, ③ along with the region of the sky ④ in which these stars are found.

20

① The post office has promised ② to resume ③ first class mail delivery to ④ area on Friday.

21

In 2009 Brazil, ① long the world's worst offender, saw its pace of jungle clearing plummet to ② the third of its historical rate. That's ③ due in part to the recession, as falling commodity prices made clearcutting for farms ④ less profitable.

22

Over the course of his career he designed over _____ for homes, offices and hotels.

① one thousand furnitures

② one thousand furniture

③ one thousand pieces of furnitures

④ one thousand pieces of furniture

23

① As job hunts became tough after the financial crisis, ② an anecdotal evidence suggested that ③ more young people ④ considered public service.

24

Air Force One was ① due to land in Washington ② in Tuesday morning after an overnight flight from the island of Oahu. The president is returning from vacation ③ the same day Republican presidential candidates square off in the Iowa caucuses, the first ④ nominating contest of the 2012 campaign.

25

These four major corporations ① have tasked their troops ② to employ all ③ means necessary to explore ④ moon for rubium deposits, ⑤ then establish and secure rubium refineries.

정답과 해설 p.169

Practice

01

The duties of the priest ① towards the secrecy of the ② confessional seemed so grave to me that I wondered ③ how anybody had ever found in himself the courage to undertake ④ it.

02

Martin Luther King Jr.'s assassination ironically ① resulted in a series of violent ② riots across nearly every major city in America, though ③ it always ④ advocated the use of nonviolent protest.

03

Researchers at the university ① are investigating a series of ② indicators that ③ could help ④ themselves ⑤ predict earthquakes.

04

Government authorities will focus their attention ① on the expansion of the nation's railway facilities, ② as ③ it is emerging ④ as the most environmentally-friendly method of transportation.

05

For the last two weeks I ① have had to ② stay up ③ the most of the night to observe star configurations ④ for a project for my astronomy class.

06

I should like to see children ① taught that they should not say they like things ② which they do not like ③ merely because certain other people say they like ④ it.

07

_____ the writers who have produced important work since our last edition have been updated.

① The most of   ② Almost all
③ The almost   ④ Almost some

08

The conflict over the past decade ① has cost more than 100,000 lives in Groznyy, the capital of Chechnya. ② Much of the city ③ remain in ruins and ④ Chechen-led terrorists are spreading the conflict to ⑤ neighboring republics.

09

Science has obviously multiplied the power of the warmakers. The weapons of the moment can kill more people more secretly and more unpleasantly than _____ of the past.

① these   ② those
③ that   ④ this

10

Two ① bus-crashes in separate locations in Morocco ② have claimed 27 lives, including ③ that of a German and a ④ Dutch tourist.

11

Every year, ① hundreds of people leave important jobs in the government to take more lucrative positions in private industry. ② Some go to work as lobbyists, ③ another as consultants to business, ④ still others as key executives in corporations, foundations and universities.

12

① Almost orders ship within 3 to 5 business days of purchase. Shipping times may ② vary due to availability of merchandise. ③ Should you change or cancel your order, please contact us immediately. ④ Once the parcel was sent to the post office, we will be unable to make ⑤ any changes.

13

Some former White House residents have remained ① in the public eye ② for life, while ③ the others have slipped ④ into obscurity.

14

① Most of critics agrees that the gothic has been ② an important presence in America beginning with Charles Brockden Brown and that ③ it continues to influence the nation's culture and to ④ permeate the nation's literature at every level.

15

In science one experiment, ① whether it ② succeeds or fails, is ③ logically followed by ④ other in a ⑤ theoretically infinite progression.

16

Although sleep disorder is ① associated with heart disease in both men and women, ② they may negatively ③ affect the heart rates of women more than ④ those of men.

17

In ① the La Sierra region you'll find the temperate weather ② patterns that give Ecuador ③ it's status ④ as the Land of Eternal Spring.

18

Acute stress is ① the most common form of stress. It ② comes from demands and pressures of ③ the recent past and ④ anticipated demands and pressures of the near future. Acute stress is thrilling and exciting in small doses, but ⑤ too many is exhausting.

19

Artificial intelligence (AI) is part of our global culture, and ① their impact on our everyday lives ② is growing. Searching for news ③ about AI presents a deluge of information. Why not ④ use a little AI of our own ⑤ to better handle the task?

20

① By the time Ralph Rogers completes his testimony, every major executive of our company but Mark Jamieson ② and I ③ will have been accused of complicity in the stock swindle. ④ No error

21

① Most of the water at the bottom of the North Pacific Ocean ② has not been exposed to sunlight in at least 800 years and ③ some of them has been down there ④ for two millennia.

22

Those who distrust science ① as a guide to conduct, ② whether individual or social, ③ seem to overlook ④ their pragmatic nature, or perhaps they scorn it for that very reason.

23

① Spending money on tablet computers may ② seem an extravagance, but some ③ of educators say they are more than ④ just a cool toy.

24

Why a person has ① none friendship is ② something that cannot ③ be adequately ④ determined by ⑤ a survey.

25

In this movie, a young woman working as a sales associate at a department store takes a mannequin that resembles _____ to the rooftop of the building and drops it to the ground, morbidly curious to know what it feels like to jump off there.

① him   ② himself
③ her   ④ herself

정답과 해설 p.169

Practice

01

① Those who pass their lives in foreign travel find they contract ② much ties of hospitality, but ③ form no ④ friendships.

02

The prime minister ① held to his long-standing goal ② of a balanced budget and, ③ alike his predecessor, ④ called for considerable ⑤ increase in public expenditure.

03

The fertility rate of women with ① higher incomes ② is higher while women who ③ pursue careers tend to have ④ less babies.

04

When I mailed ① the 200-pages manuscript ② to my editor, I didn't ③ realize that the pages were ④ completely ⑤ out of order.

05

The number of work permits ① issued to Hong Kong ② nationals during the ③ twelve-months period ④ was ⑤ eight hundred.

06

A distinction ① between 'fact' and 'fiction' seems ② unlike to get us very far, not least because ③ the distinction itself ④ is often a questionable one.

07

Although the unique circumstances of every life ① result in ② each of us having an individual way ③ of speaking, we generally tend to ④ sound alike others who share similar educational backgrounds with us.

08

It was July 10, 2012, and I was an ordinary ① 17-years-old girl, who'd been ② feeling unwell. ③ With my mother by my side, I now sat in Dr. Mahbob's office and ④ awaited my diagnosis.

09

① Many evidence ② indicates that ③ the number of gorillas ④ in the wild is decreasing ⑤ drastically.

10

Today's young people have very adult worries about the uncertainty of the future and the lack of jobs in particular, far _____.

① different to what their parents' generation
② from different their parents' generation
③ different what their parents' generation
④ different from their parents' generation

11

When a fluid is ① in motion, its flow can be characterized in one of two ways. The flow ② is said to be streamline, or laminar, if every particle that ③ passes a particular point moves along exactly ④ smooth the same path followed by previous particles passing that point.

12

The World Conference Against Racism is supposed to put ① on the table such sensitive issues ② that reparation for slavery and the question of ③ whether Zionism is racism ④ or not.

13

① None direct flights are ② currently scheduled from New York to Seoul, ③ but an airline agent can recommend ④ an alternative travel route.

14

The Olympic Games, which take place once every four ① year, are ② considered the most competitive ③ of athletic ④ competitions.

15

Recent presidents have made ① a great deal of pledges they didn't keep. You may not like everything I tell you tonight, but you ② deserve to hear the truth. On the economy we've made ③ a little progress, but we still have ④ a great deal of work to do.

16

If you want ① to be happy, here are ② a little tips ③ for overcoming six common ④ barriers to happiness.

17

Nearly ① two-thirds of Americans ② choose higher payroll taxes for Medicare and Social Security over ③ reduced benefits in either ④ programs.

18

CPRSS, the ① official news organization of China, ② disseminates information ③ to domestic ④ and internationally newspapers.

19

The company is _____, flying to 80 destinations in 55 countries.

① a world second profitable airline
② the world secondly profitable airline
③ the world's second most profitable airline
④ a world's secondly most profitable airline

20

During the past decade _____ have cobwebbed across the continent, putting cheap flights within the reach of every vocationer or jobseeker.

① the score of new routes
② scores of new route
③ scores of new routes
④ the score of new route

21

Credit insurance against default on corporate bonds costs _____ default insurance for the government debt.

① nine time as many as
② nine times as much as
③ nine times as many as
④ nine time as much as

22

_____ here is that these situations tend to repeat themselves and things seem to roughly continue the same.

① What interesting
② What an interesting
③ Being interested
④ Of interest
⑤ Having been interested

23

Government economists are taking a _____ view of the country's IT market this year, citing a recent pattern of slowing growth.

① conserved
② conserving
③ conservation
④ conservative

24

Robinson ①desired a happy marriage and hoped ②to be a great man ③in politics; he achieved ④neither goals.

25

United Nations ①is accusing the militia ②of blocking emergency food supplies to ③tens of ④thousand of people in the suburban area.

정답과 해설 p.170

Practice

01

The son ①of Italian immigrants grows up ②poorly in San Francisco and becomes the greatest baseball player ③of his day, marries an American goddess and never ④in word or deed befouls his legend and greatness.

02

①At issue is whether Treasury Inflation-Protected Securities, commonly ②known as TIPS, are ③too a good deal for investors: Opponents say the government ④has been losing money on them while defenders question ⑤the accounting.

03

It would ①thus be futile to argue that industrialization destroyed the great ②extended family of ③the past, since such a family type ④rare existed.

04

①Most people think ②of deserts as dry, flat areas with little vegetation and little ③or no rainfall, but this is ④hard true.

05

①Although mankind has ②undergone no general improvement in intelligence or ③morality, it has made ④extraordinarily progress in the accumulation of knowledge.

06

Photoperiodism is the ①functional or behavioral ②response of an organism to ③changes in duration of daily, ④seasonally, or yearly periods of light and darkness.

07

She has ①so a ②good memory ③that she can remember ④a person's exact words ⑤even a week later.

08

A scandal last month at the University of Virginia, where 122 students are ①being investigated for ②possible plagiarism of term papers, ③revealed ④how easily cheating has become.

09

Tomatoes, ①actual a fruit that is used as ②a vegetable, began ③gaining wide acceptance as ④a food plant in the United States ⑤between 1820 and 1850.

10

①A jet stream is a flat and narrow tube ②of air that moves more ③rapid than the ④surrounding air.

11

When I spoke English, people nodded ①at me, smiled ②sweet, said encouraging words. ③Even the people in my culture ④would say that I'd do well in ⑤life.

12

Bone is one of ①the hardest materials in the body and, although ②relative light in weight, it has a remarkable ability ③to resist tension and other forces ④acting on it.

13

① In spite of a tremendous amount of ② electronic gadgetry, ③ air traffic control still depends ④ heavy on people.

14

① Environmental conscious and ② socially minded travelers ③ should try to determine ④ how much of an opportunity they will have to ⑤ make a contribution at their destinations.

15

① Humans leave their ② nuclear families when they ③ get married. ④ Similar, chimpanzees often join a new group to ⑤ mate and reproduce.

16

The terrain of Antarctica, ① near one and a half ② times as big ③ as the United States, ④ is amazingly varied.

17

We think and talk _____ to have conscious awareness of and control over everything we think and say.

① at too fast a rate

② in too fast a rate

③ at a too fast rate

④ in a too fast rate

18

Due to our ① overwhelmingly growth of nearly 1,000% ② over the last three years, we have an immediate need and ③ are willing to train even ④ non-experienced individuals in local markets.

19

① The actual causes for international conflicts may differ ② substantial ③ from the reasons ④ provided in public statements.

20

①The question of ②whether computers can have ③minds is ④rapid becoming ⑤a significant issue.

21

With electronic health records ①seen ②widely as a way to make medical care better, it is ③disturbing ④how slow they are being adopted by doctors.

22

The internet now plays _____ in many people's lives that it is essential for us to try to decide whether it is good or bad.

① such important a part
② such a part important
③ so important a part
④ a part so important

23

Barbara McLintock was a creative thinker among scientists, one for whom intuition played _____ formal experimentation and analysis.

① as an important role as
② as important a role as
③ as a role important as
④ as important as a role

24

While ①being big is still an advantage — size offers ②a better survival cushion if food ③proves hard to find — there are other factors that limit ④how easy that trait is passed down.

25

After the Grimm Brothers ①had ②collected "housewives' tales" ③from around the country, they ④edited them into stories ⑤appropriately for children.

01

In a study of local brain activity in people ① performing a language task, people with ② stroke-related aphasia showed ③ high activity levels in the right half of the brain than ④ people who did not have aphasia.

02

The students whose parents let them see R-rated movies sometimes or all the time were _____ have tried smoking during the study period as those who never saw the movies.

① almost five times as likely to
② almost as five times likely to
③ as almost five times likely to
④ almost five times more likely to

03

The more I learned about the current trend in intellectual property law, _____ that novel forms of cultural copyright come with substantial risks.

① the more became it obvious
② it became the more obvious
③ the more obvious it became
④ the more it obvious became

04

Of several word processors that are ① being used these days, most of Americans and Europeans think that MS Word is ② the better since it is ③ easier to learn than other ④ ones.

05

She finally became even ① very violent in her disposition than her husband himself. She was not satisfied ② with simply doing ③ as well as he had commanded; she seemed anxious ④ to do better.

06

① Hurricane Charley is one of ② most destructive hurricanes ③ ever to hit ④ the United States. More than 20 people died ⑤ because of Charley's effects.

07

① Although ② most of the wild horses in the western range have already been ③ rounded up, the more remote the area, ④ the greatest the possibility that ⑤ they can still be found.

08

Mortgage ① approvals in Britain were more than ② a third higher in November ③ as a year earlier as government subsidies for homebuyers helped the property recovery ④ gather pace.

09

I can tell you that the new director of our department is _____ man I have ever met.

① the most quite stupid
② most the quite stupid
③ the quite most stupid
④ quite the most stupid

10

Young adults who live with their parents are ① nearly as ② likely to say they are satisfied with their housing situation ③ like those who live ④ on their own.

11

In some countries, ① higher levels of enrollment for young adult women ② are linked to improved access ③ to education, but they can also imply a later insertion into the labor market ④ then for men.

12

New York City commuters spend ① little time ② annually delayed by traffic congestion ③ than the average ④ for very large cities.

13

① Of the three main forms of fossil fuels — coal, petroleum, and natural gas — petroleum is ② the more common, providing approximately 40 percent of ③ the world's energy, ④ with coal and natural gas each providing nearly 25 percent.

14

① Many believe that people in Asian countries ② tend to be ③ more reserved than ④ the western countries.

15

Researchers have found ① in a review of studies that the density of billboards advertising tobacco products ② is ③ more than twice as high in black neighborhoods ④ than in white.

16

Babies' intelligence, ① the research shows, is very ② different from adults and ③ from the kind of intelligence we usually ④ cultivate in school.

17

The longer the treatment for snakebite is delayed, _____.

① one risks losing a limb is greater
② the greater one risks losing a limb
③ the greatest one risks losing a limb
④ the greater one risks to lose a limb
⑤ one risks to lose a limb is greater

18

My ① going to such a place was part of my mother's not so secret plan ② to change my character, which she worried ③ was becoming too much like ④ her.

19

We are as much delighted ①by benevolence ②than we are gratified by the scent ③of perfume ④or nauseated by a foul stench.

20

①One big advantage writing ②offers over speaking is that we can refine our message, making ③it as ④succinctly as possible.

21

The institutions of science mean ①that the theories and ideas that scientists have developed are far superior ②than the ③ones that we human ④beings had before the growth of modern science.

22

We really ①do perceive the sun ②as ③close to us ④than it actually is.

23

The problem of school education that John ①is experiencing is similar to ②you ③in that they both ④stem from the lack of interaction between students and teachers.

24

The placement of ①the sun at the center of the universe by Galileo was ②certainly more important than ③the principle of buoyancy and may be more important than ④any scientific discovery in the history of the world.

25

She makes ①much high grades than her sisters; however, ②they are a great deal ③more sociable than ④she is.

Practice 01   정답과 해설 p.170

01

A computerized map of the freeways using information gathered by sensors embedded in the pavement _____ on a local cable channel during rush hours.

① to air   ② airing
③ air   ④ airs

02

Beijing's decision to require that all new personal computers ① sold in China ② contain software that ③ bars access to certain Internet content ④ seem self-destructive and foolish.

03

One study found ① that those who consistently felt impatient and pressed for time ② was more than twice as likely ③ as laid-back types ④ to develop high blood pressure over ⑤ a 13-year period.

04

Writers ① intent on informing their readers often, ② without realizing it, ③ includes a word or phrase that ④ expresses their ⑤ personal point of view.

05

① Seldom we have these types of arguments, but if we're ② concerned about our friendship, we need to ③ talk about it more and try to ④ cooperate with each other.

06

① Since the end of World War II, the dynamic growth of communication systems of all types ② have provided a unique opportunity for the development of new methods ③ to influence public opinion ④ on a wide range of activities and behaviors.

07

The series ① of natural phenomena ② could be described in ③ their entirety without mentioning the value of things, and our scale of valuation remains meaningful, whether or not one of its objects ④ appear frequently or at all in reality.

08

Throughout the ① developed world, we are at a point ② in our evolution ③ at which famine, ④ which essentially governed the rise and fall of civilizations throughout history, ⑤ are no longer an acute threat.

09

Paying for union services ① only when you need ② them ③ are like paying taxes for police and fire services only if you use ④ them.

10

Only occasionally _____ reading Tom's newspaper, over his shoulder, as she sat in the station waiting room.

① found she herself
② she finds herself
③ did herself she find
④ did she find herself

11

The takeover of the New York Stock Exchange's owner illustrates ① starkly how trading in commodities and derivatives ② have become ③ much more lucrative than ④ trading in corporate shares.

12

_____ scholars who regularly publish their professional works has doubled since 2002.

① As many as
② As most of
③ The quantity of
④ The number of

13

Those who favor the new administrative law say that the present law does not set spending limits on lobbyists' gifts to politicians, _____ statewide funds.

① nor it limits
② nor does it limit
③ nor they limit
④ nor do they limit
⑤ nor they are limited

14

The religion of the Hopi Indians ① include ② several different ceremonies ③ intended to influence or ④ pay respect to nature.

15

Every non-Western society is searching for a path to modernity that it can feel _____ in some way local, authentic and, in that sense, non-Western.

① is   ② are
③ being   ④ be

16

From that act of civil disobedience _____ spawned the New Power Party, which allied with the DDP and won five legislative seats of its own.

① had   ② were
③ has   ④ was

17

It is true that ① much of the Korean Art as it ② developed through the early years ③ were influenced by ④ the Chinese.

18

Just as the early 20th century had the great master Pablo Casals, ① the latter part of the last century had Rostropovich. Despite ② being regarded as the best in his era, he was modest and humble. ③ That he recorded the entire Bach Cello Suites when he was over 60 ④ prove his modesty.

19

① Like baseball parks and basketball-hockey arenas, football stadiums have ② for decades ③ been evolving into places ④ where an increasing amount of the real estate ⑤ are devoted to premium-priced seating.

20

Each year the number of students who ① are unable to find ② a dorm room for the semester and forced to live ③ off campus without meal plans ④ are soaring.

21

_____ that everyone left the auditorium.

① So monotonously did he speak
② He so did speak monotonously
③ Monotonously did he speak so
④ So did he monotonously speak

22

Wages and the cost of living _____ in virtually equal proportions through the generations.

① have grown   ② having grown
③ growing   ④ grows

23

It ① is often remarked that the advent of the movies and the ② ever faster pace of modern life ③ has conspired to make description a ④ less essential part of prose narrative in our ⑤ own times.

24

People in a growth mindset do not just seek challenge, they ① thrive on it. The bigger the challenge, ② the more they stretch. And nowhere ③ it can be seen more clearly than in the world of sport. You can just watch people ④ stretch and grow.

25

Good parents wouldn't jump to conclusions, _____ assume that every problem was a catastrophe they needed to fix.

① never they would
② or would they
③ neither they would
④ nor would they

01

Companies ① taking a longer term view of profit with the idea of being ② socially responsible through sustainable development ③ is being rewarded both with government support and by consumers ④ as they make their purchases.

02

The danger of eating ① too much pepper, ② not to speak of drinking only soft drinks and beers, ③ do not seem to worry ④ either Susan or John.

03

Somewhere between the business newsletter, the consumer magazine, and a hobby _____ zines (pronounced "zeens").

① are periodicals called
② are called periodicals
③ periodicals are called
④ called periodicals are

04

Some scientists propose that thumb ① sucking in children ② are a habit which is ③ developed at random, but recent theory suggests that is neurologically and genetically ④ based.

05

The truth is that ① the commonest response to violence is ② one of repugnance, and ③ that a significant number of people everywhere ④ tries to oppose it ⑤ in whatever ways they can.

06

The point ① at which physical decline ② with age ③ begins adversely to affect ④ a driver's capability ⑤ have not yet been studied.

07

The lowest stockpiles in ① decades mean there ② are less grain to buffer the impact of drought, ③ floods, and crop failures, ④ making prices ⑤ more volatile.

08

① As is usual in such cases, she was the apple of his father's eye. Among his courtiers ② were young man of that fineness of blood and lowness of station common to the heroes of romance who love royal maidens. This royal maiden was well content with her lover, ③ for he was handsome and brave to a degree ④ unsurpassed in all this kingdom.

09

① Neither the Bronte sisters nor their brother Branwell ② are remembered ③ as healthy or happy. ④ No error

10

① Neither of my parents, ② who was born in Eastern Europe, ③ understands the full implications of ④ a democratic electoral system.

11

The number of countries ① capable of developing nuclear weapons ② have increased to more ③ than 20 ④ in recent years.

12

In April, Steve Jobs launched his iPad. And it was good. The iPad was not the first eReader or Tablet on the market, nor _____ as multi-functional as the iPhone. You can't make phone calls with an iPad.

① it was not   ② it was

③ was it   ④ it was so

13

Only ① <u>with</u> recent advances in genetic science ② <u>has</u> physicians been able to begin ③ <u>curing</u> genetic diseases. Doctors can now treat ④ <u>a number of</u> genetic diseases that individuals may inherit from their parents.

14

Research in ① <u>learning</u> ② <u>suggests</u> that ③ <u>getting</u> good grades ④ <u>depend</u> more on effective study skills than on a high IQ.

15

I say ① <u>with confidence</u> that neither of my children ② <u>have</u> ③ <u>ever before</u> bothered to read ④ <u>a single</u> word of this book.

16

That the committee members could not agree with each other about solving those problems _____ caused more serious problems.

① is   ② was
③ has   ④ have

17

The prominence of names like Rockefeller, Carnegie, Hill and Armour ① <u>indicate</u> that business ② <u>was still thought of</u> as a field of personal competition, ③ <u>of heroic endeavor</u>, and ④ <u>not of corporate manipulation</u>.

18

Only when the skill is repeated with consistently correct outcomes _____.

① has it truly been learned
② has been it truly learned
③ it has truly been learned
④ has it truly been learning
⑤ it has been truly learning

19

① <u>At least</u> part of their great secret ② <u>is</u> that ③ <u>they both</u> live in the same country. White and black have shared that secret for a long time now, and ④ <u>has done</u> an efficient job of keeping ⑤ <u>it</u> from each other.

20

The ①varied classes of organic compounds with their basically common pattern as well as ②with their peculiarities and reactions ③serves as groundwork for this course. ④No error

21

Beneath the epidermal cells _____ the body-wall muscle, which is relatively thick in some species under certain circumstances.

① exist   ② exists
③ exist where   ④ where it existed
⑤ where exist

22

Avery's most recent works, ①in addition to television shows, ②has been several popular movies and cable broadcast comedy programs. He also frequently ③donates his time to charity events ④to help raise money for children in need.

23

The grand, ①leading principle, ②toward which every ③argument unfolded in these pages directly converges, ④are the absolute and essential importance of human development in its richest diversity.

24

But ①what genuinely recommends the service is the public playlist facility, allowing individual users ②to curate and publish groupings of songs ③based on whatever criteria ④takes their fancy.

25

Mistinguett was not highly talented as a dancer, _____ a good voice, but she had vitality and conviction, and even in old age she was able to play young parts.

① neither had she
② nor she have
③ neither did she have
④ nor did she have

Practice 정답과 해설 p.170

01

There ① is inscribed on the walls the ② follow proverb: "Do unto others ③ as you would have ④ them unto you."

02

He cannot find a suitable job despite _____.

① has been trained thoroughly in repairing and maintaining computers

② his thorough training in the repair and maintenance of computers

③ being trained thoroughly in how to repair and maintaining computers

④ the fact of receiving a thorough computer training in their repair and their maintenance

03

Controversial matters ① involving the whole sections ② were discussed; nevertheless, ③ most of the representatives ④ remaining calm.

04

Our appetite for food, _____ many modern humans, is a natural drive for survival.

① a problem for

② is a problem for

③ being a problem

④ its problem is

05

When ① the final story has been written for that final newspaper ② sometime in the future, you can be sure ③ that it's substance will be some ④ violent act that has occurred.

06

Socrates was _____ searches for the truth and the meaning of life.

① a philosopher, a person who

② a philosopher, a person

③ a philosopher and a person who

④ a philosopher and person

07

_____ small specimen of the embryonic fluid is removed from a fetus, it will be possible to determine whether the baby will be born with birth defects.

① If a   ② That a

③ A   ④ After it is a

08

Now mobile chatting is a widely accepted phenomenon, but _____ a novelty in the telecommunications industry.

① once it being

② it was once

③ once there being

④ there was once

09

In November 1989, ①amid the tide of revolt that was sweeping Eastern Europe, ②protesters' seizing the moment and ③demand new elections ④led to the resignation of the communist leadership and ⑤to the end of communism in Czechoslovakia.

10

Chloroplasts evolved ①about 1.6 billion years ago ②then one cell, incapable of using the ③sun's energy, engulfed ④another cell that could.

11

So profuse and ①vary is our use of these words that ②it is not easy to define just ③what we mean ④by them.

12

Trucks routinely need fuel, oil, and _____ to remove road grime from the chassis and windows.

① thorough washed

② a thorough washing

③ thoroughly washed

④ a thoroughly washing

⑤ are thoroughly washed

13

Frederick Law Olmsted, who ① designed Manhattan's Central Park, ② wanting the park ③ to be a "democratic playground" ④ where everyone ⑤ was equal.

14

Our teacher ① expects us to be on time, ② to do ③ all our homework, and ④ sitting quietly ⑤ in class.

15

① Undoubtedly, Cathy was taking ② a social science class when her father went to ③ the school to see her. Anyone ④ has taken the course was not ⑤ allowed to use a mobile phone.

16

Detroit was the birthplace of ① both the industrial age and the ② nation's middle class, and the ③ city's rise and fall ④ being a window into the challenges ⑤ facing all of modern America.

17

Multinational companies _____ it increasingly important to employ internationally acceptable brand names.

① finding   ② are finding
③ they are finding   ④ that find

18

The notes are ① by Robert, who is a Dante scholar and a professor emeritus ② at Princeton, ③ where he taught the Divine Comedy ④ during forty-two years.

19

When he ① was a little boy, Mark Twain ② would walk along the piers, ③ watch the river boats, ④ swimming and fish in the Mississippi, ⑤ much like his famous character, Tom Sawyer.

20

Classroom routines are ① an important factor in keeping children ② constructively busy, in ③ encouraging self-discipline, and above all, ④ to facilitate learning.

21

Rory, a ranger in an African National Park, ① believes that people should ② do their bit to stop poaching, "whether it's putting some coins ③ in a tin, writing an article, or ④ just spread the word."

22

Only now are questions such as how a material was produced, how much energy will be used to take care of it, and what happens to it at the end of its life _____ to echo through the industry.

① begin
② begins
③ beginning
④ has begun

23

Emerson ① himself, however, writing at the dawn of ② the industrial ③ age, observing ④ with interest the proliferation of railways, ware houses, canals and factories, ⑤ wishing to make room for the possibility of alternative forms of beauty.

24

More than two-thirds of about 20,680 Olympic athletes _____ for a recent report had caffeine in their urine.

① studied
② study
③ to study
④ studying

25

① Talks with North Korea ② which may create a situation favorable ③ to the emergence of ④ a middle class that will push for ⑤ democratization.

MEMO

에듀윌 편입 솔루션 문법 Basic

발 행 일	2023년 7월 12일 초판
편 저 자	에듀윌 편입 LAB
펴 낸 이	김재환
펴 낸 곳	(주)에듀윌
등록번호	제25100-2002-000052호
주 소	08378 서울특별시 구로구 디지털로34길 55
	코오롱싸이언스밸리 2차 3층

www.eduwill.net

대표전화 1600-6700

여러분의 작은 소리
에듀윌은 크게 듣겠습니다.

본 교재에 대한 여러분의 목소리를 들려주세요.
공부하시면서 어려웠던 점, 궁금한 점,
칭찬하고 싶은 점, 개선할 점, 어떤 것이라도 좋습니다.

에듀윌은 여러분께서 나누어 주신 의견을
통해 끊임없이 발전하고 있습니다.

에듀윌 도서몰 book.eduwill.net
• 부가학습자료 및 정오표: 에듀윌 도서몰 → 도서자료실
• 교재 문의: 에듀윌 도서몰 → 문의하기 → 교재(내용, 출간) / 주문 및 배송

꿈을 현실로 만드는
에듀윌

**고객의 꿈, 직원의 꿈,
지역사회의 꿈을 실현한다**

에듀윌 편입의
독한 관리 시스템

전문 학습매니저의 독한 관리로
빠르게 합격할 수 있도록 관리해 드립니다.

독한 담임관리

· 진단고사를 통한 수준별 학습설계
· 일일 진도율부터 성적, 멘탈까지 관리
· 밴드, SNS를 통한 1:1 맞춤 상담 진행
· 담임 학습매니저가 합격할 때까지
  독한 관리

독한 학습관리

· 학습진도 체크 & 학습자료 제공
· 데일리 어휘 테스트
· 모의고사 성적관리 & 약점 보완 제시
· 대학별 배치상담 진행

독한 생활관리

· 출석 관리
· 나의 학습량, 일일 진도율 관리
· 월별 총 학습시간 관리
· 슬럼프 물리치는 컨디션 관리
· 학원과 동일한 의무 자습 관리

에듀윌
편입 솔루션

문법 BASIC   정답과 해설

문법이 어려워?

이 책을 빡!

편입 최초
프리미엄 해설 수록

eduwill

에듀윌
편입 솔루션

문법 BASIC 정답과 해설

에듀윌 편입 솔루션

문법 BASIC 정답과 해설

GRAMMAR BASIC

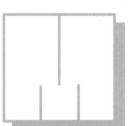
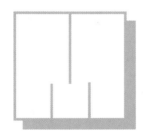

문법이 어려워?

이 책을 봐!

편입 최초
프리미엄 해설 수록

1강 동사

Practice 01

01	②	02	①	03	③	04	③	05	②
06	①	07	①	08	④	09	③	10	②
11	②	12	④	13	②	14	③	15	⑤
16	⑤	17	③	18	③	19	②	20	②
21	⑤	22	②	23	④	24	④	25	③

01
[2013 단국대]

(①In line with company safety policy,) all new workers
must first ②participate a safety ③briefing (before
④attempting to operate dangerous machinery.)

정답 ② (participate → participate in)

해석 회사 안전 방침에 의거하여, 모든 신입 사원들은 위험한
기계를 다루기 전에 안전에 관한 설명회에 참석한다.

분석 자동사 participate의 어형
② 자동사 participate은 목적어를 받을 때 전치사가 함
께 와야 한다. participate in으로 고쳐야 한다.
① in line with ~ : '~에 의거하여'라는 뜻의 문장의 의미
를 더해 주는 수식어구로 적절하다.
③ safety briefing은 복합명사로 쓰여 적절하다.
④ 전치사의 목적어로 동명사가 나와 적절하다.

02
[2015 서울여대]

Men (who ①enter into ②female-dominated fields)
easily ③move up to supervisory positions, a phenomenon
(④known as the glass escalator.)
(which is)

정답 ① (enter into → enter)

해석 여성이 주를 이루는 분야에 입성한 남자들이 쉽게 관리직
(고위직)의 위치에 오른다. 이러한 현상은 유리 천장이라
고 알려져 있다.

분석 타동사 enter의 어형

① 타동사 enter는 목적어를 받을 때 전치사를 쓰지 못
한다.
② 분야(field)가 지배하는 주체가 아니라 여성들에 의해
지배되는 대상이므로 수동의 관계인 과거분사
(dominated)는 적절하다.
③ 주어(Men)와 동사(move)의 수 일치가 적절하다.
④ 현상이 알고 있는 주체가 아니라 유리 천장이라고 알
려진 대상이므로 수동의 관계인 과거분사(known)는
적절하다.

03
[2010 성균관대]

It was (①principally) the influence of Christianity ②that
deprived beauty ③from the central place (it ④had in
⑤classical ideals of human excellence.)

정답 ③ (from → of)

해석 인간이 우월하다는 고전적 이상 속에 아름다움(美)에게서
본래 가지고 있었던 중심적 지위를 앗아간 것은 바로 기
독교의 영향력이었다.

분석 「deprive A of B」
③ 「deprive A of B」의 어형으로 쓰인다. from을 of로
고쳐야 한다.
① 단독 부사로 문장 전체에 의미를 더해 주는 부사(수식
어)로 쓰여 적절하다. 뒤에 명사(the influence)를 꾸
민다고 착각하기 쉽지만 명사를 수식하려면 정관사
the 뒤에 위치해야 한다.
② 「It is/was ~ that ...」 형태의 강조구문으로 that절 속
주어가 강조된 형태의 문장이다.
④ 주절 동사가 과거(was)이므로 종속절의 동사 역시 과
거(deprived)는 적절하다.
⑤ 형용사(classical)가 명사(ideals)를 수식하여 적절하다.

04
[2011 성신여대]

Wall Street analysts _____ optimistic (about
the performance of value stocks.)

① reached　　　　　　② resulted

③ remained　　　　　④ revealed

정답 ③

해석 월스트리트(Wall Street) 분석가들은 가치주의 실적에 대해 여전히 낙관적이었다.

분석 자동사 remain의 어형
- ③ 형용사(optimistic)를 보어로 받을 수 있는 2형식 동사는 remain이 유일하다.
- ①, ②, ④ 형용사 보어를 받을 수 없는 동사이다.

05

[2014 상명대]

The sun ①was ②raising ③over the mountain (when I
  S   V   rising   ⓟ   N   부사절 S
④rose out of bed and ⑤sat at the table.)
  V₁   V₂

정답 ② (raising → rising)

해석 태양이 산 중턱에 떠올랐을 때 나는 잠에서 깨어 식탁에 앉았다.

분석 자동사(rise)와 타동사(raise)의 구분
- ② raise는 타동사로 반드시 목적어(N)가 있어야 한다. 뒤에 전명구(over the mountain)인 수식어구만 있는 것으로 보아 자동사의 진행형인 rising으로 고쳐야 한다.
- ① when절이 과거(rose)인 것으로 보아 주절 역시 과거(was)는 적절하다.
- ③ 자동사(rise) 뒤 수식어구인 전명구는 적절하다.
- ④ 뒤에 전명구(out of bed)가 나와 자동사 rose는 적절하다.
- ⑤ 뒤에 전명구(at the table)가 나와 자동사 sat은 적절하다.

06

[2015 가톨릭대]

The committee didn't really _____ [meeting a
        S   V
lot of opposition to the new plan for traffic control.]
                       O

① anticipate   ② predict

③ expect   ④ prepare

정답 ①

해석 위원들은 교통을 통제하기 위한 새로운 계획에 그렇게나 많은 반대에 부딪힐 줄 전혀 예상하지 못했다.

분석 동명사(R-ing)를 목적어로 취하는 동사
- ① 빈칸 뒤 동명사(meeting)를 목적어로 받을 수 있는 동사는 anticipate뿐이다.
- ②, ③, ④ 전부 부정사를 목적어로 받는 동사이다.

07

[2011 동덕여대]

Visitors (to the zoo) are requested to refrain _____
  S   V   O.C
feeding the animals in their cages.

① from   ② with

③ to   ④ of

정답 ①

해석 동물원 방문객들은 우리 안에 있는 동물들에게 먹이 주는 것을 삼가도록 권고받는다.

분석 자동사 refrain의 어형
- ① 자동사 refrain은 뒤에 명사가 나올 때 전치사 from을 써야 한다.
- ②, ③, ④ refrain의 어형에 맞지 않는 전치사이다.

08

[2017 가천대]

(①Unbeknown to my parents,) I took several college
                              S   V₁   O
courses (in creative writing) and was ②excelling. (After
                               ⓟ   V₂
reading one of my short stories), my first creative writing
         동명사구   S
teacher decided [that I was ③to be a writer.] I decided
                   to follow V   명사절(O)   S   V
[④following my passion] (instead of obeying my family's
  동명사   O
decree.)

정답 ④ (following → to follow)

해석 나는 부모님도 모르게 문예 창작 전공 과정을 수강하며 두각을 나타냈다. 내가 쓴 단편 소설을 읽어 보신 후, 나의 첫 문예 창작 교수님께서는 내가 작가가 되어야만 한다고 생각하셨다. 그래서 나 역시 부모님의 바람을 따르기보다 나의 열정을 따르기로 결심했다.

분석 「decide + to R」
- ④ decide는 준동사를 목적어로 받을 때 to R를 쓰기 때문에 to follow로 고쳐야 한다.
- ① unbeknown to ~ : '~도 모르는 사이에'라는 표현이다.
- ② excel은 자동사로 쓰여 적절하다.
- ③ 「be + to R」는 예정, 의무, 의도, 가능, 운명의 뜻을 나타낸다.

09

My father believed [that family members should help
each other] and made us _____ some chores
every Saturdays.

① to do   ② does

③ do   ④ did

정답 ③

해석 나의 아버지는 매주 토요일 가족 구성원들이 서로를 도와
몇 가지의 귀찮은 일을 해야 한다고 생각하셨다.

분석 5형식 사역동사 make의 어형

③「make + O + O.C(R)」 5형식 사역동사의 어형으로
빈칸은 동사원형(do)이 와야 한다.

①, ②, ④ make의 목적보어 자리에는 동사원형(R)이 나
와야 한다.

10

It's ① very hard [to get people ② examine their life
(unless you ③ remind them it's not going to ④ last
forever.)]

정답 ② (examine their life → to examine their life)

해석 당신이 사람들에게 삶은 영원히 지속되는 것이 아니라는
것을 상기시켜 주지 않으면 사람들로 하여금 자신의 삶을
점검하도록 만드는 것은 굉장히 힘들다.

분석 5형식 동사 get의 어형

②「get + O + O.C(to R)」 5형식 동사의 어형이다. 목적
보어 자리에 동사원형을 쓰지 못하므로 to examine
their life로 고쳐야 한다.

① be동사의 보어로 hard는 형용사로 쓰여 적절하다.

③ remind는 타동사로 뒤에 대상(사람)을 목적어로 받아
적절하다. 여기서 them은 people을 대신 받고 있다.

④「be going to + R」 형태로 to 뒤에 동사원형이 나오
고 last는 자동사로 목적어가 없어 적절하다.

11

The most underrated ① of the major senses,) smell has
direct access ② at the more primitive, or basic, parts
of the brain.) Brain imaging techniques ③ have shown
[that smell can activate mood, emotion, and memory
(without ④ being consciously perceived.)]

정답 ② (at → to)

해석 인간의 주요 감각들 중 가장 과소평가 받는 후각은 뇌의
원초적인 부분에 직접적인 접근을 한다. 뇌 영상 기법은
후각이 의식적으로 인지되지 않고서도 분위기, 감정, 기억
력을 향상시킬 수 있다는 것을 보여 준다.

분석「have access to + N」

② have access to ~ : '~에 접근하다'라는 표현은 전치
사 to와 함께 쓴다. 명사 access는 뒤에 전치사를 끌
고 나올 경우 항상 to와 함께한다.

① 명사와 명사의 충돌을 피해 주기 위해 전치사는 적절하
다. (최상급 뒤에 명사가 너무 뻔하면 생략이 가능하다.)

③ 주어는 brain이 아니라 Brain imaging techniques
(뇌 영상 기법)이므로 수 일치가 적절하다.

④ 전치사의 목적어로 동명사는 적절하다. 후각이 의식적
으로 인지하는 주체가 아닌 인지되는 대상이므로 수동
태 동명사로 쓰였다.

12

(Because the rain ① fell ② all night,) the ③ clogged
drain pipe ④ bursted and ⑤ flooded the house.

정답 ④ (bursted → burst)

해석 밤새도록 비가 왔기 때문에, 꽉 막힌 배수로가 터져 집을
침수시켰다.

분석 burst – burst – burst(동사의 불규칙 3단 변화)

④ burst – burst – burst로 쓰이는 불규칙 3단 변화이므
로 burst로 고쳐야 한다.

① 자동사 fall의 과거형이므로 뒤에 부사가 나와 적절하다.

② 과거 시점을 나타내는 표현이다.

③ 배수관이 막는 주체가 아니라 막히는 대상이므로 수동
의 관계인 과거분사(clogged)는 적절하다.

⑤ burst and flooded로 과거동사가 병치되어 적절하다.

13

We ① decided [to go on a trip to the mountains] but
forgot [② taking the map,] ③ so we stopped ④ to buy
⑤ one at a gas station.)

정답 ② (taking the map → to take the map)

해석 우리는 산으로 여행을 가기로 했지만 깜빡 잊고 지도를
챙기지 않아서 지도를 사기 위해 주유소에 들렀다.

분석 「forget + to R/R-ing ~」의 의미 구분

② 「forget + to R(깜빡 잊고 ~하지 않다)/forget + R-ing(~했었던 사실을 잊다)」의 의미 차이를 묻고 있다. 우리가 산으로 여행을 가기로 결정했지만 '깜빡 잊고 지도를 챙기지 않았다'라는 의미가 적절하므로 to take로 고쳐야 한다.

① decide는 to R를 목적어로 받아 적절하다.

③ 접속사로 쓰여 문장과 문장을 연결하여 적절하다.

④ 「stop + to R(~하기 위해 멈추다)」의 표현으로 문맥상 적절하다.

⑤ one은 앞에 the map을 대신 받는 대명사로 수 일치가 적절하다.

14
[2015 한국외대]

A ① proposed law ② would make the illegal consumption or sale (of dog meat) ③ punishing (by ④ a fine of up to 5,000 euros.)

정답 ③ (punishing → punished)

해석 발의된 법안은 개고기의 불법적인 소비 혹은 판매를 하면 5,000유로의 벌금으로 처벌받는다는 내용이다.

분석 5형식 동사 make의 어형

③ 「make + O + O.C」 5형식 동사의 어형으로 쓰일 때, 목적어가 목적보어를 하는 주체, 즉 능동의 관계라면 동사원형(R)을 쓰고, 목적어가 목적보어 당하는 대상, 수동의 관계라면 p.p. 형태의 과거분사를 써야 한다. 개고기의 소비 혹은 판매가 처벌을 하는 주체가 아니라 처벌받는 대상이므로 수동의 관계인 과거분사(punished)로 고쳐야 한다.

① 법안이 발의하는 주체가 아니라 발의되는 대상이므로 수동의 관계인 과거분사(proposed)는 적절하다.

② 뒤에 동사원형이 나와 조동사는 적절하다.

④ 여기서 fine은 '벌금'이라는 뜻의 명사이다.

15
[2015 상명대]

(In ① the 1880s,) the public's ② well-justified skepticism (about doctors) encouraged ③ leading medical professors, (many of whom ④ had studied in France and Germany,) ⑤ began restructuring American medical education.

정답 ⑤ (began → to begin)

해석 1880년대에, 의사들에 대한 대중들의 정당한 회의론적인 태도가, 대다수가 프랑스와 독일에서 의학을 연구한 뛰어난 교수들로 하여금, 미국의 의학 교육에 대한 혁신을 시작하도록 자극했다.

분석 5형식 동사 encourage의 어형

⑤ 「encourage + O + O.C(to R)」 5형식 동사의 어형으로 목적보어 자리에 to R를 써야 하기 때문에 to begin으로 고쳐야 한다.

① 연도 앞에는 the를 쓰지 않지만, 연대 앞에는 the를 써야 하므로 적절하다.

② 회의론이 정당화시키는 주체가 아니라 정당화되는 대상이므로 수동의 관계를 나타내는 과거분사(justified)는 적절하다.

③ leading은 '뛰어난, 주도하는, 선도하는'이라는 뜻의 형용사로 뒤에 명사를 수식한다.

④ many of whom에서 whom은 접속사이기에 동사가 나와 적절하다. 주절이 과거이기에 종속절에 과거완료 역시 적절하다.

16
[2016 상명대]

(① As more and more teenagers socialize ② online,) middle school and high school teachers are increasingly seeing a ③ breezy form (of ④ Internet English) ⑤ to jump from e-mail into schoolwork.

정답 ⑤ (to jump → jump 또는 jumping)

해석 점점 더 많은 10대 청소년들이 온라인을 통해서 사교 활동을 함에 따라서, 중고등학교 선생님들은 인터넷상에서 사용되는 영어가 이메일 공간을 넘어서 학교 공부에까지 등장하는 것을 더 많이 목격하고 있다.

분석 5형식 지각동사 see의 어형

⑤ 「see + O + O.C(R/R-ing)」 5형식 동사의 어형으로 쓰여 목적보어 자리에 to R는 쓸 수 없다. jump 혹은 jumping으로 고쳐야 한다.

① 부사절 접속사로 쓰여 「주어 + 동사」가 나와 적절하다.

② 자동사 뒤에 부사로 쓰여 적절하다.

③ 형용사(breezy)가 명사(form)를 수식하여 적절하다.

④ Internet English는 복합명사이다.

17 [2016 경기대]

(①Anticipating a future (②in which millions of Americans will prefer [to ③shopping in the security of their living rooms,])) the mall industry is experiencing a ④full-blown mid-life crisis.

분사구문 / 형용사절 S

V / shop / S V O

S V O

정답 ③ (shopping → shop)

해석 수백만의 미국인들이 거실에서 안전하게 쇼핑하는 것을 선호하게 될 미래를 예측한 쇼핑몰 업계는 만연한 중년의 위기(성장통을 겪는다는 뜻)를 경험하고 있다.

분석 동사 prefer의 어형

　③ prefer는 to R와 R-ing를 둘 다 목적어로 받을 수 있다. prefer 뒤에 바로 to가 나왔으므로 부정사 to라는 것을 알 수 있으므로 동사원형(shop)으로 고쳐야 한다.

　① 분사구문이다. 쇼핑몰 업계가 미래를 예측하는 주체이고 뒤에 목적어(a future)도 있으므로 능동태 분사구문(Anticipating)은 적절하다.

　② 「전치사 + 관계대명사」는 절 이하의 성분이 완전하게 나와 적절하다.

　④ full-blown은 '만연한, 만개한'이라는 뜻의 형용사로 쓰여 뒤에 명사를 꾸며 적절하다.

18 [2014 경기대]

People (①with strong personal relationships) are 50% ②more likely to outlive ③than those (④without.)

S

- V - (people)

정답 ③ (than → 삭제)

해석 끈끈한 유대 관계를 형성하고 있는 사람들이 그렇지 않은 사람들보다 더 오래 살 가능성이 50% 이상이다.

분석 타동사 outlive의 어형

　③ out이 들어간 동사들은 타동사이다. 이때 out의 의미가 '~보다'의 뜻이므로 뒤에 than을 쓰고 자주 묻는다. outlive(~보다 오래 살다)는 목적어를 받는 타동사이므로 than을 삭제한다.

　① 명사와 명사의 충돌을 피해 주기 위해 전치사는 적절하다.

　② than이 없어도 의미상 필요하다면 비교 표현(-er/more ~)은 얼마든지 가능하다.

　④ without은 보통 전치사로 쓰이지만 뒤에 명사가 너무 뻔한 경우 그 명사를 생략시키고 혼자 부사로 쓰일 수 있다.

19 [2010 상명대]

effects

The study ①concerned itself mainly (with ②the affects)

S V O

(of ③anxiety) (on decision making) (④in high-risk situations.)

정답 ② (the affects → the effects)

해석 그 연구는 위험성이 높은 상황에서 하게 되는 의사 결정 과정에 대한 불안감의 효과를 주로 다루고 있다.

분석 affect(동사)와 effect(명사)의 구분

　② affect(동사)와 effect(명사)의 구분을 묻고 있다. 전치사 뒤에 동사인 affects가 나올 수 없으므로 명사 effects로 고쳐야 한다.

　① concern은 타동사로 뒤에 목적어를 받아 적절하고, 주어와 목적어가 같을 경우에 재귀대명사를 써야 한다.

　③ 전치사의 목적어로 명사가 나오고, 명사와 명사의 충돌을 피해 주기 위해 전치사도 적절하다.

　④ 앞의 making은 목적어를 받는 동명사가 아니다. decision making이 '의사 결정 과정'이라는 뜻의 복합명사이므로 뒤에 명사와 충돌을 피해 주기 위해 전명구(수식어구)는 적절하다.

20 [2016 단국대]

(While most American architects (in the early 1900s)

부사절 S

looked to Europe for ideas,) Frank Lloyd Wright found

V S V

Japanese design and art _____.

O O.C

① inspires　　　　　② more inspiring

③ is more inspiring　　④ are more inspiring

정답 ②

해석 1900년대 초창기에 대부분의 미국 건축가들은 아이디어를 떠올리기 위해 유럽 쪽으로 눈을 돌렸던데 반면, 프랭크 로이드 라이트(Frank Lloyd Wright)는 일본의 디자인과 미술이 더 큰 영감을 준다고 생각했다.

분석 5형식 동사 find의 어형

　② 「find + O + O.C(형용사)」 5형식 동사의 어형으로 쓰여 목적보어 자리에 형용사(inspiring: 영감을 주는)가 나온 ②가 정답이다.

　①, ③, ④ found 뒤에 접속사 that이 생략되어 주어, 동사가 나왔다고 생각할 수 있지만 그렇게 되면 시제의 오류가 생긴다. 주절이 과거(found)일 때 종속절에서는 현재 혹은 현재완료가 나오지 못한다.

21

One ① third (to ② nearly half of the people) (in the majority of countries) ③ surveyed) admitted [they wanted ④ their spouse ⑤ losing weight.]

정답 ⑤ (losing → to lose)

해석 조사를 실시했던 대다수의 국가들 중 3분의 1에서 거의 절반의 사람들이 자신의 배우자가 체중을 줄였으면 좋겠다고 시인했다.

분석 5형식 동사 want의 어형

⑤ 「want + O + O.C(to R)」 5형식 동사의 어형으로 쓰여 to lose로 고쳐야 한다.

① one[a] third는 '3분의 1'이라는 분수 표현이다.

② nearly는 숫자와 연관된 표현 앞에 있으면 '거의'라는 뜻으로 쓰이는 수식어이다.

③ 국가들이 조사한 것이 아니라 조사받은 대상이므로 수동의 관계인 과거분사(surveyed)는 적절하다.

④ people을 대신 받는 대명사이므로 수 일치가 적절하다.

22

Physicists often find _____ to separate a beam of particles into a spectrum according to their energy.]

① it is used
② it useful
③ useful
④ its use

정답 ②

해석 물리학자들은 입자선을 에너지에 따라 스펙트럼으로 분리하는 것이 쓸모 있다는 것을 종종 알게 된다.

분석 5형식 동사 find의 '가목적어 – 진목적어' 구문

② 「find + it + O.C(형용사) + to R ~ / that S + V ~」 5형식 '가목적어 – 진목적어' 어형이다. 목적보어인 형용사 뒤에 「to R / that S + V」와 같은 진짜 목적어가 있다면 목적어 자리에 반드시 가짜 목적어인 it을 써야 한다.

① 「find + that + S + V ~」 3형식의 어형에서 that이 생략되었다고 보면 'to R하는 것이 사용된다'라는 의미가 되어 부적절하다.

③ 목적보어 뒤에 진짜 목적어(to separate ~)가 있다면 가짜 목적어 it을 반드시 써야 한다.

④ its use가 명사로 쓰여 목적보어가 존재하지 않아 적절하지 않다.

23

The company's attorney _____ to them [that we should use caution in deciding what information to release to the public.]

① notified
② informed
③ told
④ said

정답 ④

해석 우리 회사 변호사는 대중들에게 무슨 정보를 공개할지 결정하는 데 있어 신중해야 한다고 말했다.

분석 동사 say의 어형

④ say는 대상(사람)을 목적어로 받지 못하기 때문에 대상(사람) 앞에 반드시 전치사 to를 써야 하므로 ④가 정답이다.

①, ②, ③ 전부 대상(사람)을 목적어로 받는 동사이기에 them을 목적어로 받을 때 전치사 to가 없어야 한다.

24

(Based on an analysis of the most successful ① executives' schedules and activities,) I discovered ② seven practices (you ③ should seriously consider ④ to adopt in order to make the most of your morning.)

정답 ④ (to adopt → adopting)

해석 나는 가장 성공한 임원들의 일정과 활동을 분석한 토대로 당신이 아침 시간을 활용하기 위해 진지하게 채택을 고려해야만 하는 일곱 가지 습관을 발견했다.

분석 3형식 동사 consider의 어형

④ consider은 동명사(R-ing)를 목적어로 받기 때문에 adopting으로 고쳐야 한다.

① 복수명사(Ns)의 소유격은 뒤에 아포스트로피(')만 붙이므로 적절하다. (ex. girls' room)

② discovered의 목적어로 쓰여 적절하다.

③ 부사가 동사를 수식하여 적절하다.

25

The book fair ① outdoors was ② to be opened
   S   ⓐ   V postpone
yesterday, but they were obliged ③ to postponing it
              S   V   O.C
(④ on account of the sudden blizzard.)
   = because of

정답 ③ (to postponing → to postpone)

해석 도서 박람회가 어제 야외에서 개최될 예정이었다. 그러나
주최 측은 갑작스럽게 불어 닥친 눈보라 때문에 어쩔 수
없이 도서 박람회를 연기시킬 수밖에 없었다.

분석 5형식 동사 oblige의 어형

③ 「oblige + O + O.C(to R)」 5형식 동사의 어형을 수동
태로 만든 문장이다. 이때 oblige의 목적보어는 to R
로 쓰이므로 to postpone으로 고쳐야 한다.

① outdoors은 부사로 뒤에 동사를 수식하여 적절하다.

② 도서 박람회가 여는 주체가 아니라 열리는 대상이므로
수동태 부정사(to be opened)는 적절하다.

④ 명사와 명사의 충돌을 피해 주기 위해 전명구는 적절
하다.

Practice 02

01	②	02	④	03	②	04	③	05	②
06	④	07	③	08	②	09	④	10	④
11	③	12	④	13	④	14	④	15	③
16	④	17	②	18	⑤	19	②	20	②
21	④	22	③	23	①	24	③	25	③

01
[2012 고려대]

(Nowadays) some might find emotional renewal (in
　　　　　　　 S 　　 V 　　　　　O
pleasant parks and natural lands,) but the disadvantaged
　　　　　　　　　　　　　　　　　　　 S
_____.
　　　　　V
① cannot afford reaching to them
② cannot afford [to reach them]
　　　　 V 　 부정사(O)
③ could not afford to reach to them
④ could not afford to reaching them

정답 ②

해석 요즘 몇몇 사람들은 공원이나 자연 경관을 보며 기분
전환을 하지만, 가난한 사람들은 그곳에 갈 만한 경제적
여유가 없다.

분석 afford와 reach의 어형
② afford는 to R를 목적어로 받는 동사이므로 ①, ④는
탈락되고, 타동사 reach는 목적어를 받을 때 전치사가
올 수 없기 때문에 ②가 적절하다.
① afford는 to R를 목적어로 받는 동사이다.
③ 타동사 reach는 목적어를 받을 때 전치사가 올 수 없다.
④ afford는 to R를 목적어로 받기에 to reaching이 아
닌 to reach로 써야 한다.

02
[2017 아주대]

(① Using specialized cells,) plants can sense gravity
　　 분사구문 　　　　　　　　　　 S 　 V₁ 　　 O
② and redistribute hormones, (③ called auxins,) (to
　　　 V₂ 　　　　　 O 　　　　　 (which are)
stimulate growth and allow vital features (of the plant)
　　　　　　　　　　　　　　　　 O
to develop
④ develop.) (However,) a big puzzle is [⑤ how this
O.C 　　　　　　　　　 S 　 V 　 명사절(N)
transport process occurs (at a cellular level.)]
　　 S 　　　　　 V

정답 ④ (develop → to develop)

해석 분화된 세포를 이용하여, 식물은 중력을 느끼고 옥신이라
불리는 호르몬을 재분배하여 성장을 자극하고 식물의 필
수적 특징들을 발달시킬 수 있다. 그러나 한 가지 커다란
의문점은 이러한 수송 과정이 세포 수준에서 어떻게 일어
나는가 하는 것이다.

분석 5형식 동사 allow의 어형
④ 「allow + O + O.C(to R)」 5형식 동사의 어형으로 쓰
여 목적보어 자리에 동사원형 develop을 쓸 수 없다.
to develop으로 고쳐야 한다.
① 식물이 세포를 사용하는 주체이고, 목적어(specialized
cells)도 있기 때문에 능동태 분사구문(Using)은 적절
하다.
② sense and redistribute로 병치되어 적절하다.
③ 호르몬이 부르는 주체가 아니라 auxin이라고 불려지
는 대상이므로 수동의 관계인 과거분사(called)는 적
절하다.
⑤ how는 절 이하의 성분이 완전하여 명사의 역할을 하
기에 be동사의 보어로 적절하다.

03
[2017 홍익대]

(In [① what appears to be a hallway,]) a hooded detainee
　　　 명사절 　 V 　　　　　　　　　 S
seems (② be handcuffed ③ in an awkward position)
　 V 　　 to be 　 C
(④ atop two boxes.)
　　 P

정답 ② (be → to be)

해석 복도처럼 보이는 곳에서, 복면을 한 어떤 억류된 사람이
두 개의 상자 위에 어색한 자세로 수갑이 채워져 있는 것
같다.

분석 2형식 동사 seem의 어형
② 이미 동사(seems)가 있는데 동사가 또 나올 수 없기
때문에 to be로 고쳐야 한다.
① what은 절 이하의 성분이 불완전하여 하나의 명사로
쓰인다. 전치사 in의 목적어로 쓰여 적절하다.
③ 앞에서 문장이 끝나 수식어구(전명구)는 적절하다.
④ 명사와 명사의 충돌을 피해 주기 위해 전치사는 적절
하다.

04

(① In the draft,) (② obtained by the Associated Press,)
(which is)
the Security Council demands [that all parties (in Syria)
S   V   명사절(O) S   (should)
immediately ③ to stop any violence (irrespective ④ of
V   O   Ⓟ
[where it comes from.])]]
N

정답 ③ (to stop → stop)

해석 AP 통신이 입수한 초안에서 안전 보장 이사회는 시리아
의 모든 정파들에게 그 어디에서 오는 폭력이든지에 상관
없이 즉시 모든 폭력을 멈춰야만 한다고 요구했다.

분석 동사 demand의 어형

③ demand는 어떠한 경우에도 5형식 어형(demand +
O + to R)으로 쓰일 수 없다. demand가 뒤에 that절
을 받아 「demand + that + S + (should) + R」의 어
형으로 쓰인다. that절 속에 동사는 반드시 원형으로
써야 하기에 to stop을 stop으로 고쳐야 한다.

① 수식어구(전명구)의 역할로 쓰여 적절하다.

② 초안(draft)이 입수하는 주체가 아니라 입수되는 대상
이고, 뒤에 목적어도 없기 때문에 수동의 관계인 과거
분사(obtained)는 적절하다.

④ irrespective of ~: '~와 상관없이'라는 뜻의 전치사
로 쓰여 적절하다.

05

to create
(① Having failed ② creating a consensus,) the boss
분사구문   S
asked [③ that the decision ④ be put off.]
V   명사절(O)   S   (should) V

정답 ② (creating → to create)

해석 합의된 의견을 이끌어 내지 못했기 때문에 그 사장은 결
정을 뒤로 미뤄야만 했다.

분석 동사 fail의 어형

② 「fail to R/fail in N」의 어형으로 쓰인다. fail은 to R
를 목적어로 받기 때문에 to create로 고쳐야 한다.

① 사장이 합의된 의견을 이끌어 내지 못한 시점이 주절
동사(asked)보다 이전이기에 완료분사구문(having
p.p.)은 적절하다.

③ ask는 that절을 목적어로 받을 수 있다.

④ 「ask + that + S + (should) + R」 명령형 동사의 어형
으로 쓰여 적절하다.

06

(① In addition) the founding fathers (of America)
S
② opposed a strong government (③ because it might
V   O   부사절 S
④ interfere people's freedom.)
V   N
with

정답 ④ (interfere → interfere with)

해석 게다가 미국의 헌법 제정자들은 강력한 정부를 반대했다.
그 이유는 그것이 인간의 자유를 방해할 수도 있기 때문
이다.

분석 자동사 interfere의 어형

④ 자동사 interfere은 목적어(N)를 받을 경우 전치사
with 혹은 in을 써야 하므로 interfere with로 고쳐야
한다.

① in addition: '게다가'라는 뜻의 수식어구(전명구)로 쓰
여 적절하다.

② 타동사 oppose는 전치사 없이 목적어를 받아 적절하다.

③ because는 접속사로 쓰여 주어, 동사가 나와 적절
하다.

07

William H. Johnson's ① artistic debt (to Scandinavia) is
S   V
evident (in paintings) (that ② range from sensitive
C   형용사절 V   Ⓟ   A
portraits (of citizens in his wife's Danish home,
Kerteminde,) ③ and ④ awe-inspiring views (of fjords and
to   B
mountain peaks) (⑤ in the western and northern regions
of Norway.)

정답 ③ (and → to)

해석 윌리엄 H. 존슨(William H. Johnson)이 스칸디나비아
에 예술적 영향을 받았음은 아내의 고향 덴마크, 케르테
미네(Kerteminde) 사람들을 풍부한 감성으로 그린 초상
화부터, 노르웨이 서부와 북부 지역의 피오르드와 산봉우
리를 장엄하게 그린 전경에 이르기까지 아우르는 다양한
그림들에서 분명하게 보인다.

분석 「range from A to B」 (A에서 B까지의 범위를 아우르다)

③ 「range from A to B」의 어형으로 쓰여 and를 to로
고쳐야 한다.

① 형용사(artistic)가 명사(debt)를 수식하여 적절하다.

② 자동사 range는 「from A to B」를 쓰기에 적절하다.

④ 형용사(awe-inspiring)가 명사(views)를 수식하여 적절하다.

⑤ 명사와 명사의 충돌을 피해 주기 위해 수식어구(전명구)는 적절하다.

08

[2013 동국대]

More efforts should be made (to attract ① highly skilled foreign workers) (to help keep the country's growth engine ② to move.) A serious consideration ③ should be given (to a proposal) (to permit foreigners) (④ who have stayed here for more than 10 years.)

정답 ② (to move → moving)

해석 국가의 성장 동력 활성화를 유지하는 데 도움을 주는 능숙한 외국인 노동자들을 끌어들이기 위해 많은 노력을 기울여야 한다. 10년 이상 여기서 지내온 외국인들을 수용하자는 제안을 진지하게 고려해 보아야만 한다.

분석 5형식 동사 keep의 어형

② 「find/keep + O + O.C(R-ing)」 5형식 동사의 어형으로 쓰이므로 to move를 moving으로 고쳐야 한다.

① 부사(highly)가 형용사(skilled)를 수식하여 적절하다. skilled는 '능숙한, 숙련된'이라는 뜻의 형용사이다.

③ 고려가 행하는 것이 아닌 행해지는 대상이므로 수동태는 적절하다.

④ 선행사가 사람(foreigners)이고 절 속에 주어가 불완전하여 주격 관계대명사(who)는 적절하다.

09

[2014 가천대]

"The evolutionary biologist," (Huxley says,) "is tempted (to ask [① whether the aim should not be ② to let the mammal ③ die within us,] so as the more effectually to permit the man ④ live.")

정답 ④ (live → to live)

해석 헉슬리(Huxley)가 말하기를 "진화 생물학자는, 혹시 목표가 우리 인간들이 더 효과적으로 살 수 있도록 우리들 가운데서 동물을 죽게 하는 것이어야 하는 것은 아닐까 하는 질문을 하도록 유혹을 받는다."고 하였다.

분석 5형식 동사 permit의 어형

④ 「permit + O + O.C(to R)」 5형식 동사의 어형으로 쓰여 live를 to live로 고쳐야 한다.

① whether은 절 이하의 성분이 완전하여 하나의 명사로 쓰이므로 ask의 목적어로 적절하다.

② 「be + to R」 형태로 예정, 의무, 의도, 가능, 운명의 뜻으로 쓰이는 표현이다.

③ 「let + O + O.C(R)」 5형식 동사의 어형으로 쓰여 동사 원형(die)은 적절하다.

10

[2016 상명대]

The superintendent (of the jail,) (who was standing ① apart from the rest of warders,) (② moodily ③ prodding the gravel with his stick,) ④ rose his head (⑤ at the sound.)

정답 ④ (rose → raised)

해석 침울한 표정으로 막대기로 자갈을 찌르며 나머지 교도관들로부터 떨어져 서 있던 교도소 소장은 그 소리에 고개를 들어 올렸다.

분석 rise와 raise의 구분

④ 자동사 rise는 목적어를 받지 못하는데 his head가 있으므로 타동사 raised로 고쳐야 한다.

① 자동사(stand) 뒤에 수식어구인 부사구로 나와 적절하다.

② 분사구문(prodding)을 수식하는 부사로 쓰여 적절하다.

③ 교도소 소장이 자갈을 쿡 찌르는 주체이므로 능동태 분사구문(prodding)은 적절하다.

⑤ 명사와 명사의 충돌을 피해 주기 위해 수식어구(전명구)는 적절하다.

11

[2016 홍익대]

(Yesterday) I had to have my car _____ away by the police, (since it suddenly stopped on a highway.)

① towing   ② tow
③ towed   ④ town

정답 ③

해석 어제 내 차가 고속 도로에서 갑자기 멈췄기 때문에, 경찰에게 견인시키도록 해야 했다.

분석 5형식 사역동사 have의 어형

③ 「have + O + O.C(R/R-ing/p.p.)」 5형식 사역동사의 어형이다. 이때 목적어가 목적보어 하는 주체, 즉 능동의 관계일 때 목적보어 자리에 R/R-ing를 쓰고, 목적어가 목적보어 당하는 대상, 즉 수동의 관계일 때 p.p.를 쓴다. 목적어(my car)가 견인하는 주체가 아니라 견인되는 대상이므로 수동의 관계인 과거분사(towed)를 써야 한다.

12 [2011 경기대]

(①Although a multinational investigation team blamed
부사절   S   V
the North ②to sink the South Korean warship Cheonan
A   B
③in a torpedo attack,) North Korea denies ④its
                          S   V
involvement.
O

정답 ② (to sink → for sinking)

해석 비록 다국적 조사팀은 북한이 남한의 군함인 천안함을 어뢰로 침몰시켰다고 비난했다 할지라도, 북한은 자신의 연루 사실을 부인했다.

분석 「blame A for B(N/R-ing)」의 어형

② 「blame A for B(N/R-ing)」 3형식 동사의 어형으로 쓰이므로 to sink를 for sinking으로 고쳐야 한다.

① Although는 접속사로 쓰여 뒤에 주어, 동사가 나와 적절하다.

③ 명사와 명사의 충돌을 피해 주기 위해 전치사로 적절하다.

④ North Korea(북한)을 대신 받는 대명사로 쓰여 수 일치가 적절하다.

13 [2011 가천대]

(Although you must get off (while the bus is ①being
부사절 S   V   부사절   S   V
cleaned,)) you may ②leave your suitcases and ③other
            S   laid V   O
belongings ④laying on your seats.
                  O.C

정답 ④ (laying → laid 또는 lying)

해석 버스를 청소하는 동안에 당신이 내려야 한다 할지라도, 당신의 좌석에 있던 여행 가방과 다른 소지품들을 남겨 두어도 괜찮다.

분석 lie와 lay의 구분

④ 「leave + O + O.C(R-ing)」 5형식 동사의 어형으로 쓰여 목적보어 자리에 laying이 쓰였다. 타동사 lay는 반드시 뒤에 목적어가 나와야 하는데, 뒤에 전명구(수식어구)밖에 없으므로 수동의 관계인 과거분사(laid) 혹은 자동사(lie)의 현재분사(lying)로 고쳐야 한다.

① 버스가 청소하는 주체가 아닌 청소되는 대상이므로 수동태는 적절하다. 진행은 당시의 상황을 세게 전달하는 표현일 뿐이다. 진행형 절대 불가능 동사를 제외하고 진행은 얼마든지 가능하다.

② 조동사 뒤 동사원형(leave)은 적절하다.

③ other은 뒤에 복수명사(belongings)를 수식한다.

14 [2011 홍익대]

Yet these truths are ①no solace (against the kind of
        S   S V
alienation) (that comes of ②being ever the suspect,) a
              형용사절 V   ⓟ 동명사   =
fearsome entity ③with whom pedestrians avoid ④to
                    형용사절   S   V
make eye contact.)
making

정답 ④ (to make → making)

해석 하지만, 이러한 사실들은 보행자들이 눈조차 맞추려 하지 않는 무서운 존재인 용의자가 되는 것으로부터 오는 소외감에 대한 위안이 되지 않는다.

분석 3형식 동사 avoid의 어형

④ finish, mind, avoid와 같은 동사는 목적어로 동명사(R-ing)를 받기 때문에 to make를 making으로 고쳐야 한다.

① no는 형용사로 반드시 뒤에 명사를 수식해야 한다.

② 전치사의 목적어로 동명사는 적절하다.

③ 「전치사 + 관계대명사」는 절 이하의 성분이 완전하고 선행사를 수식하여 적절하다.

15 [2011 서울여대]

ⓐ   ⓐ
①A knowledgeable and open-minded ②evaluation (of
                                  S   deciding
your current lifestyle) might ③lead to decide to make
                              V   ⓟ 동명사   Ⓝ
④a few fundamental changes.]

정답 ③ (lead to decide → lead to deciding)

해석 당신의 현재 생활 방식에 대한 해박하고 탁 트인 평가가 몇 가지 근본적인 변화를 하기로 결정하는 결과를 이끌어 낼 수 있다.

분석 동사 lead의 어형

③ 자동사의 어형 「lead to N/R-ing」과 5형식 동사의 어형 「lead + O + to R」로 쓰인다. ③에서 lead to가 붙은 것으로 보아 자동사로 쓰인 것이므로 전치사 to이므로 명사 혹은 동명사가 나와야 한다. lead to deciding으로 고쳐야 한다.

① 형용사(knowledgeable)가 명사(evaluation)을 수식하여 적절하다.

② 주어가 필요한 자리이므로 명사는 적절하다.

④ a few, few는 뒤에 복수명사만을 수식한다.

16 [2011 동국대]

The exact cause (of ①aging) is unknown, ②but genetic factors ③are known (to ④influence on longevity.)

정답 ④ (influence on → influence)

해석 노화의 정확한 원인은 아직 밝혀지지 않았지만 유전적 요소들이 장수에 영향을 미친다는 사실까지는 알려져 있다.

분석 3형식 타동사 influence의 어형

④ influence가 명사가 아닌 동사로 쓰일 때는 타동사이다. 타동사는 전치사 없이 목적어를 받아야 하므로 on을 삭제한다. 다만 「have an influence on + N」의 형태에서는 동사 have가 따로 있기에 influence는 명사로 쓰인 형태이므로 이와 구분할 줄 알아야 한다.

① 전치사의 목적어로 '노화'라는 뜻의 명사는 적절하다.

② 접속사가 문장과 문장을 연결하여 적절하다.

③ 유전적 요소들이 알고 있는 주체가 아닌 장수에 영향을 미친다고 알려져 있는 대상이므로 수동태는 적절하다.

17 [2011 서울여대]

The president's declaration (of an emergency) was a procedural maneuver (to make it easier (for hospitals,) (should they be swamped with sick people,) them to alternate sites for triage and treatment.])

① transfer　　　　② to transfer

③ will transfer　　④ transferring

정답 ②

해석 대통령의 비상사태 선포는 만약 병원들이 환자들로 가득 차면 병원들이 환자들을 임시 부상자 분류와 치료를 위한 대체 장소로 이동시키는 것을 쉽게 만들기 위한 절차상의 조치였다.

분석 5형식 동사 make의 '가목적어-진목적어' 구문

② 「make + it + O.C(형용사) + to R ~/that + S + V ~」 5형식의 '가목적어-진목적어' 어형이다. make 뒤에 가목적어(it)와 목적보어(easier)가 있는 것으로 보아 빈칸에는 진짜 목적어가 필요하므로 to R 혹은 「that + S + V」가 나와야 한다. 이 조건을 충족시키는 것은 ②이다. for hospitals는 to R의 의미상 주어이다.

18 [2012 상명대]

The psychologist William James ①believed [that ②facial expressions not only ③provide a visible sign of an emotion ④but also actually ⑤contribute the feeling itself.]

정답 ⑤ (contribute → contribute to)

해석 심리학자 윌리엄 제임스(William James)는 얼굴 표정이 감정을 시각적인 표현을 나타낼 뿐만 아니라, 사실상 감정 자체의 원인이 되기도 한다고 생각했다.

분석 자동사 contribute의 어형

⑤ 「contribute to + N/R-ing」 자동사의 어형으로 쓰여 명사를 받을 때 전치사 to가 있어야 한다.

① 목적어로 that절을 받아 능동태 동사는 적절하다.

② that절 속에 주어의 역할로 명사는 적절하다.

③ 주절이 과거시제라도 종속절의 내용이 일반적 사실이라면 현재시제를 써야 한다. 주어(facial expressions)와 동사(provide)의 수 일치 역시 적절하다.

④ 「not only A but (also) B」는 등위상관접속사로 상관관계 역시 적절하다.

19 [2012 홍익대]

They admitted nearly 200 people, (all of whom sat on simple chairs) and (①who could easily hear the accompanying music ②playing on piano by a local girl,) (who ③would attempt [to match the music ④to the tone of the particular scene.])

정답 ② (playing → played)

해석 그들은 거의 200명 정도의 사람들을 입장시켰다. 모두 간이 의자에 앉아 한 지역 소녀에 의해 피아노로 연주되는 반주 음악을 수월하게 들을 수 있었고, 그 소녀는 그 음악을 특별한 장면 속의 분위기에 어울리도록 만들려고 애썼다.

분석 5형식 지각동사 see/hear의 어형

② 「see/hear + O + O.C(R/R-ing/p.p.)」 5형식 지각동사의 어형이다. 이때 목적어가 목적보어 하는 주체, 즉 능동의 관계일 때 목적보어 자리에 R/R-ing을 쓰고, 목적어가 목적보어 당하는 대상, 즉 수동의 관계일 때 p.p.를 쓴다. 음악이 연주하는 주체가 아닌 연주되는 대상이므로 수동의 관계인 과거분사(played)로 고쳐야 한다.

① 선행사가 사람(nearly 200 people)이고 주어 자리가 불완전하여 주격 관계대명사는 적절하다.

③ 주절 동사가 과거이므로 종속절에 조동사의 과거형은 적절하다.

④ 명사와 명사의 충돌을 피해 주기 위해 전치사는 적절하다.

20
[2011 가천대]

Students dislike [_____ to fill an hour or two hours (each night) with meaningless homework.]

① have been
② having
③ to have
④ to have been

* fill A with B: A를 B로 채우다

정답 ②

해석 학생들은 매일 밤 한두 시간을 의미 없는 숙제로 채우는 것을 싫어한다.

분석 동사 dislike의 어형

② dislike는 동명사(R-ing)를 목적어로 받는 동사이기에 여기에 해당되는 ②가 정답이다.

① 이미 앞에 동사 dislike가 있으므로 또 동사가 나오면 안 된다.

③, ④ dislike는 뒤에 to R를 받을 수 없다.

21
[2013 경희대]

(However prepared or well-meaning parents may be,) it is difficult for them [to acknowledge that their children have grown up,] but it is extremely important for them [to let the children _____ their own mind.]

① to make up
② to making up
③ making them up
④ make up

정답 ④

해석 아무리 부모들이 준비가 되어 있거나 선하더라도, 그들의 자녀가 성장했다는 것을 인정하기는 힘들다. 하지만 부모가 자녀들로 하여금 스스로 자신의 마음을 결정하도록 만드는 것은 굉장히 중요하다.

분석 5형식 사역동사 let의 어형

④ 「let + O + O.C(R)」 5형식 동사의 어형으로, 빈칸은 목적보어 자리이므로 동사원형(make)이 와야 한다.

①, ②, ③ let은 목적보어 자리에 절대 「to R/R-ing」 형태를 쓰지 못한다.

22
[2012 홍익대]

You ①can't just close your eyes and wish us ②back (in Kansas) (among kindly folk) (who obligingly ③conform outdated expectations ④of age.)

정답 ③ (conform → conform to)

해석 당신은 단지 가만히 눈만 감고서, 나이에 대한 구식적인 기대치에 어쩔 수 없이 순응하는 사람들이 있는 캔자스로 우리가 돌아가 주기만을 바랄 수는 없다.

분석 자동사 conform의 어형

③ 「conform to + N/R-ing」 자동사의 어형으로 쓰이기 때문에 뒤에 명사가 나올 때 전치사 to가 있어야 한다.

① 조동사 뒤에 부사는 얼마든지 나올 수 있다.

② 「wish + O + (to be) + O.C」의 형태로 쓰여 적절하다.

④ 명사와 명사의 충돌을 피해 주기 위해 전명구는 적절하다.

23
[2011 경희대]

Maria Callas was a woman (for whom the term prima donna could have been invented.) She was an American-born Greek soprano and made her professional debut in 1942, and (since then) she _____ (to be) a singer-actress.

① long considered herself
          V   O

② was long herself considered

③ long considering herself

④ herself long considering

정답 ①

해석 마리아 칼라스(Maria Callas)는 프리마 돈나라는 용어를 세상에 만들어 낸 여자였다. 그녀는 그리스계 미국인 소프라노였으며 1942년에 데뷔를 했다. 그리고 그 이후 그녀는 자신을 오랫동안 가수 겸 배우라고 생각해 왔다.

분석 5형식 동사 consider의 어형

① 빈칸 앞에 대명사의 주격인 she가 나온 것으로 보아 빈칸은 동사가 나와야 하므로 ③, ④는 탈락되고, 「consider + O + (to be/as) + O.C」 5형식 동사의 어형으로 쓰여 ①이 적절하다. ②는 was considered라는 수동태 사이에 목적어(herself)가 나와 부적절하다.

24
[2017 상명대]

Microfinance ①enables village people (in ②developing
     S   to borrow V   O
countries) ③borrow ④small amounts of money from
          O.C   = much
Microfinance Institutions (⑤in order to set up small

community businesses.)

정답 ③ (borrow → to borrow)

해석 소액 금융 지원은 개발 도상국의 마을 사람들이 소규모 지역 공동체 사업을 설립하기 위해 소액 금융 지원 기관으로부터 적은 액수의 돈을 빌릴 수 있도록 해 준다.

분석 5형식 동사 enable의 어형

③ 「enable + O + O.C(to R)」 5형식 동사의 어형으로 쓰이므로 목적보어 자리에 동사원형이 나오지 못한다. to borrow로 고쳐야 한다.

① 주어와 동사의 수 일치와 뒤에 목적어(small amounts of money)가 나온 것으로 보아 능동태 역시 적절하다.

② developing country(개발 도상국), developed country (선진국)의 의미로 쓰인다.

④ an amount of, amounts of는 뒤에 불가산명사를 수식하므로 money는 적절하다.

⑤ 「in order to R ~」 '~하기 위해서'라는 뜻의 수식어구이다.

25
[2011 단국대]

(As more ①is understood (about the genetics and the
부사절 S   V S
brains of people) (who ②stutter,)) researchers hope [that
         형용사절   at   S   V 명사절
medication (aimed directly ③by the disorder) eventually
     S (which is)
will ④become available.]
    V   C

정답 ③ (by → at)

해석 말을 더듬는 사람들의 유전적 특질과 뇌에 대해서 더욱 많은 것이 이해됨에 따라, 연구원들은 이 질병을 직접적으로 겨냥한 약물 치료가 결국에는 상용 가능하기를 희망하고 있다.

분석 동사 aim의 어형

③ 「aim at N/aim A at B」의 어형으로 자·타동사로 둘 다 쓰일 수 있다. 무엇으로 쓰여도 전치사는 at과 함께 나와야 하는 단어이다. 구조 분석에서 보이듯이 aimed부터 disorder까지는 앞에 명사인 medication을 꾸며 주는 분사의 형태로 앞에 (which is)가 생략되어 있다. 전치사 at으로 고쳐야 한다.

① 많은 일이 이해하는 주체가 아니라 이해되는 대상이므로 수동태는 적절하다.

② 주격 관계대명사절 속의 동사(stutter)가 선행사(people)와 수 일치가 되어 적절하다.

④ 조동사 뒤에 동사원형은 적절하다.

2강 시제

Practice

01	④	02	②	03	④	04	②	05	③
06	①	07	①	08	③	09	①	10	①
11	④	12	④	13	④	14	②	15	①
16	②	17	②	18	②	19	④	20	②
21	①	22	③	23	④	24	④	25	②

01
[2014 경기대]

Tim Morrison, (①who tried [to hang ②himself] after years of ③being bullied,) ④has died (last Monday).

정답 ④ (has → 삭제)

해석 수년간 괴롭힘을 당한 후 목을 매어 자살을 하려 했던 팀 모리슨(Tim Morrison)이 지난 월요일 사망했다.

분석 시점부사와 동사의 시제 일치

④ 시점부사와 동사는 반드시 시제를 일치시켜야 한다. 절대 한국어의 해석으로 영어의 시제를 따지는 것이 아니라 시점부사를 암기하여 풀어야 한다. 「last + 명사」는 과거 시점부사로서 시점부사가 포함된 문장의 동사는 반드시 시제를 일치시켜야 하므로 현재완료 (has died)를 과거(died)로 고쳐야 한다.

① 선행사가 사람(Tim Morrison)이고 절 속에 주어가 불완전하여 주격 관계대명사는 적절하다.

② 주어랑 목적어가 같을 때 재귀대명사를 써야 한다. hang의 주어는 선행사인 Tim Morrison이고 목적어와 같기에 재귀대명사는 적절하다.

③ 전치사의 목적어로 동명사가 나와 적절하다.

02
[2015 홍익대]

There _____ several attempts (to define morality) (since Middle Ages.)
현재완료 시점부사

① has been　　②have been
③ was　　④were

정답 ②

해석 중세 시대 이후로 도덕을 정의내리고자 하는 여러 번의 시도가 있었다.

분석 시점부사와 동사의 시제 일치 / 주어와 동사의 수 일치

② 「since + 과거 시점 N」는 현재완료 시점부사이다. 과거로 나온 ③, ④는 탈락되고 there/here로 문장이 시작되면 동사 뒤에 있는 첫 번째 명사가 주어이다. 주어 (several attempts)와 동사(have been)의 수 일치가 된 ②가 정답이다.

03
[2014 동덕여대]

The instructor had gone (①over the problems) (②many times) (③before the students ④will take the final examination.)

정답 ④ (will take → take)

해석 학생들이 기말시험을 보기 전에 선생님은 문제들을 여러 번 복습했다.

분석 시간·조건의 부사절 속에서 조동사 will 불가

④ 시간·조건의 부사절(when, before, after, if 등)에서 현재시제가 미래를 대신해야 하기 때문에 조동사 will을 쓰지 못한다. 또한 주절이 과거완료(had gone)이기에 종속절에는 더욱이 미래를 쓰지 못한다. took으로 고쳐야 한다.

① go over는 '거듭 살펴보다. 탐구하다'의 의미로 쓰여 적절하다.

② '여러 번'이라는 뜻의 수식어구(부사)로 쓰여 적절하다.

③ 뒤에 주어, 동사가 나와 접속사 before는 적절하다.

04
[2011 상명대]

The Greeks began [to ①write from left to right around the fifth century B.C.] (because they ②increasingly believe [that right was "good" and left was "bad."]) This belief ③is still common (in many countries) today, and ④left-handed people suffer (because of it.)

정답 ② (increasingly believe → increasingly believed)

해석 그리스인들은 기원전 5세기경부터 왼쪽에서 오른쪽으로 글을 쓰기 시작했다. 그 이유는 오른쪽이 '좋고' 왼쪽이 '나쁘다고' 믿었기 때문이다. 이러한 믿음은 오늘날 많은 국가에서도 여전히 흔해서 그로 인해 왼손잡이들은 고충을 겪는다.

분석 주절이 과거일 때 종속절의 시제
② 주절 동사가 과거일 때 종속절에 현재/현재완료는 쓰지 못하고 과거/과거완료가 나와야 한다. 주절 동사가 과거(began)이기에 종속절(because절)에 현재를 쓰지 못하므로 과거인 believed로 고쳐야 한다.
① begin 동사는 to R와 R-ing를 둘 다 목적어로 받을 수 있어 적절하다. write은 자·타동사 둘 다 쓰일 수 있다.
③ today가 있으니 현재시제도 적절하고 be동사 뒤에 형용사 역시 적절하다.
④ 형용사(left-handed)가 명사(people)를 수식하여 적절하다.

05
[2011 아주대]

(By the end of the 1800s,) the ① output (of ② European artists, writers and scientists) ③ have accelerated (to the point) (where ④ it dwarfed the ⑤ productiveness of the 1700s.)

정답 ③ (have accelerated → had accelerated)
해석 1800년대 말까지, 유럽의 예술가들, 작가들 그리고 과학자들은 1700년대의 작품 수를 적어 보이게 만드는 지경까지 빠르게 작품을 만들어 냈다.
분석 과거완료 시점부사와 동사의 시제 일치
③ 「By + 과거 시점 N」는 「S + had p.p.」를 써야 하는 과거완료 시점부사이기 때문에 had accelerated로 고쳐야 한다. 또한 주어(the output)와 동사의 수 일치 역시 부적절하다.
① 주어의 역할로 명사는 적절하다.
② 형용사(European)가 명사들을 수식하여 적절하다.
④ the output을 대신 받는 대명사로 쓰여 수 일치 역시 적절하다.
⑤ 정관사 뒤에 명사가 나와 적절하다.

06
[2016 가톨릭대]

What causes plants to bloom? (Although you may think [that plants _____] (based on the amount of sunlight) (they receive,)) they actually bloom (according to the amount of uninterrupted darkness.)

① flower
② flowered
③ flowering
④ to flower

정답 ①
해석 무엇이 식물로 하여금 꽃을 피우도록 야기하는가? 비록 당신은 식물들이 받는 햇빛의 양을 기반으로 꽃을 피운다고 생각할지도 모르지만, 식물들은 실제로는 연속되는 어둠의 양에 따라 꽃을 피운다.
분석 일반적 사실은 항상 현재시제
① 식물이 꽃을 피우고 지는 것은 일반적 사실이다. 일반적 사실은 항상 현재시제로 표현하기에 ①이 적절하다. 여기서 flower는 동사로 쓰였다. think 뒤에 that절이 나와 절 속에 동사가 필요하므로 동사가 아닌 ③, ④는 탈락되고, ②는 시제가 부적절하다.

07
[2011 강남대]

Mr. Kim will already _____ his presentation (by the time you reach the convention center.)

① have finished
② finished
③ finish
④ have been finished

정답 ①
해석 당신이 컨벤션 센터에 도착할 때까지 김 씨는 자신의 프레젠테이션을 끝마칠 것이다.
분석 시점부사와 동사의 시제 일치 / 능동태와 수동태
① 「by the time + S + 현재V」는 「S + will have p.p.(미래완료)」를 써야 하는 미래완료 시점부사이다. 빈칸 앞에 will이 있기에 have p.p. 형태인 ①, ④로 좁혀지고, 빈칸 뒤에 목적어가 있기에 능동인 ①이 적절하다.

08
[2012 단국대]

He could remember [① driving along the road] (just ② before the accident ③ happens,) but he couldn't ④ remember the accident itself.

정답 ③ (happens → happened)
해석 그는 그 사고가 발생하기 이전에 그 길을 따라 운전했던 사실을 기억해 냈지만 그는 그 사건 자체는 기억할 수 없었다.

분석 동사의 시제

③ but 이하 문장의 내용을 보면 그가 사건 자체는 기억하지 못한다고 했으므로 사건이 벌어지긴 했다는 것을 유추할 수 있다. 그렇다면 before절 이하 현재시제는 미래를 대신하는 것이기에 의미가 상충된다. 사건이 발생한 것 역시 과거라는 것을 유추할 수 있어 happened로 고쳐야 한다.

① 「remember + to R(미래)/R-ing(과거)」의 의미로 쓰인다. 사건이 일어난 것은 이미 지난 일이므로 길을 따라 운전했던 것 역시 이미 지난 일이기에 동명사는 적절하다.

② before는 전치사와 접속사의 역할을 둘 다 가지고 있고 뒤에 주어, 동사가 나온 것으로 보아 접속사로 쓰였다.

④ 조동사 뒤에 동사원형은 적절하다.

09 [2013 가천대]

I ① ~~worked~~ (have worked) (with Peter) (② for the past five years) and I always found him ③ to be a lawyer (of ④ the highest caliber.)

정답 ① (worked → have worked)

해석 나는 지난 5년 동안 피터와 일해 왔으며 항상 그가 가장 뛰어난 역량을 가진 변호사라는 것을 알고 있었다.

분석 현재완료 시점부사와 동사의 시제 일치

① 「for the past + 기간 N」는 현재완료 시점부사이기 때문에 문장의 동사는 현재완료로 써야 한다. have worked로 고쳐야 한다.

② 「for the past + 기간 N」형태로, 현재완료 시점부사로 쓰여 적절하다. 여기서 for 대신 in을 써도 괜찮다.

③ 「find + O + (to be) + O.C」 5형식 어형으로 쓰여 to be는 생략해도 무방하고 써도 무방하다.

④ 최상급 앞에 정관사 the가 함께 나와 적절하다.

10 [2017 홍익대]

(When the Supreme Court ① ~~rules~~ (ruled) in 1896 ② in favor of the South's "separate but equal" racial doctrine,) the federal government ③ put its stamp (of approval) (④ on state laws) (requiring cradle-to-grave segregation of the races.)

정답 ① (rules → ruled)

해석 1896년에 연방 대법원이 남부 주들의 '분리 평등' 인종 정책에 대해 우호적인 판결을 내렸을 때, 연방 정부는 인종들을 하여금 평생 분리하도록 한 주법을 승인하는 도장을 찍었다.

분석 과거 시점부사와 동사의 시제 일치

① 「in + 과거 연도」는 과거 시점부사이다. 과거동사 (ruled)로 고쳐야 한다.

② in favor of ~ : '~에 찬성하여, ~에 유리하게'라는 뜻의 표현으로 전치사는 적절하다.

③ when절이 과거시제이기에 주절도 과거시제(put) 역시 적절하다.

④ 명사와 명사의 충돌을 피해 주기 위해 전치사는 적절하다.

11 [2012 국민대]

Harrisburg, ① a transportation center (in the ② days of riverboat ③ traffic,) has been Pennsylvania's capital ④ ~~in~~ (since) 1812.)

정답 ④ (in → since)

해석 배로 강을 건너던 시절에 교통의 중심지였던 해리스버그는 1812년 이후로 펜실베이니아주의 주도 역할을 하고 있다.

분석 시점부사와 동사의 시제 일치

④ 「in + 과거 연도」는 과거 시점부사인데 동사는 현재완료(has been)가 고정되어 있다. 동사에는 밑줄이 없으므로 전치사 in을 since로 고쳐 현재완료 시점부사로 만들어 준다.

① Harrisburg와 동격을 이루는 명사로 적절하다.

② 명사와 명사의 충돌을 피해 주기 위해 전치사는 적절하다.

③ 전치사의 목적어로 명사는 적절하다.

12 [2012 단국대]

Most historians ① agree [that the English alphabet descended ② from ancient Egyptian hieroglyphics] (that were first recorded (③ more than 5,000 years ④ ~~before~~ (ago)).)]

정답 ④ (before → ago)

해석 대부분의 역사가들은 영어의 알파벳이 5,000년 이상 이전에 최초로 기록된 고대 이집트의 상형 문자에서 나왔다는 사실에 동의한다.

분석 시점부사와 동사의 시제 일치

④ 「기간 N + before」는 과거완료(had p.p.) 시점부사인데, 동사는 과거시제(were recorded)로 고정이 되어 있다. 동사에는 밑줄이 없으니 ④를 ago로 고쳐야 한다. 「기간 N + ago」는 과거 시점부사이다.

① that절을 목적어로 받고 있어 능동태는 적절하다.

② 자동사 descend는 명사를 받을 때 전치사 from이 나와야 한다.

③ 숫자 앞에 more than은 숫자 '이상'이라는 뜻의 수식 어구이다.

13

[2013 동국대]

A research report (from the Ministry of Knowledge Economy) also showed [that ① prolonged global recession caused the nation's exports ② to slow and ③ dampened consumer sentiment,] (which also negatively ④affect affected labor productivity.)

정답 ④ (affect → affected)

해석 지식 경제 부처가 조사한 보고서에 따르면 지속되는 세계 경제 위기가 나라의 수출을 둔화시켰고 소비자들의 기대도 저하시켰다. 이러한 사실이 노동 생산성에 부정적인 영향을 미쳤다.

분석 주절이 과거일 때 종속절의 시제

④ 주절 동사의 시제가 과거일 때 종속절에 현재/현재완료는 쓰지 못한다. 주절 동사가 과거(caused and dampened)이므로 종속절(which절)도 과거시제(affected)로 고쳐야 한다.

① prolonged는 '지속되는'이라는 뜻의 형용사로 쓰여 명사(global recession)를 수식하여 적절하다.

② 「cause + O + to R」 5형식 동사의 어형으로 쓰여 적절하다.

③ 'caused and dampened' 동사가 and로 병치되어 적절하다.

14

[2017 상명대]

(① By the time Ryan graduates,) he ②has spent *will have spent* fours years (in college) and ③ a total of sixteen years (of his life in school.) (Like many students,) Ryan believes [that the time and money ④(spent on his education) ⑤will pay off.]

정답 ② (has spent → will have spent)

해석 라이언(Ryan)이 졸업할 즈음이면, 그는 대학에서 4년, 자신의 인생 중 총 16년을 학교에서 보낸 셈이 될 것이다. 대다수의 학생들처럼 라이언도 교육에 투자한 시간과 돈이 성공하게 해줄 것이라고 믿고 있다.

분석 시점부사와 동사의 시제 일치

② 「by the time + S + 현재V」 형태로 「S + will have p.p.(미래완료)」를 써야 하는 시점부사이므로 will have spent로 고쳐야 한다.

① 시간 · 조건 부사절에서는 의미상 미래가 필요하더라도 현재시제가 미래를 대신하기에 적절하다.

③ spend의 목적어인 시간명사가 and로 병치되어 적절하다.

④ 돈이 소비하는 주체가 아니라 교육에 소비되는 대상이므로 수동의 관계인 과거분사(spent)는 적절하다.

⑤ 주절이 현재이기에 종속절에 미래가 나와도 무방하고 pay off는 자동사로 쓰여 '성공하다'의 의미로 쓰여 적절하다.

15

[2011 서경대]

(When you ①will realize [*(that)* your bullies will be offended] (②no matter what you do,)) you'll ③stop [trying to please ④them.]

정답 ① (will realize → realize)

해석 네가 무슨 짓을 하든지 상관없이 너를 괴롭히는 아이들이 화낼 거라는 것을 깨달으면, 너는 그들을 기쁘게 하고자 노력하던 것을 멈추게 될 것이다.

분석 시간 · 조건의 부사절 속에서 조동사 will 불가

① 시간 · 조건의 부사절(when, before, after, if, as soon as 등)에서는 현재시제가 미래를 대신해야 한다. 조동사 will을 쓰지 못하기 때문에 현재시제(realize)로 고쳐야 한다.

② 앞에서 수동태로 문장이 끝나 있고 no matter what
은 부사절(수식절)의 역할이기에 적절하다.

③ stop은 R-ing(동명사)를 목적어로 취하기에 적절하다.

④ your bullies를 대신 받는 대명사로 복수명사를 대신
받는 대명사 them은 수 일치상 적절하다.

16

[2012 홍익대]

This enrichment process was [①what determined the
composition (of the Solar System) (4.5 billion years
ago,) and ultimately ②makes possible the chemistry (of
life ③on Earth) (④as per the "Big Bang" theory.)]

목적어가 전명구의 수식을
받아 길어져 뒤로 빠진 형태

정답 ② (makes → made)

해석 이러한 농축 과정이 45억 년 전에 태양계의 구성을 결정
지었고, 궁극적으로 빅뱅 이론에 따라 지구에서 생명체
의 화학 작용을 가능하게 했다.

분석 주절이 과거일 때 종속절의 시제 / 시점부사와 동사의 시
제 일치

② 주절 동사가 과거(was)이므로 종속절에 현재/현재완
료가 올 수 없다. 또한 what절 속에서도 determined
와 and로 병치가 되어 있기에 과거인 made로 고쳐
야 한다.

① what은 절 이하의 성분이 불완전하여 하나의 명사로
쓰여 be동사(was)의 보어로 적절하다.

③ 명사와 명사의 충돌을 피해 주기 위해 전치사는 적절
하다.

④ as per ~ : '~에 따라'라는 표현이므로 적절하다.

17

[2012 경희대]

Such Bohemianism could ①be construed (as affectation,)
and it's possible [that (early in life) Katherine Mathilda
Winton ②has deliberately cultivated a style] (that would
③signal her disregard (for ④a world) (she found
stultifying.))

정답 ② (has deliberately cultivated a style that →
deliberately cultivated a style that)

해석 그런 자유분방한 기질은 가식으로 받아들여질 수도 있다.
캐서린 마틸다 윈튼(Katherine Mathilda Winton)은 젊
은 시절에 자신이 무의미하다고 보았던 세상에 대해 무관
심을 암시하는 스타일을 의도적으로 만들었을 가능성도
있다.

분석 시점부사와 동사의 시제 일치

② early in life라는 과거 시점부사가 있다. 시점부사가
나온 문장의 동사는 반드시 시제 일치를 해주어야 하
므로 과거동사(cultivated)로 고쳐야 한다.

① 자유분방한 기질이 이해하는 주체가 아니라 가식으로
받아들여지는 대상이므로 수동태는 적절하다.

③ 조동사 뒤에 동사원형이 나오고 목적어도 있으므로 능
동태 동사는 적절하다.

④ 구조 분석에서 보이듯이 she 앞에 목적격 관계대명사
(that)가 생략되어 있어 found의 목적어가 불완전
하고 stultifying은 목적보어의 역할로 쓰여 적절하다.

18

[2013 경희대]

(In the eight hundred years) (①since his death,) people
②sought (in vain) (for the grave of Genghis Khan,) the
13th-century conqueror and imperial ruler (who, (at the
time of his death,) ③occupied the largest contiguous
empire,) (④stretching from the Caspian Sea to the
Pacific.)

have sought

정답 ② (sought in vain for → have sought in vain for)

해석 그의 죽음 이후 800년 동안 사람들은 징기스칸의 무덤을
찾았으나 헛수고였다. 징기스칸은 13세기의 정복자이자
제국의 통치자였고 그가 죽었을 때 카스피해부터 태평양
까지 뻗어 있는 가장 큰 제국을 점령한 상태였다.

분석 시점부사와 동사의 시제 일치

② 「since + 과거 N」는 현재완료(have/has p.p.) 시점부
사이므로 현재완료(have sought)로 고쳐야 한다.

① since는 전치사로 쓰일 때 과거 시점 N을 받아 적절
하다.

③ 주격 관계대명사 who절 속의 동사이고 목적어도 있기
에 능동태 역시 적절하다.

④ 제국이 카스피해부터 태평양까지 뻗어 있는 주체이므
로 능동의 관계인 현재분사(stretching)는 적절하다.
또한 stretch는 자동사로 쓰이기 때문에 수동의 관계
인 과거분사(p.p.)는 쓸 수 없다.

19 [2011 서강대]

I met Kerry (years ago) (when he first ① became an assistant professor.) We both taught biology, but Kerry ② liked [to use a lot of mathematics in his teaching.] This ③ upset his students, (who ④ believe [that they would escape math by studying biology.])

정답 ④ (believe → believed)

해석 나는 케리가 처음 조교수가 되었던 몇 년 전에 그를 만났다. 우리는 둘 다 생물학을 가르쳤지만 케리는 강의에 수학을 많이 활용했다. 이러한 점이 생물학을 배움으로써 수학을 피할 수 있다고 생각했던 학생들을 화나게 만들었다.

분석 주절이 과거일 때 종속절의 시제

　④ met, became, taught, liked, upset으로 보아 전부 과거 사실을 전달하고 있다. 주절이 과거(upset)라면 종속절(who절)에 현재/현재완료가 나오지 못하기 때문에 believed로 고쳐야 한다.

　① 동시 시점을 나타내는 when절이므로 주절과 같은 시제(과거)는 적절하다.

　② 별다른 시점부사가 있는 것이 아니기에 과거시제로 일관되게 연결되어 적절하다.

　③ 여기서 upset은 과거시제이다. 만약 현재였다면 수 일치를 했어야 한다. 앞 문장의 동사들의 시제와 수 일치가 맞지 않는 것으로 보아 과거동사 역시 적절하다. (upset – upset – upset)

20 [2011 가천대]

(① Once marine biologists had determined the precise migratory route of the California whale,) they ② are finding [that the distance (covered) was ③ much greater than ④ had been thought.]

정답 ② (are finding → found)

해석 해양 생물학자들이 캘리포니아 고래들의 정확한 이동 경로를 확인하자마자 그들은 고래가 이동하는 거리가 생각했던 것보다 훨씬 길다는 사실을 알게 되었다.

분석 주절과 종속절의 시제 / 문맥상의 시제

　② 부사절(once) 속에 동사도 과거완료(had determined)로 고정되어 있고, ②가 현재라면 than절 속에서 과거

완료(had been)도 쓰지 못한다. 주절이 과거일 때 종속절에 과거 혹은 과거완료가 가능하므로 are finding을 found로 고쳐야 한다.

　① once는 부사도 있지만 접속사의 역할도 있기에 주어, 동사가 나와도 적절하다.

　③ 뒤에 than이 있는 것으로 보아 앞에는 비교급이 있어야 하고 비교급 앞에 much는 비교급 강조부사로 쓰여 적절하다.

　④ 주절이 과거(was)이기에 종속절에 과거완료도 가능하고 거리가 생각하는 주체가 아닌 생각되는 대상이므로 수동태 역시 적절하다.

21 [2011 동덕여대]

Our superior location, (just next to the Jackson Wildlife Preserve,) _____ a beautiful natural environment (that will help you achieve total well-being.)

① ensures

② would ensure

③ had ensured

④ did ensure

정답 ①

해석 잭슨 야생 동물 보호 구역 바로 옆에 위치한 우리의 유리한 위치가 당신이 토털 웰빙을 실현하도록 도와주는 아름다운 자연환경을 보장한다.

분석 주절이 과거일 때 종속절의 시제

　① 주절이 과거라면 종속절(that절)에 조동사의 현재형(will)이 나오지 못한다. 주절이 현재일 때 종속절에 조동사의 현재형이 나올 수 있으므로 이 조건을 충족시키는 ①이 적절하다.

22 [2011 상명대]

(① In the coming years,) the Internet will have ② an even greater impact (on the way) (we shop, get our news, ③ entertained, conduct financial affairs, and ④ talk with friends and family.)

정답 ③ (entertained → entertain)

해석 앞으로 인터넷은 우리가 쇼핑하고, 소식을 얻고, 즐기고, 금융 업무를 수행하고, 친구와 가족들과 이야기하는 방식에 훨씬 더 큰 영향을 미치게 될 것이다.

분석 동사의 시제 병치

③ 구조 분석에서 보이듯이 A(shop), B(get), C(entertained), D(conduct), and E(talk)로 병치되고 있다. 영어는 여러 개를 병치할 경우 마지막 단어 앞에만 접속사를 쓰고 앞에 있는 접속사는 전부 콤마(,)로 대체할 수 있다. 단, 이때 A~E까지 일관되게 연결해야 하는데 전부 동사가 현재로 연결된 것으로 보아 entertained를 entertain으로 고쳐야 한다.

① 미래 시점을 나타내는 시점부사구로 미래동사(will have)와 일치되어 적절하다.

② have an impact on ~ : '~에 영향을 미치다'의 표현으로 쓰였고, 비교급 앞에 even은 강조 부사이므로 적절하다.

④ talk는 자동사로 쓰여 뒤에 전명구(수식어)가 나와 적절하다.

23
[2011 서경대]

He ①was ultimately ②known (to millions) (③who had
S   V   형용사절 V
                had
no clear idea of [what he ④has done.])
                  O ⓟ 명사절 Ⓝ

정답 ④ (has done → had done)

해석 그는 자신이 무슨 일을 했는지 잘 알지 못했던 수백만 명의 사람들에게 결국 알려졌다.

분석 주절이 과거일 때 종속절의 시제

④ 주절이 과거(had)일 때 종속절(what절)에 현재/현재완료는 쓰지 못하기에 had done으로 고쳐야 한다.

① 문장 전체가 과거 사실을 전달하기에 과거시제는 적절하다.

② 그 사람이 수백만의 사람들에게 알려지는 대상이므로 수동태는 적절하다.

③ 선행사가 사람(millions)이고 절 이하에 주어 자리가 불완전하기에 주격 관계대명사(who)는 적절하다.

24
[2011 세종대]

(In an attempt) (to prevent students from concentrating

①only on school tests,) the Seoul Office of Education
                                                    S
said [that ②it was ③considering [abolishing exams] and
      명사절(O) S   V   O
replacing
④replace them (with essays) (to encourage creativity.)]
(it was)   V   O

정답 ④ (replace → replacing)

해석 학생들이 학교 시험에만 집중하지 못하도록 하는 시도 속에, 서울시 교육청은 시험을 폐지하고 창의력을 장려하는 논술로 대체할 것을 고려 중에 있다고 말했다.

분석 접속사 and로 연결한 동사의 시제 병치

④ 주절 동사도 과거(said)이고 that절의 동사 역시 과거(was considering)이기에 ④에 현재가 올 수 없다. considering과 병치시켜 replacing으로 고쳐야 한다.

① 자동사 concentrate은 뒤에 명사가 나올 경우 전치사 on과 함께 나온다.

② 서울 교육청(the Seoul Office of Education)을 대신 받는 대명사로 수 일치가 적절하다.

③ 서울 교육청이 시험 폐지를 고려하는 주체이므로 능동의 관계는 적절하다.

25
[2012 국민대]

(After a couple of environmental researchers had drawn
부사절   S   V
                                            written
diagrams (in ①their notebooks) and ②wrote explanations
          O   (had)
of the formations) (③which they had observed,) they
                      형용사절   S
returned (to their campsite) (④to compare notes.)

정답 ② (wrote → written)

해석 두 명의 환경 연구가는 자신들의 노트에 도표를 그리고 그들이 관찰했던 형성층들에 대한 설명을 작성한 이후에, 캠프장으로 돌아와 노트를 비교해 보았다.

분석 시제의 병치

② and 앞에 있는 동사가 과거완료(had drawn)인데 뒤에 있는 동사를 과거로 연결할 수 없다. wrote를 written으로 고쳐야 한다. had drawn and (had) written으로 연결해 주는 형태이다.

① 복수명사(a couple of ~ researchers)를 대신 받는 대명사로 수 일치가 적절하다.

③ 선행사가 사물(the formations)이고 절 이하의 성분이 불완전하기에 목적격 관계대명사(which)는 적절하다.

④ to R의 부사적 역할로 결과의 뜻을 나타내어 적절하다.

3강 수동태

Practice 01

01	③	02	②	03	②	04	②	05	③
06	①	07	③	08	②	09	①	10	④
11	③	12	②	13	③	14	①	15	①
16	②	17	③	18	②	19	③	20	①
21	①	22	②	23	②	24	④	25	③

01
[2010 단국대]

(①Because gorillas have often been killed (②to permit
the capture of their young for zoos) and humans have
recently been ③occupied more and more of their
habitat,) gorillas are now threatened (④with extinction.)

정답 ③ (occupied → occupying)

해석 새끼들을 잡아 동물원에 보내려고 고릴라를 죽여 왔고 사
람들이 최근에 점점 더 많은 고릴라 서식지를 차지했기
때문에, 고릴라들은 이제 멸종 위기에 처했다.

분석 능동태와 수동태의 구분
③ 사람들이 고릴라의 서식지를 차지하는 주체이고, 동사
뒤에 목적어가 있기 때문에 능동태를 써야 한다. 능동의
진행을 표현하기 위해 occupying으로 고쳐야 한다.
① Because는 접속사로 쓰여 주어, 동사를 받아 적절하다.
② 문장이 끝난 뒤 to R의 부사적 용법으로 쓰여 적절하다.
④ 문장이 끝난 뒤 수식어구(전명구)가 나와 적절하다.

02
[2010 단국대]

Professor Bueno de Mesquita adds [that authoritarian
governments (around the world), (①including China's,)
②are shown [that they can reap the benefits of
economic development] (while ③resisting any pressure
④to relax their power.)]

정답 ② (are shown → are showing)

해석 부에노 데 메스키타(Bueno de Mesquita) 교수는 중국
을 포함한 전 세계의 권위주의적인 정부들은 자신들의 권
력을 완화시키려는 압박은 거부하는 반면 경제 개발에 따
른 이익은 챙길 것이라는 것을 보여 주고 있다고 덧붙여
말하고 있다.

분석 능동태와 수동태의 구분
② 동사 뒤에 that절(명사절)을 목적어로 받고 있는 것으
로 보아 능동태인 are showing으로 고쳐야 한다.
① 전 세계의 권위주의적인 정부가 중국을 포함하고 있는
주체이고, 뒤에 목적어도 있기 때문에 능동의 관계인
현재분사(including)로 수식하는 것은 적절하다.
③ 분사구문의 태(능동태, 수동태)를 묻고 있다. resisting
앞에 생략된 주어는 they(정부들)이고 정부들이 압박
받는 것을 거부하는 주체이고, 뒤에 목적어도 있기 때
문에 능동태 분사구문(resisting)은 적절하다.
④ to R의 형용사 역할로 앞에 나온 명사(pressure)를 수
식하여 적절하다.

03
[2010 동국대]

Art has not always been [what (we think) ①it is today.]
An object (regarded as Art today) may not ②have
perceived (as such) (when it was first made,) ③nor was
the person (who ④made it) necessarily regarded as an
artist.

정답 ② (have perceived → have been perceived)

해석 예술은 항상 오늘날 우리가 생각하는 것과 같은 것은 아
니었다. 오늘날 예술로 간주되는 대상이 처음에 이것이
형성되었을 때(과거)의 그 자체의 것으로 여겨지지 않고,
혹은 이것을 만든 사람조차도 예술가로 여겨지지 않을 수
있다.

분석 능동태와 수동태의 구분
② 주어는 대상(An object)이다. 대상이 여기는 주체가
아니라 그 자체로 여겨지는 대상이고, 뒤에 목적어도
없기 때문에 수동태인 have been perceived로 고쳐
야 한다.
① what은 절 이하의 성분(명사)이 불완전하여 하나의 명
사로 쓰이기에 is의 보어가 불완전하여 적절하다. 여기
서 it은 Art를 받는 대명사이다.
③ nor 뒤에 문장이 나올 경우 반드시 「동사 + 주어」의 어
순으로 도치를 해야 한다.

④ 주격 관계대명사(who)절 속의 동사(made)이고 An object를 받기에 대명사의 수 일치가 적절하다.

04
[2009 경희대]

(Typically,) ① more trade fairs ② are holding (in the fall) than (in ③ any other month) (④ because of the weather in this region.)

정답 ② (are holding → are held)

해석 이 지역의 날씨 때문에, 일반적으로 무역 박람회가 어느 다른 계절보다도 가을에 더 많이 열린다.

분석 능동태와 수동태의 구분
② 박람회가 개최하는 주체가 아니라 개최되는 대상이므로 수동태인 are held로 고쳐야 한다. hold가 '가지다, 보유하다'의 뜻일 경우만 수동을 쓰지 못하고 지금처럼 다른 뜻으로 쓰이면 얼마든지 수동태로 쓸 수 있다.
① 주어의 역할로 명사는 적절하다.
③ 「-er/more ~ than any other N」는 비교급을 이용한 최상급 표현 방법이므로 적절하다.
④ because of는 전치사로 쓰여 뒤에 명사가 나와 적절하다.

05
[2013 성균관대]

The researchers are developing sensors (that ① could be placed on vehicles) (that regularly cross a bridge, (② such as city buses and police cars.)) These ③ could be measured [how the bridge ④ responds to the vehicle ⑤ moving across it,] and report any suspicious changes.

정답 ③ (could be measured → could measure)

해석 연구원들이 광역 버스와 경찰차와 같이 보통 다리를 건너는 자동차에 부착될 수 있는 감지 장치를 개발하고 있다. 이 장치들은 다리를 건너는 차량에 반응하는 방식을 측정하고 어떤 의심스러운 변화를 기록할 수 있다.

분석 능동태와 수동태의 구분
③ 동사 뒤에 목적어로 how절(명사절)이 있다. 수동태는 목적어를 받을 수 없기 때문에 능동태인 could measure로 고쳐야 한다. 주어와 동사의 관계로만 접근하기는 어려운 문제이다. 장치들(These)은 어떠한

것을 측정할 수도 있고 측정될 수도 있기 때문이다. 이렇게 능동과 수동의 관계 설정이 애매하다면 목적어의 유무로 접근해야 한다.
① 선행사인 sensors가 주어로, 감지 장치가 부착하는 주체가 아니라 부착되는 대상이므로 수동태는 적절하다.
② such as는 전치사이므로 뒤에 명사가 나와 적절하다.
④ 자동사 respond는 뒤에 명사가 나올 때 전치사 to와 함께 나와야 한다.
⑤ 자동차가 다리를 건너는 주체(능동)이지, 건너지는 대상(수동)이 아니기에 능동의 관계인 현재분사(moving)는 적절하다.

06
[2013 이화여대]

Deviance is any non-conformist behavior (which ① disapproved of by society or a social group,) (② whether it is ③ illegal or not.) It is ④ norm-breaking behavior, and can range (from being ⑤ eccentric to criminal activity.)

정답 ① (disapproved → is disapproved)

해석 일탈이란 그것이 불법이건 아니건 간에, 사회와 사회단체가 허락하지 않는 비순응자의 행동이다. 그것은 규범을 깨는 행동이고, 그것의 범위는 이상한 행동부터 기이한 범죄 행동까지 다양하다.

분석 「자동사 + 전치사」의 수동태
① 원칙적으로 자동사는 수동태가 될 수 없다. 하지만 전치사 뒤에 있는 명사가 주어 자리로 이동한다면 전치사의 목적어 자리가 비워져 있다는 조건하에 가능하다. (ex. He deals with the matter. = The matter is dealt with by him.) disapproved of 뒤에 명사가 없는 것으로 보아 수동태가 되어야 한다는 것을 알 수 있다. is disapproved로 고쳐야 한다. 더 간단하게 접근하는 방법은 보기의 주어 역할을 하고 있는 선행사 behavior(행동)가 승인하는 주체가 아니라 승인되는 대상이므로 수동을 써야 한다.
② whether은 명사절과 부사절로 쓰일 수 있는데 이 문제에서는 부사절로 쓰여 수식절의 역할이다.
③ be동사의 보어로 형용사는 적절하다.
④ 행동(behavior)이 규범을 깨뜨리는 주체이기에 능동의 관계인 현재분사(breaking)는 적절하다.
⑤ 동명사(being)의 보어 역할로 형용사는 적절하다.

07 [2013 한국외대]

(In 1999,) an eighteen-year-old participant died (in a
                  S   V
gene therapy experiment). His death showed [that the
                         S   V   명사절(O)
researchers _____ the risks of their procedure.]
    S   V   O

① have not adequately assessed

② have not been adequately assessed

③ had not adequately assessed

④ had not been adequately assessed

정답 ③

해석 1999년 한 18세의 참여자가 유전자 치료 실험을 받던 도
중 숨졌다. 그의 죽음은 바로 연구원들이 그 실험 과정의
위험성을 제대로 인지하지 못했었다는 사실을 보여 준 것
이다.

분석 시제와 태의 구분

③ 주절 동사가 과거(showed)로 나와 종속절(that절)에
현재/현재완료는 나오지 못하므로 ①, ②는 탈락되고,
빈칸 뒤에 목적어(the risks)가 있기 때문에 능동태가
적절하다.

08 [2013 단국대]

(In Borneo,) (① where I was born and ② grown up,) I
            형용사절 S   V₁   V₂   S
have worked (③ in tropical conditions) (cutting survey
  V
lines) (through a forest) (that was ④ like a jungle.)
                        형용사절

정답 ② (grown up → grew up)

해석 내가 태어나고 자란 보르네오(Borneo)섬에서, 나는 열대
조건 속에서 일했으며 정글과 비슷한 숲에서 관측선을 그
렸다.

분석 자동사의 수동태 불가능

② I was born and grown은 원래 and (I was) grown
의 형태이다. grow가 '자라다, 성장하다'의 뜻으로 쓰
이면 자동사인데 영어는 원칙적으로 자동사를 수동태
로 쓰지 못한다. 과거동사 능동의 형태인 grew로 고쳐
야 한다.

① 관계부사 where은 장소의 명사를 수식하여 적절하고,
내가 낳은 주체가 아니라 태어난 대상이므로 수동태로
쓰여 적절하다.

③ 문장이 끝난 뒤 수식어구(전명구)가 나와 적절하다.

④ be like ~는 '~와 비슷하다'의 표현으로, 여기서 like
는 전치사이므로 뒤에 반드시 명사가 나온다.

09 [2013 단국대]

A total eclipse can ① be lasted (up to 7 minutes,)
     S   last
(② during ③ which time the moon's shadow moves
   부사절   N   S   V
(across Earth) (at a rate of about 0.6 kilometers) (④ per
second.))

정답 ① (be lasted → last)

해석 개기일식은 7분 정도 지속될 수 있다. 그 시간 동안 달의
그림자가 대략 초당 0.6킬로미터의 속도로 지구를 가로
질러 이동한다.

분석 수동태 불가능 동사

① 영어에는 수동태를 쓰지 못하는 수동태 절대 불가능
동사가 있다. 이 동사들은 해석의 여부, 목적어의 여부
와는 상관없이 수동태로 나오면 무조건 틀리는 동사이
니 반드시 암기를 해야 한다. last 역시 수동태 절대 불
가능 동사이기에 능동태인 last로 고쳐야 한다.

②, ③ 「전치사 + 복합관계형용사」 형태의 어려운 문장이
다. 이 부분은 심화 과정에서 자세히 다룰 테니 지금은
구조 분석의 형태만 보고 넘기는 것이 좋다.

④ per는 '~당'의 뜻으로 쓰여 초당 0.6킬로미터의 속도
라는 표현으로 적절하다.

10 [2013 동국대]

We ① take ethical investment (very seriously.) Recently
S   V   O
we ② were involved (in a project) (to build a large dam
S   V
in the Asian country of Paradiso.) We discovered [that
                                   명사절(O)
                                   S   V be forced
③ large numbers of farming people ④ would force to
  = many   S   V
leave the area flooded by the dam.]
  O.C

정답 ④ (would force → would be forced)

해석 우리는 윤리적 투자를 심각하게 받아들인다. 최근 우리는
아시아의 파라디소에 거대한 댐을 건설하는 프로젝트에
관계되어 있다. 우리는 수많은 농업 종사자들이 댐에 의
해 범람된 지역을 어쩔 수 없이 떠날 수밖에 없다는 것을
알게 되었다.

분석 능동태와 수동태의 구분(force + O + to R ~)

④ 「force + O + to R ~」 5형식 동사의 어형으로 쓰인다.
force는 문제에서 보이는 것처럼 곧바로 to R를 받지
못하기 때문에 수동인 「be forced to R ~」의 형태
로 쓰면 가능하다. would be forced로 고쳐야 한다.

① 보기 뒤에 목적어가 있어 능동태는 적절하다.

② involve는 항상 타동사로 「involve A in B」의 형태로 쓰이거나 목적어가 없다면 be involved in처럼 수동태로 쓰인다. 보기 뒤에 목적어가 없기에 수동태는 적절하다.

③ 「many = a number of, numbers of」의 표현으로 뒤에 복수명사(people)를 수식하여 적절하다.

11 [2013 서울여대]

The right hemisphere (of the human brain) is less
S   V₁
① crucial (to language production) and ② appears to be
   C   V₂
                            with
③ more concerned the ④ creation of images.
   C

정답 ③ (more concerned → more concerned with)

해석 인간의 우뇌는 언어 생산에는 덜 중요하고 이미지를 만들어 내는 데 있어 좀 더 연관된 것으로 보인다.

분석 동사의 어형(concern A with B)

③ 수동태(be concerned)는 목적어를 받을 수 없다. 「concern A with B = A be concerned with B」의 형태로 써야 하기에 보기 뒤에 with를 추가시켜야 수동태 뒤에 명사를 받을 수 있다.

① be동사의 보어로 형용사는 적절하고 문장이 끝난 뒤에 명사를 받기 위해 전치사를 쓴 것 역시 적절하다.

② is and appears로 병치도 괜찮고 appear는 to R를 보어로 받을 수 있어 적절하다.

④ 명사와 명사의 충돌을 피해 주기 위해 전명구는 적절하다.

12 [2013 세종대]

(① About) (three hundred years before Caesar,) human
                                                        S
                     was treated
geography ② treated ③ only in conjunction) (④ with
S   V
description of particular areas.)

정답 ② (treated → was treated)

해석 시저(Caesar) 이전 대략 300년 전에, 인문 지리학은 특정 지역에 대한 묘사와 함께 취급되었다.

분석 능동태와 수동태의 구분

② 인문 지리학이 취급하는 주체가 아니라 묘사와 결합된 것으로 취급되는 대상이고, 목적어도 없기 때문에 수동태인 was treated로 고쳐야 한다.

---

① 숫자 앞에 about은 '대략'이라는 뜻의 수식어구로 적절하다.

③ only는 전치초점부사로 어떠한 단어를 세게 말하고 싶을 때 그 앞에 위치하는 부사이므로 적절하다. 여기서는 in conjunction의 의미를 세게 전달한 것이다.

④ 명사와 명사의 충돌을 피해 주기 위해 전치사는 적절하다.

13 [2014 가천대]

                                          (which are)
(It) is a fact [① that pesticides ② considered unsuitable in
가S   진S   S remain   O.C
rich countries) ③ are remained in use (in many poor
                        V
④ ones.)]

정답 ③ (are remained → remain)

해석 부유한 나라에서 부적합하다고 여겨지는 살충제가 가난한 나라들에서는 여전히 사용되고 있다는 것은 사실이다.

분석 수동태 불가능 동사

③ 자동사, 타동사 할 것 없이 수동태가 되면 무조건 틀리는 수동태 절대 불가능 동사가 있다. remain 역시 수동태 절대 불가능 동사이기에 remain으로 고쳐야 한다.

① 「It(가주어) ~ that절(진주어) ...」로 쓰여 적절하다.

② 살충제가 여기는 주체가 아니라 부적합하다고 여겨지는 대상이므로 수동의 관계인 과거분사(considered)는 적절하다.

④ countries를 대신 받는 대명사이고 수 일치 역시 적절하다.

14 [2014 경기대]

The attack ① was occurred (② while they were
S   V   부사절   S   V
customers (at a ③ convenience store) (④ in March
                          C
2012.))

정답 ① (was → 삭제)

해석 2012년 3월 그들이 어느 한 편의점의 고객일 때, 그 공격이 있었다.

분석 수동태 불가능 동사

① occur은 수동태 절대 불가능 동사이다. was를 삭제해 능동태로 고쳐야 한다.

② while은 접속사이기 때문에 주어, 동사가 나와 적절하다.

③ convenience store는 '편의점'이라는 복합명사로 쓰여 적절하다.

④ 월, 연도 등 앞에는 전치사 in을 쓰기 때문에 적절하다.

15
[2014 단국대]

(So far from being a misfortune,) poverty may, by vigorous self-help,) _____ into a blessing.

① be converted

② have converted

③ is converted

④ have been converting

정답 ①

해석 가난은 결코 불행이 아니라 열심히 노력하면 축복으로 바뀔 수 있다.

분석 조동사의 특징 / 능동태와 수동태의 구분

① 「convert A into B(A를 B로 변환시키다)」로 쓰이는 동사이다. 빈칸 뒤에 「into + N」의 전명구가 나온 것으로 보아 수동태를 써야 하는데 ②, ③은 능동태라서 부적절하다. ③은 조동사 뒤에 동사원형(R)이 나오지 않아 부적절하다. 또한 주어(가난)가 축복으로 바꾸는 주체가 아니라 축복으로 바뀌는 대상이기에 수동태를 써야 한다고 접근해도 좋다.

16
[2014 상명대]

A strange ① coincidence ② was happened (when ③ the news ④ was ⑤ announced this morning.)

정답 ② (was happened → happened)

해석 그 소식이 오늘 아침 발표되었을 때, 이상한 우연의 일치가 일어났다.

분석 수동태 불가능 동사

② happen은 수동태 절대 불가능 동사이다. happened로 고쳐야 한다.

① 주어 자리에 명사가 나와 적절하다.

③ news는 불가산명사로 취급하기에 a/an은 나올 수 없지만 the는 가능하다.

④ news는 불가산명사로 항상 단수동사와 수 일치하기에 적절하다.

⑤ 소식이 발표하는 주체가 아닌 발표되는 대상이므로 수동태 역시 적절하다.

17
[2014 아주대]

The association (of Europe) (with political freedom) _____ (in ancient Greece.)

① had first been made

② which was first made

③ was first made

④ first made

⑤ was first making

정답 ③

해석 정치적 자유를 가진 유럽 연합은 고대 그리스에서 처음 이루어졌다.

분석 능동태와 수동태의 구분 / 시점부사와 동사의 시제 일치

③ 문장에 동사가 없다. 빈칸은 동사가 필요한 자리이므로 ②는 탈락되고, 유럽 연합이 만드는 주체가 아닌 만들어지는 대상이므로 수동태를 써야 한다. 능동태인 ④, ⑤는 탈락되고, ①, ③은 둘 다 수동태이지만 ①은 과거완료 수동, ③은 과거 수동으로 시제의 선택을 묻고 있다. in ancient Greece라는 과거 시점부사가 있어 ③이 적절하다. 문법에서 시제를 묻는 경우, 한국어의 해석으로는 거의 묻지 않고 지금과 같이 시점에 대한 힌트를 주고 묻는다는 것을 명심해야 한다.

18
[2015 서강대]

(① As historical databases ② relatively impoverish,) we might expect the ③ newer discipline (of quantitative sociolinguistics) to ④ cast some light on the matter.

정답 ② (relatively impoverish → are relatively impoverished)

해석 역사적 자료의 질이 비교적 빈약해짐에 따라서, 우리는 계량 사회 언어학이라는 새로운 학문이 이 문제를 밝게 비추어 주길(해결책을 모색할 방법을) 기대한다.

분석 능동태와 수동태의 구분

② impoverish는 타동사로만 쓰이는 동사이다. 목적어도 존재하지 않고 역사적 자료들이 질을 저하시키는 주체가 아니라 저하되는 대상이므로 수동태인 are relatively impoverished로 고쳐야 한다.

① As는 부사절 접속사로 쓰여 주어, 동사가 나와 적절하다.

③ expect의 목적어의 역할로 명사는 적절하고 형용사 newer은 명사를 수식하고 있다.

④ 「expect+O+to R ~」 5형식 어형으로 쓰여 적절하다.

19 [2015 성균관대]

Fifty-six people, (①including two ②retired generals,) (who were)
③were went (on trial) (in Turkey's second case) (against
a clandestine group) (④accused of ⑤plotting to (which was)
overthrow the government of Prime Minister Recep
Erdogan.)

정답 ③ (were went → went)

해석 두 명의 예비역 장군을 포함한 56명의 사람들이, 수상 Recep Erdogan의 정부를 전복시키려는 음모를 꾸민 혐의로 기소된 비밀 단체에 대한 터키의 두 번째 사건 때문에 재판을 받았다.

분석 자동사의 수동태 불가능

③ go는 자동사이다. 자동사는 원칙적으로 수동태를 쓰지 못하므로 능동태인 went로 고쳐야 한다.

① 56명의 사람들이 2명의 예비역 장군을 포함하는 주체이고, 뒤에 목적어도 있기 때문에 능동의 관계인 현재분사(including)는 적절하다.

② retired는 '은퇴한'의 뜻을 가진 형용사이다.

④ 단체가 고소한 주체가 아닌 음모를 꾸민 혐의로 고소당한 대상이므로 수동의 관계인 과거분사(accused)는 적절하다.

⑤ 전치사의 목적어로 동명사는 적절하다.

20 [2015 성균관대]

Hundreds of civilians were ①reporting (killed in reported
②shelling,) (as the army struggled ③to root out Tamil 부사절
rebels from ④the last few square kilometers of land
⑤under their control.)

정답 ① (reporting → reported)

해석 우리 군이 그들의 통제하에 있는 마지막 수백 킬로미터 지역에서 타밀 반군을 뿌리 뽑기 위해 고군분투하고 있을 때, 수백 명의 민간인들이 포격에 의해 죽었다고 보도되었다.

분석 능동태와 수동태의 구분

① 수백 명의 시민들 자신이 죽었다고 보도하는 주체가 아니라 보도되는 대상이므로 수동태인 reported로 고쳐야 한다. 앞에 이미 be동사(were)가 있어 reported로 고치면 수동태가 된다.

② '포격'이라는 뜻의 명사로 전치사의 목적어로 적절하다.

③ 「struggle + to R ~」는 '~하기 위해 고군분투하다'의 뜻으로 to R의 부사적 용법으로 쓰여 적절하다.

④ 순서를 나타내는 서수 앞에는 정관사 the가 있어야 한다.

⑤ 명사와 명사의 충돌을 피해 주기 위해 전치사는 적절하다.

21 [2015 한양대 에리카]

Scientists now know [that all objects ①compose (of are composed/consist
S   V   명사절(O) S₁   V₁
many molecules) and the ②force (of gravity) ③pulls (on
S₂   V₂
④each of them.)]

정답 ① (compose of → are composed of 또는 consist of)

해석 과학자들은 모든 물체가 수많은 분자들로 구성되어 있고, 중력의 힘이 분자들 각각을 끌어당기고 있다는 사실을 알고 있다.

분석 능동태와 수동태의 구분

① compose는 타동사로만 쓰이는 동사인데 뒤에 목적어가 없는 것으로 보아 수동태인 are composed of 혹은 자동사인 consist of로 고쳐야 한다. 또한 모든 물질이 구성하는 주체가 아니라 수많은 분자들로 구성되는 대상이므로 수동태를 써야 한다.

② 여기서 force는 명사로 쓰인 형태이다.

③ 주어(the force)와 동사(pulls)의 수 일치가 적절하다.

④ each는 대명사의 역할도 가지고 있어 전치사의 목적어로 적절하다.

22 [2015 홍익대]

(By ①the time) (when the attack ②was arrived,) the 형용사절   S   V
defenders ③could be ④disconcerted, wavering,
S   V   C₁   C₂
worried, hesitant, vacillating.
C₃   C₄   C₅

정답 ② (was arrived → arrived)

해석 공격이 시작되었을 때 방어하는 이들은 당황하고, 동요하고, 걱정하고, 주저하며, 망설일 수 있다.

분석 자동사의 수동태 불가능

② arrive는 자동사로 쓰인다. 자동사는 원칙적으로 수동태를 쓰지 못하므로 능동태인 arrived로 고쳐야 한다.

① 전치사의 목적어로 명사는 적절하다.

③ 보기 뒤에 동사원형이 있기 때문에 조동사는 적절하다.

④ 형용사 disconcerted는 보어로 쓰여 적절하다.

23

The bodily processes (behind taste) _____
S   V
unclear to date.
C

① are remained

② remain

③ have been remained

④ remaining

정답 ②

해석 맛을 느끼는 과정 이면에 있는 신체적인 과정이 지금까지도 명확하지 않은 채로 남겨져 있다.

분석 수동태 불가능 동사

② 빈칸은 동사가 필요한 자리이므로 ④는 탈락되고, remain은 수동태 절대 불가능 동사이기에 ①, ③도 탈락되어 정답은 ②이다.

24
[2016 경기대]

The public ①was brought (to the realization) [that (②if
S   V   동격   부사절
Superman could ③be paralyzed,) it could ④be
               V   S
happen S
happened (to anybody.)]
   V

정답 ④ (be happened → happen)

해석 만일 슈퍼맨의 전신이 마비된다면, 대중들은 그런 일이 누구에게나 일어날 수 있다는 사실을 깨닫게 될 것이다.

분석 수동태 불가능 동사

④ happen은 수동태 절대 불가능 동사이다. 능동태인 happen으로 고쳐야 한다.

① 「be brought to the realization that ~」은 'that절

이하 내용을 깨닫다'의 표현이다. 수동태 뒤 전명구가 나오고 that절은 앞 명사의 동격을 나타내고 있다.

② 동격의 that절 속에 가정법이 나와 if절은 조건절(부사절)의 형태이다.

③ 슈퍼맨이 마비되는 대상이므로 적절하다.

25
[2016 단국대]

The orphans (living in the rural village) _____
S
(to the amusement park.)

① considered took

② considered to take

③ were considered to be taken
        V   O.C

④ were considered being taken
        V   O.C

정답 ③

해석 시골에 살고 있는 고아들을 놀이공원으로 데리고 가는 것이 고려되었다.

분석 5형식 consider의 수동태

③ 고아들이 누군가를 놀이공원으로 데리고 가는 것을 고려하는 주체가 아닌 고려되는 대상이므로 동사는 수동태를 써야 한다. 그러므로 ①, ②는 탈락되고, consider가 3형식으로 쓰일 때 동명사를 받고 5형식으로 쓰일 때 be considered to R로 쓰이기 때문에 정답은 ③이 적절하다. 3형식으로 쓰여 동명사(R-ing)를 목적어로 받는 경우는 수동태로 쓸 수 없다.

Practice 02

01	①	02	②	03	②	04	④	05	①
06	③	07	③	08	③	09	④	10	②
11	③	12	③	13	③	14	①	15	②
16	③	17	①	18	①	19	①	20	④
21	①	22	③	23	②	24	③	25	⑤

01
[2016 홍익대]

(Because of his stupid behavior,) Max was _____
(by everybody.)

① laughed at　　　　② laughing at

③ laughed　　　　　④ laughing

정답 ①

해석 맥스(Max)의 어리석은 행동 때문에 모든 사람들이 그를 비웃었다.

분석 「자동사 + 전치사」의 수동태

① 자동사는 원칙적으로 수동태가 될 수 없다. 하지만 전치사 뒤에 있는 명사가 나와 주어가 된다면 전치사의 목적어 자리가 비워져 있는 조건하에 가능하다. (ex. They laughed at Mary. = Mary was laughed at by them.) 맥스(Max)가 어리석은 행동을 했다면 자신이 비웃는 것이 아니라 사람들에게 비웃음을 당해야 하므로 능동태인 ②, ④는 탈락되고, ①, ③ 중 자동사의 수동태는 반드시 동사에 붙은 전치사를 목적어 자리를 비워 놓고 써야 하기 때문에 ①이 정답이다.

02
[2017 경기대]

(When private property ① came into existence,) and (when private property ② could inherit by one of their sons,) fathers began [③ to look for the son] (④ to whom they could leave their property.)

정답 ② (could inherit → could be inherited)

해석 사유 재산이 생겼을 때, 그리고 사유 재산을 아들 중 한 명이 물려받을 때, 아버지들이 재산을 물려줄 수 있는 아들을 찾기 시작했다.

분석 능동태와 수동태의 구분

② 사유 재산이 상속받는 주체가 아니라 상속되는 대상이므로 수동태인 could be inherited로 고쳐야 한다.

① come은 자동사로 수식어구(전명구)를 받아 적절하다.

③ begin은 to R와 R-ing를 둘 다 의미 차이 없이 목적어로 받을 수 있기에 적절하다.

④ 「전치사 + 관계대명사(to whom)」는 절 이하의 성분이 완전하고 선행사가 사람이기에 which가 아닌 whom이 적절하다.

03
[2017 단국대]

(After careful deliberation,) the proposed merger _____ (by the CEO.)

① assent　　　　　② is assented

③ is assenting　　　④ assents

정답 ②

해석 신중하게 고려한 이후, 제안된 합병 건이 최고 경영자에 의해 승인된다.

분석 능동태와 수동태의 구분

② 합병이 승인하는 주체가 아니라 승인되는 대상이므로 수동태가 적절하다.

①, ③, ④ 전부 능동태로 나와 정답이 될 수 없다.

04
[2017 단국대]

(Although these procedures are (① most commonly) used to detect the most common genetic ② disorders — (Down syndrome, for example) — ③ they could, (in principle,) ④ use (to detect more minor genetic abnormalities.)

정답 ④ (use → be used)

해석 비록 이러한 절차들이 다운 증후군과 같은 가장 일반적인 유전 질환을 발견하는 데 흔히 사용된다 할지라도 원칙적으로 이 절차들은 좀 더 가벼운 유전 질환을 발견하는 데 사용될 수도 있다.

분석 능동태와 수동태의 구분

④ 여기서 ③의 they는 these procedures를 받는 대명사이다. 이 절차들이 사용하는 주체가 아니라 사용되는 대상이므로 수동태인 be used로 고쳐야 한다.

① most는 단독으로 부사로 쓰일 수 있어 be p.p.(수동) 사이에 부사는 적절하다.

② disorders(질환)는 가산, 불가산의 선택을 묻는 명사가 아니기에 적절하다.

③ these procedures를 대신 받는 대명사로 수 일치는 적절하다.

05

Pope Francis (on Sunday) ①was offered a Christmas hope (for peace) (in a world) (②lacerated by war and terrorism,) (urging people ③to remember migrants, refugees and those) (④hit by economic instability) (⑤caused by "idolatry of money.")

정답   ① (was offered → offered)

해석   일요일에 프란치스코 교황(Pope Francis)은 전쟁과 테러로 상처를 입은 세상에 평화를 위한 크리스마스의 희망을 선포했으며, 사람들로 하여금 이민자, 난민 그리고 '돈이라는 우상 숭배'에 의해 야기된 경제적 불안정으로 타격을 입은 사람들을 기억해야 한다고 촉구했다.

분석   능동태와 수동태의 구분

① 교황이 크리스마스의 희망을 선포받는 대상이 아니라 선포하는 주체이기 때문에 능동태인 offered로 고쳐야 한다.

② 세상이 전쟁과 테러로 상처받는 대상이고, 뒤에 목적어도 없기 때문에 수동의 관계인 과거분사(lacerated)는 적절하다.

③ 「urge + O + to R ~」 5형식 동사의 어형으로 쓰여 적절하다.

④ 사람들이 경제적 불안정으로 타격을 받은 대상이므로 수동의 관계인 과거분사(hit)는 적절하다. (hit – hit – hit)

⑤ 경제적 불안정이 돈이라는 우상 숭배에 의해 야기되는 대상이고, 뒤에 목적어도 없기 때문에 수동의 관계인 과거분사(caused)는 적절하다.

06

(To our surprise,) Erik Dickinson fell ①short of his parents' expectations, (②disappointing them (who kept the faith in their son's potential for success,) (when he ③was proved (to be) ④a failure as a statesman.)

정답   ③ (was proved → proved)

해석   우리가 놀랍게도, 정치인으로서 실패한 사람으로 밝혀졌을 때, 에릭 디킨슨(Erik Dickinson)은 부모님의 기대치에 미치지 못했으며, 아들이 성공할 수 있다는 가능성을 굳게 믿고 있던 부모님을 실망시켰다.

분석   능동태와 수동태의 구분

③ 「prove + (to be) + 명사 / 형용사 ~」 형태로 prove는 「(to be) + 명사 / 형용사」를 보어로 받을 경우, '~로 증명되다, 밝혀지다'라는 그 자체로 수동의 의미를 가지고 있는 자동사이므로 수동태를 쓰지 못한다. 능동태 proved로 고쳐야 한다.

① fall short of ~ : '~이 부족하다, ~에 못 미치다'의 의미로 적절하다.

② 에릭 디킨슨이 부모를 실망시키는 주체이므로 능동태 분사구문(disappointing)은 적절하다.

④ failure가 '실패'의 뜻일 때 불가산명사, '실패한 사람'의 뜻으로 쓰일 때 가산으로 쓰여 적절하지만 딱히 해석으로서 가산과 불가산의 선택을 묻는 단어는 아니다.

07

A distinction (between two kinds of intelligence) — (crystallized and fluid intelligence) — ①has been widely studied (by researchers) (studying adult learning.) Crystallized intelligence ②is heavily dependent (on education and experience.) It ③is consisted of the set of skills and knowledge) (that we each learn as part of growing up in any culture.) Fluid intelligence, (in contrast,) ④is thought to be a more basic set of abilities, (not so dependent on specific education.)

정답   ③ (is consisted of → consists of)

해석   두 가지 종류의 지능 – 결정성 지능과 유동성 지능 – 사이의 차이점을 성인 학습을 연구하는 학자들이 광범위하게 연구해 왔다. 결정성 지능은 교육과 경험에 크게 의존

하며 그것은 어느 문화에서든 우리들 각자가 성장하는 과
정의 일부로서 학습하는 일련의 기술과 지식으로 구성되
어 있다. 이와는 대조적으로, 유동성 지능은 특정한 교육
에 그다지 의존하기보다 좀 더 기본적인 일련의 능력들이
라고 여겨진다.

분석 수동태 불가능 동사

③ consist는 수동태 절대 불가능 동사이다. 수동태 불가
능 동사는 해석의 여부, 목적어의 여부와는 상관없이
수동태로 나오면 무조건 틀리는 동사이므로 능동태인
consists of로 고쳐야 한다.

① 주어(A distinction)와 동사(has)의 수 일치는 적절하
고, 차이점이 연구하는 주체가 아니라 연구되는 대상
이므로 수동태도 적절하다.

② 부사(heavily)가 형용사(dependent)를 수식하여 적
절하다.

④ 유동성 지능이 기본적 능력이라고 여겨지는 대상이므
로 수동태는 적절하다. 「think + O + (to be) + O.C」
5형식 동사의 어형에서 수동태가 된 문장이다.

08 [2011 경희대]

① It seems almost certain [that the 60 years (after
penicillin ② came to market) ③ will eventually view ④ as
just an interlude (in the eternal war) (between us and
them.)]

정답 ③ (will eventually view → will eventually be
viewed)

해석 페니실린이 시판된 이후 60년이라는 세월이 결국 우리(인
간)와 그들(병) 사이의 끝없는 전쟁에서 단지 막간극으로
여겨질 것은 거의 확실해 보인다.

분석 능동태와 수동태의 구분(view + O + as + O.C)

③ 「view + O + as + O.C」 5형식 동사의 어형으로 쓰였
다. 뒤에 「as + O.C」가 온 것으로 보아 수동태인 will
eventually be viewed로 고쳐야 한다. 또한 60년이
라는 기간이 막간극으로 여겨지는 대상이므로 관계를
따져 보아도 수동을 써야 한다.

① 「It(가주어) seems ~ that절(진주어) ...」 구문이다.
seem의 보어로 형용사가 쓰여 적절하다.

② come은 자동사로 수식어구(전명구)가 나와 적절하다.

④ 「view + O + as + O.C」 5형식 동사의 어형에서 수동
태가 되어 「as + O.C」는 적절하다.

09 [2011 경희대]

(Today) it emerged [that (about) 500 red-winged blackbirds
and starlings _____ (in Louisiana.) Their tiny
corpses littered a short stretch (of highway near the
city of Labarre) (after apparently falling dead from the
sky.)]

① have found dead

② found dead

③ had found dead

④ had been found dead

정답 ④

해석 오늘 500마리의 빨간 날개의 찌르레기들이 루이지애나
(Louisiana)에서 죽은 채로 발견된 것으로 알려졌다. 분
명히 하늘에서 죽은 채로 떨어지고 난 후 라바르(Labarre)
라는 도시 근처 고속 도로의 짧은 구간에 작은 새들의 시
체가 흩어져 있었다.

분석 능동태와 수동태의 구분 / 시제의 선택

④ 주절 동사가 과거(emerged)라서 종속절(that절)에 현
재/현재완료는 나올 수 없으므로 ①은 탈락된다. 또한
찌르레기들이 죽은 채로 발견되는 대상이므로 능동태
인 ②, ③도 탈락되고, 수동태로 쓰인 ④가 적절하다.

10 [2011 강남대]

(If we don't get a ① satisfying solution to the problem,)
we'll ② be forcing to ③ take action ④ against your
company.)

정답 ② (be forcing to → be forced to)

해석 만약 우리가 그 문제에 대한 만족스러운 해결책을 얻지
못하면, 우리는 어쩔 수 없이 귀사에게 조치를 취하게 될
것입니다.

분석 능동태와 수동태의 구분(force + O + to R)

② 「force + O + to R ~」 5형식 동사의 어형이다. 동사와
to take가 붙은 것으로 보아 수동태인 be forced to
로 고쳐야 한다.

① 감정·심리 동사의 분사는 사람을 과거분사(p.p.)로
수식하고, 사물을 현재분사(R-ing)로 수식하기 때문에
solution은 사물이기에 현재분사(satisfying)는 적절
하다.

③ 「be forced to R」에서 to는 부정사이기에 동사원형 (take)은 적절하다.
④ 명사와 명사의 충돌을 피해 주기 위해 전치사는 적절하다.

11 [2011 강남대]

The ① renovated business center, (② which has several restaurants, boutiques and Internet cafes,) ③ can be accommodated (④ as many as 1,000 guests).

정답 ③ (can be accommodated → can accommodate)

해석 여러 개의 식당, 양품점, 그리고 인터넷 카페들이 있는 보수된 비즈니스 센터가 1,000명 이상의 손님을 수용할 수 있다.

분석 능동태와 수동태의 구분
③ 비즈니스 센터가 1,000명 이상의 손님을 수용하는 주체이고, 보기 뒤에 목적어(1,000 guests)가 있기 때문에 능동태인 can accommodate로 고쳐야 한다.
① 센터가 보수하는 주체가 아니라 보수되는 대상이므로 수동의 관계인 과거분사(renovated)는 적절하다.
② 선행사가 사물(business center)이고 절 이하에 주어 자리가 불완전하여 관계대명사(which)는 적절하다. 또한 주격 관계대명사절 이하의 동사(has)는 선행사 (business center)와 수 일치하므로 적절하다.
④ 숫자 앞에 as many as는 '숫자 이상'이라는 뜻의 형용사로 쓰여 적절하다.

12 [2011 경기대]

Columbia ① has suffered the heaviest rain (in decades) (② due to the La Nina weather phenomenon,) (which ③ is caused water temperature (in the Pacific Ocean) ④ to drop.)

정답 ③ (is caused → causes)

해석 콜롬비아는 라니냐 기후 현상으로 인해 수십 년 동안 폭우로 고통받아 왔는데, 이 현상은 태평양의 수온을 낮아지도록 야기한다.

분석 능동태와 수동태의 구분(cause + O + to R)
③ 「cause + O + to R ~」 5형식 동사의 어형이다. 뒤에 목적어(water temperature)가 있기 때문에 능동태인 causes로 고쳐야 한다.

① suffer는 자동사와 타동사의 용법을 둘 다 가지고 있다. 예전 영어에서는 그 구분을 물어보았지만 현대 영어에서는 구분을 묻지 않기에 따질 필요가 없다.
② 명사와 명사의 충돌을 피해 주기 위해 전치사는 적절하다.
④ 「cause + O + to R ~」 5형식 동사의 어형으로 목적보어의 to R는 적절하다.

13 [2011 상명대]

(① At the meeting) (held in December,) ② it was announced [that the choice (of recipients) ③ had finally limited (④ to Dr. Evert, Professor Applebaum, or her.)]

정답 ③ (had finally limited → had finally been limited)

해석 12월에 열린 회의에서 수상하는 대상은 결국 에버트 박사, 애플바움 교수, 그리고 그녀로 제한되었다고 발표되었다.

분석 능동태와 수동태의 구분(limit A to B)
③ 「limit A to B」 3형식 동사의 어형에서 태를 묻고 있다. 주어(the choice)가 제한되는 대상이고, 뒤에 목적어도 없기 때문에 수동태인 had finally been limited로 고쳐야 한다.
① 회의가 개최하는 주체가 아니라 개최되는 대상이므로 수동의 관계인 과거분사(held)는 적절하다.
② 「it(가주어) was ~ that절(진주어) ….」 구문에서 진짜 주어는 that절의 내용이다. that절이라는 내용이 발표하는 주체가 아니라 발표되는 대상이므로 수동태는 적절하다.
④ 「limit A to B」의 어형에서 수동태가 되어 be limited to ~의 표현은 적절하다.

14 [2011 서경대]

The injury ① was occurred (when the ② 25-year-old man ③ was running through stunts ④ at England's Leavesden Studios.)

* run through: ~을 연습하다

정답 ① (was occurred → occurred)

해석 영국의 리브스덴(Leavesden) 스튜디오에서 25살의 남자가 스턴트 연기를 연습하다가 부상이 발생했다.

분석 수동태 불가능 동사
① occur은 수동태 절대 불가능 동사이다. 능동태인 occurred로 고쳐야 한다.

② 숫자와 명사가 하이픈(-)으로 연결되어 형용사로 쓰일 경우, 단수명사로 연결해야 하기 때문에 year은 적절하다.

③ 주절이 과거이기에 종속절도 과거가 나와 적절하다.

④ 명사와 명사의 충돌을 피해 주기 위해 수식어구(전명구)는 적절하다.

15

The ①lens and cornea are ②supply (with ③nutrients and oxygen) (by the ④aqueous fluid.)
supplied

정답 ② (supply → supplied)

해석 수정체와 각막은 수양액에 의해 영양분과 산소를 공급받는다.

분석 동사 두 개 불가능(supply A with B)

② 이미 보기 앞에 be동사(are)가 존재하는데 또 동사가 나올 수 없어 정답은 금방 찾을 수 있다. 또한 수정체와 각막이 제공하는 것이 아니라 제공받는 대상이므로 수동태인 supplied로 고쳐야 한다.

① '수정체'라는 뜻의 명사로 쓰여 주어 역할로 적절하다.

③ 전치사의 목적어로 명사는 적절하다. (가산, 불가산을 묻는 명사가 아니다.)

④ 형용사가 명사를 수식하여 적절하다.

16
[2011 세종대]

(To ①ring in the Year of the Rabbit,) ②three major museums ③are held exhibitions (④to introduce visitors to the mythology of the rabbit in Korean culture.)
holding

정답 ③ (are held → are holding)

해석 토끼의 해를 알리기 위해, 세 곳의 주요 박물관들은 한국 문화에 존재하는 토끼 신화를 관람객들에게 소개하는 전시회를 열고 있다.

분석 능동태와 수동태의 구분

③ 박물관이 전시회를 개최하는 주최이고, 뒤에 목적어도 있기 때문에 능동태인 are holding으로 고쳐야 한다.

① 문두에 To R의 부사적 용법으로 쓰여 적절하다.

② three가 나와 뒤에 복수명사가 나온 형태이다.

④ to R의 형용사적 용법으로 앞의 명사(exhibitions)를 수식하여 적절하다.

17
[2011 세종대]

We have ①been endured the ②successively ③higher levels (of unemployment) (during ④the past three recessions.)

정답 ① (been endured → endured)

해석 우리는 지난 3년간의 경기 침체기 동안에 계속해서 더 높아지는 실업률을 견뎌 내고 있다.

분석 능동태와 수동태의 구분

① 보기 뒤에 목적어(the levels of unemployment)가 있기 때문에 수동태를 쓰지 못한다. 능동태로 써야 하므로 been을 삭제해야 한다.

② 부사(successively)가 형용사(higher)를 수식하여 적절하다.

③ 형용사(higher)가 명사(levels)를 수식하여 적절하다.

④ 「during the past + 기간 N」는 현재완료 시점부사이므로 동사의 시제가 일치되어 적절하다.

18
[2012 광운대]

(In 1963) Maria Mayer ①awarded the Nobel Prize ②in physics) (for her ③findings) (on the ④constituents) (of the atomic ⑤nucleus.)
was awarded

정답 ① (awarded → was awarded)

해석 1963년에 마리아 메이어(Maria Mayer)는 원자핵을 구성하는 성분에 대한 조사의 결과로 노벨 물리학상을 받았다.

분석 능동태와 수동태의 구분

① 마리아가 노벨상을 수여하는 주체가 아니라 수여받는 대상이므로 수동태인 was awarded로 고쳐야 한다. award는 4형식의 어형으로 쓰여 수동태가 되어도 직접목적어가 나올 수 있다.

② 명사와 명사의 충돌을 피해 주기 위해 전치사는 적절하다.

③ finding은 '발견, 조사[연구] 결과'라는 뜻의 단순 명사로 쓰여 전치사의 목적어로 적절하다.

④ 정관사(the) 뒤에 명사는 적절하다.

⑤ 전치사의 목적어 자리에 명사는 적절하다.

19 [2012 동덕여대]

The event ①is proved (to be) a great chance (②for us)
(to meet high school ③alumni and other friends ④all at
once.)

정답 ① (is proved → proves)

해석 그 행사는 우리가 고등학교 졸업생들과 다른 친구들 모두
를 한 번에 만날 수 있는 좋은 기회로 밝혀졌다.

분석 능동태와 수동태의 구분

① 「prove + (to be) + 명사/형용사 ~」 형태로, prove 뒤
에 (to be) 명사/형용사를 보어로 받을 경우 '~로 증
명되다, 밝혀지다'라는 그 자체로 수동의 의미를 가지
고 있는 자동사이므로 수동태가 아닌 능동태 proves
로 고쳐야 한다.

② to R의 의미상 주어로 쓰여 적절하다.

③ alumnus(졸업생)의 불규칙 복수형 명사로 적절하다.

④ all at once는 '모두 함께'의 뜻으로 쓰인 부사로 적절
하다.

20 [2012 명지대]

A Hong Kong journalist (who _____ in mainland
China for nearly 16 months for spying charges) will face
trial this week.

① detains

② is detaining

③ has detained

④ has been detained

정답 ④

해석 중국 본토에서 거의 16개월 동안 스파이 혐의로 억류되었
던 홍콩 저널리스트는 이번 주에 재판을 받을 예정이다.

분석 능동태와 수동태의 구분

④ 주격 관계대명사(who)절 속에 동사의 주어는 선행사
(A Hong Kong journalist)이다. 저널리스트가 스파
이 혐의로 억류하는 주체가 아니라 억류되는 대상이므
로 ④가 적절하다. ①, ②, ③은 전부 능동태라서 부적
절하다. 보통 능동과 수동의 선택은 주어와 동사의 관
계를 설정하여 따지지만 만약 단어의 뜻을 모른다면
찍어야 하는데, 그때 목적어가 있으면 능동태, 없다면
수동태를 찍는 것은 차선책의 방법으로 쓸 수 있다.

21 [2012 서강대]

The world is ①made up (with objects.) They have
properties (②independent of any people or other
beings) (who experience them.) For example, ③take a
rock, It's a separate object and it's hard. (Even if no
people or other beings ④existed in the universe,) it
would still be a separate object and it would still be
hard.

정답 ① (made up with → made up of)

해석 세상은 물체들로 구성되어 있다. 그 물체들은 그것을 경
험하는 사람 혹은 다른 존재들로부터 독립적인 특징을 가
지고 있다. 예를 들어 돌멩이 하나를 집어라. 그 돌멩이는
하나의 독립적인 개체다. 그리고 그것은 단단하다. 심지어
우주에 사람 혹은 다른 어떤 존재도 없다고 할지라도 그
것은 여전히 하나의 독립된 개체이고, 그것은 여전히 단
단할 것이다.

분석 수동태 뒤 전치사의 선택(be made up of)

① 「be made up of」는 '~로 구성되다'라는 표현으로,
이때 전치사는 of 또는 from을 쓴다. with를 쓰지 않
기에 made up of로 고쳐야 한다. be made up of와
be made up from의 차이는 심화 과정에서 따로 다
루겠지만 현대 영어에서는 잘 묻지 않는 지식이다.

② 형용사(independent)가 전명구(of N)와 결합되어 뒤
에서 앞에 있는 명사(properties)를 수식하여 적절하
다. 또한 independent는 전치사 on이 아닌 of 혹은
from을 쓰는 형용사이다.

③ 명령문으로 쓰여 적절하다.

④ exist는 자동사로 쓰여 수식어구(전명구)를 받아 적절
하다.

22 [2012 서강대]

(In most of our practical activities,) we ①rely (upon our
senses) and develop intuitions (we can ②trust). (When
important issues ③raise,) (regardless of what others
may say,) our own senses and intuitions are our best
④guides (for action.)

정답 ③ (raise → are raised)

해석 우리가 실질적인 행동을 할 때, 우리는 감각에 의존하고, 우리가 믿을 수 있는 직관력을 발달시킨다. 중요한 이슈가 생기면, 남들이 말하는 것과는 상관없이, 우리 자신의 감각과 직관력은 행동하기 위한 최고의 길잡이가 된다.

분석 능동태와 수동태의 구분

③ raise는 타동사로만 쓰이는 동사인데 뒤에 목적어가 없기 때문에 수동태인 are raised로 고쳐야 한다. 또한 중요한 문제가 제기되는 대상이므로 수동태를 써야 한다.

① rely는 자동사로 쓰여 뒤에 명사를 받을 때 전치사 (up)on이 나와야 하기에 적절하다.

② 구조 분석에서 보이듯이 we 앞에 목적격 관계대명사 (that)가 생략되어 trust의 목적어 자리가 불완전한 것은 적절하다.

④ 명사와 명사의 충돌을 피해 주기 위해 전치사는 적절하다.

23
[2012 성균관대]

(Although the media were ① largely denied access ② with the battlefields,) the Gulf War ③ (nevertheless) gained the reputation (of the first real-time television war,) and the images (④ projected into American homes) ⑤ helped [to incite the most passionate war fever (since World War II.)]

정답 ② (with → to)

해석 매체들은 대체로 전쟁터에 접근이 불가능하지만, 그럼에도 불구하고, 걸프전은 최초의 실시간 텔레비전 전쟁이라는 명성을 얻었다. 그리고 미국 가정에 송출된 영상들은 2차 세계 대전 이래 가장 열정적인 전쟁 열병을 불러일으키는 데 일조했다.

분석 동사와 연결된 전치사의 선택(be denied access to ~)

② 「deny A(대상) access to ~ = A be denied access to ~」는 '~ 접근을 허용하지 않다'의 뜻으로 쓰이는 표현인데, 이때 access와 연결되는 전치사는 항상 to를 써야 하기에 with를 to로 고쳐야 한다.

① 수동태(be p.p.) 사이에 형용사는 쓰지 못하고 부사는 가능하다.

③ nevertheless는 '그럼에도 불구하고'라는 뜻의 부사이다.

④ 영상이 미국 가정에 송출되는 대상이므로 수동의 관계인 과거분사(projected)는 적절하다.

⑤ help는 to R를 목적어로 받을 수 있어 적절하다.

24
[2012 중앙대]

A natural harbor ① is preferred (to an artificial one,) (for ② the latter is expensive (to construct) and tends [to depreciate rapidly.]) (Hence) it is recommended [that available capital and manpower ③ expend in improving natural harbors.)] ④ No error

정답 ③ (expend in → be expended in)

해석 천연 항구가 인공 항구보다 선호된다. 그 이유는 후자(인공 항구)는 만드는 데 비용이 많이 들고, 빠르게 가치가 하락하는 경향이 있기 때문이다. 그러므로 가용 자본과 인력은 천연 항구 개발에 쓰이는 것이 권고된다.

분석 능동태와 수동태의 구분

③ 가용 자본과 인력이 무엇인가를 쓰는 주체가 아니라 쓰여지는 대상이므로 수동태인 be expended in으로 고쳐야 한다. 「recommend + that + S + (should) + R」의 어형으로 쓰이기에 ③ 앞에는 should가 생략되어 동사원형을 써야 한다.

① 항구가 선호되는 대상이므로 수동태는 적절하다.

② 숫자 둘의 개념에서 전자는 the former, 후자는 the latter로 표현한다. 천연 항구와 인공 항구 둘의 개념이기에 적절하다.

④는 ①, ②, ③ 중에 오류가 없는 경우 선택한다.

25
[2014 아주대]

We conclude [that brown bears, and perhaps other large mammals, have continuously _____ the archipelago (for at least 40,000 years.)]

① stayed　　　　　　② dwelled

③ been dwelled　　　④ been lived

⑤ inhabited

정답 ⑤

해석 우리는 갈색곰이, 그리고 아마도 다른 거대한 포유류가,
     최소한 4만년 동안 이 군도에 쭉 거주해 온 것으로 결론
     을 내렸습니다.
분석 동사의 어형
     ⑤ inhabit은 타동사로 뒤에 목적어를 받을 수 있어 정답
        으로 적절하다.
     ①, ② 자동사이기 때문에 목적어를 받을 수 없다.
     ③, ④ 자동사이기 때문에 수동태가 불가능하다.

4강 조동사

Practice

01	②	02	④	03	②	04	②	05	④
06	③	07	②	08	③	09	②	10	④
11	④	12	③	13	③	14	③	15	③
16	②	17	④	18	③	19	②	20	③
21	④	22	③	23	②	24	③	25	①

01

[2005 고려대]

①One (of the central and most difficult moral questions) (of our age) is: Do the terminally ill ②has the right (to ③take their own lives) (before they suffer great pain or become ④a burden to others?)

정답 ② (has the right → have the right)

해석 우리 시대의 중요하지만 가장 어려운 도덕적 문제 중 하나는 바로 이것이다. 불치병에 걸린 사람들이 큰 고통을 겪거나 다른 사람들에게 부담이 되기 전에 자살할 권리가 있을까?

분석 주조동사 do의 용법

② 일반동사를 의문문으로 만들 때 「Do/Did/Does + S + R ~?」 형태로 주어 뒤에는 반드시 동사원형이 나와야 하기 때문에 has를 have로 고쳐야 한다.

① 단수동사(is)가 고정되어 있어 단수주어(One)는 적절하다.

③ to R의 형용사적 역할로 앞에 명사(the right)를 수식하여 적절하다.

④ become의 보어로 명사는 적절하고, 명사와 명사의 충돌을 피해 주기 위해 전치사 역시 적절하다.

02

[2010 한국외대]

One (of the ①chief things) (in science) ②is careful observation, (for things (that ③look rather alike) may actually ④very different (when we come ⑤to look closely.))

정답 ④ (very different → be very different)

해석 과학의 주요할 점 중의 하나는 신중한 관찰이다. 그 이유는 제법 유사해 보이는 것들이 자세히 살펴보았을 때 사실은 굉장히 다르기 때문이다.

분석 서법 조동사 may의 용법

④ 조동사(may) 뒤에는 반드시 동사원형(R)이 나와야 하므로 be동사의 원형을 쓴다면 뒤에 형용사(different)도 받을 수 있다.

① 「one of the Ns(복수명사)」가 나와야 하므로 chief things는 적절하다.

② 주어가 단수명사(One)이기에 단수동사(is)의 수 일치가 적절하다.

③ 주격 관계대명사절 속의 동사(look)는 선행사(things)와 수 일치가 되어 적절하다.

⑤ 「come + to R ~」 '~하게 되다'의 표현으로 come은 뒤에 to R를 보어로 받을 수 있다.

03

[2016 국민대]

(As David Cameron was)
(①Keen on green policies,) David Cameron used to ②cycling (to work) (in a variety of ③fetching helmets) (with his brief case following ④by car.)

정답 ② (cycling → cycle)

해석 환경 정책에 관심이 많은 David Cameron은 서류 가방을 차에 실은 채 여러 개의 멋진 헬멧을 돌려가며 쓰고 자전거를 타고 일터에 가곤 했다.

분석 「used to + R ~」(~하곤 했다)

② be동사가 없는 used to는 조동사로 쓰여 반드시 뒤에 동사원형(R)이 나와야 하므로 cycle로 고쳐야 한다.

① 분사구문으로 앞에 As David Cameron was가 생략되어 형용사는 적절하다.

③ fetching은 '멋진, 매력적인'의 뜻을 가진 형용사이다.

④ 전치사 by 뒤에 교통·통신 수단의 명사가 나오면 관사를 쓰지 못하기 때문에 적절하다.

04

[2017 단국대]

(When there is no alternative for a drug,) patients and insurance companies have no choice _____ price a drug-maker set.]

① but to pay

② but to pay [whatever]

③ other than pay whatever

④ other than paying

정답 ②

해석 어떠한 약에 대한 대안이 없을 경우, 환자와 보험 회사는 제약 회사가 정한 가격을 그대로 지불할 수밖에 없다.

분석 「have no choice but + to R」

② 「cannot but + R = cannot help + R-ing = have no choice but + to R」는 '~하지 않을 수 없다'의 표현으로 ③, ④는 탈락되고, 빈칸 뒤 명사(price) 뒤에 또 「주어 + 동사(a drug-maker set)」가 나와 있기에 접속사가 필요하므로 ②가 적절하다. 여기서 whatever 는 복합관계형용사의 용법으로 쓰였다.

05   [2011 경희대]

U.S. marines (① on a recent trip) (to Afghanistan)
  S
② offered medical care (to local women) (in the village of
  V   O
Lakari,) but ③ some of these women said [they would
rather die ④ than being touched by a male doctor.]
             be   O

정답 ④ (than being touched → than be touched)

해석 최근 아프가니스탄으로 파병간 미 해병대원들이 라카리 (Lakari) 마을에 사는 여성들에게 의료 서비스를 제공해 주었지만, 몇몇 여성들은 남자 의사가 몸을 만지게 하느니 차라리 죽는 게 낫다고 말했다.

분석 「would rather A than B」

④ 「would rather A than B」는 'B하느니 A하는 편이 낫 겠다'의 표현으로, 이때 A와 B 자리에는 반드시 동사 원형이 나와야 하므로 being을 be로 고쳐야 한다.

① 명사와 명사의 충돌을 피해 주기 위해 전명구는 적절 하다.

② 뒤에 목적어도 있고 주어(미 해병대원들)가 치료를 제 공하는 주체이므로 능동태는 적절하다.

③ some은 대명사의 역할도 가지고 있어 「of + 한정사 (these) + 명사」를 받아 적절하다.

06   [2011 고려대]

(If there are any barriers to further progress,) then
  부사절   V   S
science _____ (at unprecedented speed) (just
  S   V
before it crashes into them.)
  부사절 S V

① well may to move

② well may be move

③ may well be moving

④ may well to move

정답 ③

해석 더 발전하는 데 있어 장애물이 있다면, 과학은 그러한 어려 움을 겪기 전에 유례없는 속도로 나아가는 것이 당연하다.

분석 「may well R」

③ 「may well R ~」는 '~하는 게 당연하다'의 표현으로 여기서 may well은 하나의 조동사이다. 뒤에 동사원 형을 써야 하므로 ③이 정답으로 적절하다.

07   [2011 이화여대]

(① Sensing the imminent arrival of his infant son,) Dr.
  분사구문   (should)
Frankenstein demanded [that his maid ② disinfected
  S   V   명사절(O) S   V
his house (③ in order to make sure that the baby is well
  O
④ taken care of.)]

정답 ② (disinfected → (should) disinfect)

해석 젖먹이 아들이 곧 도착한다는 것을 느낀 프랑켄슈타인 박 사는 아들을 잘 돌볼 수 있도록 하녀에게 집을 소독하라 고 지시했다.

분석 「demand + that + S + (should) + R」 명령형 동사의 용법

② 명령형 동사(suggest, insist, require, request, recommend, demand, ask, advise, move 등)가 that절을 받을 경우 「demand + that + S + (should) + R ~」와 같이 주어 뒤에 항상 조동사 should가 생 략이 되기 때문에 반드시 동사원형(R)을 써야 하므로 disinfect로 고쳐야 한다. 물론 should를 써도 무방하 지만 문제로 묻는 경우에는 거의 생략을 하고 물어본 다.

① 분사구문으로 쓰여 프랑켄슈타인이 깨닫는 주체이므 로 능동태 분사구문(Sensing)은 적절하다.

③ 「in order to R ~(~하기 위해서)」의 목적의 부사구로 적절하다.

④ 아이가 돌보는 주체가 아니라 돌보아지는 대상이므로 수동태는 적절하고, take care of의 수동태는 be taken care of 뒤에 명사가 불완전해야 한다.

08
[2010 서울여대]

Rey, (①who asked [that neither his last name ②nor his
S   S 형용사절   명사절   S
given name ③was used to protect his and his family's
          be (should)   V
privacy,]) ④grew up (in Chappaqua, the rich Westchester
              V   =
suburb.)

정답 ③ (was used to → (should) be used to)

해석 자신과 가족의 사생활을 보호하기 위해 자신의 성과 이름 모두 사용하지 말아 달라고 요청했던 레이(Rey)는 웨스트체스터(Westchester) 근교의 부촌인 차파쿠어(Chappaqua)에서 성장했다.

분석 「ask + that + S + (should) + R」 명령형 동사의 용법
③ 명령형 동사(suggest, insist, require, request, recommend, demand, ask, advise, move 등)가 that절을 받을 경우 「ask + that + S + (should) + R ~」와 같이 주어 뒤에 항상 조동사 should가 생략이 되기 때문에 반드시 동사원형(R)을 써야 하므로 was를 be로 고쳐야 한다. 물론 should를 써도 무방하지만 문제로 묻는 경우에는 거의 생략을 하고 물어본다.
① 선행사가 사람(Rey)이고 절 속에 주어 자리가 불완전하기에 주격 관계대명사(who)는 적절하다.
② 「neither A nor B」는 등위상관접속사로 상관관계가 적절하다.
④ 주어(Rey)에 대한 동사(grew up)로 쓰여 적절하다.

09
[2011 한국외대]

The yen is weakening. But Tokyo _____ its
S   V   S   V
interest rates again.
O
① dares not raise
② dare not raise
        V
③ does not dare raise
④ dare not to raise

정답 ②

해석 엔화가 약세를 보이고 있지만 오히려 일본은 대담하게 다시 이자율을 올리지 않고 있다.

분석 조동사 dare의 용법
② need, dare는 뒤에 부정어가 있으면 조동사로 쓰여 동사원형이 나와야 한다.
① 조동사일 경우 수 일치를 하지 못한다.
③ 「do/does/did not dare to R ~」와 같이 주조동사를 빌려와 동사 앞에 부정을 하면 일반동사로 쓰여 뒤에 to R가 나와야 한다.
④ need, dare 뒤에 부정어가 나오면 조동사이므로 to R 를 쓰지 못한다.

10
[2011 강남대]

He suggested [that all applicants _____ the
S   V   명사절(O)   S   (should) V₁
forms (at the front desk) and submit them.]
O   V₂   O
① filled out
② be filling out
③ should have filled out
④ fill out

정답 ④

해석 그는 모든 지원자들이 프런트 데스크에 있는 양식에 내용을 기재해 제출해야 한다고 제안했다.

분석 「suggest + that + S + (should) + R」 명령형 동사의 용법
④ 명령형 동사(suggest, insist, require, request, recommend, demand, ask, advise, move 등)가 that절을 받을 경우 「suggest + that + S + (should) + R ~」와 같이 주어 뒤에 항상 조동사 should가 생략이 되기 때문에 반드시 동사원형(R)을 써야 하므로 ④가 정답으로 적절하다. 물론 should를 써도 무방하지만 문제로 묻는 경우에는 거의 생략을 하고 물어본다.
① 동사원형이 나오지 않아 부적절하다.
② 동사원형이 나오긴 했지만 진행을 쓸 이유가 없으므로 부적절하다.
③ should를 써도 되지만 「should + have p.p. ~」는 '~했어야 했는데 …'라는 후회의 뜻이 되어 부적절하다.

11

[2011 상명대]

①The mayor disparaged our efforts (②to beautify the
town square) (by saying [that the flower bed (we had
planted) ③looked somewhat worse than the weeds
④it had replacing.)])

정답 ④ (it had replacing → it had replaced)

해석 시장은 우리가 심었던 화단이 그 자리에 원래 있던 잡초
보다도 오히려 보기 좋지 않다고 말하면서 광장을 미화하
려는 우리의 노력을 폄하했다.

분석 주조동사 have의 용법

④ 주조동사 have/had 뒤에는 반드시 과거분사(p.p.)가
나와야 하므로 replacing을 replaced로 고쳐야 한다.

① 「주어 + 동사」로 쓰여 적절하다.

② effort는 동격의 to R를 받는 명사이기에 적절하다.

③ that절 속에 주어(the flower bed)에 대한 동사로 쓰
였고 look은 오감동사로 형용사(worse)를 보어로 받
아 적절하다.

12

[2012 동덕여대]

(Only ①after the agreement was ②made) did the CEO
③decided [to forgo having his workers ④do mandatory
overtime work.]

정답 ③ (decided to → decide to)

해석 동의가 이루어지자마자 대표 이사(CEO)는 직원들이 의
무적으로 해온 야근을 없애기로 결정했다.

분석 주조동사 do의 용법

③ only after the agreement was made를 문두 강조
하여 도치가 되어 있다. 일반동사를 도치시킬 때 「do/
did/does + S + R ~」의 형태로 도치를 해야 하므로
decided를 decide로 고쳐야 한다.

① Only 뒤에 부사절(after the agreement was made)
을 문두로 끌고 나와 강조를 한 표현으로 적절하다.

② 동의가 이루는 주체가 아니라 이뤄지는 대상이므로 수
동태는 적절하다.

④ having의 have가 사역동사로 목적보어 자리에 동사
원형(do)은 적절하다.

13

[2012 한국항공대]

①Never did I dream [that he made ②such a surprising
suggestion] [that the government ③gives up the bribery
tradition] (which ④has remained for a long period of
time.)

정답 ③ (gives up → give up)

해석 그가 오랫동안 이어져 온 뇌물 주는 관례를 정부 차원에
서 없애야 한다는 놀라운 제안을 할 것이라고는 전혀 상
상도 하지 못했다.

분석 「suggestion + that + S + (should) + R」 명령형 명사
의 용법

③ 명령형 명사(suggestion, requirement, demand,
recommendation, advice 등)가 that절을 받을 경
우 「suggestion + that + S + (should) + R ~」와 같
이 주어 뒤에 항상 조동사 should가 생략이 되기 때
문에 반드시 동사원형(R)을 써야 하므로 gives up을
give up으로 고쳐야 한다. 물론 should를 써도 무방
하지만 문제로 묻는 경우에는 거의 생략을 하고 물어
본다.

① 부정어가 문두에 강조되면 도치가 되어 did I dream
은 적절하다.

② 「such + a/an + 형용사 + 명사 = so + 형용사 + a/an
+ 명사」의 어순으로 쓰여 적절하다.

④ 주격 관계대명사절 속의 동사(has remained)는 선행
사(tradition)에 수 일치하여 적절하다.

14

[2014 동덕여대]

The ①irritable sergeant ②was insistent [that nothing
③supersedes the drilling (of ④the forty new men.)]

정답 ③ (supersedes → supersede)

해석 화가 난 병장은 그 어떤 것도 40명의 신병 훈련을 대신할
수 없다고 주장했다.

분석 「insistent + that + S + (should) + R」 명령형 형용사의
용법

③ 명령형 형용사(necessary, imperative, mandatory,
essential, insistent, urgent 등)가 that절을 받을 경우
「insistent + that + S + (should) + R ~」와 같이 주어
뒤에 항상 조동사 should가 생략이 되기 때문에 반드시
동사원형(R)을 써야 하므로 supersedes를 supersede

로 고쳐야 한다. 물론 should를 써도 무방하지만 문제로 묻는 경우에는 거의 생략을 하고 물어본다.

① 형용사(irritable)가 명사(sergeant)를 수식하여 적절하다.

② 문장의 동사로 쓰여 적절하다.

④ 「관사 + 숫자 + 형용사」의 어순으로 쓰여 적절하다.

15 [2012 아주대]

They planned [to sell luxury T-shirts and shoes] (to coincide with the movie's release,) but Sarah demanded [that the merchandise _____ sold only through her Bitten line.]

① should
② were
③ be
④ being
⑤ are

정답 ③

해석 그들은 그 영화 개봉에 맞춰 비싼 티셔츠와 신발을 판매하려고 계획했다. 하지만 사라(Sarah)는 그 제품을 자신의 비튼(Bitten) 라인을 통해서만 판매해야 한다고 요구했다.

분석 「demand + that + S + (should) + R」 명령형 동사의 용법

③ 명령형 동사(suggest, insist, require, request, recommend, demand, ask, advise, move 등)가 that절을 받을 경우 「demand + that + S + (should) + R ~」와 같이 주어 뒤에 항상 조동사 should가 생략이 되기 때문에 반드시 동사원형(R)을 써야 하므로 ③이 정답으로 적절하다.

① should를 써도 무방하지만 뒤에 동사원형이 나오지 않아 부적절하다.

②, ④, ⑤는 동사원형이 나오지 않아 부적절하다.

16 [2016 한국산업기술대]

I _____ [to be a practicing doctor,] but now I'm more interested (in research).

① was used to want
② used to want
③ used to wanting
④ was used to wanting

정답 ②

해석 나는 과거에 개업 의사가 되고 싶었지만 지금은 연구에 좀 더 관심이 있다.

분석 「used to + R ~」(~하곤 했다)

② 「used to R ~」는 '~하곤 했다'의 표현으로 뒤에 동사원형이 나와야 하므로 적절하다.

① 「S(사람) be used to + N/R-ing」는 '주어(사람)가 명사/동명사에 익숙하다'의 표현으로 이때 to는 전치사로 쓰여 뒤에 동사원형이 나올 수 없다.

③ 「used to + R ~」는 '~하곤 했다'의 표현으로 뒤에 동사원형이 나와야 한다.

④ 문법적으로 틀리진 않으나 '나는 개업 의사가 되기를 원하는 것에 익숙하다'의 의미가 되어 부적절하다.

17 [2012 인천대]

A: Did you criticize his mistake?

B: Yes, but _____ it.

① I'd not rather do
② I'd rather not to do
③ I'd rather not doing
④ I'd rather not have done

정답 ④

해석 A: 네가 그의 실수를 비난했어?
      B: 응, 근데 비난하지 말걸 그랬어.

분석 「조동사 + have p.p.」의 의미

④ 「should + have p.p. = would + rather have p.p.」는 '~했어야 했는데 … (안 했다)'의 의미이고, 「should not have p.p. = would rather not have p.p.」는 '~하지 말았어야 했는데 …(했다)'의 의미이다. 그의 실수를 비난했냐 물었을 때 '응'이라고 했지만 but이 있으니 후회의 표현인 ④가 적절하다.

① 과거의 후회 표현이 아니라서 부적절하다.

② would rather은 조동사로 뒤에 동사원형이 와야 한다.

③ would rather은 조동사로 뒤에 동사원형이 와야 한다.

18 [2009 광운대]

The professor requested [that the student _____ his paper as soon as possible.]

① should finish to write

② should finish the writing

③ finish writing

④ finishes writing

⑤ finished writing

정답 ③

해석 교수는 학생으로 하여금 가능한 빨리 논문 쓰는 것을 마치라고 요구했다.

분석 명령형 동사의 용법 / finish의 어형

③ 명령형 동사(suggest, insist, require, request, recommend, demand, ask, advise, move 등)가 that절을 받을 경우 「request + that + S + (should) + R ~」와 같이 주어 뒤에 항상 조동사 should가 생략이 되기 때문에 반드시 동사원형(R)을 써야 하므로 ④, ⑤는 탈락되고 finish는 동명사를 목적어로 받는 동사이기에 ③이 적절하다.

① finish는 동명사(R-ing)를 목적어로 받기에 to write은 부적절하다.

② should를 쓰는 것은 상관없지만 동명사 앞에 정관사(the)는 오지 못한다.

19

[2008 총신대]

They couldn't but _____ (at the funny scene.)
S   V

① laughing   ② laugh

③ laughed   ④ to laugh

정답 ②

해석 그들은 웃긴 장면을 보고 웃지 않을 수 없었다.

분석 「cannot but + R ~」

② 「cannot but + R = cannot help + R-ing = have no choice but + to R」는 '~하지 않을 수 없다'의 표현으로 동사원형(laugh)이 나온 ②가 정답으로 적절하다.

20

[2009 영남대]

① It is mandatory [② that a registered student
  가S   진S   S
③maintains his or her GPA ④of B⁺ (in the major field.)]
(should) V   O

정답 ③ (maintains → maintain)

해석 소속 학생이 전공 분야에서 B⁺ 성적을 유지해야 하는 것은 필수적이다.

분석 「mandatory + that + S + (should) + R」 명령형 형용사의 용법 / 가주어(It) ~ 진주어(that절)

③ 명령형 형용사(necessary, imperative, mandatory, essential, insistent, urgent 등)가 that절을 받을 경우 「mandatory + that + S + (should) + R ~」와 같이 주어 뒤에 항상 조동사 should가 생략이 되기 때문에 반드시 동사원형(R)을 써야 하므로 maintains를 maintain으로 고쳐야 한다. 물론 should를 써도 무방하지만 문제로 묻는 경우에는 거의 생략을 하고 물어본다.

①, ② 「It(가주어) is ~ that절(진주어) ....」의 형태로 쓰여 적절하다.

④ 명사와 명사의 충돌을 피해 주기 위해 전치사는 적절하다.

21

[2007 총신대]

She worked very hard (so that she _____ pass
S   V   부사절   S   V
the entrance exam.)
                O

① will   ② shall

③ may   ④ could

정답 ④

해석 그녀는 입학시험에 합격하기 위해 열심히 공부했다.

분석 so that절 이하 조동사의 현재형과 과거형의 구분

④ so that이 붙어 나와 절 속에 조동사가 쓰일 경우 주절 동사의 시제와 맞춰 써야 한다. 주절 동사가 과거(worked)이므로 so that절 이하 조동사도 과거형(could)으로 쓰인 ④가 정답으로 적절하다.

①, ②, ③ 조동사의 현재형으로 쓰여 부적절하다.

22

[2008 총신대]

                              (should)
Some students moved [that Kim _____ elected
  S   V   명사절 S   V
the next chair.]
              (O)

① will be   ② was

③ be   ④ had been

정답 ③

해석 몇몇 학생들이 김 군을 차기 의장으로 선출해야만 한다고 제안했다.

분석 「move + that + S + (should) + R」 명령형 동사의 용법

③ 명령형 동사(suggest, insist, require, request, recommend, demand, ask, advise, move 등)가 that절을 받을 경우 「move + that + S + (should) + R ~」와 같이 주어 뒤에 항상 조동사 should가 생략이 되기 때문에 반드시 동사원형(R)을 써야 하므로 ③이 정답으로 적절하다. 물론 should를 써도 무방하지만 문제로 묻는 경우에는 거의 생략을 하고 물어본다.

③ 이 문제는 소거법으로 풀어내는 것이 좋다. 「If + S + Vs(현재)」의 형태로 왔기 때문에 가정법 과거와 가정법 과거완료인 ①, ②는 탈락되고 ③, ④로 좁혀진다. 여기서 빈칸 앞에 in the past라는 과거 시점이 있으므로 조동사 뒤에 have p.p.를 써야 과거를 나타내므로 ③이 정답으로 적절하다.

23

[2000 단국대]

The scientists could not ①help ②but [talking about the
                 S   V
success ③of the Voyager missions ④among themselves.]
               O

정답 ② (but talking → talking)

해석 과학자들은 보이저호의 임무를 성공한 것에 대해 자기들끼리 얘기할 수밖에 없었다.

분석 「cannot help + R-ing」

    ② 「cannot but + R = cannot help + R-ing = have no choice but + to R」는 '~하지 않을 수 없다'의 표현으로 could not help가 나온 것으로 보아 but talking을 talking으로 고쳐야 한다.

    ① 「cannot help + R-ing」의 용법으로 쓰여 적절하다.

    ③ 명사와 명사의 충돌을 피해 주기 위해 전치사는 적절하다.

    ④ among themselves는 '자기들끼리'라는 표현으로 적절하다.

24

[2006 경희대]

(If the universe is expanding,) then (in the past) it
   부사절   S   V   S
_____ now.
  V

① would have been smaller than it is

② would be smaller than it is

③ must have been smaller than it is

④ must be smaller than it is

정답 ③

해석 만약 우주가 팽창하고 있다면 과거의 우주는 지금보다 더 작았음에 틀림없다.

분석 「조동사 + have p.p.」의 용법

25

[2009 동덕여대]

A: I am surprised that John didn't return your call.

B: He _____ not have gotten my message.

① must   ② could

③ should   ④ ought

정답 ①

해석 A: 나는 존이 너의 전화에 회신하지 않았다는 사실에 놀랐어.

    B: 그가 메시지를 받지 못했음에 틀림없어.

분석 「조동사 + have p.p.」의 용법

    ① 「must + have p.p. ~」는 '과거에 ~했음에 틀림없다'라는 표현으로 의미상 ①이 적절한 표현이다.

5강 가정법

Practice

01	②	02	②	03	①	04	②	05	②
06	②	07	③	08	④	09	④	10	③
11	④	12	④	13	④	14	④	15	③
16	③	17	④	18	①	19	①	20	①
21	①	22	①	23	④	24	③	25	⑤

01

[2011 동덕여대]

(If the convenience store provided more various products,) the residents _____ shopping more often.

① will go
② would go
③ went
④ would have gone

정답 ②

해석 만약 편의점이 좀 더 다양한 상품을 판매한다면, 주민들이 더 자주 물건을 사러 갔을 것이다.

분석 가정법 과거의 시제

② 가정법 과거 「If + S + Ved/were ~, S + would/ should/could/might + R ...」 형태로 ②가 정답으로 적절하다.

02

[2013 성균관대]

(① In the mid-19th century,) (if you ② wanted [to have a scientific fight,]) you could have ③ picked no better subject ④ than paleontology.

정답 ② (wanted → had wanted)

해석 19세기 중반, 당신이 과학적 투쟁을 하길 원했다면 고생물학보다 더 나은 주제를 선택하지는 못했을 것이다.

분석 가정법 과거완료의 시제

② 가정법 과거완료 「If + S + had p.p. ~ , S + would/ should/could/might have p.p. ...」의 형태로 쓰인 것을 주절 동사(could have picked)를 보아 알 수 있다. wanted를 had wanted로 고쳐야 한다.

① 「in the 세기」에서 전치사는 in을 써야 한다.

③ 이미 앞에 could have까지 나와 있어 p.p. 형태는 적절하다.

④ 앞에 비교급(better)이 있어 than은 적절하다.

03

[2015 숙명여대]

(If I ① was [were] in his place,) I ② would be very much ③ concerned (about the future) and would certainly be ④ taking steps (to improve my situation.)

정답 ① (was → were)

해석 만일 내가 그의 상황이라면, 나는 미래에 대해 엄청나게 걱정했을 것이고, 내가 처한 상황을 개선하기 위한 조치를 확실히 취했을 것이다.

분석 If + S + were (O) / If + S + was (X)

① If절 속에 be동사의 과거형은 주어의 수와 상관없이 were을 써야 한다. was를 were로 고쳐야 한다.

② 가정법 과거 「If + S + Ved/were ~, S + would/ should/could/might + R ...」 형태로 적절하다.

③ be concerned about ~ : '~대해 걱정하다'의 표현으로 적절하다.

④ 내가 조치를 취하는 주체이므로 능동태는 적절하다.

04

[2013 경희대]

= If the former President had not endorsed

(Had the former President not endorsed him during the last campaign,) the first-time presidential candidate _____ lost the election (by a narrow margin.)

① could not have
② might have
③ shall have
④ ought to have

정답 ②

해석 만약 마지막 선거 운동 기간 동안 전 대통령이 그를 지지하지 않았었다면, 처음으로 대통령 후보가 된 사람은 아슬아슬하게 선거에서 떨어졌을 것이다.

분석 가정법 과거완료의 도치

② Had the former President not endorsed = If the former President had not endorsed의 가정법 과

거완료의 도치된 표현이기에 주절에는 「would/should/could/might + have p.p.」의 형태가 와야 하므로 ③, ④는 탈락된다. ①, ②는 의미 차이를 묻고 있는데 '전직 대통령이 그를 지지하지 않았었더라면'이라는 문맥을 토대로 '처음 대선에 나간 후보자는 떨어졌을 텐데'라는 의미가 나와야 하기에 부정어가 없는 ②가 정답으로 적절하다.

05

부사절
(If my boss _____) (while I'm out,) please tell
      S   V   부사절   R
her [that I'll be back] (as soon as I finish [interviewing
I.O   D.O   부사절   S   V   O
the candidates.])

① call   ② should call
③ will call   ④ called

정답 ②

해석 만약 제가 밖에 있는 동안 사장님이 전화하시면, 후보자 인터뷰가 끝나자마자 돌아오겠다고 말해 주세요.

분석 가정법 미래의 시제
  ② 가정법 미래 「If + S + should + R ~, S + will/would + R ...」, 「If + S + should R ~, R ...(명령문)」의 형태로 쓰여 ②가 정답으로 적절하다.
  ① 주어와 동사의 수 일치가 되어 있지 않아 부적절하다.
  ③ 시간 · 조건(if)의 부사절에서 will은 절대 쓰지 못한다.
  ④ 「If + S + Ved」를 쓰게 되면 가정법 과거의 형태로 주절은 「S + would/should/could/might + R」의 형태가 되어야 한다.

06

(If today I lived in a Communist country) (where certain
부사절 S   V   형용사절
principles (dear to the Christian faith) are suppressed,)
S   V
_____ that country's antireligious laws.]
                         O

① I will openly advocate disobeying
② I would openly advocate [disobeying
                 V
③ I will have openly advocated disobeying
④ I would have openly advocated disobeying

정답 ②

해석 만약 내가 지금 기독교 신앙에 어떤 중요한 원리가 억압받는 공산주의 국가에 산다면 그 국가의 반종교법에 대한 불복종을 공개적으로 옹호했을 것이다.

분석 가정법 과거의 시제
  ② 가정법 과거 「If + S + Ved/were ~, S + would/should/could/might + R ...」 형태로 ②가 정답으로 적절하다.
  ①, ③ 조동사의 현재형이 나와 부적절하다.
  ④ 가정법 과거완료 형태이다.

07

(If qualitatively diverse products were to be offered on
부사절   S   V
one-dimensional consumers,) (incapable of absorbing
                            (who are)
the diversity,) consumption _____ be limited.
                 S   V

① will   ② can
③ would   ④ shall

정답 ③

해석 만약 다양성을 받아들일 수 없는 1차원적인 소비자에게 질적으로 다양한 제품들이 제공된다면, 오히려 소비는 제한될 것이다.

분석 가정법 과거의 시제
  ③ 가정법 과거 「If + S + Ved/were ~, S + would/should/could/might + R ...」 형태로 주절에는 조동사의 과거형이 나와야 하므로 ③이 정답으로 적절하다.

08

                    (that)
The author _____ [her article was so controversial]
    S   O
(had it not been for the spate of correspondence.)
= if it had not been
① would never think
② have never thought
③ have never been thought
④ would never have thought

정답 ④

해석 만약 수많은 편지가 오지 않았었더라면 그 작가는 자신의 기사가 그렇게 논란이 되고 있다는 것을 생각도 못했었을 것이다.

분석 가정법 과거완료의 도치
  ④ 빈칸 뒤 「had it not been for ~ = if it had not been for ~」는 가정법 과거완료의 도치된 표현이다. 주절에는 「S + would/should/could/might + have

46 _에듀윌 편입 솔루션 문법 Basic

p.p. ~」의 형태가 나와야 하므로 ④가 정답으로 적절하다.

09
[2013 가천대]

부사절
(If you _____ English harder (when you were
 S   V   O   부사절   S   V
young,)) now you could speak English better.
  C   S   V   O

① had been studying

② studied

③ should have studied

④ had studied

정답 ④

해석 만약 네가 어렸을 때 더 열심히 영어를 공부했었더라면 지금 너는 영어를 더 잘할 수 있었을 것이다.

분석 가정법 혼합의 시제

④ 가정법 혼합 「If + S + had p.p. ~, S + would/should/could/might + R + now/today(현재 시점)」의 형태로 쓰인 문장이다. 주절의 동사만 보면 ②로 착각할 수 있지만, if절 안에 과거 시점(when you were ~)을 단서로 주고 있다. if절 속에서는 시제를 한 단계 이전으로 당겨쓰기 때문에 과거 시점이 있다면 한 단계 당겨서 과거완료를 써야 하므로 ④가 정답으로 적절하다.

① 과거완료까지는 좋았지만 '젊었을 때'라는 정확한 시점이 왔기에 진행은 부적절하다.

10
[2013 고려대]

(_____ empirical evidence to support his views and to finding ways to test them statistically,) his influence (on economics) would have been greater.
                                                     S   V   C

① If he devoted much effort to gather

② Did he devoted more effort to gather

③ Had he devoted more effort to gathering
   = If he had devoted

④ If he had devoted much effort gathering

정답 ③
* devote A to B: A를 B에 바치다, 전념[헌신]하다

해석 만약 그가 자신의 견해를 뒷받침할 수 있는 경험에 의한 증거를 수집하고 그 견해를 통계적으로 검증할 수 있는 방법을 찾는 데에 더 많은 노력을 기울였었더라면, 경제학에 끼치는 그의 영향력이 훨씬 더 컸을 것이다.

분석 가정법 과거완료의 시제 / devote의 어형

③ 주절 동사(would have been)를 보아 가정법 과거완료를 써야 한다는 것을 유추할 수 있다. 이때 가능한 것은 「If + S + had p.p. ~ = Had + S + p.p. ~」의 형태이므로 이에 해당하는 보기는 ③, ④로 좁혀진다. ③과 ④의 차이는 전치사 to의 유무인데 「devote A to B」의 형태로 쓰이므로 ③이 정답으로 적절하다.

11
[2013 세종대]

(_____,) I would take them (on a night
                        S   V   O
cruise on the river.)

① If I have been asked to take visitors on a tour of my city

② If I would be asked to take visitors on a tour of my city

③ If I had asked to take visitors on a tour of my city

④ If I were asked to take visitors on a tour of my city
   부사절
   S   V   O.C

정답 ④

해석 만약 내가 여행객을 데리고 안내하기를 요구받으면, 여행객들로 하여금 강에서 야간 유람선을 타게 할 것이다.

분석 가정법 과거의 시제

④ 가정법 과거 「If + S + Ved/were ~, S + would/should/could/might + R ...」의 형태를 묻고 있다. 주절 동사(would take)를 단서로 잡아 「If + S + Ved」 형태를 찾으면 ④가 정답으로 적절하다.

12
[2013 세종대]

(_____,) my sister would not have been
                        S   V
able to live out her dream (as a prominent fashion
                    O
designer today.)

① If it was not an open admission policy

② If there has not been for an open admission policy

③ If it would not have been for an open admission policy

④ (If it had not been for an open admission policy)
   부사절

정답 ④

해석 만약 개방적인 입학 정책이 없었더라면 나의 누이는 오늘날 저명한 패션 디자이너로서의 꿈을 실현하지 못했을 것이다.

분석　가정법 과거완료의 시제

④ 가정법 과거완료 「If + S + had p.p. ~, S + would/should/could/might + have p.p. ...」의 형태를 묻고 있다. 주절 동사(would not have been)를 단서로 잡아 「If + S + had p.p.」 형태로 쓰인 ④가 정답으로 적절하다.

13

I felt (_____ I were living two people's lives.)
S　V　부사절　　　　　　　S　　V　　　　　O
① although　　　　　　　② even though
③ even if　　　　　　　　④ as if

정답　④

해석　나는 마치 두 사람의 삶을 사는 것인 양 느껴졌다.

분석　가정법으로 쓰일 수 있는 접속사의 선택

④ 빈칸 뒤 주어가 I임에도 동사가 were가 나온 것으로 보아 빈칸에는 가정법과 연관된 접속사가 필요하다는 것을 알 수 있다. 보기 중 ④가 유일하게 가정법과 연관된 접속사이다.

14

The French philosopher Pascal remarks [① that
　　　　　　　　S　　　　　　　　V　　　　　명사절(O)
seemingly trivial occurrences (we might not even be
　　　　　　　　S　　　　　　(that)
aware ② of) ③ affect geopolitical event.] He famously
　　　∅　　　　V　　　　　　　　　　S
wrote, ["(Cleopatra's nose, ④ were it been shorter,) the
V　　　　　　　　　　　　　　had
　　　　　　　　　　　= if it had been
whole face (of the world) would have been changed."]
　　S　　　　　　　　　　　V

정답　④ (were → had)

해석　프랑스 철학자 파스칼(Pascal)은 우리가 심지어 인식하지 못한 겉보기에는 사소한 것처럼 보이는 사건들이 지정학적인 사건들에 영향을 미친다고 말한다. 그는, '클레오파트라(Cleopatra)의 코가 조금만 낮았더라면 세계사의 모든 국면이 바뀌었을 것이다.'라고 유명한 글을 남겼다.

분석　가정법 과거완료의 도치

④ 마지막 행 주절 동사(would have been)를 보아 가정법 과거완료의 형태가 쓰여야 한다. 「Were + S ~ = If + S + were ~」는 가정법 과거의 형태이므로 시제가 맞지 않는다. were를 had로 고쳐야 한다.

① that절은 remarks의 목적어로 쓰여 적절하다.

② 구조 분석에서 보이듯이 we 앞에 목적격 관계대명사

that이 생략되어 전치사 of의 목적어 자리가 불완전한 형태로 적절하다.

③ that절 속에 주어(trivial occurrences)에 대한 동사(affect)로 쓰여 수 일치가 적절하다.

15

부사절
(If I had been the CEO,) I _____ the company
S　V　　　　　C　　　S　　　V₁　　　　　　O
and hired more staff.
(would have) V₂　O
① restructured
② would restructure
③ would have restructured
④ would have been restructured

정답　③

해석　만약 내가 CEO였다면, 그 회사를 구조 조정하여 더 많은 직원들을 고용했을 것이다.

분석　가정법 과거완료의 시제

③ 가정법 과거완료 「If + S + had p.p. ~, S + would/should/could/might + have p.p. ...」의 형태를 묻고 있다. ③, ④의 형태가 가능한데 능동태와 수동태를 묻고 있다. 빈칸 뒤에 목적어(the company)가 있기에 능동인 ③이 정답으로 적절하다.

16

The security (of England) depends (on (gentlemen) [being
　　S　　　　　　　　　　V　　　ⓟ　　의미상 주어
allowed to live peaceably in their homes as decent
landlords and masters.]) (_____ the aristocrats
동명사구　　　　　　　　　　　　　　　　　　　S
(of France) followed our example,) they would not have
　　　　　　p.p.　　　　　　　　　　S　　　　V
found themselves severed at the neck.
　　　O　　　O.C
① If　　　　　　　　　　② Unless
③ Had　　　　　　　　　④ With

정답　③

해석　영국의 안보는 그들의 고향에서 존경받는 지주와 주인으로써 평화롭게 사는 것이 허락된 신사에게 의존하고 있다. 만일 프랑스의 귀족들이 우리 영국 귀족의 예를 따랐다면, 그들의 목이 잘리지는 않았을 것이다.

분석　가정법 과거완료의 도치

③ 가정법 과거완료 「If + S + had p.p. ~, S + would/should/could/might + have p.p. ...」의 도치 형태

를 묻고 있다. 마지막 행 주절 동사(would not have found)를 보아 가정법 과거완료(If + S + had p.p. ~ = Had + S + p.p. ~)의 형태가 쓰여야 하므로 ③이 적절하다.

①, ② 가정법 과거의 형태가 되어 주절에 「S + would + R ~」의 형태가 나와야 하므로 부적절하다.

④ 전치사 뒤에 주어, 동사는 나올 수 없다.

분석 가정법 과거완료의 도치

① 가정법 과거완료 「If + S + had p.p. ~, S + would/ should/could/might + have p.p. ...」의 도치 형태를 묻고 있다. 주절 동사(would not have been)를 보아 「If + S + had p.p. ~ = Had + S + p.p. ~」 형태가 나와야 하는데 이 조건을 충족하는 ①이 정답으로 적절하다.

---

17 [2017 아주대]

부사절
(If sales had not improved,) we _____ to
  S   V   S   V
consider [selling the company last year.]
             O

① have
② will have
③ will have had
④ would have had
⑤ would have been had

정답 ④

해석 만약 매출이 나아지지 않았더라면, 우리는 작년에 회사 매각을 고려했을 것이다.

분석 가정법 과거완료 / 능동태와 수동태의 구분

④ 가정법 과거완료 「If + S + had p.p. ~, S + would/ should/could/might + have p.p. ...」의 형태를 묻고 있다. ④, ⑤의 형태가 가능한데 have는 수동태를 쓰지 못하는 동사이므로 ④가 정답으로 적절하다.

---

19 [2011 단국대]

(It seems [that few businessmen participated in the
 가S   진S   S   V
charity ball for the street children;] (otherwise,) more
                                          ad   S
money _____.
          V

① would have been raised
② was being raised
③ had been raised
④ might have been raising

정답 ①

해석 거리의 가난한 아이들을 위한 자선 무도회에 사업가들이 거의 참여하지 않은 것 같다. 그렇지 않았더라면, 더 많은 돈이 모금되었을 것이다.

분석 otherwise의 용법 / 능동태와 수동태의 구분

① otherwise는 직설법과 가정법을 혼용하여 쓰는 접속사이다. 빈칸에는 조동사의 과거형이 나와야 하기 때문에 ①, ④로 좁혀지고, 돈이 모금하는 주체가 아니라 모금되는 대상이므로 수동태인 ①이 정답으로 적절하다.

---

18 [2016 서울여대]

The travels (of Marco Polo) (in the twelfth century)
    S
would not have been so well known (_____ for
        V
the book he wrote while in jail.)

① had it not been = if it had not been
② it had not been
③ were it not
④ it were not

정답 ①

해석 만약 마르코 폴로(Marco Polo)가 감옥에 있는 동안 저술한 책이 없었더라면, 그가 했던 12세기의 여행은 그렇게 널리 알려지지 않았을 것이다.

---

20 [2011 가천대]

                         (that)
Years later, she said, [(had her father told me the truth,)
              S   V   = if her father had told
I _____ a much better girl.]
S   V   O

① could have been
② can have been
③ will have been
④ had been

정답 ①

해석 몇 년 뒤에, 만약 그녀의 아버지가 나에게 진실을 말했더라면, 내가 훨씬 더 나은 여자아이가 되었을 것이라고 그녀는 말했다.

분석 가정법 과거완료의 도치

① 가정법 과거완료 「If + S + had p.p. ~, S + would/should/could/might + have p.p. ....」의 도치 형태를 묻고 있다. 「If + S + had p.p. ~ = Had + S + p.p. ~」의 형태이므로 주절에는 조동사의 과거형 뒤에 have p.p.가 나와야 한다.

21

[2011 국민대]

I ①would buy this fancy ②furniture yesterday, (③had I had enough cash ④on hand.)

> have bought (위 ①)
> S · V · O
> = if I had had

정답 ① (would buy → would have bought)

해석 만약 내가 수중에 충분한 현금이 있었다면, 어제 그 화려한 가구를 구입했을 것이다.

분석 가정법 과거완료의 도치

① 가정법 과거완료 「If + S + had p.p. ~, S + would/should/could/might + have p.p. ....」의 도치 형태를 묻고 있다. had I had의 원래 문장은 if I had had의 형태이기 때문에 주절에는 조동사의 과거형 뒤에 have p.p.가 나와야 하므로 would buy를 would have bought로 고쳐야 한다. 혹 ③을 if I로 고쳐야 한다고 생각할 수 있지만 이미 주절에 yesterday라는 과거 시점부사가 있기 때문에 가정법의 주절에서 과거 시점이 있다면 조동사의 과거형 뒤에 have p.p.를 써야 한다.

② furniture는 절대 불가산명사(집합적 물질명사)이므로 a/an 혹은 복수형을 쓰지 못하므로 적절하다.

③ 가정법 과거완료의 도치 형태이므로 적절하다.

④ 명사와 명사의 충돌을 피해 주기 위해 전명구는 적절하다.

22

[2012 경기대]

I often found myself regretting my own existence, and
S · V · O · O.C

wishing myself dead; and (_____ the hope of
O.C · O · O.C

being free), (I have no doubt but that) I should have
삽입절 · S · V

killed myself.
O

① but for = if it had not been for

② unless

③ concerning

④ no less than

정답 ①

해석 나는 종종 내 자신의 존재에 대해 후회했고, 내가 죽었으면 좋겠다고 생각했다. 만약 자유로워질 희망이 없었더라면, 나는 분명히 자살했을 것이다.

분석 if it had not been for의 대용어구 but for

① 「if it had not been for N = but for / without N」의 형태로 대체할 수 있는데 이 부분을 묻고 있다. 주절에 should have killed를 보아 가정법 과거완료 if it had not been for의 대용어구인 but for가 정답으로 적절하다.

23

[2012 가톨릭대]

(_____ I visited the company earlier,) I could
= If I had visited · S

have obtained enormous help (from lots of different
V · O

sectors of its management.)

① Since   ② If

③ Unless   ④ Had

정답 ④

해석 만약 내가 그 회사를 좀 더 일찍 방문했더라면, 나는 많은 경영 지원 부서로부터 엄청난 도움을 받을 수 있었을 것이다.

분석 가정법 과거완료의 도치

④ 가정법 과거완료 「If + S + had p.p. ~, S + would/should/could/might + have p.p. ....」의 도치 형태를 묻고 있다. 「If + S + had p.p. ~ = Had + S + p.p. ~」의 형태이므로 주절 동사(could have obtained)를 보아 가정법 과거완료의 도치 형태인 ④가 정답으로 적절하다.

24

[2012 단국대]

(On Sunday afternoon,) John planted flowers (in his
S · V · O · 부사절

garden by himself.) He might _____ $350 (if he
S · V · O · S

had hired someone to do the job.)
V · O

① paying   ② be paid

③ have paid   ④ have been paid

정답 ③

해석 일요일 오후에, 존(John)은 정원에 직접 꽃을 심었다. 만약 그가 그 일을 할 사람을 고용했었더라면, 아마 350달러는 지불했을 것이다.

분석 가정법 과거완료의 시제

③ 가정법 과거완료 「If + S + had p.p. ~, S + would/
should/could/might + have p.p. ...」의 형태를 묻
고 있다. if he had hired를 보아 주절에 조동사의 과
거형 뒤에 have p.p.가 나와야 하므로 ③, ④로 좁혀
진다. 빈칸 뒤 목적어($350)가 있기 때문에 능동태인
③이 정답으로 적절하다.

25
[2012 숙명여대]

An insurance company might send investigators (to
      S   V   O
determine the cause of a mysterious fire.) (If the

investigators sent back a report [that the fire was
      S   V   O   S   동격
caused by the presence of oxygen in the atmosphere,])
  V
they would not keep their jobs very long. And yet they
  S   V   O
would be right. (Had there been no oxygen present,)
                = If there had been
there _____ no fire.
        V   S

① has been   ② is

③ will be   ④ would be

⑤ would have been

정답 ⑤

해석 보험 회사는 원인을 알 수 없는 화재의 조사를 위해서 조
사관을 파견할 수 있다. 만일 조사관들이 공기 중의 산소
의 존재에 의해서 화재가 일어났다는 보고서를 보낸다면,
그들은 직업을 오래 유지하지 못할 것이다. 하지만 그들
이 옳은 점도 있다. 만약 산소가 없었다면 화재는 없었을
것이다.

분석 가정법 과거완료의 도치

⑤ 가정법 과거완료 「If + S + had p.p. ~, S + would/
should/could/might + have p.p. ...」의 도치 형태
를 묻고 있다. 「If + S + had p.p. ~ = Had + S + p.
p. ~」의 형태이므로 Had there been을 보고 가정법
과거완료라는 것을 파악할 수 있다. 가정법 과거완료
의 형태인 ⑤가 정답으로 적절하다.

6강 부정사

Practice

01	②	02	④	03	④	04	④	05	④
06	②	07	④	08	②	09	④	10	④
11	②	12	③	13	③	14	④	15	①
16	②	17	③	18	④	19	④	20	④
21	④	22	④	23	③	24	②	25	②

01
[2011 서울여대]

Cellphones, (① which are usually ② used to helping people keep track of each other,) are ③ starting [to take on quite a different function] — [helping users ④ hide their whereabouts.]

정답 ② (used to helping → used to help)

해석 주로 서로의 소식을 계속하여 듣기 위해 쓰이던 휴대 전화가 사용자들의 행방을 감추는 완전히 다른 용도로 쓰이기 시작하고 있다.

분석 「S(사물) + be used to R ~」의 용법

② 「S(사물) + be used to R ~」는 '주어가 ~하기 위해 사용되다', 「S(사람) + be used to + N/R-ing」는 '주어가 N/R-ing에 익숙하다', are used to의 주어가 사물(Cellphones)이므로 used to help로 고쳐야 한다.

① 선행사가 사물이고 절 이하의 성분이 불완전하여 관계대명사 which는 적절하다.

③ start는 to R와 R-ing를 둘 다 목적어로 받을 수 있다.

④ 「help + O + (to) R ~」 help는 목적보어 자리에 to R를 써도 되고 to를 생략해도 된다.

02
[2011 인천대]

George _____ improve his test score,] but he did not have enough time to study.

① knew
② knew how that
③ knew how
④ knew [how to

정답 ④

해석 조지는 시험 성적을 향상시킬 수 있는 법을 알았지만 공부를 할 충분한 시간이 없었다.

분석 know의 어형

④ 「know + to R ~(X)」, 「know + 의문사 + to R ~(O)」의 형태로 쓰인다. know는 to R를 목적어로 받을 수 없고, 「의문사 + to R」를 목적어로 받는 것은 가능하다. 「의문사 + to R」는 항상 '명사'이다.

① know 뒤에 동사원형이 나올 수 없다.

② 「know + 의문사 + to R」는 가능하지만 「know + 의문사 + that」은 부적절하다.

③ 「know + 의문사 + to R」는 가능하지만 R은 부적절하다.

03
[2013 경기대]

(When ① it comes to the economic expansion,) the 1990s ② was a very special period (③ that is unlikely ④ to repeat for a while in recorded American history.)

정답 ④ (to repeat → to be repeated)

해석 경제 성장에 관해서 1990년대는 미국 역사에 한동안 다시 일어나지 않을 것 같은 굉장히 특별한 시기였다.

분석 부정사의 태(to R / to be p.p.)

④ 특별한 시기(a special period)가 반복하는 주체가 아니라 반복되는 대상이므로 수동태 부정사(to be repeated)로 고쳐야 한다.

① when it comes to ~: '~에 관하여'라는 표현으로 이 경우 it은 뜻이 없는 대명사이다.

② 주어가 '1990년대'라는 단수이므로 수 일치는 적절하다. 연대를 쓰려면 숫자 뒤에 -s를 붙여야 하고 복수가 아닌 단수 취급한다.

③ 관계대명사 that은 선행사의 종류(사람, 사물)와 격(주격, 목적격)과 상관없이 쓸 수 있다.

04
[2016 경기대]

You may ① well have misunderstandings (about forgiveness) ② that ③ lead you to ④ rejecting it out of hand.)

정답 ④ (rejecting → reject)

해석 당신은 당연하게도 용서에 대해 오해하고 있을 것이며, 그러한 오해는 당신이 용서를 고민 없이 거부하게 만든다.

분석 「lead + O + to R」의 어형

④ 「lead + O + to R ~」 5형식 동사의 어형으로 쓰여 여기서 to는 부정사이므로 동사원형(reject)으로 고쳐야 한다.

① may well R ~ : '~하는 게 당연하다'의 뜻으로 쓰이는 조동사이다.

② 관계대명사 that은 선행사의 종류(사람, 사물)와 격(주격, 목적격)과 상관없이 쓸 수 있다.

③ 주격 관계대명사절 속의 동사(lead)는 선행사(misunderstanding)와 수 일치하여 적절하다. 여기서 선행사를 forgiveness와 misunderstandings 중 구분하는 것은 해석으로 해야 한다. 오해가 당신으로 하여금 용서하는 것을 거부하게 만드는 것이므로 수 일치는 적절하다.

05

[2013 서울여대]

(By 1901) there were **enough** automobiles (on New York's roadways) _____ the state to rule [that they had to be registered.]

① caused

② would cause

③ causing

④ **to cause**

정답 ④

해석 1901년에 들어 뉴욕 도로의 많은 차들은 주에서 자동차 등록이라는 규정을 만들게 하였다.

분석 「enough + to R」의 용법

④ enough는 뒤에서 준동사로 부연 설명을 하는 경우 반드시 부정사(to R)로 하기 때문에 ①, ②, ③은 탈락되고 ④가 적절하다.

06

[2014 상명대]

(① In order ② to be not late for the flight and ③ have ④ enough time for breakfast,) I suggest ⑤ [getting up at five in the morning.]

정답 ② (to be not → not to be)

해석 비행기 시간에 늦지 않고, 아침을 먹을 수 있는 충분한 시간을 가지기 위해 나는 아침 5시에 일어날 것을 제안한다.

분석 부정사(to R)의 부정어 위치

② to R의 부정은 반드시 to 앞에 위치해야 하므로 not to be로 고쳐야 한다.

① in order to R ~ : '~하기 위해서'라는 목적을 나타내는 표현이다.

③ to be and (to) have의 병치로 적절하다. to R를 and로 연결하는 경우 to는 얼마든지 생략이 가능하다.

④ enough가 명사를 수식할 때 위치는 명사 앞, 명사 뒤에 모두 쓰일 수 있다.

⑤ suggest가 준동사를 목적어로 받을 경우 동명사(R-ing)를 받아 적절하다.

07

[2013 서울여대]

Some people say [it's asking **too** little of Rio _____ man-made structures to represent the city's aspirations.]]

① expects

② has expected

③ is expected

④ [to expect]

정답 ④

해석 몇몇 사람들은 인간이 짓는 건물들로 리우의 열망을 나타내도록 하는 것은 그 도시에게 너무 과소하게 요구하는 것이라 말한다.

분석 「too ~ to R ...」의 용법

④ '너무 ~하여 ...할 수 없다, ...하기에 너무 ~하다'라는 뜻의 「too + 형용사/부사 + to R ...」 용법으로 ④가 적절하다.

①, ②, ③ 이미 문장에 동사가 있기 때문에 동사가 또 나올 수 없다.

08

[2016 가천대]

Medical bills (in the United States) have risen (outrageously) (since the beginning of the 1960's) and steps need [_____ to reverse this trend] or the average American will not be able to afford medical care.

① to take

② to be taken

③ to being taken

④ being taken

정답 ②

해석 미국의 의료비는 1960년대 초반부터 터무니없이 가파르게 상승해 왔고 이러한 추세를 뒤집을 조치가 취해지지 않는다면 일반적인 미국인들은 의료 서비스 비용을 감당할 수 없을 것이다.

분석 need의 어형 / 부정사의 태(to R/to be p.p.)

② need는 to R를 목적어로 받는 동사이므로 ③, ④는 탈락되고, 조치(steps)가 취하는 주체가 아니라 조치(steps)가 취해지는 대상이므로 수동태 부정사로 쓰인 ②가 적절하다.

09 [2015 경기대]

The US government had been ①preparing (for a
S   V₁
hurricane) (in New Orleans) (for ②a number of years)
and had ③already decided (on a plan) ④getting people
        V₂   =
out of the city.)

정답 ④ (getting → to get)

해석 미국 정부는 수년 동안 뉴올리언스의 허리케인에 대비해 왔고, 시민들을 뉴올리언스 밖으로 대피시킬 계획을 이미 세워 놓았다.

분석 명사 뒤 동격의 to R

④ plan, effort, ability, attempt는 R-ing가 아닌 to R로 동격을 표현하기 때문에 to get으로 고쳐야 한다.

① 미국 정부가 허리케인에 대비하는 주체이므로 능동의 진행형은 적절하다.

②「a number of = many」이므로 복수명사(years)를 수식하여 적절하다.

③ 수식어(부사)로 쓰여 동사의 의미를 돕기 위해 나와 적절하다.

10 [2015 상명대]

Constantinople ①could win the battle ②but not the
S   V   O   B
war, (③for there were ④very many Bulgarians (for
부사절   V   too   S   의미상
Greeks) ⑤to rule.)   주어

정답 ④ (very → too)

해석 그리스인들이 우위를 차지할 수 없을 만큼 불가리아인의 수가 많았기 때문에 콘스탄티노플은 전투에서는 승리했으나 전쟁에서는 승리할 수 없었다.

분석 「too ~ to R …」의 용법

④ '너무 ~해서 …할 수 없다'라는 뜻의 「too + 형용사/부사 + to R …」 용법으로, 뜻이 같다고 very를 쓰지 못하므로 too로 고쳐야 한다.

① 조동사 뒤에 동사원형이 나오고 목적어도 있어 능동태는 적절하다.

②「not A but B」의 변형 구문인 「B but not A」의 형태로 쓰여 적절하다.

③ 여기서 for는 앞 문장에 대한 원인을 나타내는 접속사로 쓰여 적절하다.

⑤ '너무 ~하여 …할 수 없다'라는 뜻의 「too + 형용사/부사 + to R …」 용법으로 쓰여 적절하다.

11 [2017 경기대]

Many researchers have strived (①toward a theory) (that
S   V   ①toward   S
is ②enough eclectic to encompass all of ③their   형용사절
insights in ④some form.)
C

정답 ② (enough eclectic → eclectic enough)

해석 많은 연구원들은 그들의 모든 통찰을 어떤 형태로 포괄할 수 있을 만큼 충분히 절충적인 이론을 세우고자 노력해 왔다.

분석 「형용사/부사 + enough」의 어순

② enough가 형용사를 수식할 경우 반드시 형용사 뒤에 위치해야 하므로 eclectic enough로 고쳐야 한다.

① strive는 자동사로 쓰여 뒤에 전명구가 나와 적절하다.

③ 복수명사(Many researchers)를 대신 받는 대명사로 수 일치가 적절하다.

④ some은 불가산명사(N)와 가산명사의 복수형(Ns)을 둘 다 수식할 수 있다.

12 [2017 한국외대]

(While I wished [to obtain ①a sound knowledge of ②all
부사절 S V
aspects of zoology,]) I planned [③to devote especially
                        S   V   O
④to insects.]
                be devoted   O

정답 ③ (to devote → to be devoted)

해석 나는 동물학의 모든 면에 정통한 지식을 얻기를 희망하면서 특히 곤충에 전념할 계획을 세웠다.

분석 「devote A to B」

③ 「devote A to B」의 어형으로 쓰여 항상 타동사로 쓰인다. 목적어가 없는 것으로 보아 수동태인 to be devoted로 고쳐야 한다.

① knowledge는 보통 불가산명사로 쓰이지만 지금처럼 앞에 형용사의 수식을 받아 구체적으로 어떠한 지식인지 설명하는 경우, 가산으로 쓰일 수 있어 적절하다. 여기서 sound는 '건전한, 정통한, 타당한'의 뜻을 가진 형용사이다.

② all은 불가산명사(N)와 가산명사의 복수형(Ns)을 둘 다 수식할 수 있다.

④ 「devote A to B = A be devoted to B」의 형태로 devote는 항상 전치사 to와 함께 쓰인다.

13

[2011 서울여대]

(In 1798) the circulation (of the journal) was 3,000
             S   V
copies and that number is estimated (to _____
  C   S   V
by 1809.)
        지시형용사

① double

② be doubling

③ have doubled

④ have had doubled

정답 ③

해석 1798년에 그 저널의 발행 부수는 3,000부였고 그 수는 1809년에 두 배가 된 것으로 추정된다.

분석 to R vs to have p.p. (부정사의 시제 비교 표현)

③ 부정사는 단순부정사(to R)와 완료부정사(to have p.p.)가 있다. 이 둘의 구분은 시제가 아니라 주절 동사와 해석 비교를 통해 동사와 부정사가 같은 시점이라면 단순부정사(to R)를 쓰고 주절 동사보다 부정사가 이전 시점이라면 완료부정사(to have p.p.)를 쓴다. 문장의 동사가 현재(is)인데 반해 빈칸 뒤에 「by + 과거 시점」이 나와 부정사가 동사보다 이전 시점이라는 것을 알 수 있다. 완료부정사 to have doubled를 써야 하므로 ①, ②, ④는 탈락되고 ③이 적절하다. ④는 완료를 두 번 쓰지 못하기 때문에 부적절하다.

14

[2011 성신여대]

London restaurants use old newspapers (_____
          S   V   O
"fish and chips," a traditional Britain dish.)
                =

① wrap

② wraps

③ wrapped

④ to wrap

정답 ④

해석 런던의 식당들은 영국의 전통 음식인 '피시앤칩스'를 싸기 위해 날짜가 지난 신문을 사용한다.

분석 「use + O + to R ~」의 용법

④ 「use + O + to R ~」는 '~하기 위해 목적어를 사용하다'라는 의미이다.

①, ②, ③ 한 문장에 동사가 두 개는 나올 수 없다.

15

[2011 세종대]

The city is _____ by one man.)
    S   V

① small enough (to be run)
                 C

② too small for being running

③ too small to run

④ small enough to have run

정답 ①

해석 그 도시는 한 사람이 운영할 수 있을 정도로 작다.

분석 「형용사/부사 + enough to R」

① 충분히 작아서 한 사람에 의해 운영될 수 있다는 의미는 「enough to R」이다.

② 「too ~ to R ...」의 표현은 「for R-ing」로 쓰지 못한다.

③ 도시가 너무 작아서 운영할 수 없다는 의미도 맞지 않을뿐더러 도시가 운영하는 주체가 아니라 운영되는 대상이므로 능동태 부정사도 부적절하다.

④ 도시가 운영하는 주체가 아닌 운영되는 대상이므로 능동태 부정사는 부적절하다. have p.p.는 완료일 뿐 수동태가 아닌 능동태이다.

16

[2011 세종대]

_____ [that years ago, the quality and styling of many GM vehicles fell away behind Toyota.]

① Sufficiently is it to say

② Suffice it to say

③ Suffice this to say

④ Sufficient this is to say

정답 ②

해석 몇 년 전에는 많은 GM 차량의 퀄리티와 스타일이 도요타에 뒤처졌었다고만 말해 두자.

분석 「suffice + it + (to say) + that + S + V ~」의 용법

② suffice + it + (to say) + that + S + V ~ : '~라고 말하면 충분하다'의 표현으로 ②가 적절하다.

17 [2011 세종대]

It remains _____ [whether a respected
가S   진S   S
economist will have the necessary clout (to stick to the
                V   O
reform path.)]

① to see ② for seeing
③ to be seen ④ for being seen

정답 ③

해석 존경받는 경제학자가 개혁의 행보를 고수하기 위해 필요한 영향력을 가지는지는 아직 지켜봐야 할 일이다.

분석 「remain + to R」의 어형 / 부정사의 태(to R/to be p.p.)

③ remain은 to R를 보어로 받기 때문에 ②, ④는 탈락되고 남은 것은 부정사의 태이다. It은 가주어이고 whether절이 진짜 주어이기 때문에 whether절의 내용이 직접 바라보는 주체가 아니라 보여지는 대상이므로 수동태 부정사인 ③이 적절하다.

18 [2011 숭실대]

(Unfortunately,) ①the differences (in the range of roles)
                              ∅   S
(that languages play frequently) ②lead some people to
형용사절 S   V   V
believe [that some languages (which do not fulfill ③a
O.C   명사절   S   형용사절 ∅   V   of doing
wide range of functions) are (in fact) ④incapable to do
O   V   C
so.]

정답 ④ (incapable to do → incapable of doing)

해석 언어의 역할에 있어 범위의 차이는 불행하게도 종종 넓은 범위의 기능을 수행하지 못하는 언어들은 사실상 그 역할을 수행할 능력이 없다고 사람들로 하여금 믿게 만든다.

분석 「(in)capable of R-ing」의 용법

④ 「(un)able to R = (in)capable of R-ing」의 형태로 쓰이므로 of doing으로 고쳐야 한다.

① 주어(the differences)와 동사(lead)의 수 일치가 적절하다.

② 「lead + O + to R ~」 5형식 동사의 어형으로 쓰여 적절하다.

③ a wide range of ~ : '다양한 ~'의 의미로 쓰이는 수식어구이다.

19 [2011 홍익대]

It would be like [①drinking whisky simply] (②to get
S   V   형용사절 ⓟ   N
drunk,) (which ③is likely (in the long run) ④diminishing
앞 문장 전체   ∅   to diminish
your pleasure in the stuff.)

정답 ④ (diminishing → to diminish)

해석 그것은 취하기만 위해 위스키를 마시는 것과 같으며, 이는 장기적으로 그것의 즐거움을 약화시킬 수 있다.

분석 「be likely to R ~」 (~할 가능성이 있다)

④ 「be likely to R ~」는 '~할 가능성이 있다'의 표현으로 be likely 뒤에는 to R가 나와야 하므로 to diminish로 고쳐야 한다.

① 전치사(like) 뒤에 동명사(drinking)의 역할로 쓰여 적절하다.

② to R의 부사적 용법(목적)으로 쓰여 적절하다.

③ 관계대명사 which는 앞 문장 전체를 받을 수 있다. 이 경우 which절 속 동사는 단수 취급한다.

20 [2012 경희대]

The magnitude 9.0 Tohoku earthquake ①(on March 11,
                              ∅   S
2011), (②which occurred near the northeast coast of
형용사절   V
Honshu, Japan,) ③was estimated ④to be caused
                      V   to cause
between 30,000 and 40,000 deaths.)

정답 ④ (to be caused → to cause)

해석 3월 11일에 일본 혼슈의 북동부 해안에서 발생한 진도 9.0의 도호쿠 지진은 약 3~4만 명의 사망자를 낸 것으로 추정되었다.

분석 부정사의 태(to R/to be p.p.)

④ 주어(The magnitude ~ earthquake)가 3~4만 명의 사상자를 야기하는 주체이므로 능동태 부정사인 to cause로 고쳐야 한다.

① 연도와 월은 전치사 in과 함께 쓰지만, 날짜 앞에는 반드시 전치사 on을 써야 한다.

② 선행사가 사물(The magnitude ~ earthquake)이고

절 속에 주어 자리가 불완전하여 관계대명사 which는 적절하고, occur은 자동사로 쓰여 적절하다.

③ 주어(The magnitude ~ earthquake)와 동사(was)의 수 일치가 적절하고, 지진이 추정하는 주체가 아니라 추정되는 대상이므로 수동태 역시 적절하다.

21

(In 1991,) (in the aftermath of Anita Hill's testimony) (against Supreme Court nominee Clarence Thomas,) President George Bush ① signed a law (② granting sexual-harassment plaintiffs the right) to ③ trial by jury and ④ claiming to financial damages.)

정답 ④ (claiming → (to) claim)

해석 대법관 후보자 클래런스 토마스에 대한 아니타 힐의 증언으로 조지 부시 대통령은 성폭력 원고가 배심원단으로부터 재판을 받고, 금전적 배상을 청구할 수 있는 권리를 부여하는 법안에 서명하였다.

분석 부정사(to R)의 병치
④ to trial and (to) claim으로 병치되는 형태이다. (to) claim으로 고쳐야 한다.
① 주어(President George Bush)가 법안에 서명하는 주체이므로 능동태는 적절하다.
② 법안이 원고(성폭행을 당한 사람)에게 권리를 승인하는 주체이고, 뒤에 간접목적어와 직접목적어가 있어 능동의 관계인 현재분사(granting)로 수식하여 적절하다.
③ 부정사의 형용사적 용법으로 명사(the right)를 수식하여 적절하다.

22
[2012 홍익대]

Sisyphus's continuous pushing (of the stone) (up the hill) (only _____ it roll down again) served (as the literary model) (for the third of Zeno's paradoxes.)

① having
② having been
③ have
④ to have

정답 ④

해석 어차피 다시 굴러 떨어질 돌을 끊임없이 언덕 위로 밀어 올리는 시시포스의 이론은 제논의 세 번째 역설에 문학적인 모델의 역할을 하였다.

분석 「only to R」의 용법
④ only는 to R와 결합하여 결과의 의미로 쓰이므로 ④가 적절하다.
①, ② only는 R-ing와 함께 쓰이지 않는다.
③ 구조 분석에서 보이듯이 이미 동사(served)가 있어 동사가 또 나올 수 없다.

23
[2013 서울여대]

(Around ① the globe,) temperatures ② are said ③ to climb about ④ 1.1 degrees in the 20th century.)

정답 ③ (to climb → to have climbed)

해석 20세기에 지구 전역 온도가 약 1.1도 올랐다고 알려져 있다.

분석 to R vs to have p.p. (부정사의 시제 비교 표현)
③ 주절 동사가 현재(are said)인데 사람들이 말함과 동시에 온도가 올라가는 것이 아니라 먼저 온도가 올라간 사실을 후에 사람들이 언급하는 것이므로 완료부정사인 to have climbed로 고쳐야 한다. 또한 동사는 현재(are said)인데 과거 시점부사(in the 20th century)가 있어 이전 시점이라는 것을 파악할 수 있다.
① 전치사의 목적어로 명사는 적절하다.
② 온도가 말하는 것이 아니라 온도가 올라갔다고 언급되는 대상이므로 수동태는 적절하다.
④ 1도가 아닌 이상 온도를 표현할 때 전부 복수로 표현한다.

24
[2015 가천대]

His customers are too worried (about [① affording the necessities of life,]) (like food and health care,) ② splurging on games, and those (who ③ do make a purchase) tend [to ④ look for the cheapest items on the shelves.]

* splurge on: ~에 돈을 펑펑 쓰다

정답 ② (splurging → to splurge)

해석 그의 고객들은 식료품이나 의료 서비스 같은 생활필수품을 감당하는 것을 너무나 심각하게 걱정하기 때문에, 게

임에 돈을 마음껏 쓰지 못하며 구매하는 사람들은 진열대에서 가장 저렴한 제품만을 찾는 경향이 있다.

분석 「too ~ to R ...」의 용법

② 해석이 수반돼야 하는 문제이다. 그의 고객들이 생필품을 감당하는 것에도 너무 걱정을 하는데 게임에 돈을 쓴다는 것은 문맥에 맞지 않다. 생필품을 구매하는 것을 너무나도 걱정하여 게임에도 돈을 쓸 수 없다는 의미가 어울리므로 「too ~ to R ...」의 용법을 써야 하므로 to splurge로 고쳐야 한다.

① 전치사의 목적어로 동명사는 적절하다.

③ 주격 관계대명사절 속의 동사(do)는 선행사(those)와 수 일치되어 적절하다. 긍정문의 do는 강조 표현이다.

④ tend는 to R를 목적어로 받는 동사이다.

25

① Repairs (to the Washington Monument) will require
massive scaffolding ② to build (around the obelisk) and
may keep it ③ closed (into 2014) (after ④ it was damaged
by an earthquake last year.)

정답 ② (to build → to be built)

해석 워싱턴 기념비의 수리 작업은 방첨탑 주위에 거대한 발판을 설치해야 할 것이며, 작년 지진으로 손상된 이후로 2014년까지 폐쇄될 수도 있다.

분석 부정사의 태(to R/to be p.p.)

② 「require + O + to R ~」5형식 동사의 어형에서 목적어가 목적보어 하는 주체라면 to R(능동태)를 쓰고 목적어가 목적보어 당하는 대상이라면 to be p.p.(수동태)를 써야 한다. 목적어는 거대한 발판(massive scaffolding)인데 발판이 짓는 주체가 아니라 지어지는 대상이므로 to be built로 고쳐야 한다.

① 주어 자리에 명사가 쓰여 적절하다.

③ 워싱턴 기념탑(it)이 폐쇄하는 주체가 아닌 폐쇄되는 대상이므로 수동의 관계인 과거분사(closed)는 적절하다.

④ 워싱턴 기념탑(Washington Monument)을 받는 대명사로 수 일치가 적절하다.

7강 동명사

Practice

01	①	02	③	03	③	04	③	05	③
06	②	07	④	08	④	09	④	10	③
11	③	12	③	13	①	14	④	15	③
16	①	17	④	18	①	19	③	20	②
21	③	22	①	23	②	24	③	25	①

01

[2010 경기대]

(When it comes ①to praise or blame people for [②what they do,]) we tend [to use a standard] (③that is ④relative to some conception of normal behavior.)

정답 ① (to praise or blame → to praising or blaming)

해석 사람들의 행동을 칭찬하거나 비난하는 것에 관해서 우리는 정상적인 행동의 개념과 관련된 기준을 적용하는 경향이 있다.

분석 「when it comes to N/R-ing」

① 「when it comes to N/R-ing」는 '~에 관하여'라는 표현으로, 이때 to는 전치사이므로 뒤에 명사 혹은 동명사가 올 수 있다. 동사원형은 절대 쓰지 못하므로 to praising or blaming으로 고쳐야 한다. 전치사 to의 관용적 구문들을 반드시 암기해야 한다.

② what절은 절 이하의 성분(명사)이 불완전하여 하나의 명사로 쓰이기 때문에 전치사 for의 목적어로 적절하다.

③ 선행사의 종류(사람, 사물)와 격(주격, 목적격)과 상관없이 전부 쓸 수 있는 that은 적절하다.

④ be동사의 보어로 형용사는 적절하고 relative는 전치사를 쓸 때 to와 함께 온다.

02

[2013 경희대]

(Meanwhile) the lighthouse ①had been growing slowly larger. It had now almost assumed color, and appeared (like a little gray shadow on the sky.) The man (at the

oars) ②could not be prevented (③from being turned his head) (rather often ④to try for a glimpse of this little gray shadow.)

정답 ③ (from being turned → from turning)

해석 그동안 등대는 천천히 더 커져가고 있었다. 등대는 이제 거의 색을 띄며 하늘의 회색 그림자처럼 보였다. 노 젓는 사람은 이 회색 그림자를 보기 위해 머리를 꽤 자주 돌릴 수밖에 없었다.

분석 동명사의 능동태와 수동태 구분(R-ing/being p.p.)

③ 뒤에 목적어(his head)가 있으므로 수동태 동명사를 쓸 수 없다. 능동태 동명사인 from turning으로 고쳐야 한다.

① grow는 자동사이므로 능동태는 적절하다.

② 「조동사 + 부정어 + 동사원형」은 적절하다.

④ to R의 부사적 용법으로 쓰여 적절하다.

03

[2013 한양대]

Neighborhoods are very clearly ①demarcated (according to income level,) and there is not much overlap. Poor people live (in poor neighborhoods) (that are characterized by ②dilapidated buildings, broken glass, graffiti, and a general state of disrepair.) People are not dedicated (to ③create an aesthetically ④pleasing environment.)

정답 ③ (create → creating)

해석 구역 간 경계는 소득 수준에 따라 매우 뚜렷하고, 이 경계가 모호한 지역은 많지 않다. 가난한 자들은 낙후된 건물, 깨진 유리, 그라피티, 그리고 전체적으로 황폐한 모습이 특징인 가난한 동네에 산다. 사람들은 미적으로 보기 좋은 환경을 만드는 데 열심이지 않다.

분석 「dedicate A to N/R-ing = be dedicated to N/R-ing」

③ 「be dedicated to」에서 to는 전치사이므로 동사원형이 나오지 못한다. creating으로 고쳐야 한다.

① 경계가 표시되는 대상이므로 수동태는 적절하다.

② 건물이 붕괴시키는 주체가 아니라 붕괴되는 대상이므로 수동의 관계인 과거분사(dilapidated)는 적절하다.

④ pleasing은 '즐거운, 만족스러운'의 뜻을 가진 형용사로 쓰여 명사를 수식하고 있다.

04

[2013 세종대]

I would <u>prefer</u> [having an assigned roommate]
S   V   A

_____.

① to have to choose a roommate on my own
② than to have to choose a roommate on my own
③ to [having to choose a roommate on my own]
   ⓟ   B
④ than have to choose a roommate on my own

정답 ③

해석 나는 스스로 룸메이트를 고르는 것보다 배정받은 룸메이트가 있는 것을 선호한다.

분석 「prefer to R ~ rather than (to) R ~ = prefer R-ing ~ to R-ing ~」

③ 「prefer to R ~ rather than (to) R = prefer R-ing(A) ~ to R-ing(B) ~」는 'B보다 A하는 것을 선호하다'의 표현으로 둘 중 무엇을 써도 상관없지만 prefer 뒤에 having이 왔으므로 ③이 적절하다.

05

[2014 단국대]

She still <u>has</u> nightmares (from _____ in a small
S   V   O   ⓟ   Ⓝ
dark cupboard for hours.)

① locking up
② having locked up
③ having been locked up
④ locked up

정답 ③

해석 그녀는 작고 어두운 벽장에 몇 시간 동안 갇혀 있었던 이유로 악몽을 여전히 꾼다.

분석 동명사의 능동태와 수동태 구분(R-ing/being p.p.)

③ 그녀가 벽장을 가두는 주체가 아니라 벽장에 갇히는 대상이므로 수동태 동명사(being p.p.)인 ③이 적절하다.

①, ② 능동태 동명사이므로 '그녀가 벽장을 가둬야 한다'는 뜻으로 쓰여 부적절하다.

④ 전치사 뒤에 명사가 없어 부적절하다.

06

[2015 가천대]

(Instead of [_____ formal and well rehearsed,])
       ⓟ   Ⓝ
the performance was spontaneous, contradictory and
          S   V   C₁   C₂
mutually respectful.
             C₃

① that
② being
③ its
④ such

정답 ②

해석 그 공연은 격식 있고 잘 연습되어 있었다기보다는 즉흥적이고 모순적이면서도 그 두 가지가 공존하는 종류의 것이었다.

분석 「전치사 + 명사 / 동명사」

② 전치사 뒤에는 명사 혹은 동명사가 나올 수 있으므로, 그 조건을 성립하는 것은 ①과 ②인데 빈칸 뒤 형용사 formal까지 받을 수 있어야 하므로 be동사의 동명사 형태인 being이 적절하다.

① 전치사 뒤 대명사로 쓰인 것까지는 괜찮지만 뒤에 형용사 formal and rehearsed와 연결이 되지 않아 부적절하다.

③, ④ 전치사 뒤 명사가 없어 부적절하다.

07

[2013 동국대]

We are all <u>looking forward</u> (with eager anticipation)
S   V
_____ what James and Bradley will say.

① hear
② to hear
③ hearing
④ to hearing

정답 ④

해석 제임스와 브래들리가 무엇이라 말할지 우리 모두가 열렬히 기대하고 있다.

분석 「look forward to N/R-ing」

④ 「look forward to N/R-ing」는 '~을 학수고대하다'의 표현으로, 이때 to는 전치사로 쓰여 뒤에 반드시 명사 혹은 동명사가 와야 하기 때문에 ④가 적절하다.

① 전치사 to도 없고 동사원형이 나와 부적절하다.

② 전치사 to 뒤에 동사원형은 쓰지 못한다.

③ 전치사 to가 빠져 부적절하다.

08

[2014 가톨릭대]

(From researches) (①conducted by biologists,) ②it is
                   (which are)   가S
<u>known</u> [that <u>ants</u> are <u>guided</u> (by a secretion) ③<u>paid</u>
진S   S   V   (which is)
<u>onto the soil</u> through the sting,) (in the manner of (ink)
                                            ⓟ 의미상
④~~drawing~~ out of a pen.)]   주어
being drawn   Ⓝ

정답 ④ (drawing → being drawn)

해석 생물학자들이 수행한 연구에 따르면, 개미는 펜에서 흘러나온 잉크처럼 침을 이용해 땅에 쏜 분비물에 의해 길을 찾는다고 알려져 있다.

분석 동명사의 능동태와 수동태 구분(R-ing/being p.p.)

④ 동명사의 의미상 주어는 바로 앞 명사인 ink이다. 잉크가 추출하는 주체가 아닌 추출되는 대상이므로 수동태 동명사인 being drawn으로 고쳐야 한다.

① 연구가 행하는 주체가 아니라 행해지는 대상이고, 뒤에 목적어도 없기 때문에 수동의 관계인 과거분사(conducted)는 적절하다.

② 「가주어(it) ~ 진주어(that절) ...」 구문이다. that절의 내용이 아는 주체가 아니라 알려지는 대상이므로 수동태는 적절하다.

③ 분비물이 배출하는 주체가 아니라 배출되는 대상이므로 수동의 관계인 과거분사(paid)로 수식하여 적절하다.

09
[2015 가천대]

(①With the help of modern mass communication,) an ②increasing number of governments (in the developing world) ③are committed (to ④support family-planning programs.)
- S
- V
- ℗ supporting
- Ⓝ

정답 ④ (support → supporting)

해석 더 많은 개발 도상국 정부들은 현대 대중 매체의 도움으로 가족계획 프로그램을 지원하는 데 힘쓰고 있다.

분석 「commit A to N/R-ing ~ = be committed to N/R-ing ~」

④ 「be committed to ~」 '~에 전념하다'의 표현으로, 이때 to는 전치사이므로 명사 혹은 동명사가 나와야 한다. supporting으로 고쳐야 한다.

① 전치사 뒤에 명사가 나와 수식어구로 적절하다.

② increasing은 '늘어나는'이라는 뜻의 형용사이다.

③ commit의 목적어가 없는 것으로 보아 수동태는 적절하고, 주어와 동사의 수 일치 역시 적절하다.

10
[2015 경기대]

A recidivist is a person (who keeps ①going back to a life of crime) (②even ③after punished;) (in other words,) an ④incurable criminal.
- S
- V
- C = 형용사절
- ℗ being punished

정답 ③ (after punished → after being punished)

해석 상습범은 처벌을 받고 난 뒤에도 범죄를 저지르는 삶으로 돌아가는 사람으로, 다시 말하자면 구제 불능의 범죄자를 뜻한다.

분석 전치사 after의 용법

③ after가 전치사로 쓰여 뒤에는 명사 혹은 동명사가 나와야 하므로 after being punished로 고쳐야 한다. 이때 ③을 접속사를 남겨 놓은 형태의 분사구문으로 보는 학생들이 있다. 물론 분사구문에서 의미를 명확하게 전달하기 위해 접속사를 남기는 경우가 있는데, 이 경우 after 혹은 before는 남길 수 없다.

① 「keep R-ing」는 '계속 ~하다'의 표현으로 쓰여 적절하다.

② even은 뒤에 나온 단어의 의미를 세게 전달하는 전치 초점부사이다.

④ 형용사(incurable)가 명사(criminal)를 수식하여 적절하다.

11
[2016 국민대]

(①While many museums are strictly no-go zones for ②photography,) (for one "museum" in the Philippines) [taking happy snaps] ③are an ④essential part (of the visitor's experience.)
- 부사절
- S
- V
- C
- is
- S
- V
- C

정답 ③ (are → is)

해석 많은 미술관은 사진 찍는 것을 엄격히 규제하지만, 필리핀의 한 미술관에서는 행복한 사진을 찍는 것이 방문객의 경험의 중요한 일부이다.

분석 동명사(R-ing)가 주어일 경우 동사의 수 일치

③ 주절 주어가 동명사(taking happy snaps)이다. 동명사가 주어일 경우 동사는 단수 취급하므로 is로 고쳐야 한다.

① while은 접속사로 쓰여 「주어 + 동사」를 받아 적절하다.

② 전치사의 목적어로 명사는 적절하다.

④ 형용사(essential)가 명사(part)를 수식하여 적절하다.

12

[2016 서울여대]

There is ① no objection (his) [joining the party] (② provided he is willing to ③ fit in with the plans of the group and is ready and able to ④ do his share of the work.)

정답 ① (no objection → no objection to)

해석 그가 그 단체의 계획에 자신을 맞출 의지가 있고, 그의 몫을 할 준비가 되어 있고 능력이 된다면 그가 당에 입당하는 것을 반대하지 않을 것이다.

분석 명사와 명사의 충돌

① 동명사(joining) 앞에 대명사의 소유격(his)은 동명사의 의미상 주어이다. 그렇다면 이미 앞에 명사(objection)가 나와 있는데 또 뒤에 동명사(joining the party)가 나와 명사와 명사가 충돌되기 때문에 이를 피해 주기 위해 no objection to로 고쳐야 한다.

② provided는 if를 대신하여 쓸 수 있는 접속사이므로 「주어 + 동사」를 받아 적절하다.

③ 「be willing to R ~」는 '기꺼이 ~하다'의 뜻으로 적절하다.

④ able to는 부정사이기에 동사원형은 적절하다.

13

[2016 홍익대]

The patrollers got used ① to [see Alice ② wander about) and she became just another fixture (in the patrollers' night,) (worthy of no more attention ③ than a hooting owl or a rabbit) (④ hopping across the road.)

정답 ① (to see → to seeing)

해석 순찰하는 사람들은 앨리스가 정처 없이 떠돌아다니는 모습을 보는 데 익숙해졌고, 그들에게 그녀는 울고 있는 올빼미나 길을 깡충깡충 뛰어다니는 토끼만큼이나 주의를 기울일 필요가 없는, 그저 밤마다 마주치는 고정 인물이 되었다.

분석 「S(사람) + get/be used to + N/R-ing」

① 「S(사람) + get/be used to + N/R-ing」는 '~에 익숙하다'의 뜻으로, 이때 to는 전치사로 쓰여 명사 혹은 동명사가 나와야 한다. to see를 to seeing으로 고쳐야 한다.

② 「see + O + R/R-ing ~」 5형식 지각동사의 목적보어로 쓰여 적절하다.

③ 앞에 비교급(more)이 있기에 than은 적절하다.

④ 토끼가 깡충깡충 뛰는 주체이므로 능동의 관계인 현재분사(hopping)로 수식하여 적절하다.

14

[2017 단국대]

(① Examining the link between nationality and prosperity in the age of globalism,) Milanovic has concluded [that ② a human being's place and culture ③ have become the dominant factor ④ in determination standard of living.)]

정답 ④ (in determination → in determining)

해석 세계화 시대에 국적과 번영 간 상관관계가 있는지를 검토한 밀라노비치는 인간의 거주지와 문화가 생활 수준을 결정하는 데 있어 지배적인 요소가 되었다는 결론을 내렸다.

분석 명사와 명사의 충돌

④ 명사(determination)와 명사(standard)가 충돌되어 부적절하다. 전치사의 목적어 역할을 함과 동시에 뒤에 명사를 받을 수 있도록 in determining으로 고쳐야 한다.

① 밀라노비치가 연결 고리를 검토하는 주체이므로 능동태 분사구문(Examining)은 적절하다.

② 뒤에 명사(place and culture)를 받을 수 있도록 소유격을 써서 적절하다.

③ 주어가 a human being's place and culture로 복수이므로 동사(have become)의 수 일치도 적절하다.

15

[2011 서울여대]

Women tend [to spend (as) much time (as they can) (in) _____ those (they love.)]

① support, help, and nurture

② to support, to help, and to nurture

③ supporting, helping, and nurturing

④ supported, helped, and nurtured

정답 ③

해석 여성은 그들이 사랑하는 사람을 부양하고, 도와주며, 양육하는 데 가능한 한 많은 시간을 쓰는 경향이 있다.

분석 「spend + O + (in) + R-ing」

③「spend + O(시간/돈) + (in) + R-ing ~」는 '~하는데 시간/돈을 소비하다'의 표현이다. 위의 구조 분석에도 표시되어 있지만 문제에서 spend의 목적어는 much time이고「as ~ as they can」은 '가능한 한'이라는 뜻의 수식어구이다. 결국「spend much time (in) 동명사」의 자리를 묻고 있는 것이므로 ③이 적절하다.

16

[2011 덕성여대]

(In spite of some earlier ①~~confuse~~) (②concerning the
    P   confusion   = about
opening date of the new plant,) we are ③confident [that
                                  S   V   C
we will be ready ④by September 1.]

정답 ① (confuse → confusion)

해석 새 공장 단지를 여는 날짜에 대한 초기에 일부 혼란이 있었음에도 불구하고 우리는 9월 1일까지 준비를 마칠 것이라 확신하고 있다.

분석 「전치사 + 동사원형 (X)」

① in spite of는 전치사이므로 뒤에 동사원형은 쓰지 못한다. 명사인 confusion으로 고쳐야 한다.

②「concerning = about」으로 분사형 전치사로 쓰여 뒤에 명사를 받아 적절하다.

③ be동사의 보어로 형용사는 적절하다.

④ by는 '~까지'의 뜻을 가진 전치사로 쓰여 적절하다.

17

[2011 동국대]

Some galleries obtain money (through sponsorship.)
     S   V   O
Works of art are often expensive and galleries
     S   V   C   S
_____.

① can buy rarely them without organize a public appeal

② can buy rarely them without organized a public appeal

③ can rarely buy them without a public appeal organizing

④ can rarely buy them (without organizing a public appeal)
       V   O   P   N

정답 ④

해석 몇몇 화랑들은 후원을 통해 자금을 조달한다. 예술 작품은 대개 값비싸므로 대중적인 지지를 조직하지 않고는 그러한 작품을 거의 구매할 수 없다.

분석 전치사(without) 뒤 품사

④ 전치사(without)의 목적어로 동명사구(organizing ~ appeal)를 받아 적절하다.

①, ② 전치사 뒤에 동사가 나올 수 없어 부적절하다.

③ 전치사의 목적어를 a public appeal으로 본다면 organizing은 분사가 되어 앞에 명사를 수식해야 하지만 대중적인 지지를 조직하는 주체, 즉 능동의 관계로 쓰이지 못하므로 부적절하다.

18

[2011 상명대]

                      의미상 주어
                        your
I appreciate ①you [helping me ②to do the dishes,]
S   V   (that)   O
but I wish [you would ③lay them down on the table
    S   V   O
more ④carefully.]

정답 ① (you → your)

해석 내가 설거지하는 것을 네가 도와준 것은 고맙지만, 접시를 식탁 위에 내려놓을 때 조금 더 조심해 주면 좋겠다.

분석 동명사의 의미상 주어

① 동명사의 의미상 주어를 인칭대명사(사람)로 쓰는 경우 반드시 소유격으로 써 주어야 하므로 you를 your로 고쳐야 한다.

②「help + O + to R」의 5형식 어형으로 쓰여 적절하다.

③ 뒤에 목적어(them)가 있으므로 타동사 lay는 적절하다.

④ 문장이 끝나 수식어구인 부사가 나와 적절하다.

19

[2011 서울여대]

(① Instead of ② sticking to one study location,)
     P   changing
③simply) [~~change~~ the room] ④where a person studies)
        S   형용사절
improves retention.
  V   O

정답 ③ (simply change → simply changing)

해석 한 곳의 공부 장소를 고집하는 것보다 단순히 공부하는 장소를 바꾸는 것만으로도 기억력을 향상시킬 수 있다.

분석 한 문장에 동사 2개 (X)

③ 구조 분석에서도 보이지만 이미 뒤에 동사(improves)가 있다. 동사가 또 나오면 안 되기에 동사(improves)의 주어 역할을 할 수 있도록 동명사(changing)로 고쳐야 한다.

① 전치사 뒤에 동명사를 받아 적절하다.

② 전치사의 목적어로 동명사는 적절하다. stick은 자동사로 쓰여 전치사 to를 받는다.

④ 관계부사 where은 앞에 장소명사(the room)를 수식
하여 적절하다.

20
[2017 상명대]

The Belts zoo spend ① a lot of time (on ② ~~educating~~
~~children~~) (about the ③ importance) (of ④ rare species)
(⑤ in their homeland.)

S V O children's education

정답　② (educating children → children's education)

해석　벨츠 동물원은 어린아이들에게 그들의 국가적 희귀 동물
의 중요성에 대해 가르치는 데 많은 시간을 보낸다.

분석　「spend + O(시간/돈) + on + N」

　② 「spend + O + (in) + R-ing」에서 이와 같이 목적어
　　뒤에 동명사를 쓰는 경우는 전치사 in이 생략이 가능
　　하다. 하지만 「spend + O + on + N」처럼 목적어 뒤
　　에 단순명사가 나오는 경우는 전치사 on이 반드시 나
　　와야 한다. 보기에서 spend a lot of time 뒤에 on이
　　나왔다는 것은 뒤에 동명사가 아닌 명사가 나와야 한
　　다는 단서이기 때문에 children's education으로 고
　　쳐야 한다.

　① spend는 시간 혹은 돈을 목적어로 받아 적절하고, a
　　lot of는 가산과 불가산을 둘 다 수식하여 적절하다.

　③ 전치사의 목적어로 명사는 적절하다.

　④ 형용사(rare)가 명사(species)를 수식하여 적절하다.

　⑤ 명사와 명사의 충돌을 피해 주기 위해 전치사는 적절
　　하다.

21
[2011 성신여대]

Samuel Walton ① pioneered the first ② mail-order
business (by ③ ~~pay~~ cash for merchandise ④ directly
from manufacturers.)

S paying V O directly

정답　③ (pay cash for → paying cash for)

해석　샘 월튼은 제조업자로부터 직접 상품을 받고 현금을 지불
함으로써 통신 판매업의 선구자가 되었다.

분석　「전치사 + 동명사」

　③ 전치사(by) 뒤에는 동사가 쓰일 수 없고 명사 혹은 동
　　명사가 나올 수 있다. paying cash for로 고쳐야 한다.

　① 타동사로 쓰여 목적어를 받아 적절하다.

② mail-order business(통신 판매 사업)는 복합명사로
쓰여 적절하다.

④ 동명사(paying ~ merchandise)를 수식하는 부사로
쓰여 적절하다.

22
[2011 숭실대]

(In Monmouth County, New Jersey,) snow drifts (of up
to five feet) contributed (to ① ~~stall~~ a passenger bus on
the Garden State Parkway,) (where snow plows were
having a difficult time ② clearing) (because there were
so many ③ stranded cars ④ cluttering the ramps,))
(state police spokesman Steve Jones said.)

stalling / (in) 형용사절 S V / 부사절 V / S / 삽입절

정답　① (stall → stalling)

해석　뉴저지 먼마우스 지역에서는 5피트까지 쌓인 눈으로 가
든 스테이트 파크웨이로 가는 여객 버스를 오도 가도 못
하게 하고 있고, 너무 많은 차들이 비탈길을 어지럽히며
발이 묶여 있어 제설기들로 눈을 치우는 데 어려움을 겪
고 있다고 스티브 존스 주립 경찰 대변인이 전했다.

분석　「contribute to + N/R-ing」

　① 「contribute to + N/R-ing」는 '~에 기여하다'의 표현
　　으로, 이때 to는 전치사이므로 동사원형(stall)을 쓰지
　　못하기 때문에 동명사(stalling)로 고쳐야 한다.

　② 「have a difficult time (in) R-ing」는 '~하는 데 어려
　　움을 겪다'라는 의미로, 전치사 in이 생략되어 동명사
　　clearing은 적절하다.

　③ 자동차가 발이 묶인 대상이므로 수동의 관계인 과거분
　　사(stranded)로 수식하여 적절하다.

　④ 뒤에 목적어(the ramps)를 받아 능동의 관계인 현재
　　분사(cluttering)는 적절하다.

23
[2012 동덕여대]

(① Once you become accustomed to ② ~~use~~ this new
system,) you'll find it ③ much easier [④ to operate than
the previous one.]

부사절 S V P / using / S V 가O O.C 진O

정답　② (use → using)

해석　이 새로운 시스템을 사용하는 데 익숙해지면, 이전의 것보
다 이것이 훨씬 조작하기 쉽다는 것을 알게 될 것입니다.

분석 「be accustomed to + N/R-ing」

② 「be accustomed to + N/R-ing」는 '~에 익숙하다'의 표현으로, 이때 to는 전치사이다. 전치사 뒤에 동사원형 (use)은 나올 수 없어 동명사(using)로 고쳐야 한다.

① once는 부사도 있지만 접속사로도 쓰일 수 있어 「주어 + 동사」를 받아 적절하다.

③ find의 5형식 어형으로, 목적보어의 역할로 형용사는 적절하고 비교급을 강조하는 부사(much) 역시 괜찮다.

④ 「find + it + O.C(형용사) + to R/that + S + V」 형태의 「가목적어(it)–진목적어(to R)」 구문으로 쓰여 적절하다.

분석 전치사 뒤 품사의 선택

① 전치사(far from) 뒤에 동사원형을 쓰지 못하기에 동명사(being)로 고쳐야 한다.

② 「of + 추상명사 = 형용사」로 쓰여 being의 보어로 적절하다.

③ 뒤에 목적어도 있어 능동태 동사는 적절하다.

④ 명사와 명사의 충돌을 피해 주기 위해 전치사는 적절하다.

24

[2012 인천대]

Governor Hester sees small business as the best hope
　　　　S　　　V　　　O　　　　　　O.C
(for ＿＿＿＿＿＿ the state's economy.)
　　ⓟ

① revitalize　　　　　　② revitalized

③ revitalizing　　　　　④ revitalization

정답 ③

해석 헤스터 주지사는 소기업들이 주 경제를 활성화시킬 가장 큰 희망으로 본다.

분석 전치사 뒤 품사의 선택

③ 전치사(for)의 목적어 자리이다. 다만 빈칸 뒤에 명사(the state's economy)가 나온 것으로 보아 전치사의 목적어 역할을 할 수 있음과 동시에 빈칸 뒤 명사를 처리할 수 있는 동명사로 나온 ③이 정답으로 적절하다.

① 전치사 뒤에 동사원형은 쓰지 못한다.

② 전치사 뒤에 과거동사 역시 쓰지 못한다.

④ 전치사 뒤에 명사로는 가능하지만 빈칸 뒤 명사와 충돌이 일어나 부적절하다.

25

[2012 홍익대]

　　　　　　　being
(Far from ①be ②of no consequence,) this confusion
　ⓟ　　　　동명사　└ = consequent ┘　　　S
③plays a positive role (④in his theoretical edifice.)
　V　　　　O

정답 ① (be → being)

해석 이 혼란은 별일이 아니긴커녕 그의 이론적 체계에 긍정적인 역할을 한다.

Practice 01

01	①	02	④	03	①	04	③	05	④
06	④	07	①	08	②	09	③	10	③
11	①	12	④	13	①	14	③	15	②
16	③	17	②	18	④	19	③	20	③
21	③	22	①	23	①	24	③	25	④

01
[2017 상명대]

Kansas farmers ①used the weed killer 2, 4-D had a
② higher-than-average risk (③ of ④ contracting
malignant ⑤ lymphoma.)

using (위에 표기)
S / V / O / p / N

정답 ① (used → using)

해석 2, 4-D 제초제를 사용한 캔자스주의 농부들은 악성 림프
종에 걸릴 위험이 평균보다 높았다.

분석 현재분사(R-ing)와 과거분사(p.p.)의 구분

① 뒤에 이미 동사(had)가 있는 것으로 보아 used는 동
사가 아닌 과거분사로 앞에 나온 명사(farmers)를 수
식하고 있다는 것을 알 수 있다. 농부들이 제초제를 사
용하는 주체이고, 뒤에 목적어도 있기 때문에 능동의
관계인 현재분사(using)로 고쳐야 한다.

② 형용사(higher-than-average)가 명사(risk)를 수식하
여 적절하다.

③, ④ risk는 동격을 표현할 때 「of + R-ing」로 쓰기 때
문에 적절하다.

⑤ contracting의 목적어로 쓰여 적절하다.

02
[2010 단국대]

The ①absence (of organic materials,) (some scientists
② speculated,) was the result (of intense ultraviolet
③radiation) (penetrating the atmosphere of Mars) and
④destroyed organic compounds in the soil.)

삽입절 / V / C / ⓐ₁ / destroying / ⓐ₂
S

정답 ④ (destroyed → destroying)

해석 유기물의 결핍은 화성의 대기권을 통과해 토양의 유기 화
합물을 파괴하는 강력한 자외선 때문이라고 몇몇 과학자
들은 추측했다.

분석 현재분사(R-ing)와 과거분사(p.p.)의 구분

④ destroyed부터 끝까지 앞에 명사(ultraviolet
radiation)를 수식하고 있다. 자외선이 유기 화합물을
파괴하는 주체이고, 뒤에 목적어도 있기 때문에 능동
의 관계인 현재분사(destroying)로 고쳐야 한다.

① 주어의 역할인 명사로 쓰여 적절하다.

② 구조 분석에서도 보이지만 some ~ speculated까지
삽입절로 쓰여 적절하다.

③ 전치사의 목적어로 명사는 적절하다.

03
[2017 한국항공대]

Another interesting application (of ultrasound) is the
ultrasonic ranging unit (①using (in some cameras) ②to
provide an ③almost instantaneous measurement of
the distance) (between the camera and the objects)
④to be photographed.)

used / (which is) / S / V / C

정답 ① (using → used)

해석 초음파의 또다른 흥미로운 적용 예시는 일부 카메라에서
카메라와 피사체 간의 거리를 거의 즉시 측정하기 위해
사용하는 초음파 거리 측정 기구이다.

분석 현재분사(R-ing)와 과거분사(p.p.)의 구분

① 기구(unit)가 직접 사용하는 주체가 아니라 카메라에서
사용되는 대상이므로 수동의 관계인 과거분사(used)
로 고쳐야 한다.

② to R의 부사적 용법(목적)으로 쓰여 적절하다.

③ almost는 부사로서 형용사(instantaneous)를 수식
하여 적절하다.

④ 피사체가 사진 찍히는 대상이므로 수동태 부정사는 적
절하다.

04
[2010 경희대]

(_____ as an opera singer,) John McCormack
made his Covent Garden debut (in 1907,) (at age 23.)
Later he expanded his singing style (to include
elements of Irish ballads and traditional folk songs.)

분사구문 / S / V / O / S / V / O

① Was trained   ② To train

③ Trained   ④ Training

정답 ③

해석 오페라 가수로서의 훈련을 받은 존 맥코맥은 1907년에 코벤트 가든에서 23살의 나이에 데뷔했다. 이후 아일랜드 발라드와 전통 민요의 요소들을 포함시키는 것으로 자신의 가창법의 범위를 확대하였다.

분석 분사구문의 태(능동태와 수동태의 구분)

③ 빈칸 앞에 As John McCormack was가 생략되어 있는 분사구문이다. 분사구문 앞에 주어가 없다는 것은 주절 주어와 같아서 생략된 것이기에 존 맥코맥(John McCormack)이 오페라 가수로 훈련받은 대상이고, 뒤에 목적어도 없기 때문에 수동태 분사구문(Trained)인 ③이 적절하다.

① 뒤에 주어, 동사가 나와 있어 동사가 또 나올 수 없다.

② to R의 부사적 용법(목적)으로 쓰였지만 의미도 맞지 않고 능동태도 부적절하다.

④ 빈칸 뒤에 목적어도 없기에 능동태 분사구문은 부적절하다.

05

[2010 성균관대]

(A few years ago) Canadian lottery officials ①learned the importance (of careful ②counting) (the hard way) (when they ③decided to give back some ④unclaiming prize money) (that had ⑤accumulated.)

(S) learned (V) the importance (O), counting, unclaimed 표기, 부사절 S V O, 형용사절 V

정답 ④ (unclaiming → unclaimed)

해석 캐나다의 복권 담당 직원들은 몇 년 전 누적된 미청구 당첨금을 반환하기로 결정했을 때 곤욕을 치르고서야 정확한 계산의 중요성을 깨닫게 되었다.

분석 현재분사(R-ing)와 과거분사(p.p.)의 구분

④ 상금이 주장하는 주체가 아니라 소유권이 주장되는 대상이므로 수동의 관계인 과거분사(unclaimed)로 고쳐야 한다.

① 타동사로 쓰여 목적어를 받아 적절하다.

② 전치사의 목적어 역할로 '계산'이라는 뜻의 명사로 쓰여 적절하다.

③ to R를 목적어로 받는 타동사로 쓰여 적절하다.

⑤ 관계대명사 that절 속에 주어가 불완전한 형태이며 accumulate은 자동사로 쓰여 적절하다.

06

[2014 상명대]

I finally ①reached Tom (②in his office,) and he said [he (that) ③ would ship the ④redesigning brochures ⑤ by express mail.]

(S) reached (V) Tom (O), S V, redesigned 표기, O

정답 ④ (redesigning → redesigned)

해석 사무실에 있던 톰과 드디어 연락이 닿았고, 그는 새롭게 디자인된 브로슈어를 속달 우편으로 보내 줄 것이라 말했다.

분석 현재분사(R-ing)와 과거분사(p.p.)의 구분

④ 브로슈어(책자)가 디자인하는 주체가 아니라 디자인되어지는 대상이므로 수동의 관계인 과거분사(redesigned)로 고쳐야 한다.

① reach는 타동사로 목적어(Tom)를 받아 적절하다.

② 문장이 앞에서 완성되어 있어 수식어구인 전명구로 쓰여 적절하다.

③ 주절이 과거(said)이기에 종속절에 조동사의 과거형(would)은 적절하고 ship은 동사원형의 형태이다.

⑤ by 뒤에 교통 혹은 통신 수단의 명사가 나올 경우 관사를 쓰지 못하므로 적절하다.

07

[2010 이화여대]

(①Consisted of 93 percent water,) ②the banana tree, (③which is the largest plant ④on Earth without a woody stem,) is a very fragile plant.

Consisting, 분사구문 S, 형용사절, V C

정답 ① (Consisted of → Consisting of)

해석 93퍼센트가 물로 이루어져 있고 지구상 목질 줄기 없이 가장 큰 식물인 바나나 나무는 매우 허약한 식물이다.

분석 분사구문의 태(능동태와 수동태의 구분)

① 분사구문 앞에 주어가 없다는 것은 주절 주어와 같아서 생략된 것이다. 주절 주어(the banana tree)가 구성되는 것이므로 수동의 관계인 consisted가 맞다고 생각될 수 있다. 하지만 consist는 그 자체로 '~로 구성되다'의 수동의 의미를 가진 자동사로 수동태로 절대 쓰지 못하기 때문에 능동태 분사구문(Consisting of)으로 고쳐야 한다.

② 주어의 역할인 명사로 쓰여 적절하다.

③ 선행사가 사물이고 절 속에 주어가 불완전하여 관계대명사 which는 적절하다.

④ 명사와 명사의 충돌을 피해 주기 위해 전명구는 적절하다.

08
[2013 서강대]

Luis Chiappe, an expert (on early birds) (at the Natural History Museum of Los Angeles County,) suggests [that flight ① likely occurred (as a by-product of arm flapping) (② in ground-dwelled dinosaurs,)] (as the predecessors (of birds) used their ③ feathered arms to increase their running speed or balance themselves) (④ as they made fast turns.)

정답 ② (in ground-dwelled dinosaurs → in ground-dwelling dinosaurs)

해석 로스앤젤레스 자연사 박물관의 초기 조류 전문가인 루이스 치아피는 조류의 조상인 육지 공룡이 깃털 덮인 날개를 뛰는 속도를 증가시키고, 빠르게 방향을 전환할 때 균형을 유지하기 위해 사용하면서 이 날갯짓의 결과로 비행이 발생했을 것이라 주장한다.

분석 현재분사(R-ing)와 과거분사(p.p.)의 구분

② 하이픈(-)으로 연결된 복합분사이다. 이 경우 항상 뒤에 수식받는 명사와의 관계를 따지면 된다. 공룡이 거주하는 주체이므로 능동의 관계인 현재분사(ground-dwelling)로 고쳐야 한다.

① that절 속에 자동사 occur로 쓰인 것이고 likely는 부사로 쓰여 동사를 수식하는 것은 적절하다.

③ feathered는 '깃털을 가진, 깃털로 덮인'이라는 의미의 형용사로 쓰여 명사(arms)를 수식하여 적절하다.

④ 부사절 접속사 as로 쓰여 「주어＋동사」를 받아 적절하다.

09
[2013 성균관대]

Brazil's economy performed ① much worse (than ② expected in the third quarter,) ③ grown by less than 1%) (④ compared with the same period a year ⑤ earlier.)

정답 ③ (grown → growing)

해석 브라질 경제는 3분기에 예상보다 훨씬 악화되어 1년 전 동기간 비교 시 1% 이하의 성장률을 보였다.

분석 분사구문의 태(능동태와 수동태의 구분)

③ 분사구문 앞에 주어가 없다는 것은 주절 주어와 같아서 생략된 것이다. 브라질 경제가 성장 당하는 대상이 아니라 성장하는 주체이므로 능동태 분사구문(growing)으로 고쳐야 한다.

① much, still, even, a lot은 비교급 앞에 위치하여 강조부사로 쓰이므로 적절하다.

② 브라질 경제가 예상하는 주체가 아니라 예상되는 대상이므로 수동의 관계인 과거분사는 적절하다.

④ 브라질 경제가 1년 전 같은 시기와 비교되는 대상이므로 수동의 관계인 과거분사는 적절하다.

10
[2013 한국외대]

(① Buoyed by the winter sports season,) consumption (of instant noodles) ② has spiked, (with the monthly sales (for last December) ③ exceeded 40 billion won ④ for the first time.)

정답 ③ (exceeded → exceeding)

해석 겨울 스포츠 시즌의 영향으로 즉석 라면의 소비는 작년 12월 판매량이 처음으로 400억 원을 넘어서며 급등하였다.

분석 with 분사구문의 태(능동태와 수동태의 구분)

③ 「with＋N＋R-ing/p.p.」의 선택을 묻고 있다. 이때 with 뒤에 있는 명사와의 관계를 따져 능동의 관계라면 R-ing를, 수동의 관계라면 p.p.를 써야 한다. 월간 판매량이 400억 원을 초과하는 주체이고, 뒤에 목적어도 있기 때문에 능동의 관계인 현재분사(exceeding)로 고쳐야 한다.

① 분사구문의 태를 묻고 있다. 분사구문 앞에 주어인 명사가 없다면 주절 주어와 같아서 생략된 것이기에 주절 주어와 관계를 따지면 된다. 즉석 라면의 소비가 유지하는 주체가 아니라 유지되는 대상이기에 수동태 분사구문은 적절하다.

② 주어(consumption)와 동사(has spiked)의 수 일치도 적절하고 spike는 자동사로 쓰였다.

④ 명사와 명사의 충돌을 피해 주기 위해 전명구는 적절하다.

11

[2013 가톨릭대]

The Kyoto Protocol is an ambitious effort (to reduce the man-made emissions) (_____ responsible for global warming.)

(S / V / C / (which are))

① believed
② believing
③ to believe
④ have believed

정답 ①

해석 교토 의정서는 지구 온난화에 책임져야 할 인간이 만들어 내는 배기가스를 줄이도록 한 엄청난 시도이다.

분석 문의구성 / 현재분사(R-ing)와 과거분사(p.p.)의 구분

① 빈칸부터 끝까지 앞의 명사구(the man-made emissions)를 수식하고 있는 자리이다. 배기가스가 믿고 있는 주체가 아니라 원인이라고 여겨지는 대상이 므로 수동의 관계인 과거분사(believed)로 수식해야 한다.

② 배기가스가 원인이라고 믿는 주체가 아니라서 부적절 하다.

③ to R 역시 형용사의 역할로 앞에 명사를 수식할 수 있 지만 to believe는 능동태 부정사이므로 적절하지 않다.

④ 앞에 동사(is)가 있기 때문에 동사가 또 나올 수 없다.

12

[2013 경기대]

Law enforcement officials say [that (① in theory) the bureau could take a lead role (② in reducing gun crime,)] ③ but [that it is hindered by ④ politically ~~driving~~ laws.]

(S / O₁ / O₂ / driven)

정답 ④ (politically driving laws → politically driven laws)

해석 경찰은 이론상 그들이 총기 범죄를 줄이는 데 주도적 역 할을 할 수 있지만, 그것은 정치적인 영향으로 만들어진 법에 의해 방해받고 있다고 말한다.

분석 현재분사(R-ing)와 과거분사(p.p.)의 구분

④ 법안이 추진하는 주체가 아니라 추진되는 대상이므로 수동의 관계인 과거분사(driven)로 고쳐야 한다.

① 수식어구인 전명구로 적절하다.

② 전치사의 목적어로 명사 혹은 동명사가 가능하므로 적 절하다.

③ 「say + that + S + V + but + (say) + that + S + V」 의 형태로 병치되어 있고, it은 앞에 나온 동명사구

(reducing gun crime)를 대신 받고 있어 적절하다. 대 명사 it은 앞에 나온 명사, 구, 절을 대신 받을 수 있다.

13

[2013 세종대]

Some snorers (who have a condition (① ~~calling~~ sleep apnea)) stop breathing (② up to thirty or forty times ③ an hour) (because the throat muscles relax ④ too much and block the airway.)

(S / 형용사절 V / called / (which is) / V / O / 부사절 S / V₁ / ad / V₂ / O)

정답 ① (calling → called)

해석 수면 무호흡이라는 질병을 가진 몇몇 코 고는 이들은 인 후 근육이 지나치게 이완되어 기도를 방해하여 많으면 한 시간에 삼사십 번까지 호흡을 멈춘다.

분석 현재분사(R-ing)와 과거분사(p.p.)의 구분

① 진단(a condition)이 수면 무호흡(sleep apnea)을 부 르는 주체가 아니라 수면 무호흡이라 불리는 대상이므 로 수동의 관계인 과거분사(called)로 고쳐야 한다.

② 명사와 명사의 충돌을 피해 주기 위해 전치사는 적절 하다.

③ 「a/an + N」는 '~당, ~마다'의 뜻으로 쓰이는 표현으 로 적절하다.

④ 부사(too much)가 동사(relax)를 수식하여 적절하다.

14

[2013 아주대]

China's first emperor was buried (_____ 7,000 life-sized clay figures of soldiers) (standing in battle formation) (along by life-sized ceramic chariots.)

(S / V / 분사구문)

① surrounded
② surrounding
③ surrounded by
④ surround with
⑤ surrounding with

정답 ③

해석 중국 최초의 황제는 실물 크기의 도자기 전차들을 따라 전투 형태로 서 있는 7천여 명의 실물 크기 찰흙 병사에 둘러싸여 매장됐다.

분석 분사구문의 태(능동태와 수동태의 구분)

③ 빈칸 앞에서 문장이 끝나고 분사구문이 시작되는 형태 이다. 분사구문의 주어가 없다는 것은 주절 주어와 같 기 때문에 생략된 형태이다. 중국의 첫 번째 황제가

7,000명의 전사들에 의해 둘러싸인 대상이므로 수동의 관계인 surrounded로 쓰여야 하기 때문에 ①, ③으로 좁혀진다. 수동태 분사구문은 목적어를 받을 수 없기에 전치사 by와 함께 나온 ③이 적절하다.

① 수동태 분사구문은 목적어를 받을 수 없다.

②, ⑤ surrounding은 능동의 관계를 나타내기 때문에 부적절하다.

④ 동사가 또 나올 수 없다.

15 [2013 단국대]

(When Spielberg was a teenager,) his parents divorced,
부사절   S   V
and the ①hurtful impact (of that event) would become
       recurring S   V
a ②recurred theme (in his movies)—children
        C
(③uprooted and ④traumatized by parents' divorce.)
   ⓐ₁   ⓐ₂

정답 ② (recurred → recurring)

해석 스필버그가 십대일 때 그의 부모가 이혼하였고, 이로 인한 고통스러운 충격은 그의 영화에 되풀이되는 주제가 되었다. 그것은 부모의 이혼으로 정든 집을 떠나야만 하고 상처 입은 아이이다.

분석 분사형 완전 형용사

② 영어에는 분사로 쓰이다가 형용사로 굳어진 단어들이 있다. 이 단어들은 나올 때마다 추가하여 암기를 해야 한다. recurring은 '되풀이하는, 반복되는'이라는 뜻의 형용사로 쓰이는 단어이지만 recurred라는 형용사는 존재하지 않는다. recurring으로 고쳐야 한다.

① 형용사(hurtful)가 명사(impact)를 수식하여 적절하다.

③ 아이들이 쫓겨나는 대상이므로 수동의 관계인 과거분사(uprooted)는 적절하다.

④ 아이들이 상처를 받은 대상이기에 수동의 관계인 과거분사(traumatized)는 적절하다.

16 [2014 홍익대]

Holmes compares himself (to Dupin and Lecoq,)
   S   V   O
(_____ them as really existing historical
분사구문   O
figures.)

① treated   ② being treated

③ treating   ④ having been treated

정답 ③

해석 홈스는 듀팡과 르코크를 실재했던 역사적 인물처럼 취급하면서 그들과 자신을 비교한다.

분석 분사구문의 태(능동태와 수동태의 구분)

③ 문장이 끝나고 분사구문이 시작되고 있다. Holmes가 그들을 역사적 인물로 취급하는 주체이고, 또한 빈칸 뒤에 목적어(them)도 있기 때문에 능동태 분사구문(treating)이 적절하다.

①, ②, ④ 전부 수동태 분사구문으로 태가 부적절하다.

17 [2015 상명대]

The integral connection (between vassal ①and serf)
                                        S
(who was)
②depicting in conventional accounts) ③was destined
   depicted   V
(to come ④under intense scrutiny) (among a new
⑤breed of analyst.)

정답 ② (depicting → depicted)

해석 구전에서 표현되는 봉신과 농노 사이의 필수적 연관성은 새로운 유형의 분석가들 사이에서 면밀한 조사를 받을 운명에 놓였다.

분석 현재분사(R-ing)와 과거분사(p.p.)의 구분

② 봉신(vassal)과 농노(serf)를 수식하는 분사이다. 봉신과 농노가 묘사하는 주체가 아니라 이야기에서 묘사되는 대상이고, 뒤에 목적어도 없기 때문에 수동의 관계인 과거분사(depicted)로 고쳐야 한다.

① 「between A and B」의 형태로 상관관계는 적절하다.

③ 주어(connection)와 동사(was)의 수 일치가 적절하고, 연결 고리가 조사를 받을 운명에 처해진 대상이므로 수동태도 적절하다.

④ come은 자동사로 전명구가 나와 적절하다.

⑤ 「a breed of + N(사람)」은 '어떠한 유형의 사람'이라는 표현으로 쓰여 적절하다.

18 [2016 가천대]

Political and economic relations (between countries)
                                  S
①are to ②be based (upon complete equality) (③of the
 V   C
parties ④concern.)
          concerned

정답 ④ (concern → concerned)

해석 국가들 사이의 정치적 및 경제적 관계는 연관된 모든 당사자의 완전 평등에 기초해야 한다.

분석 문의구성

④ concern은 명사와 동사로 쓰일 수 있다. 하지만 이미 앞에 동사(are)가 존재하기 때문에 동사로 쓰일 수 없고 앞에 명사(parties)가 있기 때문에 명사로도 쓰이지 못한다. 수식할 수 있는 분사 형태(concerned)로 고쳐야 한다.

① 주어가 복수명사(Political ~ relations)이기에 수 일치는 적절하다.

② 관계가 기반으로 하는 주체가 아니라 평등을 기반으로 만들어지는 대상이므로 수동태 부정사는 적절하다. 또한 「base A (up)on B」의 형태로 쓰이는 동사이기에 뒤에 목적어가 없는 것으로 보아 수동태가 쓰여야 한다는 것을 알 수 있다.

③ 명사와 명사의 충돌을 피해 주기 위해 전치사는 적절하다.

19
[2017 한국외대]

Every successful ① advertisement uses a creative strategy (② based on an idea) (that will attract the attention of the ③ targeting consumer ④ audience.)

정답 ③ (targeting → targeted)

해석 모든 성공적인 광고는 목표하는 소비층의 관심을 끌 수 있는 아이디어에 기초한 창의적 전략을 사용한다.

분석 현재분사(R-ing)와 과거분사(p.p.)의 구분

③ 소비층이 표적으로 정하는 주체가 아니라 표적화되는 대상이므로 수동의 관계인 과거분사(targeted)로 고쳐야 한다.

① every는 해석은 '모든'이라고 하지만 항상 단수명사만을 수식하기에 적절하다.

② 전략이 기반으로 삼는 주체가 아니라 생각을 기반으로 만들어지는 대상이므로 수동의 관계인 과거분사(based)는 적절하다.

④ consumer audience는 복합명사로 쓰여 적절하다.

20
[2011 상명대]

I had a really interesting conversation (① with a fellow) (working in the industry) (② who claims [that a lot of movies ③ making these days) are modeled conceptually after ④ amusement park rides.])

정답 ③ (making → made)

해석 나는 최근에 만들어진 많은 영화들이 개념적으로 놀이 기구를 따라 만들어졌다고 주장하는 영화 산업에 종사하는 한 친구와 매우 흥미로운 대화를 가졌다.

분석 현재분사(R-ing)와 과거분사(p.p.)의 구분

③ 영화가 만드는 주체가 아니라 만들어지는 대상이므로 수동의 관계인 과거분사(made)로 고쳐야 한다.

① 명사의 충돌을 피해 주기 위한 전명구도 이상 없고, 친구가 일하는 주체이므로 능동의 관계인 현재분사(working)도 적절하다.

② 선행사가 사람(a fellow)이고 절 속에 주어 자리가 불완전하기에 주격 관계대명사 who는 적절하고, 주격 관계대명사절 속의 선행사(a fellow)와 수 일치를 해야 하므로 동사 claims 역시 적절하다.

④ 전치사(after)의 목적어로 복합명사는 적절하다.

21
[2016 가천대]

The fear (that animals feel) is carved (① deeply) (in the amygdaloid portion of the brain.) (When a rat spots a cat,) its sympathetic nerve ② tenses (because its amygdaloid body is stimulated,) (③ caused the rat to stiffen and ④ let out deep breaths.)

정답 ③ (caused → causing)

해석 동물이 느끼는 공포는 뇌의 편도체 부위에 깊이 새겨져 있다. 쥐가 고양이를 발견하면 쥐의 편도체가 자극되어 쥐의 교감 신경이 긴장하게 되며, 이러한 긴장 상태는 쥐를 경직시키고 심호흡을 하게 만든다.

분석 분사구문의 태(능동태와 수동태의 구분)

③ 앞 문장 전체를 받는 분사구문이다. 교감 신경이 긴장된다는 사실이 쥐로 하여금 경직시키는 주체이므로 능동태 분사구문(causing)으로 고쳐야 한다. 또한 뒤에 이미 목적어와 목적보어가 전부 나와 있어 수동태 분사구문은 쓰지 못한다.

① 동사(is carved)를 수식하는 부사(deeply)로 쓰여 적절하다.

② 주어(its sympathetic nerve)와 동사(tenses)의 수 일치가 적절하다.

④ to stiffen and (to) let으로 병치된 형태로 적절하다.

22

People ①sign up through the Affordable Care Act's
marketplaces) tend [to be older,] (officials said Monday,)
a demographic mix (that ②could cause premiums ③to
rise in the future) (if the pattern ④persists.)

정답 ① (sign up → signing up)

해석 월요일, 관련자에 따르면 오바마케어 시장을 통해 가입하
는 사람들은 고령일 가능성이 크며 이 패턴이 지속된다면
이러한 인구 통계는 미래에 보험료가 상승하게 할 수 있다.

분석 문의구성

① 주어(People)와 동사(tend)가 있기 때문에 동사가 또
나올 수 없다. 수식어구인 현재분사(signing up)로 고
쳐야 한다.

② 조동사 뒤에 동사원형이 나와 적절하다.

③「cause + O + to R ~」5형식 어형으로 쓰여 to rise
는 적절하다.

④ if절 속에 자동사로 쓰여 적절하다.

23

It had been startling and ①disappointed to me [to find
out [that story books ②had been written by people,]
[that books ③were not natural wonders,] (④coming up
⑤of themselves like grass.)]

정답 ① (disappointed → disappointing)

해석 이야기책이 사람들에 의해 쓰여졌으며 책들이 잔디처럼
스스로 생겨나는 자연의 경이가 아니라는 것을 알게 된
건 놀라운 동시에 실망스러운 일이었다.

분석 감정·심리 유발동사의 분사의 태(능동태와 수동태의 구
분)

①「가주어(It) – 진주어(to find ~)」구문으로 진짜 주어는
to find부터 끝까지이다. 감정동사의 분사는 사람을 꾸
밀 때 p.p. 형태로, 사물을 꾸밀 때 R-ing 형태로 수식
하기로 약속되어 있는데 진짜 주어가 to R ~이므로
disappointing으로 고쳐야 한다.

② 주절 동사가 과거완료(had been)가 나와 종속절에 과
거완료(had been)는 적절하다.

③ 주절 동사가 과거완료(had been)가 나와 종속절에 과
거시제(were) 역시 가능하다.

④ 능동태 분사구문으로 쓰였는데 come은 자동사로만
쓰이는 동사이기에 수동의 관계인 과거분사는 어차피
쓰지 못하므로 능동의 관계인 현재분사(coming)는 적
절하다.

⑤ of oneself는 '스스로'라는 표현으로 쓰여 적절하다.

24

(_____ for many years,) this house will
not withstand the cold weather this winter.

① Not having painted

② Having not painted

③ Not having been painted

④ Having not been painted

정답 ③

해석 이 집은 몇 년 동안 페인트칠을 하지 않아 이번 추운 겨울
날씨를 견디지 못할 것 같다.

분석 분사구문의 태(능동태와 수동태의 구분) / 부정어의 위치

③ 분사구문 앞에 주어가 없다는 것은 주절 주어와 같기
때문에 생략된 것이다. 주절 주어(this house)가 페인
트칠하는 주체가 아니라 페인트칠 되어지는 대상이므
로 수동태 분사구문인 ③, ④로 좁혀진다. 또한 분사구
문의 부정은 반드시 앞에 써 주어야 하기 때문에「not
+ R-ing」형태의 어순으로 쓰여야 한다. ①, ②는 태
가 부적절하고, ④는 부정어의 위치가 부적절하다.

25

Songs were passed (among musicians orally,) (although
the works (of trouveres in northern France) were
sometimes documented by literary groups.)
(_____ their mostly oral tradition,) the songs
were typically not documented.

① Give   ② To give

③ Giving   ④ Given

정답 ④

해석 프랑스 북부에서 음유 시인들의 작품들은 때때로 문학 단
체에 의해 기록되기도 했지만, 노래는 음악가들 사이에서
구두로 전달되었다. 그들의 전통이 주로 구전이었다는 것
을 고려하면, 노래들은 주로 문서화되지 않았다.

분석 분사형 전치사

　④ given은 '~을 고려해 볼 때'라는 뜻의 전치사로 쓰일
　　 수 있다. 마지막 행에 the songs were라는 주어, 동
　　 사로 완전한 문장이 나와 있기 때문에 빈칸부터 뒤에
　　 나온 명사까지 수식어구로 만들어 줄 수 있는 전치사
　　 given이 적절하다.

　① 주절이 완전하게 나와 있으므로 동사가 나올 수 없다.

　② to R의 부사적 용법으로 쓰였는데 노래가 제공하는 것
　　 이 아니고 의미 또한 맞지 않다.

　③ 분사구문으로 보기에는 노래가 제공한다는 뜻이 되어
　　 야 하는데 의미가 성립되지 않는다.

Practice 02

01	②	02	②	03	②	04	①	05	④
06	②	07	③	08	①	09	④	10	②
11	④	12	③	13	②	14	①	15	③
16	③	17	④	18	②	19	④	20	②
21	④	22	④	23	②	24	③	25	④

01
[2017 상명대]

It believes [it is time [①to reconsider our ②long-holding belief] [that animals ③should be kept out of hospitals and ④away from ⑤sick people.]]

정답 ② (long-holding → long-held)

해석 그것(들)은 동물들을 병원 안으로 출입시키면 안 되며 아픈 자들로부터 분리해야 한다는 오래된 믿음을 다시 생각해 볼 때라고 생각한다.

분석 현재분사(R-ing)와 과거분사(p.p.)의 구분

② 하이픈(-)이 연결된 분사의 경우 뒤에 수식받는 명사와의 관계를 따져 풀어야 한다. 믿음이 보유하는 주체가 아니라 보유되는 대상이므로 수동의 관계인 과거분사(long-held)로 고쳐야 한다.

① that절 안에서 「it is time + to R ~(~할 때이다)」 형태의 '가주어-진주어' 구문으로 쓰여 적절하다.

③ 동물들이 병원 외부에 격리되는 대상이므로 수동태는 적절하다.

④ 전명구(out of hospitals)와 전명구(away from sick people)를 and로 연결하여 적절하다.

⑤ 형용사(sick)가 명사(people)를 수식하여 적절하다.

02
[2011 가천대]

The Good-People Charity Foundation, (_____ about a decade ago,) is now the world's largest complex (of museums, art galleries and research facilities.)

① found
② founded
③ being found
④ was founded

정답 ②

해석 10년 전에 설립된 Good-People 자선 재단은 현재 세상에서 가장 큰 박물관, 미술관, 그리고 연구 시설의 복합체이다.

분석 문의구성 / find와 found의 구분

② 주어(The Good-People Charity Foundation)와 동사(is)가 전부 나온 완전한 문장이다. 빈칸부터 a decade ago까지 수식어구의 자리인데 자선 재단이 설립하는 주체가 아니라 설립되는 대상이므로 '설립하다(found – founded – founded)'의 수동의 관계인 과거분사(founded)가 적절하다.

① find의 과거분사로 보면 자선 재단이 발견된다는 뜻으로 의미가 부적절하다.

③ ①과 같은 이유로 부적절하다.

④ 동사가 나올 자리가 아니다.

03
[2011 경기대]

(①For those) ②wanted a luxury stay at the heart of Seoul's business and tourist districts,) many people ③say [that ABC Hotel Seoul is the best ④option.]

정답 ② (wanted → wanting)

해석 많은 사람들이 서울의 사업과 관광 지구의 중심에 호화로이 머물고 싶어 하는 자들에게 ABC 호텔이 최고의 선택이라고 말한다.

분석 현재분사(R-ing)와 과거분사(p.p.)의 구분

② 사람들이 호화로운 생활을 원하는 주체이고 뒤에 목적어도 있기 때문에 능동의 관계인 현재분사(wanting)로 고쳐야 한다. 여기서 for를 접속사로 보고 wanted를 동사로 보는 학생들도 있지만 접속사 for는 문두에 위치하지 못하기 때문에 여기에서 for는 전치사로 쓰였다는 것을 알 수 있다.

① 전치사(for)로 쓰여 뒤에 명사(those)를 받아 적절하다.

③ 주어(many people)와 동사(say)의 수 일치가 적절하다.

④ 정관사(the) 뒤에 명사가 쓰여 적절하다.

04
[2017 단국대]

The Thinker, a famous bronze and marble sculpture (by August Rodin,) depicts a pensive man, (that is,) one (_____ in deep thought.)

① captured

② captures

③ capturing

④ has been captured

정답 ①

해석 오귀스트 로댕의 청동과 대리석으로 된 유명한 조각상인 '생각하는 사람'은 생각에 빠져 있는 사람, 다시 말하자면 깊은 생각에 잠겨 있는 사람을 묘사한다.

분석 현재분사(R-ing)와 과거분사(p.p.)의 구분

　① a pensive man과 one은 동격을 이루는 명사이고 빈칸부터 수식어구이다. 사람(one)이 깊은 생각에 사로잡힌 대상이므로 수동의 관계인 과거분사(captured)로 수식하는 것이 적절하다.

　② 접속사가 없이 동사가 또 나올 수 없다.

　③ 사람이 깊은 생각을 사로잡는 주체가 아니므로 능동의 관계인 현재분사는 부적절하다.

　④ 접속사가 없이 동사가 또 나올 수 없다.

05　[2013 가천대]

The result (of a lack of clarity) (①on questions of poetics) ②has been the astonishing helplessness (of ③most scholars) (when ④confronting with the task of actually analysing and evaluating a work of art.)

S V C 분사구문 confronted

정답 ④ (confronting → confronted)

해석 시학의 문제들에 명료성이 결여된 결과로 대부분의 학자는 예술 작품을 실제로 분석하고 평가하는 작업을 직면할 때 놀라울 정도로 무기력하다.

분석 분사구문의 태(능동태와 수동태의 구분)

　④ confront는 항상 타동사로만 쓰이는 동사이다. 이 동사를 능동태 분사구문(confronting)으로 쓰게 되면 반드시 목적어가 있어야 하는데 뒤에 목적어가 없이 수식어구인 전명구가 나온 것으로 보아 수동의 관계인 수동태 분사구문(confronted)으로 고쳐야 한다. 「confront A with B = A be confronted with B」의 형태를 기억하면 쉽게 풀리는 단어이다.

　① 명사와 명사의 충돌을 피해 주기 위해 전치사는 적절하다.

　② 주어(The result)와 동사(has been)의 수 일치가 적절하다.

　③ most는 형용사의 역할로 명사를 수식하여 적절하다.

06　[2011 서강대]

(_____ high school,) the job applicant was not considered (for the position.)

분사구문 S V

① Not finished

② Not having finished

③ Having not finished

④ Having not been finished

정답 ②

해석 그 지원자는 고등학교를 마치지 않아서 그 직책에 적합하다고 고려되지 않았다.

분석 분사구문의 태(능동태와 수동태의 구분) / 부정어의 위치

　② 분사구문 앞에 주어가 없다는 것은 주절 주어와 같아서 생략된 것이다. 지원자(the job applicant)가 고등학교를 마치는 주체이기 때문에 수동태 분사구문인 ①, ④는 탈락되고, 분사구문의 부정은 반드시 「not + R-ing」와 같이 분사구문 앞에 써야 하기 때문에 ②가 적절하다.

07　[2017 국민대]

(① Buffered by oceans to the east and west, and ② peaceful neighbors to the north and south,) America enjoys a degree of security ③unmatching by world powers) (④in earlier ages.)

분사구문 ⑫ N₁ N₂ S V O unmatched

정답 ③ (unmatching → unmatched)

해석 동서로는 대양, 남북으로는 평화로운 이웃 국가들의 완충 작용으로 미국은 초기에 세계의 세력들이 필적할 수 없는 정도의 안보를 누린다.

분석 분사형 완전 형용사

　③ 영어에는 분사로 쓰이다가 형용사로 굳어진 단어들이 있다. 이 단어들은 나올 때마다 추가하여 암기를 해야 한다. unmatching이라는 단어는 존재하지 않고, unmatched는 '필적할 수 없는, 타의 추종을 불허하는'이라는 뜻을 가진 형용사이므로 unmatched로 고쳐야 한다.

　① 분사구문의 태를 묻고 있다. 미국이 바다에 의해 보호받는 대상이므로 수동태 분사구문(Buffered)은 적절하다.

　② 형용사(peaceful)가 명사(neighbors)를 수식하여 적절하다.

④ 명사와 명사의 충돌을 피해 주기 위해 전명구는 적절
하다.

08

All passengers (① travel on commercial jets) ② are
　S　　　　　　　travelling
advised ③ to allow an hour ④ for boarding.
　V　　　　　O.C

정답　① (travel on → travelling on)

해석　여객기로 여행하는 모든 승객은 탑승을 위해 한 시간 정
도 여유를 둘 것이 권고된다.

분석　문의구성

　① 주어(All passengers)와 동사(are advised)가 이미
　　　존재하기 때문에 동사가 또 나올 수 없으므로 수식할
　　　수 있도록 travelling on으로 고쳐야 한다.

　② 주어(All passengers)와 동사(are advised)의 수 일
　　　치가 적절하다.

　③ 「advise + O + to R ~」 5형식 동사의 어형의 수동태
　　　로 쓰여 적절하다.

　④ 명사와 명사의 충돌을 피해 주기 위해 전명구는 적절
　　　하다.

09
　　　　(who is)
[2011 동국대]

Any executive (_____ how to keep workers
　S　　　　　　　　　　　　　　　　　　　Ⓝ
healthy) is invited (to a seminar to be held on July 5, at
　　　　　　V
the Seoul Center.)

① concerning about

② concerning

③ who concerned about

④ concerned about

정답　④

해석　근로자의 건강에 유의하는 경영자라면 누구라도 7월 5일
에 서울 센터에서 열리는 세미나에 초대 드립니다.

분석　현재분사(R-ing)와 과거분사(p.p.)의 구분

　④ 「concern A about B = A be concerned about B」
　　　는 'A가 B에 대해 걱정 · 근심하다'의 표현을 수식어구
　　　인 분사로 만든 것이다. 분사가 명사 뒤에서 수식할 경
　　　우 분사 앞에는 「주격 관계대명사 + be동사(that is)」가 생
　　　략된 형태로 ④는 Any executive (who is) concerned
　　　about ~의 형태로 쓰여 적절하다.

---

① 능동의 관계인 현재분사를 쓰면 concerning의 목적
　어가 없어 부적절하다.

② 능동의 관계인 현재분사인 concerning의 목적어는
　대상(사람)을 받아야 한다. 「의문사 + to R」를 받을 수
　없다.

③ 주격 관계대명사절 속에 concerned가 타동사로 쓰였
　는데 목적어가 없어 부적절하다.

10
[2011 동국대]

(① Within developed countries,) there are ② well-
　　　　　　　　　　　　　　　　　　　　　V
documented
documenting differences (③ in mortality rates) (④ by
　　　　　　S
race, income, or education.)

정답　② (well-documenting → well-documented)

해석　선진국 내에서는 인종, 수입, 또는 교육 수준에 따른 사망
률에 대해 문서로 충분히 입증된 차이가 있다.

분석　현재분사(R-ing)와 과거분사(p.p.)의 구분

　② 하이픈(-)이 연결된 분사의 경우 뒤에 수식받는 명사와
　　　의 관계를 따져 풀어야 한다. 차이점이 입증하는 주체
　　　가 아니라 입증되는 대상이므로 수동의 관계인 과거분
　　　사(well-documented)로 고쳐야 한다.

　① 수식어구(전명구)로 쓰여 적절하다.

　③ 명사와 명사의 충돌을 피해 주기 위해 전명구는 적절
　　　하다.

　④ 명사와 명사의 충돌을 피해 주기 위해 전치사는 적절
　　　하다.

11
　　　　　　　　　　　　　　　　　　(that)
[2011 동국대]

SBL Group, ① a Colorado-based company, said [Mr.
　S　　　　　　　　　=　　　　　　　　　V
Sam Butler will ② resign (as CEO) (③ due to a long
health problem) ④ followed a stroke three years ago.)]
　　　　　　　　　following

정답　④ (followed a stroke → following a stroke)

해석　콜로라도 기반의 SBL 그룹은 샘 버틀러 씨가 3년 전 뇌
졸중 이후로 오래 앓아 온 건강 문제로 CEO 직에서 사임
할 것이라 말했다.

분석　현재분사(R-ing)와 과거분사(p.p.)의 구분

　④ followed 뒤에 이미 목적어(a stroke)가 있기 때문에
　　　수동의 관계인 과거분사로 수식할 수 없다. 능동의 관
　　　계인 현재분사(following)로 고쳐야 한다.

76 _에듀윌 편입 솔루션 문법 Basic

① 회사가 콜로라도 지역을 기반으로 만들어진 대상이므로 수동의 관계인 과거분사는 적절하다.

② resign은 자동사로 쓰여 전명구를 받아 적절하다.

③ due to는 '~때문에'라는 전치사로 뒤에 명사가 나와 적절하다.

12

[2011 서경대]

All construction contractors are required to adhere to
　　　S　　　　　　　　　　V　　　　　　　O.C
the legal guidelines in the building code (when _____
　　　　　　　　　　　　　　　　　　　　　　　　분사구문
existing structures.)

① to renovate　　　　② renovated

③ renovating　　　　④ renovation

정답　③

해석　모든 건축 도급업자들은 이미 존재하는 구조물을 보수할 때 건축법의 법적 지침을 준수해야 한다.

분석　분사구문의 태(능동태와 수동태의 구분)

　　　③ 부사절(when) 안에 「주어 + 동사」가 없는 것으로 보아 분사구문이라는 것을 알 수 있다. when절 속에 주어인 명사가 없다는 것은 주절 주어와 같아서 생략된 것이다. 주절 주어(All construction contractors)가 건축물을 보수하는 주체이므로 능동태 분사구문인 ③이 적절하다.

　　　① 「의문사 + to R ~」는 통째로 하나의 명사의 역할이므로 앞 명사와 충돌되어 부적절하다.

　　　② 건축 도급업자가 보수되는 대상도 아닐뿐더러 빈칸 뒤에 목적어가 있기 때문에 수동태 분사구문은 부적절하다.

　　　④ 명사와 명사가 충돌되어 부적절하다.

13

[2011 서경대]

(① Though ② ~~knowing~~ as a soybean tycoon,) Maggi
　　　　　분사구문　known (to)　　　　　　　　　　　　　S
③ has helped [④ make that nation the world's No.1
　　V　　　　　　　　O　　　　　　　　　　O.C
beef exporter.]

정답　② (knowing → known)

해석　콩을 판매하는 거상이라 알려져 있긴 하지만 매기는 고국이 세계 소고기 수출국 1위가 되는 데 도움을 주었다.

분석　분사구문의 태(능동태와 수동태의 구분)

　　　② 부사절(Though) 안에 「주어 + 동사」가 없는 것으로 보아 분사구문이라는 것을 알 수 있다. 주절 주어(Maggi)가 거상으로 알려지는 대상이고, 뒤에 목적어

가 없기 때문에 수동태 분사구문(known)으로 고쳐야 한다.

　　　① 단순 분사구문에서 의미를 명확하게 전달하기 위해 접속사는 얼마든지 남길 수 있다.

　　　③ 주어와 동사의 수 일치도 적절하고 뒤에 목적어를 받아 능동태도 적절하다.

　　　④ help + (to) R ~ : help는 to R를 목적어로 받을 때 to는 생략해도 되고 써도 된다.

14

[2011 서울여대]

Bolivia today is undergoing ① profound change, and
　S　　　　　　V　　　　　　　　　　O
those (② ~~bring it about~~) are the very people (③ that
　S　　　bringing　　　　　　V　　　C　　　　　　형용사절
have been kept in a state of paralyzed submission
　V
④ for centuries.)

정답　② (bring it about → bringing it about)

해석　볼리비아는 오늘날 큰 변화를 겪고 있고, 이 변화의 주역들은 수백 년 동안 무능한 복종 상태에 있어야 했던 바로 그 사람들이다.

분석　문의구성

　　　② 주어(those)와 동사(are)가 있기 때문에 동사가 또 나올 수 없으므로 수식할 수 있도록 bringing it about으로 고쳐야 한다.

　　　① 형용사(profound)가 명사(change)를 수식하여 적절하다.

　　　③ 관계대명사 that은 선행사(사람, 사물)와 격(주격, 목적격)에 상관없이 쓸 수 있어 적절하다.

　　　④ 문장이 끝나고 수식어구(전명구)로 쓰여 적절하다.

15

[2011 성신여대]

Those (most recently _____ in the insurance
　S
program) will have to pay higher premiums (for the
　　　　　　V　　　　　　　O
same coverage.)

① enroll　　　　　　② enrolling

③ enrolled　　　　　④ enrollment

정답　③

해석　가장 최근에 보험에 가입한 사람들은 같은 보장 내용이더라도 더 높은 비용을 지불해야 할 것이다.

분석 문의구성 / 현재분사(R-ing)와 과거분사(p.p.)의 구분
③ 주어(Those)와 동사(will have to pay)가 있기 때문에 수식어구가 필요한 자리이다. 빈칸 뒤에 목적어가 없이 전명구만 있는 것으로 보아 수동의 관계인 과거분사(enrolled)로 수식해야 한다.
① 주어와 동사가 있기 때문에 동사가 또 나올 수 없다.
② 수식어구로는 문제가 없지만 태가 틀렸다. 빈칸 뒤에 목적어가 없어 현재분사로 수식할 수 없다. 또한 enroll은 '가입시키다'라는 뜻의 동사이고 수동을 써야 '가입되다'의 의미로 쓰인다.
④ 명사(Those)와 명사(enrollment)의 충돌은 부적절하다.

16
[2012 경기대]

[What happened] was [that (in my ① forties,) (back in the Dublin of my birth,) I began ② working for the most ③ respecting newspaper in the country — (The Irish Times) — ④ (as an opinion columnist.)]

정답 ③ (respecting → respected)
해석 내가 40대 때에 내 고향 더블린에서 일어났던 일은 내가 나라에서 가장 유명한 신문인 'The Irish Times'에서 오피니언 칼럼니스트로 일을 시작했던 것이다.
분석 분사형 완전 형용사
③ 현재분사(respecting)로 수식하게 되면 '존경하는 신문'이라는 의미가 되어 부적절하다. '유명한, 훌륭한'이라는 뜻의 respected로 고쳐야 한다.
① '30대, 40대'를 표현할 때 복수로 표현한다.
② begin은 to R와 R-ing를 둘 다 목적어로 받을 수 있어 적절하다.
④ 문장이 끝난 뒤 수식어구(전명구)가 나와 적절하다.

17
[2012 상명대]

We ① were terrified by sounds; ② the screaming of the wind; the ③ restless rustle of leaves in the trees; and the sudden, ④ overwhelmed ⑤ explosions of thunder.

정답 ④ (overwhelmed → overwhelming)

해석 우리는 소리, 즉, 울부짖는 바람 소리, 끊임없이 바스락거리는 나뭇잎, 갑작스럽고 너무나도 강력한 천둥소리에 겁에 질렸다.
분석 분사형 완전 형용사
④ overwhelmed는 '압도된', overwhelming은 '압도적인, 너무나도 강력한'이라는 의미로 굳어진 형용사들이다. '강력한 폭발'이라는 의미로 쓰여야 자연스럽기 때문에 overwhelming으로 고쳐야 한다.
① 우리가 겁을 주는 것이 아니라 겁을 먹은 대상이므로 수동태는 적절하다.
② 소리(sounds)에 대한 동격의 명사를 나타내어 적절하다.
③ 소리(sounds)에 대한 동격의 명사를 나타내어 적절하다.
⑤ 소리(sounds)에 대한 동격의 명사를 나타내어 적절하다.

18
[2012 홍익대]

① A series of recalls ② involved contaminated foods this year,) (including an outbreak of salmonella from tainted peanuts) ③ that killed at least eight people and sickened 600,) has consumers ④ rightly worried about the safety of their meals.

정답 ② (involved → involving)
해석 최소 8명의 사망자와 600명의 피해자를 만든 부패한 땅콩의 살모넬라균 발생을 포함해 올해 일어난 부패한 음식에 대한 일련의 리콜 사태는 소비자들이 음식의 안전성에 대해 당연히도 걱정하게 만들고 있다.
분석 현재분사(R-ing)와 과거분사(p.p.)의 구분
② 주어(A series of recalls)와 동사(has)가 있기 때문에 분사라는 것을 알 수 있다. 뒤에 목적어가 있기 때문에 수동의 관계인 과거분사(involved)로 쓰지 못하고 능동의 관계인 현재분사(involving)로 고쳐야 한다.
① a series of ~: '일련의 ~'라는 의미의 표현으로 적절하다.
③ 관계대명사 that은 선행사(사람, 사물)와 격(주격, 목적격)에 상관없이 쓸 수 있어 적절하다.
④ 소비자들이 걱정시키는 주체가 아니라 걱정하고 있는 대상이므로 수동의 관계인 과거분사는 적절하다.

19
[2011 성신여대]

(In 1066), a bright comet (_____ in the sky)
_S
attracted much attention.
_V   _O

① appears   ② appearing

③ it appeared   ④ was appearing

정답 ②

해석 1066년에 하늘에 나타난 밝은 혜성 하나가 큰 관심을 불러 모았다.

분석 문의구성

     ② 주어(a bright comet)와 동사(attracted)가 있기 때문에 수식어가 나와야 하는 자리이므로 보기 중에 수식어구는 ②가 유일하다.

     ①, ③, ④ 수식어가 아닌 동사가 나와 부적절하다.

20
[2011 가톨릭대]

(While the cold air is expected to leak out of the region,)
부사절 S V O.C
it could be a mightly slow leak, (_____ the
S V C ℗
duration of the cold and the snow cover.)
Ⓝ

① give   ② given

③ giving   ④ to give

정답 ②

해석 차가운 공기가 그 지역에서 새어 나올 것으로 예상되지만, 추위가 지속되고 눈이 덮여 있다는 점을 고려했을 때 이는 매우 느릴 것이다.

분석 분사형 전치사

     ② 빈칸 앞에 주어(it)와 동사(could be)가 있기 때문에, 빈칸부터 끝까지 수식어구로 만들어 줘야 한다. 「given ＋N(~을 고려해 볼 때)」와 같이 전치사로 굳어진 단어들이 있다. 빈칸 뒤 명사와 함께 하나의 전명구로 만들어 줄 수 있는 ②가 적절하다.

21
[2016 서울여대]

(According to a recent study,) ① depressed patients are
℗ Ⓝ S
② more likely to stand (with ③ their necks bent forward,
V 분사구문 Ⓝ ⓐ
shoulders collapsed, and ④ arms drew in toward the
Ⓝ p.p. Ⓝ drawn
body.)

정답 ④ (arms drew in → arms drawn in)

해석 최근 연구에 따르면 우울증 환자들은 목을 앞으로 내밀고 어깨를 늘어뜨리고 팔을 몸 쪽으로 당겨 서 있을 가능성이 크다.

분석 「with + 분사구문」

     ④ 「with + N + R-ing/p.p.」의 분사구문이다. 결국 with는 전치사이기 때문에 절대 동사를 쓸 수 없다. 동사(drew)를 과거분사(drawn)로 고쳐야 한다.

     ① depressed는 '우울한'이라는 뜻을 가진 형용사이므로 태를 따지지 않는다.

     ② 「be likely to R ~」는 '~할 가능성이 있다'의 표현으로 쓰여 적절하다.

     ③ 「with + N + 형용사」 형태로 쓰인 분사구문이다. 이때 bent는 '구부린'이라는 뜻의 형용사로 쓰였다.

22
[2016 경기대]

          V
French authorities are still hunting (for suspects) (① linked
S (who are)
to ② planned terrorist attacks,) (including an ③ alleged
        targeting
suicide bomb plot) ④ targeted New Year celebrations
    (which is)
in Paris.)

정답 ④ (targeted → targeting)

해석 프랑스 정부는 파리에서 새해 기념행사를 타깃으로 한 자살 폭탄 테러 추정 음모를 포함해 계획된 테러 공격들과 관련된 용의자들을 지속해서 추적 중이다.

분석 현재분사(R-ing)와 과거분사(p.p.)의 구분

     ④ 자살 폭탄 테러 음모(suicide bomb plot)가 새해 기념행사를 표적화하는 주체이고, 뒤에 목적어도 있기 때문에 능동의 관계인 현재분사(targeting)로 고쳐야 한다.

     ① 용의자들(suspects)이 연결 짓는 주체가 아니라 계획된 테러 공격과 연결되는 대상이므로 수동의 관계인 과거분사(linked)는 적절하다.

     ② 테러 공격(terrorist attacks)이 계획하는 주체가 아니라 계획되는 대상이므로 수동의 관계인 과거분사(planned)는 적절하다.

     ③ alleged는 '추정되는'이라는 뜻의 형용사로 쓰여 명사를 수식하는 것은 적절하다.

23

[2016 가천대]

The desire (to help ①correct the worst injustices of the
economic system in our own countries) also leads us
to reach out to help ②impoverishing people in other
lands. [What makes ③such an effort feasible today] is
the fact [that so much (of what people suffer from) ④is
preventable with science and technology.]

정답 ② (impoverishing → impoverished)

해석 우리나라 경제 체제가 가지고 있는 최악의 불공정을 바로
잡는 데 도움을 주고자 하는 열망은 우리로 하여금 다른
나라에 살고 있는 가난한 사람들에게 도움의 손길을 내밀
도록 이끌었다. 오늘날 그와 같은 노력을 실행 가능하게
만든 것은 사람들이 겪고 있는 고통의 상당 부분이 과학
과 기술을 통해 예방될 수 있다는 사실에 기반하고 있다.

분석 분사형 완전 형용사

　② impoverished는 '빈곤한'이라는 뜻의 형용사로 쓰이
　는 단어다. '빈곤한 사람들'이라는 의미로 쓰일 수 있도
　록 impoverished로 고쳐야 한다. impoverishing이
　라는 형용사는 존재하지 않는다.

　① 「help + (to) R ~」 help는 to R를 목적어로 받을 때
　to를 생략해도 되고 써도 된다.

　③ such는 지시형용사로 뒤에 명사를 수식할 수 있다.

　④ 주어(much)가 단수 취급하는 대명사이기 때문에 동사
　와의 수 일치는 적절하다.

24

[2017 국민대]

Korea has long ①lost any claim (to ②being a land of
clean air and clear water,) but the ongoing controversy
(③surrounded the safety of ④drinking water) is another
wake-up call (against possible contamination of this
most basic resource.)

정답 ③ (surrounded → surrounding)

해석 한국은 공기가 깨끗하고 물이 맑은 나라의 지위를 잃어버
린 지 오래지만, 식수의 안전을 둘러싸고 지속되는 논란
은 이런 가장 기본적인 자원도 오염될 가능성이 있다는
것에 대해 또 다른 경종을 울리고 있다.

분석 현재분사(R-ing)와 과거분사(p.p.)의 구분

　③ 뒤에 목적어(the safety)가 있기 때문에 능동의 관계
　인 현재분사(surrounding)로 고쳐야 한다.

　① 현재완료(have p.p.)를 쓰기 위해 has lost는 적절하다.

　② 전치사(to) 뒤에 동명사(being)로 쓰여 적절하다.

　④ 전치사(of) 뒤에 동명사(drinking)로 쓰여 적절하다.

25

[2017 숭실대]

Functionalists generally maintain [that sex differentiation
①contributes to overall social stability,] but conflict
theorists charge [that the relationship (②between
females and males) is ③one of unequal power, (with
④men dominate women.)]

정답 ④ (men dominate women → men dominating
women)

해석 기능주의자들은 일반적으로 성 분화가 전반적인 사회적
안정에 기여한다고 주장하지만, 갈등 이론가들은 남녀의
관계가 남성이 여성을 지배하는 불평등한 힘의 관계라고
주장한다.

분석 「with + 분사구문」

　④ 아무리 「with + 분사구문」이라 불러도 결국 with는 전
　치사이다. 전치사 뒤에 동사가 나올 수 없기에 men
　dominating women으로 고쳐야 한다.

　① 자동사 contribute은 전치사 to와 함께 나오는 동사
　이다.

　② 「between A and B」의 어형으로 쓰여 적절하다.

　③ one은 relationship을 대신 받는 대명사로 쓰여 적절
　하다.

9강 접속사

Practice 01

01	④	02	③	03	②	04	③	05	③
06	②	07	②	08	①	09	④	10	③
11	①	12	①	13	④	14	②	15	②
16	③	17	④	18	④	19	④	20	①
21	①	22	③	23	①	24	③	25	②

01
[2010 가톨릭대]

명령문
Dream (_____ you'll live forever) but live each
R   부사절   S   V   R
명령문
day (_____ you'll die tomorrow.)
        부사절   S   V

① even though　　　② unless

③ in case　　　④ as though

정답 ④

해석 영원히 살 것인 양 꿈꿔라. 하지만 내일 죽을 것인 양 하루하루를 살아라.

분석 적절한 의미의 접속사의 선택

④ 보기가 전부 부사절 접속사로 쓰여 적절한 의미의 선택을 묻고 있다. '당신이 영원히 살 것인 양 꿈꾸고, 내일 죽을 것인 양 살아라.'의 의미가 가장 적절하다.

①, ②, ③ 뒤 문장과 앞 문장과의 해석을 해보면 의미가 어색하여 부적절하다.

02
[2010 가톨릭대]

(_____ unavoidable the Civil War may have
   ⓒ   ⓐ   S   V
been,) it was more devastating and exhausting than
       S   V   C₁   C₂
any European war between 1815 and 1914.

① Whatever　　　② Whether

③ However　　　④ Otherwise

정답 ③

해석 아무리 피할 수 없었다 하더라도, 남북 전쟁은 1815년에서 1914년 사이에 벌어진 그 어떤 유럽의 전쟁보다 더 파괴적이고 소모적이었다.

분석 부사절 접속사 however의 특징

③ 동사(may have been)의 보어인 형용사(unavoidable)가 앞으로 끌려 나와 있다. 이 어순으로 쓰일 수 있는 접속사는 ③이 유일하다. 「however + 형용사/부사 + S + V ~」는 '아무리 ~일지라도'라는 표현의 부사절이다.

①, ②, ④ 빈칸 뒤 어순으로 쓰일 수 없는 접속사이다.

03
[2010 경기대]

No sooner ①had Mr. Obama abandoned U.S. plans (for
            had S   p.p.   O
the missile defense system) ②then Moscow announced
                            than   S   V
[it was dropping ③its plans (④to deploy the
(that)   interceptors.)]

정답 ② (then → than)

해석 오바마 대통령이 미사일 방어 체계를 구축하려는 계획을 포기하자마자, 러시아는 요격기를 배치하려는 계획을 철회하겠다고 공식적으로 발표했다.

분석 「동사의 수 − 1 = 접속사의 수」

② 「No sooner + had + S + p.p. ~ than + S + Ved ...」는 '~하자마자 …하다'의 표현으로 동사가 두 개라면 접속사는 반드시 하나가 있어야 한다. then은 부사일 뿐 접속사가 아니기에 then을 접속사 than으로 고쳐야 한다.

① No sooner을 강조하기 위해 문두로 이동시켰기 때문에 주어, 동사가 도치된 형태이다.

③ Moscow(모스크바)를 대신 받는 대명사로 쓰여 수 일치는 적절하다.

④ plan to R ~ : plan은 동격을 나타낼 때 to R로 표현하는 명사이다.

04
[2010 단국대]

(_____ of heights,) that roller coaster is one
        분사구문   지시형용사   S   V   C
ride (I'll never go on.)
(that)

① Terrified

② Being terrified

③ Since I'm terrified

④ It was the terror

정답 ③

해석 나는 높은 곳을 끔찍이 무서워해서, 그 롤러코스터는 내가 결코 탈 일이 없는 놀이 기구이다.

분석 문의구성 / 분사구문
③ 주절(that roller coaster is ~)이 있기 때문에 빈칸부터 of heights까지는 수식어로 쓰여야 하기에 「since + S + V ~(부사절)」로 쓰여 적절하다.
①, ② 분사구문으로 쓰인 형태인데 분사구문 앞에 주어인 명사가 없다는 것은 주절 주어와 같아서 생략된 것이다. ①, ②를 쓰게 되면 '롤러코스터가 무서워한다'는 의미가 되어 부적절하다.
④ 접속사가 없이 두 개의 문장이 나올 수 없다.

05
[2010 명지대]

I ①look upon myself as very fortunate (in that I ②have
S V   O.C   부사절 S
found men so interesting ③whom I am almost
V   O   O.C   that
incapable ④of being bored by them.)

정답 ③ (whom → that)

해석 나는 굉장히 운이 좋은 사람이라 생각한다. 그 이유는 내가 너무 재밌는 사람들을 알고 있어서 지루할 일이 없기 때문이다.

분석 인과 관계를 나타내는 결과의 「so ~ that + S + V ...」
③ 결과를 나타내는 「so ~ that + S + V ...」절은 상관관계를 맞춰 써야 하기 때문에 that 자리에 다른 접속사를 쓰지 못한다. whom을 that으로 고쳐야 한다.
① 「look upon + O + as + O.C」 5형식 동사의 어형으로 쓰였고, 주어와 목적어가 같기 때문에 재귀대명사를 쓴 것은 적절하다.
② 뒤에 목적어와 목적보어가 있어 능동태는 적절하다.
④ 「be (un)able to R ~ = be (in)capable of R-ing」 형태로 쓰여 적절하다.

06
[2013 가천대]

        ┌─── 강조구문 ───┐
It was (due to his lateness) _____ such a thing
      ⓟ   S
plunged him into the disaster, (which eventually
                                    형용사절
changed his whole life.)

① when   ② that
③ as   ④ what

정답 ②

해석 결국 그의 전반적인 삶을 재난이라 부를 수 있는 상황까지 이끈 것은 바로 그의 지각 때문이었다.

분석 「It is/was ~ that ...」 강조구문
② It is/was 뒤에 전명구가 나오면 100% 「It ~ that ...」 강조구문으로 쓰인 형태의 문장이다. It was 뒤에 전명구(due to his lateness)가 있기 때문에 강조구문의 접속사 that이 적절하다.

07
[2013 단국대]

                                                 가S
A fairly good income is very important; (however,) it is
     S   V   C
still more important [that a man should follow the
                      진S   S   V
vocation (for which he is best fitted,)] (_____ it
  O   형용사절   부사절
happens to be well paid.)

① what   ② whether
③ where   ④ how

정답 ②

해석 상당히 괜찮은 소득은 굉장히 중요하다. 하지만 임금을 잘 받는 것과는 상관없이, 사람은 자신에게 가장 잘 맞는 직업(천직)을 고르는 것이 훨씬 더 중요하다.

분석 올바른 접속사의 선택
② 빈칸 앞에 「It is + important + that + S + V ~」의 주절이 있는 형태이다. 빈칸부터 끝까지 수식의 역할을 할 수 있는 부사절 접속사가 필요한 자리이기 때문에 부사절 「whether + S + V ~」 '~하든 말든 상관없이'가 적절하다.
①, ④ 명사절을 이끄는 접속사인데 빈칸은 명사가 나올 수 없는 자리이다.
③ where은 명사절, 형용사절, 부사절로 전부 쓰일 수 있지만 부사절로 보더라도 '임금을 잘 받는 곳에서'라는 의미가 맞지 않아 부적절하다.

08
[2013 단국대]

       (the orange juice is)
(If freshly ①squeezing,) the orange juice (in a one-cup
  분사구문   squeezed   S
② serving) provides ③twice the minimum daily
              V   O
requirement ④for vitamin C.)

정답 ① (squeezing → squeezed)

해석 만약 오렌지주스를 신선하게 짜내면, 오렌지주스 한 컵이 비타민 C 일일 최저 필요량의 2배의 함유량을 제공한다.

분석 분사구문의 태(능동태와 수동태의 구분)

① If절 안에 주어, 동사가 없는 것으로 보아 분사구문이라는 것을 알 수 있다. 분사구문 앞에 주어가 없다는 것은 주절 주어와 같아서 생략된 것이다. 오렌지주스가 압착하는 주체가 아니라 압착되는 대상이므로 수동태 분사구문(squeezed)으로 고쳐야 한다.

② serving은 '1인분'이라는 뜻의 명사로 one-cup serving은 복합명사로 쓰여 적절하다.

③ '두 배'의 뜻을 가진 twice는 「as ~ as ...」, 「the N」보다 앞에 위치하기 때문에 적절하다.

④ 명사와 명사의 충돌을 피해 주기 위해 전치사는 적절하다.

09
[2013 서울여대]

(While we sleep,) (research indicates,) the brain replays
　　부사절　　　　삽입절　　　　　　　S　　　V
the patterns of activity (①it experienced during waking
　　　　　　O　　　　　(that)　　　ø
hours,) (②allowing us to ③enter [what one psychologist
　　　　　분사구문　O　　O.C　　　　S
calls ④it a neural virtual reality.])
　V　ø　　　　O.C

정답 ④ (it → 삭제)

해석 연구가 보여 주기를, 우리가 자는 동안 뇌는 깨어 있는 시간에 경험했던 활동 패턴을 재연한다. 이러한 사실로 인해 우리는 한 심리학자가 소위 말하는 신경계의 가상 현실에 들어갈 수 있다.

분석 명사절 접속사 what의 특징

④ what절은 항상 명사로 쓰이고 반드시 절 이하의 성분(명사)이 한 군데 불완전해야 한다. it을 삭제하여 명사 자리를 비워야 한다.

① 앞에 목적격 관계대명사 that이 생략되어 있는 형태이고 it은 the brain을 대신 받는 대명사로 수 일치 역시 적절하다.

② 앞 문장 전체를 받는 분사구문으로 뒤에 목적어(us)와 목적보어(to enter)가 나와 있어 능동태 분사구문은 적절하다.

③ 「allow + O + to R ~」 5형식 동사의 어형으로 쓰여 적절하다.

10
[2013 세종대]

It always seems to taste ①wonderful (no matter ②how
S　　　　 V　　　　 C　　　　　　　　부사절
③sloppy I measure ④things.)
　sloppily　S　　　V　　　　O

정답 ③ (sloppy → sloppily)

해석 아무리 내가 물건들(음식들)에 대해 엉성하게 평가하더라도, 그것은 항상 환상적인 맛이 난다.

분석 how 뒤 형용사와 부사의 선택

③ how 바로 뒤에 형용사 혹은 부사에 밑줄이 있다면 반드시 그 선택을 묻게 된다. 이때 형용사와 부사의 선택은 형용사/부사 뒤를 잘라 구조를 살펴보면 된다. 동사 뒤에 형용사 자리가 불완전하다면 형용사를, 완전하다면 부사를 써야 한다. sloppy 뒤에 「주어 + 동사 + 목적어(I measure things)」가 완전하게 나와 있으므로 how sloppily로 고쳐야 한다.

① taste는 2형식 오감동사로 형용사 보어를 받아 적절하다.

② 「however = no matter how」이다.

④ measure의 목적어로 쓰여 적절하다.

11
[2014 경기대]

[①That most students need above all else] is practice
　What　　　　　S　　　　V　ø　　　　　　　C
(②in writing,) and particularly (in writing) (about things)
　　S
(that ③matter to them,) (so that they will begin to feel
형용사절　S　　　　　　　부사절　　　S　　V
the satisfaction (that comes from getting important
　　O　　　　　　　형용사절
thoughts ④down in words.))

정답 ① (That → What)

해석 대부분의 학생들이 그 무엇보다도 가장 필요로 하는 것은 글쓰기 연습, 즉, 특히 자신들에게 중요한 일에 대해 글을 쓰는 연습이다. 그러면 학생들이 중요한 생각을 글로 적어내는 데서 오는 만족감을 느끼기 시작할 것이다.

분석 명사절 접속사 what과 that의 구분

① 동사(is) 앞까지는 전부 주어(명사)의 역할이다. 명사절 that은 절 이하의 성분(명사)이 완전해야 하고, 명사절 what은 절 이하의 성분(명사)이 불완전해야 한다. 절 속에 need의 목적어가 불완전하므로 What으로 고쳐야 한다.

② 명사와 명사의 충돌을 피해 주기 위해 전치사는 적절하다.

③ 주격 관계대명사(that)절 속의 동사(matter)가 선행사(things)와 수 일치가 되어 적절하다.

④ 수식어(부사)로 쓰여 적절하다.

12

[2015 서강대]

논쟁에 대한 예시

The ①debate (over if language is natural,) (I.e., do we
call ②a table a table because that's the way it is?, or
conventional, ie., do we call it a table because that's
what we decided to call it?) (in Plato's Cratylus) is ③the
very question (that (everyone ④agrees) opens
Saussure's teachings and ties them together.)

정답 ① (debate over if language → debate over whether
language)

해석 언어가 자연적인지에 대한 논쟁 — 예를 들어, 우리는 원
래 그런 것이기 때문에, 테이블을 테이블이라고 부르는
것일까? 아니면 예를 들어, 우리는 우리가 그렇게 부르자
고 결심했기 때문에, 테이블을 테이블이라고 부르는 것일
까? 플라톤의 저서 '크라틸로스(Cratylus)'에는 모두가
동의하며, 소쉬르의 가르침을 인도하고, 그것들을 하나로
결합시키는 바로 그 의문점이 있다.

분석 명사절 접속사 whether과 if의 차이점

① 접속사 whether과 if는 둘 다 명사절로 쓰일 경우 '~인
지 아닌지'의 같은 의미로 쓰여 구분을 묻는다. 명사절
whether은 모든 명사의 자리(주어, 목적어, 보어, 전
치사의 목적어)에 들어갈 수 있지만, 명사절 if는 타동
사의 목적어 자리에만 쓰일 수 있다. 지금은 전치사
(over)의 목적어 자리이기에 whether로 고쳐야 한다.

② 「call + O(a table) + O.C(a table)」 5형식 동사의 어
형으로 쓰여 적절하다.

③ 「the very + N」는 '바로 그 명사'의 뜻으로 쓰이는 표
현인데 이 경우 very는 형용사로 쓰인 것이다.

④ 주격 관계대명사(that)절 속에 삽입절(everyone
agrees)이 나온 것이고 that절 속에 동사는 opens로
선행사와 수 일치 역시 적절하다.

13

[2015 서강대]

①(Mating done,) the female yucca moth ②climbs (atop
one of the flower's six stamens) and gathers ③a cache
of pollen, ④used tentacles for the tusk.)

정답 ④ (used tentacles → using tentacles)

해석 짝짓기가 이루어지면, 암컷 유카 나방은 꽃의 여섯 개의
수술 가운데 하나의 꼭대기까지 올라서서, 상아에 있는
촉수를 활용하여 꽃가루를 모은다.

분석 분사구문의 태(능동태와 수동태의 구분)

④ 분사구문 앞에 주어가 없다는 것은 주절 주어와 같아
서 생략된 것이다. 암컷 유카 나방이 촉수를 사용하는
주체이고 뒤에 목적어(tentacles)도 있기 때문에 능동
태 분사구문(using)으로 고쳐야 한다.

① 주절 주어와 달리 분사구문 앞에 주어가 남겨진 형태
의 독립 분사구문이다. 짝짓기가 행하는 주체가 아니
라 행해지는 대상이므로 수동태 분사구문(done)은 적
절하다.

② climb은 자동사로 쓰여 뒤에 전명구를 받은 것이 적절
하다.

③ 동사(gathers)의 목적어(a cache of pollen)로 쓰여
적절하다.

14

[2015 경기대]

The ①long-suffering smartphone maker reported a
surprise bump (in operating profits,) ②provided some
hope [that ③its turnaround efforts are starting ④to
gain traction.]

정답 ② (provided → providing)

해석 오랜 시련을 겪고 있는 스마트폰 제조 회사는 영업 이익
이 놀랄 정도로 증가했다고 발표했다. 이러한 사실이 회
사의 확 달라진 노력이 탄력을 받고 있다는 희망을 주고
있다.

분석 분사구문의 태(능동태와 수동태의 구분)

② 뒤에 목적어(some hope)가 있기 때문에 능동태 분사
구문(providing)으로 고쳐야 한다.

① 스마트폰 제조사가 고통을 겪는 주체이므로 능동의 관
계인 현재분사(suffering)는 적절하다.

③ smartphone maker을 대신 받는 대명사의 소유격으
로 수 일치는 적절하다.

④ start는 뒤에 to R와 R-ing를 둘 다 목적어로 받을 수
있어 적절하다.

15

[2015 경기대]

(①Saying [that the Miss World pageant should be
focused more on ②that a woman could ③do with a
title like Miss World,]) the organization announced [that
④future pageants will not include a swimsuit round.]

정답 ② (that → what)

해석 미스 월드 미인 대회가 미스 월드라는 타이틀을 가진 여성이 할 수 있는 것에 더 많은 초점이 맞춰 줘야 한다고 말하면서, 그 단체는 앞으로 있을 미스 월드 대회는 수영복 심사를 포함시키지 않겠다고 발표했다.

분석 명사절 접속사 what과 that의 구분

② 아무리 명사절이라 할지라도 전치사 뒤에는 절대로 that절을 쓰지 못한다. 또한 절 속에 동사(do)의 목적어가 불완전하기 때문에 명사절 접속사 what으로 고쳐야 한다.

① 분사구문의 태를 묻고 있다. 미스 월드 미인 대회가 that절의 내용을 말하는 주체이므로 능동태 분사구문은 적절하다.

③ 명사절 what은 절 이하의 성분(명사)이 불완전해야 하므로 do의 목적어가 불완전하고 수식어구(전명구)가 나와 적절하다.

④ that절의 주어 자리에 명사는 적절하다.

16
[2015 홍익대]

(Only after Al Gore left politics) ① did he ② find a
　　　　　　　　　　　 강조　　　　　　 V　 S
formula (for accomplishing his life's work,) ③created a
　　　O　　　　　　　　　　　　　　　　　　 creating
global media brand around the PowerPoint presentation)
(that became his aptly ④titled book and documentary
형용사절
An Inconvenient Truth.)

정답 ③ (created → creating)

해석 앨 고어(Al Gore)는 정계를 은퇴하자마자 자신의 일생일대 임무를 완수하기 위한 방법을 발견했다. 그래서 그는 '불편한 진실(An Inconvenient Truth)'이라는 적절한 제목이 붙은 책과 다큐멘터리로 제작된 파워 포인트를 이용한 발표를 통해서 세계적인 미디어 브랜드를 창안했다.

분석 분사구문의 태(능동태와 수동태의 구분)

③ 분사구문 앞에 주어가 없다는 것은 주절 주어와 같아서 생략된 것이다. 앨 고어(Al Gore)가 미디어 브랜드를 만드는 주체이고 뒤에 목적어도 있기 때문에 능동태 분사구문(creating)으로 고쳐야 한다.

①, ② Only ~ politics를 문두로 이동시켜 강조를 했기 때문에 도치(did he find)를 한 것은 적절하다.

④ titled는 '제목을 가진, 이름 있는'이라는 뜻의 형용사로 쓰여 명사(book)를 수식하여 적절하다.

17
[2016 가천대]

(In *As You Like It*), Rosalind began a journey,
　　　　　　　　　　　　 S　　　　　V　　　 O
(①disguising herself as a man) (when she earned the
　 분사구문　　　　　　　　　　　 부사절　 S　 V₁
wrath of her uncle and was ②driven out of the house.)
　 O　　　　　　　　　　　　 V₂
The common point here is [③that the love affair got
　　　 S　　　　 because of　 V　 명사절　 S
entangled ④because women) (who mistook heroines
　 V　　　　　　　　　　 형용사절 S　 V　　　 O
(in men's attire) as men.)]
　　　　　 O.C

정답 ④ (because → because of)

해석 'As You Like It(셰익스피어의 희극)'에서, 로잘린드는 숙부를 화나게 해서 집에서 쫓겨났기 때문에 남장을 하고 여행을 시작하게 되었다. 여기서 (다른 작품들과의) 공통점은 연애 사건이 남성복을 입은 여자 주인공을 남성으로 오해한 여자들 때문에 뒤얽히게 된다는 것이다.

분석 접속사(because)와 전치사(because of)의 구분

④ 같은 뜻으로 쓰이지만 접속사(because) 뒤에는 「주어＋동사」를 써야 하고, 전치사(because of)는 명사를 써야 한다. 뒤에 women이라는 명사만 있기 때문에 전치사 because of로 고쳐야 한다.

① 분사구문의 태를 묻고 있다. 로잘린드가 변장을 하는 주체이므로 능동태 분사구문(disguising)은 적절하다.

② 그녀가 내쫓기는 대상이므로 수동태는 적절하다.

③ be동사의 보어로 명사절(that절)이 나왔다. 명사절 that은 절 이하의 성분(명사)이 완전해야 하므로 주어, 동사, 목적어가 완전하게 나와 적절하다.

18
[2016 가천대]

You do not educate a person's palate (by ①telling him
 S　 V　　　　　 O　　　　　　　　　 I.O　　　 V
[that ②what he ③has been in the habit of eating is
명사절　　　　　　　　　　　　　　　　　　　　 S　　 V
disgusting,] but ④persuaded him to try a dish of
　 C　　　　　 persuading
properly cooked food.)
　 (by)

정답 ④ (persuaded → persuading)

해석 그가 습관적으로 먹던 음식이 역겨운 것이라고 말하는 것이 아니라, 적절하게 요리된 음식을 한번 먹어보라고 그를 설득함으로써 그의 미각을 길러 줄 수 있다.

분석 등위접속사의 병치

④ 전치사(by) 뒤 telling ~, but persuading의 병치 형태이다. 등위접속사는 앞과 뒤를 대등하게 연결시켜 줘야 하므로 동명사 persuading으로 고쳐야 한다.

① 전치사(by)의 목적어로 동명사(telling)는 적절하다.

② what절 이하 eating의 목적어가 불완전하여 통째로 하나의 명사로 쓰여 that절 속의 주어의 역할로 적절하다.

③ 「be in the habit of + R-ing」는 '~하는 습관이 있다'라는 의미로, 별다른 시점부사가 없으므로 현재완료는 적절하다.

19

[2012 서울여대]

(_____ to be comprehended today,) America Online started out (in 1985) (as simply one of many service firms) (providing customers with a new way to connect to the Internet.)

① Difficult is
② It is difficult
③ Though is it difficult
④ Difficult as it may be = Though it may be difficult
    ⓐ 부사절 S   V

정답 ④

해석 비록 오늘날 이해하기 힘들더라도, 고객들에게 인터넷에 접속하는 새로운 방법을 제공한 많은 회사들 중의 하나인 아메리카 온라인(America Online)은 1985년에 사업에 착수했다.

분석 양보의 부사절 접속사로 쓰일 수 있는 as의 어순

④ 「(Al)though + S + V + 명사/형용사/부사 ~, S + V ...」 형태의 양보의 부사절을 「명사/형용사/부사 + as[though] + S + V ~, S + V ...」의 형태로 바꿔 쓸 수 있다. 둘 중 무엇을 써도 상관없지만 해당되는 어순을 가진 ④가 적절하다.

① 접속사 없이 동사가 또 나올 수 없다.

② 접속사 없어 주어, 동사가 또 나올 수 없다.

③ 접속사 뒤에 「주어 + 동사」의 어순으로 써야 한다.

20

[2016 아주대]

Convicted of
(①Convicting for stealing a loaf of ②bread for his
분사구문
sister's ③starving children,) Jean Valjean ④was
                                          S
sentenced (to five years of hard labor and ⑤another
  V   ⓟ   Ⓝ₁
fourteen years for attempting to escape.)
              Ⓝ₂

정답 ① (Convicting for → Convicted of)

해석 굶주리고 있던 누이의 어린 자식들을 위해 빵 한 덩어리를 훔친 것 때문에 유죄 판결을 받은 장 발장(Jean Valjean)은 5년의 노역형을 선고받았고, 탈옥을 시도한 것 때문에 14년 형을 추가로 선고받았다.

분석 분사구문의 태(능동태와 수동태의 구분) / 동사의 어형

① 분사구문 앞에 주어가 없다는 것은 주절 주어와 같아서 생략된 것이다. 장 발장(Jean Valjean)이 유죄 판결을 받는 대상이므로 수동태 분사구문(Convicted of)으로 고쳐야 한다. 또한 「convict A of B(A에게 B 때문에 유죄 판결을 선고하다)」의 어형은 전치사 of를 써야 하기 때문에 전치사 for도 틀렸다.

② bread는 불가산명사로 앞과 뒤에 a/an, -(e)s가 나올 수 없어 적절하다.

③ 아이들이 굶주리는 주체이므로 능동의 관계인 현재분사(starving)는 적절하다.

④ 「sentence A to B(A에게 B의 형량을 선고하다)」의 표현에서 수동태로 쓰여 적절하다.

⑤ another은 단수명사를 수식하는 것이 일반적이지만, 지금처럼 뒤에 숫자 2이상이 있다면 복수명사를 수식할 수 있다.

21

[2016 아주대]

                                                    how
The most fundamental questions (of ①what humans
                                  S   ⓟ   명사절 S
came to be the kind of animal) (②we are)) can only be
  V   C   (that)   V
answered (by a theory) (③in which culture has its
                                    형용사절
proper role) and (④in which it is intimately ⑤intertwined
with other aspects of biology.)

* come to R ~: ~하게 되다

정답 ① (what → how)

해석 어떻게 인간이 우리 자신과 같은 그런 종류의 동물이 되었는가 하는 가장 근본적인 질문들은, 문화가 적절한 역할을 하며, 생물학의 다른 측면들과 긴밀하게 뒤얽혀 있는 이론을 통해서만 답해 질 수 있다.

분석 명사절 접속사 what과 how의 선택

① what절은 명사절을 이끌고 반드시 절 이하의 성분(명사)이 불완전해야 한다. 하지만 what절 속에 주어, 동사, 보어까지 완전하게 나와 what이 틀렸다는 것을 알 수 있다. 의미상 how로 고쳐야 한다.

② 앞에 관계대명사(that)가 생략되어 be동사(are)의 보어 자리가 불완전한 형태로 쓰여 적절하다.

③ 「전치사 + 관계대명사」는 절 이하의 성분이 완전해야
한다. 절 속에 주어, 동사, 목적어가 완전하게 나와 적
절하다.
④ 문화가 엮는 주체가 아니라 엮이는 대상이기에 수동태
로 쓰여 적절하다.
⑤ 문화가 생물학의 다른 측면들과 뒤얽히는 대상이므로
수동태는 적절하다.

22
[2016 한국외대]

The zookeeper must make sure [the bear is completely
     S   V   (that)   O
off the ground] (_____.)
                    부사절

① as is it weighed
② as to weigh up
③ as it is weighed
④ as it weighs itself

정답 ③

해석 동물원 사육사는, 곰의 무게를 측정할 때 곰이 땅에서 완
전히 떨어지도록 만들어야 한다.

분석 문의구성
③ 앞에서 문장이 완전하게 나온 형태로 빈칸은 수식어가
나오면 된다. 부사절(as + S + V ~)이 쓰인 ③이 적절
하다.
① 부사절(as ~) 속에 「주어 + 동사」의 어순을 써야 한다.
도치가 될 이유가 없다.
② as to 뒤에 동사원형이 나오려면 「so ~ as to + R」의
형태로 나와야 한다.
④ '곰이 자신의 무게를 잰다'라는 의미가 부적절하다.

23
[2016 홍익대]

But _____ the other's desire and the subject's
                         A   and   B
possession are fantasies of the subject.
              S   V   C

① both
② alike
③ not
④ not only

정답 ①

해석 그러나 다른 사람의 욕망과 소유는 둘 다 본인의 환상에
불과하다.

분석 등위상관접속사의 상관관계(both A and B)
① 등위상관접속사는 상관관계를 묻는다. 빈칸 뒤 and가
있는 것으로 보아 「both A and B」로 쓰인다는 것을
알 수 있다.

② alike는 앞에서 뒤에 나온 명사를 수식할 수 없고, 뒤
에서 앞에 있는 명사를 수식하는 단어이다.
③ 「not A but B」의 형태이므로 and와 연결될 수 없다.
④ 「not only[just/merely/simply] A but (also) B」의
형태이므로 and와 연결될 수 없다.

24
[2016 홍익대]

(In the Disney version at least), it is Geppetto's wish,
                                        가S   B
not Pinocchio's, [_____ the puppet become real.]
              A   진S

① what
② which
③ that
④ as

                          * not A but B = B, not A

정답 ③

해석 최소한 디즈니 버전에서, 그 인형이 현실이 되는 것은 피
노키오의 소원이 아니라, 제페토의 소원이다.

분석 「It is/was ~ that + S + V ...」의 '가주어-진주어' 구문
③ 「It is ~ that + S + V ...」의 '가주어-진주어' 구문이다.
진짜 주어 자리에는 that절을 써야 하므로 ③이 적절
하다.
①, ②, ④ '가주어-진주어' 구문에서 진짜 주어 자리에
what, which, as는 나올 수 없다.

25
[2016 한국외대]

(Compared to Korea and Japan), controversy (over
   분사구문   S
globalization) began a little later in Taiwan. There are a
               V   V
couple of reasons (to explain _____.)
         S   명사절

① why was this the case
② why this was the case
③ the case was why this
④ the case why was this

정답 ②

해석 한국 및 일본과 비교했을 때, 타이완에서는 세계화에 대
한 논쟁이 좀 더 나중에 시작됐다. 그것이 왜 사실인지를
설명할 수 있는 두 가지 이유가 있다.

분석 명사절(간접의문문)의 어순(접속사 + 주어 + 동사)
② 빈칸은 explain의 목적어 자리이다. 모든 명사절(간접
의문문)의 어순은 「접속사 + 주어 + 동사」의 어순으로
써야 하므로 ②가 적절하다.

Practice 02

01	④	02	①	03	①	04	①	05	③
06	②	07	③	08	③	09	③	10	④
11	③	12	①	13	③	14	④	15	④
16	②	17	①	18	③	19	③	20	①
21	③	22	③	23	①	24	③	25	②

01
[2017 가톨릭대]

She wondered [if children loved pink and blue (out of instinct,) (_____ a social compulsion) (that they are not aware of.)]

① because
② because of
③ or because
④ or because of

정답 ④

해석 그녀는 아이들이 본능적으로 분홍색과 파란색을 좋아하는 것인지 아니면 그들이 인지하지 못하는 사회적 강요 때문에 그런 것인지 궁금했다.

분석 because와 because of의 구분 / 등위접속사의 유무
- ④ 빈칸 뒤 「주어 + 동사」가 아닌 명사만 있기 때문에 전치사 because of를 써야 하고, 전명구(out of instinct)와 전명구(because of a social compulsion)를 연결해야 하므로 등위접속사 or이 필요하다.
- ①, ③ because는 접속사로 쓰여 뒤에 「주어 + 동사」가 나와야 한다.
- ② 전명구와 전명구를 연결하는 접속사가 필요하다.

02
[2017 단국대]

The Fed is raising rates and the dollar is rising, but the rest of the world is still moving (in the opposite direction,) (_____ a "Great Divergence" in monetary policy.)

① creating
② creates
③ is creating
④ created

정답 ①

해석 연방 준비은행이 금리를 올리고, 달러의 가치가 상승하고 있다. 하지만 전 세계의 나머지 국가들은 여전히 반대되는 움직임을 보이고 있으며, 이로 인해 통화 정책에서 '대분열(Great Divergence)'을 초래하고 있다.

분석 분사구문의 태(능동태와 수동태의 구분)
- ① 빈칸 앞에 주절이 있기 때문에 빈칸부터 수식어구가 필요하다. 앞 문장 전체를 받는 분사구문이며 빈칸 뒤에 목적어(a "Great Divergence")가 있으므로 능동태 분사구문(creating)이 적절하다.
- ②, ③ 접속사 없이 동사가 나올 수 없다.
- ④ 빈칸 뒤 목적어가 있기 때문에 수동태 분사구문(created)은 부적절하다.

03
[2017 서울여대]

(①Defining in a limited sense), a tale is a story, (usually short,) (that ②sets forth strange and wonderful events (in more or less ③bare summary,) (without ④detailed character-drawing.))

정답 ① (Defining → Defined)

해석 제한된 관점에서 정의될 때, 설화란 대개 자세한 인물 묘사 없이 낯설지만 놀랄 만한 사건을 날것 그대로 요약하여 설명하는 짧은 이야기다.

분석 분사구문의 태(능동태와 수동태의 구분)
- ① 분사구문 앞에 주어가 없다는 것은 주절 주어와 같아서 생략된 것이다. 이야기(a tale)가 정의 내리는 주체가 아니라 정의 내려지는 대상이고, 뒤에 목적어도 없기 때문에 수동태 분사구문(Defined)으로 고쳐야 한다.
- ② 주격 관계대명사(that)절 속의 동사(sets)는 선행사(a story)와 수 일치가 되어 적절하다.
- ③ 형용사(bare)가 명사(summary)를 수식하여 적절하다.
- ④ detailed는 '상세한, 자세한'이라는 뜻의 형용사이다.

04
[2017 서울여대]

(It is assumed [(①what Homo erectus ②must have had a communication system (③more complex than ④any of today's living primates.)]

정답 ① (what → that)

해석 호모 에렉투스는 오늘날 살아 있는 영장류의 그 어떤 것보다도 더 복잡한 의사소통 체계를 가지고 있었음에 틀림없다고 추정된다.

분석 　명사절 접속사 what과 that의 구분

　① what절은 항상 명사절을 이끌고 반드시 절 이하의 성분(명사)이 불완전해야 하는데 절 속에 주어, 동사, 목적어가 전부 나와 있으므로 명사절 접속사 that으로 고쳐야 한다. 또한 '가주어–진주어'는 「it ~ what ...」으로 표현하지 않는다.

　② 「must + have p.p.」는 '과거에 ~했음에 틀림없다'의 표현으로 쓰여 적절하다.

　③ 뒤에 than이 있기 때문에 비교급 more은 문제없고, 형용사(complex)는 앞에 명사(system)를 수식하여 적절하다.

　④ any가 명사로 쓰여 비교 대상은 적절하다.

05
[2017 서울여대]

Exactly [_____ we can replace our soil
　　　　　　명사절(S)　　　　S　　　V　　　　O
(disappearing through erosion)] is not known.
　　　　　　　　　　　　　　　V

① unless ② since
③ how ④ what

정답 　③

해석 　우리가 침식으로 인해 사라지고 있는 토양을 어떻게 대체할 수 있는지는 여전히 알려지지 않았다.

분석 　문의구성 / 명사절 접속사의 선택

　③ 뒤에 동사(is not known)가 있기 때문에 그 앞은 전부 주어(명사)의 역할이 나와야 한다. 빈칸 뒤에 있는 문장(we can replace our soil)을 하나의 명사로 만들어 줄 수 있는 명사절 접속사가 필요한 자리이기 때문에 ③, ④로 좁혀지고, 절 이하의 성분이 완전(주어 + 동사 + 목적어)하기 때문에 how가 적절하다. what은 명사절을 이끌지만 절 이하의 성분이 불완전해야 한다.

06
[2017 아주대]

(_____,) the answer (to many
　　　　　　　　　　　　　　S
kinds of pain,) (from sore joints and back pain to
headaches and stomachaches,) may be in the kitchen
　　　　　　　　　　　　　　　　　V　　　　C
(rather than in the medicine cabinet.)

① As may it sound surprising
② Surprising as it may sound = Though it may sound surprising
　　　　　　　ⓐ　　S　　V
③ Sound surprising as it may
④ May sound surprising as it
⑤ It may sound surprising as

정답 　②

해석 　비록 놀랍게 들릴 수도 있지만, 관절통과 요통에서부터 두통과 복통에 이르기까지 수많은 종류의 통증에 대한 해결책은 약이 수납된 곳이 아니라 부엌에 있을 수 있다.

분석 　양보의 부사절 접속사로 쓰일 수 있는 as의 어순

　② 「(Al)though + S + V + 명사/형용사/부사 ~, S + V ...」와 같이 쓰이는 양보의 부사절을 「명사/형용사/부사 + as[though] + S + V ~, S + V ...」의 형태로 바꿔 쓸 수 있다. 둘 중 무엇을 써도 상관없지만 해당되는 어순을 가진 ②가 적절하다.

　①, ③, ④, ⑤ 어순이 부적절하다.

07
[2017 한국외대]

(Despite the freedom of the press,) (in the U.S.) there
are limits (on _____.)
　V　　S　　ⓟ　　　ⓝ
① what can the press publish
② can the press publish what
③ what the press can publish
④ the press what can publish

정답 　③

해석 　언론의 자유에도 불구하고, 미국에서는 언론이 출판할 수 있는 것에 대한 제한이 있다.

분석 　명사절(간접의문문)의 어순(접속사 + 주어 + 동사)

　③ 명사절(간접의문문)의 어순은 「접속사 + 주어 + 동사」로 써야 하므로 ③이 적절하다. what절은 절 이하의 성분이 불완전해야 하기 때문에 타동사(publish)의 목적어가 불완전한 상태이다.

08
[2011 이화여대]

(While touring the deserts of Argentina and Chile)
　분사구문
(① which many travellers found ② spectacular,) ③ it was
　　형용사절　　　　S　　　　V　　　　O.C　　　　they found
found [that Dr. Smith ④ contracted malaria.]
　　　　　　　　　　　　　　O
　　　S　　V

정답 　③ (it was found → they found)

해석 　수많은 여행객이 멋지다고 생각했던 아르헨티나와 칠레의 사막을 여행하는 동안, 그들은 스미스 씨가 말라리아에 걸렸다는 것을 알게 되었다.

분석 　분사구문의 특징

③ 부사절 접속사(While) 이하에 「주어＋동사」가 나오지 않고 touring이 나온 것으로 보아 분사구문이라는 것을 알 수 있다. 분사구문 앞에 주어가 없다는 것은 주절 주어와 같아서 생략된 것인데 주절 주어가 뜻이 없는 가짜 주어 it이라면 touring의 주어가 될 수 없다. 그래서 주절 주어에 여행을 할 수 있는 주어인 they (= travellers) found로 고쳐야 한다.
① 선행사가 사물(the deserts)이고, 절 이하의 성분 (found의 목적어)이 불완전하기에 관계대명사 which는 적절하다.
② found의 목적보어로 형용사는 적절하다.
④ that절 속에 동사로 쓰여 적절하다.

09
[2011 가천대]

Such house chores, (＿＿＿＿＿ important for home
S (they are) 분사구문 ⓐ
management,) may not be favorite job (for anyone.)
V C

① they are   ② as
③ though   ④ despite

정답 ③

해석 비록 집안을 관리하는 데 있어 중요하다 하더라도, 집안의 허드렛일은 누구에게나 선호하는 일은 아닐 것이다.

분석 분사구문의 특징
③ 이미 문장에 주어(Such house chores)와 동사(may be)가 있기 때문에, 빈칸부터 management까지는 수식어구가 나와야 한다. 분사구문을 만들 때 접속사는 보통 생략을 하지만 의미를 명확하게 전달하고 싶을 때 남겨 주어도 괜찮다. 주어가 같아 주어(Such house chores)가 생략되고 are는 being이 되어 생략된 분사구문에서 접속사가 남겨진 ③이 적절하다.
① 접속사 없이 주어, 동사가 또 나올 수 없다.
② 분사구문에서 의미를 명확하게 전달하고 싶어 남겨 주는 접속사는 확실하게 하나의 뜻을 가진 접속사가 남겨진다. as는 모든 뜻으로 해석이 가능하여 분사구문에서 접속사로 남기지 않는다.
④ 전치사 뒤에는 형용사가 나올 수 없다.

10
[2011 단국대]

Researchers have discovered [that body fat produces
S S V 명사절(O) S
proteins (that trigger inflammation,)] (thus ＿＿＿＿＿
O 형용사절 V 분사구문

to the development of heart disease, stroke, and diabetes.)
① contributes   ② has contributed
③ being contributed   ④ contributing

정답 ④

해석 연구원들은 체지방이 염증을 불러일으키는 단백질을 생성해 낸다는 사실을 발견했다. 이와 같은 사실이 심장병, 뇌졸중, 당뇨병의 발생에 있어 원인이 되고 있다.

분석 문의구성 / 분사구문의 태(능동태와 수동태의 구분)
④ 빈칸 앞에 이미 문장이 완전하게 나와 있기 때문에 콤마(,)부터는 수식어구인 분사구문이 나와야 한다. contribute은 자동사이기 때문에 수동태는 쓰지 못하므로 능동태 분사구문(contributing)이 적절하다.
①, ② 접속사 없이 동사가 또 나올 수 없다.
③ contribute은 자동사이기 때문에 수동태를 쓰지 못하므로 수동태 분사구문(being contributed) 역시 쓰지 못한다.

11
[2011 상명대]

①I am still undecided [②whether I should insist (upon
S V C 명사절 S V
complete performance of the contract) ③or to forgive
V
the obligation (④in anticipation of concessions in later
O
negotiating sessions.)]

정답 ③ (or to forgive the obligation → or forgive the obligation)

해석 나는 계약의 완벽한 이행을 주장해야 할지 아니면 추후에 있을 협상 기간에 양보를 기대하고 지켜야 할 의무를 못 본 체해야 할지 아직 결정하지 못했다.

분석 등위접속사의 병치
③ insist or forgive로 연결되는 표현으로 등위접속사는 앞과 뒤를 대등하게 연결시켜야 한다. 앞에 어디를 보아도 to R가 없기 때문에 or 뒤 to R를 연결할 수 없다. forgive로 고쳐야 한다.
① undecided는 '결정하지 못한'이라는 뜻의 형용사로 쓰여 적절하다.
② undecided 뒤에 명사절이 나오는 경우는 undecided (about)처럼 전치사가 생략되기 때문에 적절하다.
④ 명사와 명사의 충돌을 피해 주기 위해 전명구는 적절하다.

12

[2011 서울여대]

Timothy J. McVeigh was convicted (of bombing a
federal office building in Oklahoma city,) (_____
the deaths of 168 people.)

① causing

② and caused

③ it caused

④ which it caused

정답 ①

해석 티모시 J. 멕베이(Timothy J. McVeigh)는 오클라호마
에 있는 한 연방 관공서 건물을 폭파시킨 혐의로 유죄 판
결을 받았다. 이 폭발은 168명의 사상자를 낳았다.

분석 문의구성 / 분사구문의 태(능동태와 수동태의 구분)

① 빈칸 앞에 주절이 완전하게 나와 있기 때문에 수식어
구가 필요한 자리이다. 동시 시점을 나타내는 능동태
분사구문(causing)이 적절하다.

② and 이하에 Timothy가 생략되었다고 하면 ①과 똑같
다고 생각할 수 있지만 ②는 시제가 틀렸다. and는 시
간을 앞에서 뒤로 흘려 주기 때문에 ②를 쓰면 '유죄
판결을 받고 나서 그 이후 168명을 죽였다'라는 의미
가 되어 부적절하다.

③ 접속사 없이 주어, 동사가 또 나올 수 없다.

④ 관계대명사 which는 반드시 절 이하의 성분(명사)이
불완전해야 하는데 완전하게 나와 부적절하다.

13

[2011 성신여대]

Planets are ① probably formed (as a ② result of both
gases ③ or particles) (drawn ④ together in space by
gravity.)

정답 ③ (or particles → and particles)

해석 행성들은 아마도 중력으로 인해 우주에서 한데 모인 기체
와 작은 입자의 결과로 생성된 것이다.

분석 등위상관접속사의 상관관계(both A and B)

③ 등위상관접속사 both는 A and B의 형태로 쓰인다.
or을 and로 고쳐야 한다.

① 행성들이 형성하는 주체가 아니라 형성되는 대상이므
로 수동태는 적절하다.

② 「as a result of ~」는 '~의 결과로서'의 뜻을 가진 전
치사로 쓰여 적절하다.

④ 수동의 관계인 과거분사(drawn)가 나와 수식어구(전
명구)는 적절하다.

14

[2011 세종대]

_____ you can't talk right.]

① The reason you can't get a job is because

② The reason for you can't get a job is because

③ The reason for you can't get a job is that

④ The reason (you can't get a job) is [that

정답 ④

해석 네가 직업을 얻을 수 없는 이유는 말을 똑바로 하지 못하
기 때문이다.

분석 「The reason is + that + S + V ~」(O) / 「The reason
is + because + S + V ~」(X)

④ that과 because의 선택 문제이다. The reason is의
보어로 명사절(that절)은 가능하지만 해석이 된다고 하
여 부사절(because절)은 쓰지 못한다. 「The reason
is + that + S + V ~」의 형태로 암기하는 것이 좋다.

①, ② The reason이 주어로 나왔을 경우 be동사 뒤에
는 because절을 쓰지 못한다.

③ 「The reason (why) + S + V ~」의 형태처럼 관계부사
why는 가능하지만 for는 쓰지 못한다.

15

[2011 세종대]

(Historically,) ① the most dangerous part (of a lawmaker's
job) ② has been [③ not violence, but ④ to travel.]

정답 ④ (to travel → travel)

해석 역사적으로 보면, 국회 의원의 업무 중 가장 위험한 부분
은 폭력이 아니라 여행이었다.

분석 등위상관접속사에서 A와 B의 품사 일치(not A but B)

④ 등위상관접속사 「not A but B」에서 A와 B의 품사를
맞춰 써야 한다. A에 명사(violence)가 나왔으므로 B
에도 역시 명사가 나와야 한다. to travel을 travel로
고쳐야 한다.

① 최상급 앞에는 정관사 the를 써야 하기 때문에 적절
하다.

② 주어(the most dangerous part)와 동사(has been)
의 수 일치가 적절하다.

③ 「not A but B」는 등위상관접속사로서 상관관계가 적
절하다.

16

Historians have long been reluctant (①to recognize [that
Queen Victoria was not just a monarch ②and one of
the most prominent working mothers in history]) —
③one (who was both deeply in love with her husband
④and resentful of the demands on her as a mother
and a wife.)

* be reluctant to R ~: ~하기를 꺼리다

정답 ② (and → but)

해석 역사가들은 빅토리아 여왕이 군주일 뿐만 아니라 역사상
가장 유명한 워킹 맘들 중 하나라는 사실을 인정하기 꺼
렸다. 그녀는 남편을 깊이 사랑했고 엄마와 아내로서 그
녀에게 해오는 요구에 분개하기도 했던 사람이었다.

분석 등위상관접속사의 상관관계(not only A but (also) B)

② 등위상관접속사 「not only A but (also) B」에서 not
only는 and가 아닌 but과 상관관계를 맞춰야 하기 때
문에 and를 but으로 고쳐야 한다.

① 「reluctant to R ~」는 '~하기를 꺼리는'의 표현으로
reluctant는 준동사를 받을 경우 to R와 쓰이는 형용
사이다.

③ 빅토리아 여왕을 대신 받는 대명사로 쓰여 적절하다.

④ 「both A and B」의 형태로 쓰여 상관관계가 적절하다.

17

Bone is one (of the hardest materials) (in the body) and,
(_____,) it has a remarkable ability (to
resist tension and other forces acting on it.)

① although relatively light in weight
(it is)
② having been relatively light in weight
③ that it is relatively light in weight
④ to be relatively light in weight

정답 ①

해석 뼈는 신체에서 가장 단단한 물질 중 하나이며, 비록 상대
적으로 무게는 가볍지만, 뼈에 작용하는 다른 힘과 긴장
을 견뎌 낼 수 있는 놀라운 능력을 갖고 있다.

분석 문의구성 / 분사구문의 특징

① 빈칸 앞뒤로 문장(Bone is ~)과 문장(it has ~)이 온전
히 쓰여 있기 때문에 빈칸은 수식어구가 나와야 한다.
주어가 같아 생략되고 being이 생략된 분사구문에서

의미를 명확하게 전달하기 위해 접속사를 남겨 놓은
①이 적절하다.

② 분사구문에서 접속사는 얼마든지 생략할 수 있지만 완
료분사구문(having been)은 부적절하다. 완료분사구
문은 주절 동사보다 이전 시점을 전달할 때 써 주는 표
현인데 뼈가 놀라운 능력을 갖기 이전에 비교적 가벼
웠던 것이 아니라 뼈가 가볍지만 놀라운 능력을 가지
고 있는 것은 동시 시점이기에 부적절하다.

③ that절이 완전하면 명사절로 쓰이는데 빈칸은 명사가
나올 자리가 아니다.

④ to R의 부사적 용법으로 봐야 하는데 '뼈가 비교적 가
벼워지기 위해서'라는 의미가 되어 부적절하다.

18

It may be worth ①noting [that the hijackers (②themselves)
correctly foresaw ③what the threat (to their mission)
would come (from the passengers) and (not from a
military source external ④to the plane.)]

정답 ③ (what → that)

해석 공중 납치범들이 그들의 임무에 대한 위협은 비행기 외부
에 있는 군대로부터가 아니라 승객들로부터 올 것이라고
정확하게 예측했던 사실을 주목할 만한 가치가 있다.

분석 명사절 접속사 what과 that의 구분

③ what절은 절 이하의 성분(명사)이 불완전하여 하나의
명사절을 이끈다. 뒤에 성분이 완전하게 나와 명사절
접속사 that으로 고쳐야 한다.

① worth는 전치사적 형용사로 쓰여 뒤에 명사 혹은 동
명사가 나와야 하므로 적절하다. worth 뒤에 절대 to
R는 쓰지 못한다.

② 명사 뒤 재귀대명사는 동격을 나타내는 표현이다.

④ 「external to ~」는 '~의 외부에'라는 표현으로 external
은 전치사를 쓸 때 to와 함께 쓰는 형용사이다.

19

I ①used to work (②as a salesman,) and I know [how
image is
important ③is image (in ④any job.)]
ⓐ

정답 ③ (is image → image is)

해석 나는 과거에 영업 사원으로 일했다. 그래서 나는 어떤 직
업에서 이미지가 얼마나 중요한지를 알고 있다.

분석 명사절(간접의문문)의 어순(접속사 + 주어 + 동사)

　　③ 모든 명사절(간접의문문)의 어순은 「접속사 + 주어 + 동사」의 어순으로 쓰여야 하기 때문에 image is로 고쳐야 한다.

　　① 「used to + R ~」는 '~하곤 했다'의 표현으로 쓰여 적절하다.

　　② 문장이 앞에서 끝나 있기 때문에 수식어구(전명구)로 쓰여 적절하다.

　　④ 형용사(any)가 명사(job)를 수식하여 적절하다.

20
[2012 아주대]

Just as <u>Napoleon faced</u> defeat (in Russia,) _____
　　　　　　　S　　　V　　　O

<u>Hitler saw</u> his dreams (of conquest) evaporate (at the
　　S　　V　　O　　　　　　　　　O.C
siege of Leningrad.)

① so　　　　　　　　② and

③ as　　　　　　　　④ yet

⑤ but

정답 ①

해석 나폴레옹이 러시아에서 패배를 맛본 것과 마찬가지로, 히틀러는 레닌그라드 공격에서 정복의 꿈이 물거품이 되는 것을 목격했다.

분석 「(Just) as + S + V ~, so + S + V ...」

　　① 「(Just) as + S + V ~, so + S + V ...」는 '~하는 것과 마찬가지로 ...하다'의 표현으로 Just as와 연결된 so가 적절하다.

　　②, ③, ④, ⑤ 접속사의 상관관계가 부적절하다.

21
[2012 아주대]

(Although he ① <u>has worked</u> in other ② <u>media</u> and other
부사절　　S　　V

forms,) ③ <s>but</s> Bean <u>gained</u> <u>considerable success</u> (with
　　　　　　　　S　　V　　　　O

his ④ <u>pit-fired</u> earthenware ⑤ <u>bowls</u>.)

정답 ③ (but → 삭제)

해석 비록 빈(Bean)이 현재는 다른 매체와 형태를 가지고 작업하고 있지만, 화로에서 굽는 도기 그릇과 더불어 큰 성공을 거두었다.

분석 although와 but의 공존 불가

　　③ 어떠한 경우에도 although와 but은 함께 쓰이지 못하기 때문에 but을 삭제해야 한다. 문장이 두 개라면 접

속사는 한 개를 써야 하기 때문에 접속사 두 개는 틀린 것이라는 접근 방법도 괜찮다.

　　① 완료를 표현하기 위한 has p.p.는 적절하다.

　　② other은 복수명사를 꾸며 주는 형용사로 media는 medium의 복수형 명사이다.

　　④ 도기 그릇이 불을 붙이는 주체가 아니라 불이 붙여지는 대상이므로 수동의 관계인 과거분사(fired)는 적절하다.

　　⑤ 전치사(with)의 목적어로 명사(earthenware bowls)는 적절하다.

22
[2012 한국항공대]

　　　　　　　　　　　　　　　(which was)

The most general charge (① <u>brought</u> by its
　　　　　　　　　　S

contemporaries) (② <u>against</u> the schoolroom of the

　　　　　　　　　　　　　　　　it failed

seventeenth century) <u>was</u> [that ③ <s>its failure</s> to adapt its
　　　　　　　　　　　　V　　명사절　　S

ideals to the profound changes (which were becoming
　　　　　　　　　　　　　　　　　　형용사절

④ <u>manifest</u> in social life.)]

정답 ③ (its failure to adapt → it failed to adapt)

해석 17세기 교실에 대해 동시대인들에 의해 행해진 가장 일반적인 비난은 사회생활에서 분명히 보이고 있는 근본적인 변화에 교실이 이상을 발맞추어 나가지 못하고 있다는 것이었다.

분석 문의구성

　　③ be동사(was) 뒤에 that은 명사절 접속사이다. 접속사 뒤에는 주어, 동사가 나와야 하므로 it failed to adapt로 고쳐야 한다.

　　① 비난이 행하는 주체가 아니라 행해지는 대상이므로 수동의 관계인 과거분사(brought)는 적절하다.

　　② 명사와 명사의 충돌을 피해 주기 위해 전치사는 적절하다.

　　④ become의 보어로 형용사(manifest)는 적절하다.

23
[2012 홍익대]

Chicken pox and measles, (① <s>despite</s> common and
　　　　　　　S　　　　　　　　　　　though　　　　ⓐ

rarely <u>fatal</u> among Europeans,) often ② <u>proved</u> lethal
　　　　ⓐ　　　　　　　　　　　　　　　　　V　　C

(③ <u>to</u> Native Americans,) <u>and</u> more dangerous diseases
　　　　　　　　　　　　　　　　　　　　　　　S

(such as small pox) ④ <u>were</u> especially deadly.
　　　ⓟ　　　ⓝ　　　　V　　　　　　C

정답 ① (despite → though)

해석 비록 유럽인들 사이에서는 흔하고 그다지 치명적이지 않지만, 수두와 홍역은 미국 원주민에게는 치명적으로 판명되었으며, 천연두와 같은 더욱 위험한 질병은 특히 치명적이다.

분석 접속사(though)와 전치사(despite)의 구분

① 명사가 없고 형용사(common and fatal)만 있기 때문에 전치사는 쓸 수 없다. 접속사 though로 고쳐야 한다. though는 접속사로 뒤에 주어, 동사가 나와야 하는데 주어가 같아서 생략되고 being이 생략된 분사구문에서 접속사를 남겨 준 형태이다.

② 주어(Chicken pox and measles)에 대한 동사(proved)로 쓰여 적절하다.

③ 문장이 끝난 뒤 수식어구(전명구)는 적절하다.

④ 주어(more dangerous diseases)와 동사(were)의 수 일치가 적절하다.

24   [2010 가톨릭대]

(In the past,) inexperienced young adults, (when
                     S   분사구문
_____ with crucial life decisions,) tended [to
                                                    V
accept the judgement of parents and other authority
                              O
figures.]

① be faced   ② facing
③ faced   ④ to face

정답 ③

해석 과거에는 경험이 없는 젊은이들이 중대한 삶의 결정에 직면하였을 때, 부모님과 다른 권위 있는 인물들의 판단을 따르는 경향이 있었다.

분석 분사구문의 태(능동태와 수동태의 구분)

③ 접속사(when) 뒤에 주어가 없는 것으로 보아 분사구문이라는 것을 알 수 있다. 빈칸 뒤 목적어가 없이 수식어구(전명구)가 있는 것으로 보아 수동태 분사구문(faced)이 적절하다.

① when절 속에 주어 없이 동사만 나올 수 없다.

② 목적어가 없어 능동태 분사구문(facing)은 부적절하다.

④ 「의문사 + to R ~」의 형태는 통째로 하나의 명사로 쓰여 부적절하다.

25   [2013 국민대]

The cost (of college education) ① has risen ② ~~too~~
       S   V
rapidly (③ during the past several years) that it is now
 ⓐd   that it is now
④ beyond the reach of many people.

정답 ② (too rapidly → so rapidly)

해석 지난 몇 년간 대학 등록금이 너무 급격하게 올라서 현재는 많은 사람들이 감당할 수 있는 수준을 아득히 뛰어넘었다.

분석 결과의 「so ~ that + S + V ...」 상관관계

② 결과의 「so ~ that + S + V ...」에서 so 자리에 very, too, as는 불가능하다.

① 「during the past + 기간 N」는 현재완료 시점부사이므로 현재완료(has risen)는 적절하다.

③ 동사와 시점부사의 시제 일치는 적절하다.

④ 전명구는 형용사의 역할로 쓰일 수 있기 때문에 be동사의 보어로 적절하다.

10강 관계사

Practice 01

01	①	02	③	03	④	04	③	05	④
06	①	07	②	08	①	09	④	10	②
11	③	12	④	13	④	14	①	15	④
16	④	17	④	18	②	19	④	20	①
21	①	22	①	23	⑤	24	②	25	③

01
[2011 성신여대]

Virginia Woolf, ①which developed new literary ideas ②for effecting social change,) ③led the intellectual movement (for ④freedom from the British government.)

정답 ① (which developed → who developed)

해석 사회 변화를 초래하기 위해 새로운 문학적 이상을 발전시킨 버지니아 울프는 영국 정부로부터의 자유를 위한 지적 운동을 이끌었다.

분석 관계대명사 who와 which의 구분
  ① 관계대명사 which는 선행사로 사물을 수식해야 하는데 수식받는 명사가 사람(Virginia Woolf)이므로 사람을 수식하는 관계대명사 who로 고쳐야 한다.
  ② 전치사의 목적어로 동명사는 적절하다.
  ③ 주어(Virginia Woolf)에 대한 동사(led)로 쓰여 적절하다.
  ④ 명사와 명사의 충돌을 피해 주기 위해 전치사는 적절하다.

02
[2010 세종대]

(As women have ①moved away from the traditional status of ②homemaker,) notions (of ③that a marriage ④should be) have changed (to accommodate the new reality.)

정답 ③ (that → what)

해석 여성들이 가정주부라는 전통적 위치에서 이동함에 따라, 결혼이라고 하는 것이 무엇인지에 대한 개념도 새로운 현실에 발맞추어 변화해 가고 있다.

분석 명사절 접속사 that과 what의 구분
  ③ that절은 절 이하의 성분(명사)이 완전하게 나와 명사절로 쓰이는데 should be의 보어가 불완전하여 부적절하고, 전치사 뒤에 that절은 절대 쓰지 못하기 때문에 명사절 접속사 what으로 고쳐야 한다.
  ① move가 자동사로 쓰였고, 별다른 시점부사가 없기에 현재완료(have moved) 역시 적절하다.
  ② 전치사의 목적어로 명사는 적절하다.
  ④ 명사절 접속사 what은 절 이하의 성분(명사)이 불완전해야 하므로 should be의 보어가 불완전하여 적절하다.

03
[2013 성균관대]

The closer you get to an election, ①the harder it can be [to tell ②where the candidates stand ③on the issues] ④what matter ⑤most.)]

정답 ④ (what → that 또는 which)

해석 선거에 점점 더 가까워질수록 후보자들이 가장 중요한 문제에서 어떠한 입장을 취하는지를 알아보는 것이 점점 더 어려워질 것이다.

분석 명사절 접속사 what과 관계대명사(형용사절) that의 구분
  ④ what절은 항상 명사절을 이끈다. 앞에 명사(the issues)와 충돌되어 명사절(what)을 쓰지 못하기 때문에 관계대명사(형용사절) that 혹은 which로 고쳐야 한다.
  ① 「the -er/more 형용사/부사＋S＋V ~, the -er/more 형용사/부사＋S＋ V ...」의 구문으로 쓰여 적절하다.
  ② 여기서 where절은 명사절로 쓰여 tell의 목적어의 역할로 쓰였다.
  ③ stand는 자동사이므로 전명구가 나와 적절하다.
  ⑤ most는 단독으로 부사의 역할로 쓰일 수 있다.

04
[2013 이화여대]

There is something (①uncanny about the clarity) (with which he ②recognized his hopeless position,) and the calm (③which he accepted ④the inevitable) ⑤was superhuman (in its aspect:) "I am absent-minded and could not direct my own life now."

정답 ③ (which → with which)

해석 그는 자신의 절망적인 상황을 느꼈던 명료함에 대해 묘한 것이 있고, 불가피한 것들을 받아들였던 침착함은 초인적이라 생각했다. "나는 정신이 팔려 있고 당장의 나의 삶을 이끌어 갈 수 없을 것이다."

분석 관계대명사와 「전치사 + 관계대명사」의 구분

③ 관계대명사 which는 선행사로 사물을 수식해야 하고 반드시 절 이하의 성분(명사)이 불완전해야 한다. 보기 뒤에 「주어 + 동사 + 목적어(he accepted the inevitable)」가 완전하게 나와 있어 which는 부적절하다. 절 이하의 성분이 완전해야 하는 「전치사 + 관계대명사(with which)」로 고쳐야 한다.

① 형용사(uncanny)가 명사(something)을 수식하여 적절하다.

② with which절 속에 동사로 쓰여 적절하다.

④ 「the + 형용사 = 명사」이므로 accepted의 목적어로 적절하다.

⑤ 주어(the calm)와 동사(was)의 수 일치가 적절하다.

05

①Feminist theory has assumed [that there is some
  S   V   명사절(O)   V
②existing identity, (understood ③through the category
  S
of women,)] (who not only initiates feminist interests
  (which is)   형용사절 S V(A)   O
and goals within discourse, but constitutes the subject
                             V(B)   O
④whom political representation is pursued.)
 for whom
 형용사절   S   V

정답 ④ (whom → for whom)

해석 페미니스트 이론은 여성의 범주를 통해서 이해되는 현존하는 몇몇 정체성이 있다고 가정해 왔는데, 여성은 담론 내에서 페미니스트적인 관심사와 목표를 떠올리고, 정치적 대표성을 추구하는 주체를 구성하기도 한다.

분석 관계대명사와 「전치사 + 관계대명사」의 구분

④ 관계대명사 whom은 선행사로 사람을 꾸미고 절 이하 목적어(명사) 자리가 불완전해야 하는데 뒤에 「주어(political representation) + 동사(is pursued)」가 완전하게 나와 부적절하다. 절 이하의 성분이 완전해야 하는 「전치사 + 관계대명사(for whom)」로 고쳐야 한다.

① 동사의 주어 역할로 명사는 적절하다. Feminist theory는 복합명사이다.

② 정체성이 존재하는 주체이고, exist는 자동사이기에

능동의 관계인 현재분사(existing)는 적절하다.

③ 수동의 관계인 과거분사(understood)가 앞에 명사를 수식하여 수식어구(전명구)는 적절하다.

06

Insulin is a substance (①for which enables muscles
 S   V   C   형용사절   S
②to absorb sugar from the blood, and ③to break it up
 O.C₁   O.C₂
④for the purpose of obtaining energy.)

정답 ① (for which → which)

해석 인슐린은 근육으로 하여금 혈액에서 당을 흡수하고 에너지를 얻기 위하여 당을 분해하는 역할을 하는 물질이다.

분석 관계대명사와 「전치사 + 관계대명사」의 구분

① 「전치사 + 관계대명사」는 항상 절 이하의 성분(명사)이 완전해야 하는데 enables의 주어가 불완전하므로 관계대명사(which)로 고쳐야 한다.

② 「enable + O + to R ~」 5형식 동사의 어형으로 쓰여 적절하다.

③ to absorb and to break로 병치된 형태이다.

④ for the purpose of R-ing ~ : '~하기 위한 목적으로'의 표현으로 적절하다.

07

Mark had been ①an excellent student (at the college,)
 S   V   C
but he found [that the abstract concepts ②what he
                                          that
had learned in the classroom) left him ③ill-equipped (to
           ∅ 명사절(O)   V   O   O.C
deal with ④the concrete circumstances of life.)]

정답 ② (what he had learned → that[which] he had learned)

해석 마크(Mark)는 학교에서 우수한 학생이었으나 교실에서 배운 추상적인 개념이 삶의 구체적인 상황을 다루기에는 쉽지 않다는 것을 알았다.

분석 명사절 접속사 what과 관계대명사(형용사절) that의 구분

② what절은 항상 명사절을 이끈다. 앞에 명사(the concepts)와 충돌되어 명사절(what)을 쓰지 못하기 때문에 관계대명사(형용사절) that 혹은 which로 고쳐야 한다.

① be동사의 보어인 명사로 쓰여 적절하다.

③ 「leave + O + O.C(형용사)」 5형식 동사의 어형으로

96 _에듀윌 편입 솔루션 문법 Basic

목적보어 자리에 형용사(ill-equipped)로 쓰여 적절하다. to deal 이하는 to R의 부사적 용법으로 쓰였다.
④ 전치사의 목적어로 명사는 적절하다.

08 [2013 가천대]

[① <del>That</del> she said] seems (to be) not ② so much an opinion ③ as a criticism (about ④ the way) (the company has been operated.)
- What (①)
- Ø
- S (she said)
- V (seems)
- C(A) (an opinion)
- C(B) (a criticism)
- (how) (the way)

정답　① (That → What)

해석　그녀가 말했던 것은 회사가 운영하는 방식에 대해 자신의 의견이라기보다 비난처럼 보인다는 것이었다.

분석　명사절 접속사 that과 what의 구분
- ① 이미 동사(seems)가 있기 때문에 그 앞 전부 주어 (명사)의 역할로 쓰여야 한다. that절 역시 명사로 쓰일 수 있지만 명사절 that은 절 이하의 성분(명사)이 완전하게 나와야 하는데 said의 목적어가 불완전하여 부적절하다. 절 이하의 성분(명사)이 불완전하여 하나의 명사로 만들어 줄 수 있는 명사절 접속사 what으로 고쳐야 한다.
- ② not so much A as B: A라기보다 B
- ③ not so much A as B: A라기보다 B
- ④ 전치사의 목적어로 명사는 적절하다. 뒤에 문장이 나온 이유는 관계부사 how가 생략되어 the way를 수식하고 있다.

09 [2013 가톨릭대]

Reports (nationwide) indicate [that DWI (driving while intoxicated) is a factor (in one-fourth of all reported auto crashes) (_____.)]
- S (Reports)
- V (indicate)
- 명사절(O) (that...)
- S (DWI)
- V (is)
- C (a factor)

① called by the police
② calling the police
③ when the police are called
④ (in which the police are called)
- 형용사절 / S (the police) / V (are called)

정답　④

해석　전국적인 보고서에 따르면 음주 운전이 경찰이 출동하는 신고된 모든 자동차 사고 중 1/4을 차지하는 요소라는 것이다.

분석　「전치사 + 관계대명사」
- ④ 「전치사 + 관계대명사」는 항상 절 이하의 성분(명사)이 완전하게 나와 선행사를 수식한다. in which절 속에

주어, 동사가 완전하게 나와 명사(auto crashes)를 수식하는 것이 적절하다.
- ① 수식어구로 명사를 꾸밀 수 있지만 자동사 사고가 불린다는 의미가 맞지 않아 부적절하다.
- ② 자동차 사고가 경찰을 부르는 주체가 될 수 없으므로 부적절하다.
- ③ '경찰이 불렸을 때'라는 의미가 연결되지 않아 부적절하다.

10 [2013 동국대]

Farmers sold their ① crops (to a trader,) ② when sold them to another trader) (and ③ so on) (until ④ they ended up in a shop.)
- S (Farmers)
- V (sold)
- O (crops)
- who (when)
- S
- 형용사절 (them to another trader)
- 부사절 (until they ended up in a shop)

정답　② (when → who)

해석　농부들은 자신들의 작물을 상인에게 판매하고, 그 상인은 또 다른 상인에게 팔고, 결국 그 작물들은 상점에 다다르게 된다.

분석　관계대명사 who의 특징
- ② when은 명사절, 형용사절, 부사절의 역할로 모두 쓰일 수 있지만 반드시 절 이하의 성분이 완전해야 한다. 동사 sold의 주어가 불완전하고 선행사가 사람(a trader) 인 것으로 보아 주격 관계대명사 who로 고쳐야 한다.
- ① sold의 목적어로 쓰여 적절하다.
- ③ and so on: '기타 등등'의 수식어구(부사)의 표현으로 쓰여 적절하다.
- ④ their crops를 대신 받는 대명사로 쓰여 수 일치가 적절하다.

11 [2013 세종대]

There are ① a lot of ② times ③ how we need to talk to people) (④ who come from other countries.)
- V (are)
- S (a lot of)
- S (times)
- when (how)
- 형용사절 (who)

정답　③ (how → when)

해석　우리는 다른 나라에서 온 사람들과 말할 때가 많다.

분석　관계부사 how와 when의 구분
- ③ how는 방법명사(way, manner)를 수식하고, when은 시간명사(time, day 등)를 수식하기 때문에 times를 수식할 수 있도록 when으로 고쳐야 한다.
- ① a lot of는 가산명사와 불가산명사를 둘 다 수식할 수 있어 틀린 것으로 물어볼 수 없고 항상 맞는 보기로 출제된다.

② there are 뒤에 주어의 역할인 명사로 쓰여 적절하다.
④ 선행사인 people을 수식하고 절 속에 주어 자리가 불완전하므로 주격 관계대명사 who는 적절하다.

③ 사람들이 동기를 부여받은 대상이므로 수동태는 적절하다.
⑤ 동사(have)의 목적어(명사) 역할로 쓰여 적절하다.

12

Language is a tool (for saying (as well as possible)
S V C Ø 가능한 한
[_____ we intend to say.])
명사절(O)

① which
② when
③ where
④ what

정답 ④

해석 언어는 우리가 말하고자 하는 것을 가능한 한 잘 말하기 위한 도구이다.

분석 명사절 접속사 what

④ saying의 목적어가 필요한 자리이다. 절 속에 to say 의 목적어 자리가 불완전한 것으로 보아 절 이하의 성분(명사)이 불완전해야 하는 명사절 접속사 what이 적절하다.

① which는 명사절이 아닌 형용사절을 이끄는 접속사이므로 부적절하다.

②, ③ when과 where은 명사절로 쓰일 수 있지만 절 이하의 성분이 완전해야 한다.

13

[2013 상명대]

Textrix, the company (①for which Alex works part-
S = 형용사절 S
time,) ②tends [to employ people] (who are ③highly
V O 형용사절1
motivated) and (④who has at least ⑤10 years of
형용사절2 S have
experience in the field.)

정답 ④ (who has → who have)

해석 알렉스(Alex)가 파트타임으로 일했던 회사인 텍스트릭스(Textrix)는 동기 부여가 많이 되어 있고 그 분야에서 최소한 10년의 경력이 있는 사람을 고용하는 경향이 있다.

분석 주격 관계대명사절 이하 동사의 수 일치

④ 주격 관계대명사(who)절 이하 동사(has)는 선행사 (people)에 수 일치해야 하므로 who have로 고쳐야 한다.

① 「전치사 + 관계대명사」는 절 이하의 성분이 완전하게 나와 선행사를 수식하므로 적절하다.

② 주어(Textrix)와 동사(tends)의 수 일치가 적절하다.

14

[2015 가천대]

which
The Centuriate assembly, (①what only an official
S S
(②with imperium) could summon,) was organized (like
V Ø V
the army) (with the ③presiding official acting (④as a
분사구문 R-ing
commander) and the voters as soldiers.)
(N) (acting)

정답 ① (what → which)

해석 절대적인 지배권을 가진 관리만이 소집할 수 있는 Centuriate 의회는 의회를 주재하는 관리가 지휘관처럼 행동하고 유권자들이 병사들처럼 행동하는 군대처럼 조직되었다.

분석 명사절 접속사 what과 관계대명사(형용사절) which의 구분

① what절은 항상 명사절을 이끈다. 앞에 명사(assembly) 와 충돌되어 명사절(what)을 쓰지 못하기 때문에 관계대명사(형용사절) which로 고쳐야 한다. 관계대명사 that은 콤마(,) 뒤에 쓰지 못하기 때문에 여기서는 that 으로 고칠 수 없다.

② 명사와 명사의 충돌을 피해 주기 위해 전명구는 적절하다.

③ 관리가 회의를 주재하는 주체이므로 능동의 관계인 현재분사(presiding)는 적절하다.

④ 자격의 전치사 as로 쓰여 적절하다.

15

[2015 서강대]

Some studies have ①called (into question) [whether
S V 명사절(O)
②high and variable pitch and exaggerated stress ③are
S₁ S₂ to which V
the crucial elements (in the baby talk) ④which infants
C 형용사절 S
respond.)]

정답 ④ (which infants respond → to which infants respond)

해석 일부 연구는 높고 변화가 심한 음의 높이와 과장된 강조가 유아들이 반응하는 베이비 토크에 있어서 중요한 요소들인지에 대해서 의문을 제기해 왔다.

분석 관계대명사와 「전치사 + 관계대명사」의 구분

98 _에듀윌 편입 솔루션 문법 Basic

④ 관계대명사 which는 반드시 절 이하의 성분(명사)이 불완전해야 하는데 주어(infants)와 자동사(respond)로 완전하게 나와 부적절하다. 절 이하의 성분이 완전해야 하는 「전치사 + 관계대명사(to which)」로 고쳐야 한다.

① 「call + O + into question」은 '~에 대한 의문을 제기하다'의 뜻으로, 이때 목적어가 본문처럼 길게 나올 경우 into question 뒤로 옮겨 써도 괜찮다.

② 형용사(high and variable)가 명사(pitch)를 수식하여 적절하다.

③ 주어(pitch and stress)와 동사(are)의 수 일치가 적절하다.

16
[2017 경기대]

Governments are paying ① increasing attention (to
S   V   O
international ② comparisons) (as they search ③ for
                                        부사절
effective policies) (④ <s>whose</s> enhance individuals' social
                  형용사절 S   V
and economic prospects.)
      O

정답 ④ (whose → which)

해석 정부가 개개인의 사회적·경제적 전망을 향상시키는 효과적인 정책을 찾아가며 국가 간의 비교에 더 많은 관심을 쏟고 있다.

분석 소유격 관계대명사 whose의 특징

④ 소유격 관계대명사(관계형용사)는 반드시 명사를 받고 나서 그 명사 뒤를 잘라 불완전해야 하는데 whose 뒤에 명사가 없이 동사(enhance)가 나와 부적절하다. 관계대명사 which로 고쳐야 한다.

① increasing은 '늘어나는'이라는 뜻의 형용사로 쓰여 명사(attention)을 수식하고 있다.

② 전치사의 목적어로 명사는 적절하다.

③ 명사와 명사의 충돌을 피해 주기 위해 전치사는 적절하다.

17
[2015 숭실대]

Advances (① in technology) now allow us to prolong life
S   S   V   O   O.C
(② in ways) (that were unimaginable decades ago.) But
        형용사절
should people be forced or expected to prolong lives
의문문 어순
(that ③ are unbearable painful,) or (that ④ is in effect
                                            are
"lifeless"?)

정답 ④ (is → are)

해석 지금 기술의 발전은 우리로 하여금 수십 년 전에는 상상조차 할 수 없던 방식으로 삶을 연장하는 것을 허용하고 있다. 그러나 사람들은 참을 수 없을 정도로 괴롭거나 혹은 사실상 '죽은 것이나 다름없는' 삶을 어쩔 수 없이 연장하거나 연장할 것으로 기대해야만 하는 것인가?

분석 주격 관계대명사절 이하 동사의 수 일치

④ 주격 관계대명사(that)절 이하 동사(is)의 수 일치는 선행사(lives)와 수 일치해야 한다. is를 are로 고쳐야 한다.

① 명사와 명사의 충돌을 피해 주기 위해 전치사는 적절하다.

② 명사와 명사의 충돌을 피해 주기 위해 전치사는 적절하다.

③ 주격 관계대명사(that)절 이하 동사(are)가 선행사(lives)와 수 일치되어 적절하다.

18
[2017 가톨릭대]

The plastic waste (in the ocean) breaks down (into tiny
S   V
pieces) (known as microplastics,) (_____ or
                              형용사절
(which are)
even toxic to sea creatures) (who ingest it.)

① which (scientists believe) can harm
                     삽입절
② which (scientists believe) can be harmful
형용사적절   삽입절
        S
③ in which (scientists believe) can harm
                     삽입절
④ in which (scientists believe) can be harmful
                     삽입절

정답 ②

해석 해양의 플라스틱 폐기물은 미세 플라스틱이라고 알려진 작은 조각으로 분해되는데, 과학자들은 미세 플라스틱을 먹는 바다 생물에게 해로울 수 있고 심지어 독이 될 수 있다고 생각한다.

분석 관계대명사와 「전치사 + 관계대명사」의 구분 / 조동사 뒤 동사의 선택

② scientists believe는 삽입절로 쓰였다. 결국 can be의 주어가 불완전하여 관계대명사 which를 써야 하고, 빈칸 뒤에 or 형용사(toxic)가 있기 때문에 harmful과 병치가 된 ②가 적절하다.

① 동사(harm)와 형용사(toxic)의 병치는 부적절하다.

③, ④ can의 주어 자리가 불완전하기에 「전치사 + 관계대명사」는 부적절하다.

19

[2016 홍익대]

These experiences, and others (which can't all be
① enumerated here,) ② help us ③ to find a place of
fullness, (④ which we orient ourselves morally or
spiritually.)

정답 ④ (which → to which)

해석 이와 같은 경험들과 여기서 전부 열거할 수 없는 다른 경험들이 우리로 하여금 도덕적이며 정신적으로 우리 자신의 방향으로 이끄는 완전한 장소를 찾는 일에 도움을 준다.

분석 관계대명사와 「전치사 + 관계대명사」의 구분

④ 관계대명사 which는 반드시 절 이하의 성분(명사)이 불완전해야 하는데 주어, 동사, 목적어가 완전하게 나와 부적절하다. 절 이하의 성분이 완전하게 나와야 하는 「전치사 + 관계대명사(to which)」로 고쳐야 한다.

① 경험들이 열거하는 주체가 아닌 열거되는 대상이므로 수동태는 적절하다.

② 주어(These experiences and others)와 동사(help)의 수 일치가 적절하다.

③ 「help + O + (to) R ~」 5형식 동사의 어형으로 쓰여 적절하다.

20

[2017 가톨릭대]

Many germs have had to devise tricks (to let them
spread between potential victims,) and many of those
tricks are [_____ we experience as "symptoms
of disease."]

① what
② that
③ while
④ which

정답 ①

해석 많은 세균들은 잠재적인 희생자들 사이에서 자신들이 뻗어 나갈 수 있는 수법을 고안했다. 그리고 이런 수법 중 대부분은 우리는 '질병의 증상'으로 경험하고 있는 것이다.

분석 명사절 접속사 what과 that의 구분

① be동사(are)의 보어로 명사가 필요한 자리이다. 명사절 접속사로 쓰일 수 있는 ①, ②로 좁혀지고 빈칸 뒤에 동사(experience)의 목적어 자리가 불완전한 것으로 보아 명사절 접속사 what이 적절하다.

② 명사절 that은 반드시 절 이하의 성분(명사)이 완전해야 하는데 experience의 목적어가 불완전하여 부적절하다.

③, ④ 명사절 접속사로 쓰이지 못한다.

21

[2015 동덕여대]

Knowledge (of the rate) ① which a ship is traveling
through ② the water) is important (if the navigator
③ needs to estimate the time ④ of arrival.)

정답 ① (which → at which)

해석 만약 항해사가 도착 시간을 추정하고자 한다면, 배가 바다를 가로질러 이동하는 속도에 관한 지식이 중요하다.

분석 관계대명사와 「전치사 + 관계대명사」의 구분

① 관계대명사 which는 반드시 절 이하의 성분(명사)이 불완전해야 하는데 주어(a ship), 자동사(is travelling)가 완전하게 나와 부적절하다. 「전치사 + 관계대명사(at which)」로 고쳐야 한다. 선행사가 rate, speed와 같은 명사라면 다른 전치사를 쓰지 못하고 항상 at which로만 수식한다.

② 전치사의 목적어로 명사는 적절하다.

③ 시간 · 조건의 부사절 속에서 조동사 will을 쓰지 못하기 때문에 현재시제는 적절하고, need는 to R를 목적어로 받는 동사로 쓰여 적절하다.

④ 명사와 명사의 충돌을 피해 주기 위해 전명구는 적절하다.

22

[2017 국민대]

Pending folder is [① which you put messages] ② that
you do not need to respond to immediately) but (③ that
you need to keep 'active' for the time being) — (for
example,) ④ if someone promised to get back to you
and you need a reminder to follow up.)

정답 ① (which → where)

해석 미결 폴더는 당신이 바로 대응할 필요는 없지만 당분간 '유효한' 상태로 유지할 필요가 있는 메시지를 넣어 두는 곳이다. 예를 들어 누군가가 당신에게 나중에 다시 연락하겠다고 약속을 했고 후속 조치를 취할 수 있도록 상기

시켜 줄 것이 필요한 경우를 말한다.

분석 관계대명사 which의 특징

① 관계대명사 which는 형용사절의 역할로 반드시 선행사를 수식해야 한다. be동사의 보어 자리에는 쓰일 수 없기 때문에 의미상 어울리는 명사절 접속사 where로 고쳐야 한다.

② 절 속에 respond to의 목적어 자리가 불완전하여 관계대명사 that은 적절하다.

③ 관계대명사 that절(형용사절) and that절로 병치된 형태로 적절하다.

④ 문장이 끝난 뒤 부사절의 역할로 쓰여 적절하다.

23
[2017 상명대]

The new e-ticketing system, (_____ was installed last month,) is working well.

① what   ② whom
③ where   ④ that
⑤ which

정답 ⑤

해석 지난달에 설치된 새 전자 티켓 시스템이 잘 돌아가고 있다.

분석 관계대명사의 선택

⑤ 이미 주어(The new e-ticketing system)와 동사(is working)가 있기 때문에 빈칸부터 last month까지 앞 명사를 수식할 수 있는 관계대명사가 필요한 자리이다. 선행사(The new e-ticketing system)가 사물이기에 관계대명사 which가 적절하다.

① what은 명사절을 이끄는데 빈칸은 명사 자리가 아니다.

② 선행사가 사람이 아니기 때문에 부적절하다.

③ where은 반드시 절 이하의 성분이 완전해야 한다.

④ 관계대명사 that은 콤마(,) 뒤에 쓰지 못한다.

24
[2017 한국외대]

There are two other bodies (① orbiting near Earth) (② that is sometimes ③ referred to as moons,) (though they are not strictly ④ worthy of the title.)

정답 ② (that is → that are)

해석 엄격히 말하면 위성(달)이라는 명칭을 가질 자격이 없지만, 지구 가까이에서 궤도를 돌면서 때때로 위성(달)이라 불리는 두 개의 다른 천체들이 있다.

분석 주격 관계대명사절 이하 동사의 수 일치

② 주격 관계대명사(that)절 이하 동사는 선행사(two other bodies)와 수 일치해야 한다. that is를 that are로 고쳐야 한다. 이 경우 선행사가 Earth인지 two other bodies인지의 구분의 핵심은 바로 해석이다. 지구가 달들로 간주되는 것이 아니라 다른 두 개의 천체들이 달들로 간주되는 것이라는 것을 해석으로 잡아야 한다.

① 다른 두 개의 천체들이 궤도를 돌아가는 주체이므로 능동의 관계인 현재분사(orbiting)는 적절하다.

③ 「refer to + O + as + O.C」 5형식 동사의 어형을 수동태로 쓴 형태이다.

④ 「worth + N = worthy of + N」처럼 worth는 바로 명사를 받고, worthy는 「of + 명사」를 받는다.

25
[2014 경기대]

The physicians favored a program (① guaranteed to save two hundred ② lives over one) ③ who had a one-third probability of saving everyone) and a ④ two-thirds probability (of saving no one.)

정답 ③ (who → which)

해석 의사들은 모든 사람들을 살릴 수 있는 1/3의 가능성과 아무도 살릴 수 없는 2/3의 가능성을 가진 프로그램보다는, 200명의 생명이라도 살리는 것이 보장된 프로그램을 선호했다.

분석 관계대명사 who와 which의 구분

③ who는 선행사로 사람을 수식하고, which는 선행사로 사물을 수식한다. 선행사인 one은 a program을 대신 받는 대명사이므로 사물을 꾸며 주는 which로 고쳐야 한다.

① 프로그램이 보장하는 주체가 아니라 보장되는 대상이므로 수동의 관계인 과거분사(guaranteed)는 적절하다.

② lives는 동사가 아니라 life의 복수형 명사로 쓰여 적절하다.

④ 분수 표현이다. 분자(기수)가 2이상이면 분모(서수)를 복수로 표현한다.

Practice 02

01	③	02	④	03	④	04	③	05	②
06	④	07	③	08	③	09	①	10	⑤
11	③	12	④	13	③	14	①	15	②
16	②	17	①	18	②	19	①	20	③
21	①	22	②	23	②	24	⑤	25	③

01
[2015 가천대]

Early studies ① have also shown an increase (in physical ailments) — (sore backs, dry eyes, painful necks) — (among kids) (who ② are asked to work most of the day on computers) (③ which using desks) (④ designed for pencil and paper.)

정답 ③ (which → while)

해석 초창기 연구들은 연필과 종이를 사용하도록 만들어진 책상을 사용하면서 하루 대부분을 컴퓨터로 공부하도록 요구받는 아이들 사이에서 요통, 건성 결막염, 목의 통증과 같은 신체적 질병이 늘어나고 있는 것을 보여 주고 있다.

분석 관계대명사 which의 특징
- ③ 관계대명사 which는 선행사로 사물을 수식하고 반드시 절 이하의 성분(명사)이 불완전해야 한다. 다만 절 속에 명사가 불완전한 것이지, 동사만큼은 반드시 있어야 하는데 보기 뒤에 동사가 없는 것으로 보아 ③이 부적절하다는 것을 알 수 있다. 분사구문에서 남길 수 있는 부사절 접속사 while로 고쳐야 한다.
- ① 연구가 증가 수치를 보여 주는 주체이므로 능동태는 적절하다.
- ② 선행사(kids)와 주격 관계대명사절 속에 동사(are)의 수 일치가 적절하다. 「ask + O + to R ~」 5형식 동사의 어형을 수동태로 쓴 문장이다.
- ④ 책상이 디자인하는 주체가 아니라 디자인되는 대상이므로 수동의 관계인 과거분사(designed)는 적절하다.

02
[2016 가천대]

(① To Warren Buffet,) his father's library ② must have been like a recommended booklist. (When he was eight years old,) Buffet started [③ reading the books in the library.] His reading habit might have been [④ that turned him into the Oracle of Omaha.]

* be like Ⓝ = be similar to Ⓝ

정답 ④ (that → what)

해석 워런 버핏(Warren Buffet)에게, 아버지의 서재는 권고 도서 목록과 비슷함에 틀림없었다. 여덟 살 때부터 버핏은 아버지의 서재에서 책을 읽기 시작했다. 그의 이런 독서 습관이 그를 오마하의 귀중한 정보를 주는 사람으로 변화시킨 것인지도 모른다.

분석 명사절 접속사 that과 what의 구분
- ④ be동사 뒤에 접속사 that이 나오면 무조건 명사절 접속사의 역할이다. 명사절 that은 반드시 절 이하의 성분(명사)이 완전해야 하는데 동사(turned)의 주어 자리가 불완전한 것으로 보아 명사절 접속사 what으로 고쳐야 한다.
- ① 전치사 뒤에 명사가 나와 수식어의 역할로 적절하다.
- ② must have p.p.: '과거에 ~했음에 틀림없다'의 표현으로 적절하다.
- ③ start는 to R와 R-ing를 둘 다 목적어로 받을 수 있어 적절하다.

03
[2011 가톨릭대]

The city is struggling (with a $26.5 million budget gap,) the result (of a long decline) (in Camden's property tax base and Gov. Christie's decision) (to cut state aid,) (made up more than 80 percent of Camden's budget last year.)

① who
② that
③ what
④ which

정답 ④

해석 그 도시는 2,650만 달러의 예산 차이를 메우려 고군분투하고 있다. 이 예산 차이는 캠던(Camden)의 오랜 재산세의 하락과 작년에 캠던의 예산 80% 이상을 차지했던 주정부 보조금을 삭감하겠다는 주지사 Christie의 결정의 결과이다.

분석 관계대명사 which
- ④ 사물인 선행사(state aid)를 꾸며 주는 관계대명사 which가 적절하다.
- ① who는 선행사로 사람을 수식해야 한다.

② 관계대명사 that은 콤마(,) 뒤에서 절대 쓰지 못한다.

③ what은 항상 명사절을 이끈다. 앞에 명사와 충돌되어 부적절하다.

04
[2010 상명대]

The city fathers allocated ①a substantial sum (for the ② restoration of the train station) ③but (which was soon ④dissipated (in research and planning.)

정답 ③ (but which → which)

해석 시의 행정 담당자는 상당한 금액의 돈을 기차역 복원에 할당했지만, 조사와 계획 때문에 금세 없어졌다.

분석 접속사의 수

③ 두 개의 문장이 있다. 「동사의 수 - 1 = 접속사의 수」이 기 때문에 동사가 두 개라면 접속사는 하나만 있어야 하는데 but과 which 두 개가 나와 부적절하다. but을 삭제해야 한다.

① 동사(allocated)의 목적어로 쓰여 적절하다.

② 명사와 명사의 충돌을 피해 주기 위해 전명구는 적절하다.

④ 상당한 금액이 낭비되는 대상이므로 수동태는 적절하다.

05
[2011 강남대]

You ①don't seem to understand [②that ③I'm trying to do (④with the new pricing system.)]

정답 ② (that → what)

해석 당신은 새로운 가격 체계에서 내가 무엇을 하려고 노력하는가를 이해하지 못하는 것 같다.

분석 명사절 접속사 what과 that의 구분

② understand의 목적어 자리이다. 명사절 that은 반드시 절 이하의 성분(명사)이 완전해야 하는데 to do의 목적어 자리가 불완전하여 부적절하다. 절 이하의 성분이 불완전하여 하나의 명사로 만들어 주는 what으로 고쳐야 한다.

① 일반동사는 주조동사(do)를 빌려 와 부정을 해주는 것이 적절하다.

③ try는 to R와 R-ing를 둘 다 목적어로 받을 수 있어 적절하다.

④ 문장이 끝난 뒤 전명구가 나와 적절하다.

06
[2011 강남대]

The regional manager has been looking (for an applicant) (_____ language skills include Korean and Chinese.)

① who   ② which

③ whom   ④ whose

정답 ④

해석 그 지역 매니저는 한국어와 중국어를 포함한 언어 능력을 가지고 있는 지원자를 찾고 있다.

분석 소유격 관계대명사(관계형용사) whose

④ 소유격 관계대명사(관계형용사) whose는 반드시 명사를 받고 그 명사 뒤를 잘라 절 이하의 성분이 불완전해야 한다. whose language skills 뒤를 잘라 동사(include)의 주어 자리가 불완전하여 적절하다.

①, ②, ③ 절 이하 성분(명사)이 불완전해야 하는 관계대명사로, 빈칸 뒤 성분이 완전하게 나와 부적절하다.

07
[2011 명지대]

The passive (in the English language) ①is very useful (②when you want to emphasize the object) ③which the action is happening) rather than the person (④carrying out the action.)

* A rather than B: B라기보다는 A

정답 ③ (which the action is happening → to which the action is happening)

해석 영어에서 수동태는 행동을 하는 사람보다 행위가 일어나는 대상을 강조하기를 원할 때 굉장히 유용하다.

분석 관계대명사와 「전치사 + 관계대명사」의 구분

③ 관계대명사 which는 반드시 절 이하의 성분(명사)이 불완전해야 하는데 주어(the action), 자동사(is happening)가 완전하게 나와 부적절하다. 완전한 절을 이끄는 「전치사 + 관계대명사(to which)」로 고쳐야 한다.

① 주어(The passive)와 동사(is)의 수 일치가 적절하고, be동사의 보어로 형용사 역시 적절하다.

② when절은 문장의 의미를 돕기 위한 부사절이다. want는 to R를 목적어로 받는 동사이다.

④ 사람이 행동을 하는 주체이므로 능동의 관계인 현재분사(carrying)는 적절하다.

08 [2011 상명대]

(①When going out to hunt,) Brazilian Indians (from the
  분사구문
Xavante tribe) ②follow a complex hierarchy, ③that
          S   V   O   which
                                                형용사절
specifies the tasks) (the old and young should do)
                                                  ∅
④when capturing animals.)
    (that)
  분사구문

정답 ③ (that specifies the tasks → which specifies the tasks)

해석 사냥하러 갈 때 샤반테(Xavante) 부족의 브라질 원주민들은 복잡한 위계질서를 따르는데, 이것은 노인과 젊은이들이 동물을 포획할 때 해야 하는 임무를 구체적으로 기술하고 있다.

분석 관계대명사 that
  ③ 선행사의 종류(사람, 사물)와 격(주격, 목적격)과 상관없이 전부 나올 수 있는 관계대명사 that을 유일하게 쓰지 못하는 경우가 선행사 뒤에 콤마(,)가 있을 때이다. 콤마(,) 뒤에 관계대명사 that을 쓰지 못하기 때문에 which로 고쳐야 한다.
  ① 분사구문의 태를 묻고 있다. 브라질 인디언들이 사냥하러 가는 주체이므로 능동태 분사구문(going)은 적절하다.
  ② 주어(Brazilian Indians)와 동사(follow)의 수 일치가 적절하다.
  ④ 분사구문의 태를 묻고 있다. 노인과 젊은이들이 동물을 포획하는 주체이므로 능동태 분사구문(capturing)은 적절하다.

09 [2011 아주대]

(In this book,) Mary Evans explores _____
                 S   V
social theory has engaged with and illuminated the
       S   V₁   V₂
question of relations between genders and the social
    O
world.)

① the extent (to which
     O   형용사절
② the extent to what
③ the extent which
④ the extent to those
⑤ the extent that it

정답 ①

해석 이 책에서, 메리 에반스(Mary Evans)는 사회 이론이 맞물리고 밝혀 온 성(性)과 사회 사이의 관계에서 발생하는 의문점에 대한 범위를 탐구하고 있다.

분석 extent to which
  ① 선행사가 extent일 때 관계대명사는 반드시 to which로만 수식한다. 이 경우 절 이하의 성분은 항상 완전하게 나오기 때문에 which 역시 쓰지 못하고 항상 extent to which의 형태로 쓰인다.

10 [2011 성균관대]

(Despite the current oil glut,) ①the world's known
                                    S
reserves (of both petroleum and natural gas) ②are
  S   V
expected to be declining (③by the end of the century,)
   V   O.C
and ④it would be folly [to burn [⑤which remains to
        가S   진S   what
generate electricity.]]

정답 ⑤ (which remains → what remains)

해석 현재 석유의 공급 과잉에도 불구하고 세계적으로 알려진 석유와 천연가스 보유량은 세기말이면 감소할 것으로 예측되고 있고, 전기를 생산하기 위해 남은 것을 태우는 것은 어리석은 짓이다.

분석 명사절 접속사 what과 관계대명사(형용사절) which의 구분
  ⑤ 관계대명사 which는 절 이하의 성분(명사)이 불완전하여 반드시 앞에 수식받는 명사가 있어야 한다. 지금은 burn의 목적어가 필요한 자리이기에 명사절 접속사 what으로 고쳐야 한다.
  ① 석유와 천연가스의 보유량이 알고 있는 주체가 아니라 알려지는 대상이므로 수동의 관계인 과거분사(known)는 적절하다.
  ② 주어(the world's known reserves)와 동사(are)의 수 일치가 적절하고, 「expect + O + to R ~」 5형식 동사의 어형을 수동태로 쓴 형태이다.
  ③ decline은 자동사이므로 수식어구(전명구)는 적절하다.
  ④ 「가주어(it) ~ 진주어(to R) ....」 구문으로 쓰인 문장이다.

11 [2012 명지대]

(Although English ①is widely accepted today as being
 부사절   S   V
the universal language of business,) most multinational
companies will expect you ②to speak the language of
    S   V   in which O.C
one of the countries (③which they do business,) (④in
                        형용사절 S V   O
addition to English.)

정답 ③ (which → in which)

해석 비록 영어가 오늘날 보편적인 비즈니스 언어로 폭넓게 받아들여지고 있지만, 대부분의 다국적 기업은 당신이 영어 외에 자신들이 사업을 하는 대상의 나라들 중 하나의 언어를 구사할 것을 기대할 것이다.

분석 관계대명사와 「전치사 + 관계대명사」의 구분

③ 관계대명사 which는 반드시 절 이하의 성분(명사)이 불완전해야 하는데 주어, 동사, 목적어가 완전하게 나와 부적절하다. 완전한 절을 이끄는 「전치사 + 관계대명사(in which)」로 고쳐야 한다.

① 영어가 폭넓게 받아들여지는 대상이므로 수동태는 적절하다.

② 「expect + O + to R ~」 5형식 동사의 어형으로 쓰여 적절하다.

④ 문장이 끝나고 나서 수식어구(전명구)로 쓰여 적절하다.

12
[2016 한양대 에리카]

① Careful measurements reveal [that the reaction rate
　　　　　　S　　　　　　　V　　　명사절(O)　　S
is ② too slow to account for ③ the ozone concentrations
V　　　　C　　　　　　　　　　　S
observed,] i.e. the process predicts higher peak ozone
　　　　　　　S　　　　　V
concentrations ④ that are observed.)
　　O　　　　than S
　　　　　형용사절

정답 ④ (that are observed → than are observed)

해석 신중한 측정으로 인해 반응 속도가 너무나 느려서 관찰된 오존 농도를 제대로 설명할 수 없다는 점을 보여 준다. 즉, 다시 말해서 그 과정은 관찰되는 것보다 더 높은 최대치의 오존 농도 수치를 예상한다.

분석 유사관계대명사 than

④ 수식받는 선행사 앞에 '-er/more ~'과 같은 비교급이 있다면 관계대명사는 who(m), which, that 대신에 유사관계대명사 than을 써야 한다. that을 than으로 고쳐야 한다.

① 형용사(Careful)가 명사(measurements)를 수식하여 적절하다.

② 「too ~ to R ...」 용법으로 쓰여 적절하다.

③ 오존 농도가 관찰하는 주체가 아니라 관찰되는 대상이므로 수동의 관계인 과거분사(observed)는 적절하다.

13
[2011 경기대]

Korea (① successfully) hosted the Group (of 20 ② summit)
S　　　　　　　　　V　　　　　O　　　　　　　which
(in Seoul on November 11–12), ③ what is believed to
　　　　　　　　　　　　　　　　　　　S　　V
have helped ④ boost the nation's diplomatic clout and
　　　　　(to)
international reputation.)

정답 ③ (what → which)

해석 한국은 11월 11~12일에 서울에서 G20 정상 회의를 성공적으로 개최했다. 이는 한국의 외교적 영향력과 국제적인 명성을 드높이는 데 도움이 되었다고 여겨진다.

분석 명사절 접속사 what과 관계대명사(형용사절) which의 구분

③ 앞에 명사구(the Group of 20 summit)가 있기 때문에 명사절을 이끄는 what은 부적절하다. 앞에 나온 명사를 수식할 수 있도록 관계대명사 which로 고쳐야 한다.

① 목적어(the Group of 20 summit)을 받고 있어 능동태 동사는 적절하다.

② the Group of 20 summit는 'G20 정상 회의'라는 뜻의 고유명사이다.

④ help + (to) R ~ : help는 to R를 목적어로 받아도 좋고 to를 생략시켜 동사원형만 나와도 괜찮다.

14
[2011 서경대]

Another area (① which bits and bytes are ② used) is
　　　　S　　　in which　　형용사절　　S　　　　V
③ measuring computer memory ④ storage capacity.
　　　V　　　　　　　　O

정답 ① (which → in which)

해석 비트(bit)와 바이트(byte)가 사용되는 또 다른 영역은 컴퓨터 메모리 저장 용량을 측정하는 것이다.

분석 관계대명사와 「전치사 + 관계대명사」의 구분

① 관계대명사 which는 반드시 절 이하의 성분(명사)이 불완전해야 하는데 주어, 동사가 완전하게 나와 부적절하다. 완전한 절을 이끄는 「전치사 + 관계대명사(in which)」로 고쳐야 한다.

② 비트와 바이트가 사용되는 대상이므로 수동태는 적절하다.

③ 주어(Another area)에 대한 동사(is measuring)로 나온 형태이다. 뒤에 목적어가 있기 때문에 능동태는 적절하다.

④ computer memory storage capacity가 통째로 하나의 명사로 쓰인 복합명사이다.

15 [2017 광운대]

Did you know [that ① most flight attendants fly with
their own food?] It is because the meals (airlines ② give
them to passengers) ③ have gotten smaller (④ over the
year) and leave them still hungry.) So it is not unusual
for flight attendants ⑤ [to bring their own snacks like
fruit, protein bars and sandwiches.]

정답 ② (give them to → give to)

해석 대부분의 승무원들이 자신의 음식을 가지고 비행한다는 사실을 아십니까? 이는 항공사에서 승객들에게 제공하는 식사가 최근 1년 동안 점점 양이 줄어서 승객들을 배고프게 만들기 때문입니다. 따라서 승무원들이 과일, 단백질 바, 샌드위치 등과 같은 간단한 식사를 가져오는 것은 흔한 일입니다.

분석 관계대명사의 특징

② airlines 앞에는 목적격 관계대명사 which[that]가 생략되어 있다. 목적격 관계대명사가 생략되어 있다는 것은 절 속에 목적어 자리가 불완전해야 한다는 것을 의미한다. give의 목적어인 them을 삭제해야 한다.

① 형용사(most)가 명사(flight attendants)를 수식하여 적절하다.

③ 주어(the meals)와 동사(have gotten)의 수 일치가 적절하다.

④ 앞에 문장이 완성되어 있어 수식어구(전명구)는 적절하다.

⑤ 「가주어(it) ~ 진주어(to R) ...」 구문으로 쓰여 적절하다.

16 [2013 세종대]

(As older people have accumulated their own know-
how in their careers,) they have many resources and
skills (_____).

① teach and guide younger people

② (with which to teach and guide younger people)

③ which they might teach and guide younger people

④ what might teach and guide younger people

정답 ②

해석 나이든 사람들은 자신의 영역에서 본인만의 노하우를 축적해 왔기 때문에, 그들은 어린 사람들을 가르치고 인도할 수많은 자료와 기술을 가지고 있다.

분석 「전치사 + 관계대명사」와 to R의 결합

② 「전치사 + 관계대명사」는 절 이하의 성분(명사)이 완전한 형태의 문장을 받는 것이 일반적이지만, 「전치사 + 관계대명사」는 to R와의 결합도 가능하기 때문에 ②가 수식어구로 적절하다.

① 이미 주어, 동사(they have)가 있기 때문에 동사가 또 나올 수 없다.

③ 관계대명사 which는 절 이하의 성분이 불완전해야 하는데 완전하게 나와 부적절하다.

④ what은 명사절을 이끄는 접속사이므로 앞 명사와 충돌되어 부적절하다.

17 [2011 세종대]

[_____] cannot be an extremist.

① [Whoever is doing such activities]

② Who is doing such activities

③ No matter how is doing such activities

④ How is doing such activities

정답 ①

해석 그러한 활동을 하는 사람이 극단주의자 일리가 없다.

분석 복합관계대명사 whoever

① 빈칸 뒤에 동사(cannot be)가 나온 것으로 보아 빈칸은 주어의 역할을 할 수 있는 명사가 와야 한다. 복합관계대명사 whoever는 '~한 사람'이라는 뜻의 명사절로 쓰일 수 있어 정답으로 적절하다.

② who절은 선행사로 사람을 꾸며 주는 관계대명사이지만 명사절로 쓰이지 못하는 것은 아니다. 하지만 여기서 who절을 명사절로 보면 '누가 그런 활동을 했는지'라는 뜻이 되어 동사와의 의미가 연결되지 않아 부적절하다.

③ no matter how는 부사절일뿐더러 절 이하의 성분이 완전해야 한다.

④ how는 명사절을 이끌지만 절 이하의 성분이 완전해야 한다.

18

[2011 상명대]

Frog skin allows both water and oxygen ① to pass through, ② which mean (if the air or water ③ is contaminated,) [the contaminant ④ can easily enter and damage the frog's body.])

정답 ② (which mean → which means)

해석 개구리 피부는 물과 산소가 모두 통과하도록 허용하고, 이것은 공기나 물이 오염되었다면 그 오염 물질이 개구리의 몸에 쉽게 침투해서 해를 끼칠 수 있다는 것을 의미한다.

분석 주격 관계대명사절 이하 동사의 수 일치

② 콤마(,) which는 앞 문장 전체를 선행사로 받을 수 있다. 앞 문장 전체를 선행사로 받을 경우, 주격 관계대명사절 속의 동사는 단수로 일치시키기 때문에 which means로 고쳐야 한다.

① 「allow + O + to R」 5형식 동사의 어형으로 쓰여 적절하다.

③ 공기와 물이 오염되는 대상이므로 수동태는 적절하다.

④ enter는 타동사로 쓰여 목적어(the frog's body)를 전치사 없이 받은 것이 적절하다.

19

[2013 한국외대]

A satellite is composed (of 30 modular units,) _____ equipped with a set of sensors.

① each (of which) is
② each of which are
③ some of which is
④ which of them are

정답 ①

해석 인공위성은 30개의 모듈 유닛으로 구성되어 있고, 그것들 각각에 여러 센서가 장착되어 있다.

분석 「부정대명사 + of + which + V ~」

① 문장이 끝난 뒤 「부정대명사(all, some, most, each ...) + of + which + V ~」 수식절의 형태로 쓰인다. 원문은 and each of them(30 modular units) is equipped에서 and와 them을 합쳐 관계대명사 which로 줄여 쓴 표현이다.

② 주어가 each일 때 동사는 단수 취급해야 한다.

③ 주어가 some일 때 동사는 복수 취급해야 한다.

④ 「부정대명사 + of + which」의 어순으로 써야 한다.

20

[2011 홍익대]

The strike (① for increased wages) ② consisted (of hundreds of immigrants), most (of ③ them) ④ were earning (less than) minimum wages.

정답 ③ (them → whom)

해석 임금 인상을 위한 파업은 수많은 이민자들로 구성되어 있고, 그들 대부분은 최저 임금보다도 적게 벌고 있는 사람들이다.

분석 「부정대명사 + of + whom + V ~」

③ 두 개의 문장이 나왔는데 접속사가 없다. 대명사(them)와 접속사(and)를 합친 관계대명사 which로 고쳐야 한다. 원문 The strike consisted ~ and most of them were earning ~에서 and와 them을 합쳐 관계대명사 whom으로 고치면 동사 두 개를 접속사로 이어 줄 수 있다.

① 명사와 명사의 충돌을 피해 주기 위해 전치사는 적절하다.

② consist는 자동사로 「of + N」 형태를 받아 적절하다.

④ 주어가 most(수백 명의 이민자들 대부분)이므로 복수 동사(were)와 수 일치가 되어 적절하다.

21

[2012 경기대]

Morgan Stanley, the financial firm (① who shares ② have declined 45 percent this year,) ③ plans [to cut about 1,600 jobs] (amid an industrywide ④ drop) (in revenue from investment banking and trading.)

정답 ① (who → whose)

해석 올해 주식이 45%가량 떨어진 금융 회사 모건 스탠리(Morgan Stanley)는 투자 은행과 무역 분야의 수익이 산업 전반에 걸쳐 줄어든 상황 때문에, 대략 1,600개의 일자리를 삭감할 계획이다.

분석 주격 관계대명사 who와 소유격 관계대명사 whose의 구분

① 주격 관계대명사 who는 반드시 절 이하 주어 자리가 불완전해야 하는데 절 속에 주어(shares)가 있어 부적절하다. 명사를 받고 그 명사 뒤를 잘라 불완전한 형태의 문장을 받는 whose로 고쳐야 한다.

② 완료를 나타내기 위한 have p.p.는 적절하다.

③ 주어(Morgan stanley)와 동사(plans)의 수 일치가 적절하다.

④ 전치사의 목적어로 명사는 적절하다.

22
[2012 단국대]

①One college professor developed **the idea** [②<del>which</del> (that)
S   V   O
rats might perform better on the detection test] (③if
S   V   부사절
they lived in a rich environment ④<u>than</u> in a small barren
cage.)

정답 ② (which → that)

해석 한 대학교수가 쥐들이 작고 척박한 우리보다 여유로운 환경에서 살면 탐색 실험을 더 잘 수행할 것이라는 개념을 발달시켰다.

분석 관계대명사 which와 동격의 that의 구분

② 관계대명사 which는 반드시 절 이하의 성분(명사)이 불완전해야 하는데 주어, 동사가 완전하게 나와 부적절하므로 동격의 that으로 고쳐야 한다.

① '한 명의 대학교수'로 쓰여 적절하다.

③ 부사절 접속사 if로 가정법 과거를 표현한 형태이다.

④ 전명구와 전명구를 비교하여 앞에 better이 있어 than을 쓴 것은 적절하다.

23
[2011 명지대]

①The period (in American history) ②during <del>when</del> (which) the
S
③sale of alcohol ④was banned) was called Prohibition.
                           V   O.C

정답 ② (during when → during which 또는 when)

해석 미국 역사상 술의 판매가 금지된 기간을 금주법 시대라고 부른다.

분석 전치사 + 관계대명사 / 관계부사

② during which를 합쳐 쓴 것이 관계부사 when이다. 반대로 얘기하면 when을 풀어쓴 것이 during which이다. 그러므로 전치사 뒤에 관계부사(when)를 쓰지 못하기 때문에 during which로 고치거나 혹은 during을 삭제하여 when만 남겨 준다.

① 주어의 역할로 쓰여 적절하고 명사와 명사의 충돌을 피해 주기 위한 전치사도 적절하다.

③ 절 속의 주어의 역할로 쓰여 적절하다.

④ 술 판매가 금지시키는 주체가 아니라 금지되는 대상이므로 수동태와 수 일치까지 적절하다.

24
[2012 아주대]

This study does not attempt a fully-fledged account (of
S   V₁   O
these concerns,) but simply points to their importance
                    V₂   O
(when considering _____ state theories are
        분사구문
constructed.))

① way in which   ② the way how
③ way which   ④ way that
⑤ the way (in which
                 형용사절

정답 ⑤

해석 이 연구는 관심사에 대해 전반적인 설명을 시도하는 것이 아니라, 상태 이론이 구성된 방식을 고려해 보았을 때, 그 관심사들의 중요성을 지적하려는 것이다.

분석 관계대명사의 특징

⑤ 방법의 명사는 정관사 the와 함께 the way로 쓰는 명사이므로 ①, ③, ④는 탈락되고, the way와 how는 어떠한 일이 있어도 함께 쓰이지 못해 둘 중 하나는 반드시 생략해야 한다. 그러므로 「전치사 + 관계대명사 절」 이하의 성분이 완전하게 나와 선행사(the way)를 수식하는 ⑤가 적절하다.

25
[2013 서울여대]

(In 1921,) a movement started (in several parts of the
          S   V
world,) _____ was to make table tennis a
                         V   O
serious sport.
    O.C

① which goal   ② its goal
③ the goal (of which   ④ which of the goal
    S   = and + it(a movement)

정답 ③

해석 1921년, 한 운동이 세계의 여러 곳에서 시작되었다. 그리고 그 운동의 목적은 탁구를 정식 스포츠로 만들고자 하는 것이었다.

분석 「the N + of + which」 / 「of + which + the N」

③ 소유격 관계대명사(관계형용사) whose를 풀어쓴 형태는 「of + which + the N = the N + of + which」이다. 이 조건을 만족시키는 ③이 적절하다.

① 관계대명사 which는 절 이하의 성분이 불완전해야 하는데 완전하게 나와 부적절하다.

② 접속사 없이 주어, 동사가 또 나올 수 없다.

④ 어순이 틀렸다.

11강 명사와 관사

Practice

01	②	02	②	03	③	04	③	05	③
06	④	07	③	08	②	09	③	10	②
11	①	12	②	13	④	14	④	15	①
16	①	17	③	18	①	19	②	20	④
21	②	22	④	23	②	24	②	25	④

01
[2010 가톨릭대]

Many of the mammals (that dwell in the desert) are active (only at _____) (as the intense heat of a desert day can be fatal to warm-blooded animals.)

① a night　　② night
③ the night　　④ nights

정답　②

해석　사막에 서식하는 많은 포유류들은 낮의 뜨거운 열기가 항온 동물에게 치명적일 수 있기 때문에 밤에만 활동한다.

분석　「at night」(밤에)

② at night은 '밤에'라는 뜻을 가진 하나의 표현이다. in the night 역시 같은 뜻이지만 뉘앙스가 약간 다르다. 「at noon / in the afternoon」, 「at night / in the night」과 같이 전치사를 무엇으로 쓰냐에 따라 관사의 유무도 결정된다.

02
[2010 서울여대]

The number (of Americans) (who are obese) ①continues [to increase ②at alarming rate] (while (in Italy) ③the percentage (of obese people) is half of [④what it is in the United States.])

정답　② (at alarming rate → at an alarming rate)

해석　미국의 비만 인구수는 위험한 속도로 증가하는 반면에 이탈리아의 비만 인구의 비율은 미국의 반 정도에 그친다.

분석　가산명사로 쓰이는 rate

② 영어에서 '속도, 비율'을 뜻하는 rate는 항상 가산명사로 쓰인다. 가산명사는 반드시 명사 앞뒤에 a/an 또는 -(e)s가 붙어야 하기 때문에 at an alarming rate로 고쳐야 한다.

① 「The number of + Ns」 형태가 주어로 나오면 항상 the number에 수 일치를 하여 단수동사(Vs)를 써야 하기 때문에 적절하다.

③ while절 속에 주어의 역할로 명사는 적절하다.

④ what은 항상 절 이하의 성분(명사)이 불완전하여 명사절을 이끌기에 전치사(of)의 목적어로 적절하다.

03
[2010 세종대]

(In the United States,) [①having chosen ②to purchase ③same item] created an immediate affinity (④among Americans.)

정답　③ (same → the same)

해석　미국에서는 같은 제품을 구입하기로 결정하는 일이 미국인들 사이에 즉각적인 친밀감을 일으켰다.

분석　「the same + N」

③ 「the same + N」 형태로 same이 뒤에 명사를 수식하는 형태라면 반드시 앞에 정관사 the를 함께 써야 한다. same을 the same으로 고쳐야 한다.

① 동명사구(having chosen ~ item)가 주어의 역할로 나와 적절하다.

② choose는 to R를 목적어로 받는 동사이기에 적절하다.

④ 명사와 명사의 충돌을 피해 주기 위해 전치사는 적절하다.

04
[2010 이화여대]

The story (you hear all the time) — (of ①a stagnant economy (in which high taxes and generous social benefits have undermined incentives,) ②stalling growth and innovation) — bears ③few resemblance (to ④the surprisingly positive facts.)

정답　③ (few resemblance → little resemblance)

해석　당신이 항상 듣는 높은 세금과 풍부한 사회 복지 혜택이 성장의 동기를 저하시켜 결국 성장과 개혁을 더디게 한다는 경기 침체 이야기는 놀라울 정도로 긍정적인 사실들과는 닮은 점이 거의 없다.

분석 수량형용사 few와 little의 구분

③ (a) few는 반드시 뒤에 복수형 가산명사(Ns)를 수식하는 형용사이다. 같은 뜻이지만 (a) little은 반드시 a/an 혹은 -(e)s가 없는 불가산명사(N)를 수식하는 형용사이다. 이 둘의 구분은 해석이 아니라 수식받는 명사의 형태를 보고 판단하면 된다. little resemblance로 고쳐야 한다.

① economy는 가산명사로 쓰일 수 있어 부정관사(a/an)와 함께 나온 것은 적절하지만 딱히 문제로 물어보는 명사는 아니다.

② 분사구문의 태를 묻고 있다. 높은 세금과 사회 복지 혜택이 성장과 혁신을 멈추게 하는 주체이고, 목적어(growth and innovation)가 있어 능동태 분사구문(stalling)은 적절하다.

④ 「관사 + 부사 + 형용사 + 명사」의 어순이 적절하다.

05

It might appear (to ① any casual visitor) (who may have taken a few rides ② about town ③ by a taxicab) [that all New Yorkers are filled (with a ④ loud-mouthed ill will) toward each other.]

정답 ③ (by a taxicab → by taxicab)

해석 몇 번 택시를 타고 도시를 돌아다녔을 수도 있는 평범한 방문객에게 모든 뉴욕 사람들은 서로에게 악의 가득한 소란을 떠는 사람들로 보였을 것이다.

분석 「by + 교통 · 통신 수단」

③ by 이하에 교통 · 통신 수단의 명사가 나오면 절대 관사(a/an, the)를 쓰지 못하기 때문에 by taxicab으로 고쳐야 한다.

① 전치사의 목적어로 명사는 적절하다.

② 명사와 명사의 충돌을 피해 주기 위해 전명구는 적절하다.

④ loud-mouthed는 '시끄러운, 상스러운'의 뜻을 가진 형용사로 명사(ill)를 수식하여 적절하다.

06
[2013 서울여대]

Most people ① are accustomed (to thinking of lie detectors ② as foolproof) — (as machines) (that can,

(without error,) ③ separate the guilty from ④ the innocence.)
innocent

정답 ④ (the innocence → the innocent)

해석 대부분의 사람들은 거짓말 탐지기가 틀리지 않는다고 믿는 데 익숙하다. 마치 유죄인 사람과 무죄인 사람을 오류 없이 구별할 수 있는 기계처럼 말이다.

분석 「the + 형용사 = 명사」

④ 전치사의 목적어로 명사가 나온 것은 오류가 없지만 해석이 매끄럽지 못하다. the innocence를 쓰면 '유죄인 사람들과 결백을 구분하다'의 의미가 되어 문맥에 맞지 않는다. '유죄인 사람들과 결백한 사람들을 구분 짓다'의 의미가 될 수 있도록 the innocent로 고쳐야 한다. (the + 형용사=명사: ex. the poor=poor people / the rich=rich people)

① be accustomed to N/R-ing: '~에 익숙하다'의 표현으로 쓰여 적절하다.

② 「think of + O + as + O.C」 5형식 동사의 어형으로 쓰여 적절하다.

③ 조동사(can) 뒤에 동사원형이 나와 적절하다.

07
[2013 한국외대]

Football, (often ① confused with soccer in some countries,) is a ② fast-moving ③ team sports (④ played mainly in the U.S. and Canada.)

정답 ③ (team sports → team sport)

해석 몇몇 국가에서 축구와 종종 혼동되는 미식축구는 미국과 캐나다에서 주로 경기가 행해지며, 빠르게 움직이는 팀 스포츠이다.

분석 「a/an + N」(O) / 「a/an + Ns」(X)

③ 부정관사 a/an 뒤에는 단수형 가산명사가 나와야 하기 때문에 team sport로 고쳐야 한다.

① Football이 soccer와 혼동되는 대상이고, 뒤에 목적어도 없기 때문에 수동의 관계인 과거분사(confused)는 적절하다.

② fast-moving은 '전개가 빠른'의 뜻을 가진 형용사로 명사(team sport)를 수식하여 적절하다.

④ 스포츠가 행하는 주체가 아니라 행해지는 대상이므로 수동의 관계인 과거분사(played)는 적절하다.

110 _에듀윌 편입 솔루션 문법 Basic

08

(According to a Washington Post poll) (①taken in 1999,)
(which was)
eighty-seven ②percents of Americans ③want the U.S.
　　　　　　　　　　　　　　　S　　　　　　　　　V　　　O
and China ④to sign an ⑤arms agreement.
　　　　　　　O.C

정답　② (percents → percent)

해석　워싱턴 포스트가 시행한 1999년의 여론 조사에 따르면
　　　　미국인의 87%가 미국과 중국이 무기 협약을 체결하기를
　　　　바란다.

분석　percent (O) / percents (X)

　　② 앞에 숫자가 몇이 나온다 할지라도 percent는 절대 복
　　　　수형(percents)으로 쓰지 못하는 명사이므로 percent
　　　　로 고쳐야 한다. percent는 「per=a/an」의 용법에서
　　　　파생되었기 때문이다.

　　① 여론 조사가 행하는 주체가 아니라 행해지는 대상이
　　　　고, 뒤에 목적어도 없기 때문에 수동의 관계인 과거분
　　　　사(taken)는 적절하다.

　　③ 「percent of + N / Ns」 형태가 주어로 나오면 of 뒤에
　　　　있는 명사와 동사의 수 일치를 해야 한다.

　　④ 「want + O + to R ~」 5형식 동사의 어형으로 쓰여 적
　　　　절하다.

　　⑤ arms agreement는 복합명사로 쓰였다. 원칙적으로
　　　　복합명사는 앞 명사를 단수로 연결하지만 arms를 써
　　　　야 '무기'의 뜻이 되기 때문에 가능한 형태이다. arm은
　　　　'팔'이라는 뜻으로 쓰인다.

09

(①In popular terminology,) ②any long snowstorm (with
　　　　　　　　　　　　　　　　　　　　　　S
③large amount of wind) is ④called a blizzard.
　↑　　　　　　　　　　　　V　　　　O.C
　a

정답　③ (large amount → a large amount)

해석　장시간에 걸쳐 많은 양의 바람과 함께 진행되는 폭설을
　　　　일상적인 단어로 눈보라라고 부른다.

분석　「much = an amount of」

　　③ an amount of는 much의 대용어구로 불가산명사를
　　　　수식하는 수량형용사이다. 「an amount of + N(불가
　　　　산명사)」의 형태로 써야 하고, 다만 amount 앞에는 부
　　　　정관사(a/an)가 반드시 있어야 한다. a large amount
　　　　of로 고쳐야 한다.

　　① 주절이 완전하게 나와 수식어구(전명구)의 역할로 쓰
　　　　여 적절하다.

　　② 형용사(long)가 명사(snowstorm)를 수식하여 적절하
　　　　다. any는 형용사, 대명사로 전부 쓰일 수 있어 얼마든
　　　　지 명사 앞에 나올 수 있다.

　　④ 폭설이 눈보라라고 불려지는 대상이므로 수동태는 적
　　　　절하다. 「call + O + O.C」 5형식 동사의 어형을 수동
　　　　태로 썼기 때문에 목적보어(a blizzard)가 남은 것도
　　　　적절하다.

10

Language, (in all aspects), ①consists (of abstract units
　S　　　　　　　　　　　　　　S　　　V
of ②informations) (that are ③organized and combined)
　　　　　　　　　　　　　　　　　형용사절
(④following specific computational procedures.)

정답　② (informations → information)

해석　언어는 모든 면에서 특정한 연산 절차들을 따라 구성되고
　　　　결합된 정보의 추상적인 단위들로 구성되어 있다.

분석　절대 불가산명사(집합적 물질명사) information

　　② 대부분의 명사는 가산과 불가산으로 둘 다 쓰인다. 그
　　　　래서 문법 문제에서 해석을 통하여 가산과 불가산을
　　　　구분하는 문제가 거의 나오지 않는 것이다. 하지만 절
　　　　대 불가산명사(집합적 물질명사)는 어떠한 경우에도
　　　　불가산으로만 쓰이는 명사이기에 절대로 a/an 혹은
　　　　-(e)s가 붙어 나올 수 없다. information으로 고쳐야
　　　　한다.

　　① 주어(Language)와 동사(consists)의 수 일치가 적절
　　　　하고, 자동사이기 때문에 뒤에 명사가 나올 때 전치사
　　　　of가 있어야 한다.

　　③ 정보가 구성하는 주체가 아니라 구성되는 대상이므로
　　　　수동태는 적절하다.

　　④ 뒤에 목적어(specific ~ procedures)가 있기 때문에
　　　　능동의 관계인 현재분사(following)는 적절하다.

11

One (of the best-known ①kind) (of predictably irrational
　S　　　　　　　　　　kinds
behavior) ②has been called the endowment effect ―
　　　　　　　　　　V　　　　　O.C　　　　　부연 설명
the idea [that (once something is ③in your possession,)
　Ⓝ　　동격　　　부사절
it becomes more valuable ④to you (because it's yours
S　　V　　　C　　　　　　　　　　부사절
and you don't want to lose it.)]

정답 ① (kind → kinds)

해석 가장 널리 알려진 예측 가능한 비이성적인 행동의 종류들 가운데 하나는 소유 효과라고 불려 왔다 – 소유 효과란, 어떤 것이 당신의 소유가 되고 나면, 그것이 당신에게 더 귀중해진다는 개념인데, 이는 그것이 당신의 것이며 잃어버리길 원하지 않기 때문이다.

분석 「one of + the Ns(복수명사)」

① 「one of the books(여러 권의 책 중 한 권의 책)」와 같이 one of the 뒤에는 반드시 복수명사(Ns)를 써야 한다. kind를 kinds로 고쳐야 한다.

② 주어(One)와 동사(has)의 수 일치가 적절하다.

③ be in possession은 '소유되다'의 표현이다.

④ 「valuable to ~」는 '~에 가치 있는, 소중한'의 표현으로 형용사와 전치사의 연결이 적절하다.

12

[2016 경기대]

There are concerns (for the safety) (of ① scores of people) (after a ship (carrying 118 passengers and ② crews) lost power in rough ③ waters off an Indonesian island ④ on Saturday.)

정답 ② (crews → crew)

해석 토요일 118명의 승객과 승무원을 태운 배가 인도네시아의 어느 섬 부근에서 거친 물살로 엔진 고장을 일으키고 난 후, 수십 명의 사람들의 안전이 우려되고 있는 상황이다.

분석 단수와 복수의 형태가 같은 명사(crew, staff, series, species 등)

② crew는 '선원단(단수), 선원들(복수)'이라는 뜻의 단수와 복수로 둘 다 쓰이는 단어이다. 그러므로 crew에는 복수형이라고 하여 crews를 쓰지 못한다.

① 수단위 명사(score, hundred, thousand, million 등)는 단수와 복수의 형태를 묻는다. 뒤에 of가 있으면 복수형(thousands of eggs)으로 쓰고, of가 없다면 단수형(two thousand eggs)으로 써야 하므로 적절하다.

③ water는 '물(불가산), 바다, 물결(가산)'처럼 가산과 불가산으로 둘 다 쓰일 수 있다. 하지만 모든 명사를 이렇게 암기해서 구분할 수 없기 때문에 명사는 절대 불가산명사 혹은 반드시 출제되는 명사 형태 몇 가지를 제외하고서는 가산과 불가산을 구분하지 않는 것이 좋다.

④ 요일 앞에 전치사는 항상 on을 쓴다.

13

[2016 아주대]

Ebola, a ① highly infectious virus (② that can kill up to 90 ③ percent of the people) (who catch it,) is one (of the ④ world most deadly diseases,) (⑤ causing terror among infected communities.)

정답 ④ (world → world's)

해석 감염자의 90%까지도 죽일 수 있는 전염성 강한 바이러스인 에볼라는 세상에서 가장 치명적인 질병 중 하나로, 그 바이러스에 감염된 공동체에 공포를 야기한다.

분석 명사와 명사의 충돌

④ 명사(world)와 명사(diseases)가 충돌되어 앞 명사를 소유격의 형태인 world's로 고쳐야 한다.

① highly는 '매우, 굉장히'라는 뜻의 부사로 형용사(infectious)를 수식하는 것은 적절하다.

② 선행사의 종류(사람, 사물)와 격(주격, 목적격)과 상관없이 전부 쓰일 수 있는 관계대명사 that은 적절하다.

③ percent는 항상 단수명사로 쓰이는 명사이므로 적절하다.

⑤ 에볼라가 공포를 야기하는 주체이고, 뒤에 목적어가 있으므로 능동태 분사구문(causing)은 적절하다.

14

[2016 한국외대]

(_____,) Sasha rarely misses three-point shots.

① Her excellent basketball play
② Excellent basketball player
③ An excellent basketball player is
④ An excellent basketball player

정답 ④

해석 뛰어난 농구 선수인 사샤는 3점 슛을 놓치는 일이 거의 없다.

분석 동격의 명사 / 신분 · 직업의 가산명사

④ 주절 주어와 동격의 뜻을 가진 명사를 쓰는 자리이다.

① '사샤 = 뛰어난 농구 경기(X)'라는 동격의 의미가 성립되지 않아 부적절하다.

② 사람의 신분 · 직업의 명사는 보통 가산명사로 쓰여 a/an 혹은 -(e)s의 형태가 붙어 나와야 한다.

③ 접속사 없이 동사가 또 나올 수 없다.

15

The ① evidences show [that children (of women) (② who work) are not more ③ likely to have lower school achievement than children of stay-at-home moms.]

정답 ① (evidences show → evidence shows)

해석 그 증거는 직장 여성의 자녀가 전업주부의 자녀보다 학업 성취도가 낮을 가능성이 더 높지 않다는 것을 보여 준다.

분석 절대 불가산명사(집합적 물질명사) evidence

① 절대 불가산명사(집합적 물질명사)는 a/an 혹은 -(e)s 가 붙을 수 없다. evidence shows로 고쳐야 한다.

② 선행사가 사람(women)이고 절 속에 주어 자리가 불완전하여 주격 관계대명사(who)는 적절하고, 선행사 (women)와 주격 관계대명사절 속의 동사(work)와 수 일치가 적절하다.

③ 「be likely to + R ~」는 '~할 가능성이 있다'의 표현으로 쓰인다.

④ school achievement는 '학업 성취도'의 뜻으로 복합명사로 쓰여 적절하다.

16

(In order to arrest a person,) the police ① has to be reasonably sure [that a crime ② has been committed.] The police must give the suspect the reasons (why he ③ is being arrested) and ④ tell him his rights (under the law.)

정답 ① (has → have)

해석 경찰이 누군가를 체포하기 위해선 범죄가 일어났다는 합리적인 확신이 있어야만 한다. 경찰은 용의자에게 체포 이유를 알려 줘야 하며 법적 권리도 말해 주어야 한다.

분석 the police are (O) / the police is (X)

① the police는 경찰관 전체를 지칭하는 명사로 항상 복수 취급하기로 약속이 되어 있다. 반드시 복수동사와 수 일치해야 하기 때문에 has를 have로 고쳐야 한다.

② 별다른 시점부사가 없기 때문에 현재완료(has been) 는 적절하다.

③ 그가 체포당하는 대상이므로 수동태는 적절하고, 진행형 절대 불가능 동사가 아닌 이상 당시의 상황을 세게 전달하는 표현인 진행은 얼마든지 쓸 수 있다.

④ must give and tell로 병치된 형태이다.

17

① The housekeeping problems (of living in a shelter) begin (② as soon as the shelter is occupied.) ③ Medical supplies, utensils, and equipments, (as well as food,) (if not already stored in the shelter,) ④ must be quickly gathered up and carried inside.

정답 ③ (Medical supplies, utensils, and equipments → Medical supplies, utensils, and equipment)

해석 보호 시설에서의 살림살이 문제는 그 시설에 사람이 들어오자마자 시작된다. 식료품뿐 아니라 의약품, 식기류, 그리고 장비가 그 시설에 구비되어 있지 않은 경우, 그것들을 빠르게 모아서 시설에 구비해야 한다.

분석 절대 불가산명사(집합적 물질명사) equipment

③ 절대 불가산명사(집합적 물질명사)는 a/an 혹은 -(e)s 가 붙을 수 없다. equipment로 고쳐야 한다.

① 주어의 역할로 명사가 나와 적절하다.

② 부사절(as soon as)로 쓰여 문장의 의미를 더해 주는 수식어구이며, 주거지가 거주되는 대상이므로 수동태 역시 적절하다.

④ 여러 가지의 장비들이 모여지는 대상이므로 수동태는 적절하다.

18

(Though the term *individualism* did not appear ① until late 1820s,) (when market societies were well established,) the principles (② it encompasses) ③ were already instated (④ by the mid-eighteenth century.)

정답 ① (until late 1820s → until the late 1820s)

해석 비록 '개인주의'라는 용어가 시장 경제가 확립된 1820년대 후반까지 등장하지 않았음에도 불구하고, 개인주의가 포괄하는 원리들은 18세기 중반에 이미 정립되어 있었다.

분석 연도와 연대의 차이

① in 1783과 같이 연도 앞에는 정관사 the를 쓰지 못하지만, in the 1890s와 같이 연대 앞에는 반드시 정관사 the와 함께 써 주어야 한다. until the late 1820s 로 고쳐야 한다.

② individualism을 대신 받는 대명사로 쓰여 수 일치가 적절하다.

③ 주어(the principles)와 동사(were)의 수 일치가 적절하고, 원칙이 정립되는 대상이므로 수동태 역시 적절하다.

④ 수동태 뒤 수식어구(전명구)는 적절하다.

19   [2017 서울여대]

① The constellation Orion includes ② the all stars (in the familiar pattern of the hunter,) ③ along with the region of the sky) ④ in which these stars are found.)

정답 ② (the all stars → all the stars)

해석 오리온자리는 하늘에서 이 별이 발견되는 지역과 우리에게 익숙한 사냥꾼 모양을 이루는 모든 별을 포함한다.

분석 한정사의 어순(전치 한정사)

② all, both, half 등의 단어들은 여러 역할이 있지만 그 중 the(한정사)와 함께 나올 때 한정사보다 앞에 위치해야 하는 전치 한정사로 쓰인다. 따라서 all the stars로 고쳐야 한다.

① The constellation과 Orion은 동격을 나타내는 명사이다.

③ 문장이 끝난 뒤 수식어구(전명구)의 역할로 쓰여 적절하다.

④ 「전치사 + 관계대명사」는 절 이하의 성분(명사)이 완전하게 나와 적절하다.

20   [2011 세종대]

① The post office has promised [② to resume ③ first class mail delivery (to ④ area) (on Friday.)]

정답 ④ (area → the area)

해석 우체국은 그 지역으로의 특급 우편 발송을 금요일에 재개하겠다고 약속했다.

분석 가산명사 area

④ area는 영어에서 항상 가산명사로만 쓰이는 명사이다. 따라서 a/an 혹은 -(e)s가 없어 틀렸다는 것을 파악할 수 있다. 다만 알맞게 고치려면 구체적 지역을 나타내도록 정관사 the를 활용하여 the area로 고쳐야 하지만, 우리는 정답을 찾아내려는 수험생일뿐이니 어떻게 고쳐야 하는지 몰라도 왜 틀린지 알면 정답을 골라낼 수 있다.

① 주어의 역할로 명사는 적절하다.

② promise는 to R를 목적어로 받는 동사이므로 적절하다.

③ first class mail은 '특급 우편'의 뜻으로 쓰이는 하나의 명사이다. 보통 the first man처럼 서수 뒤에 명사가 나오면 정관사 the를 써야 하지만 first class mail delivery는 하나의 표현으로 보고 넘어가면 된다.

21   [2011 숭실대]

(In 2009) Brazil, (① long) the world's worst offender, saw its pace (of jungle clearing) plummet (to ② the third of its historical rate.) That's ③ due (in part) to the recession, (as falling commodity prices made clearcutting for farms ④ less profitable.)

정답 ② (the third → one[a] third)   * be due to+Ⓝ: ~ 때문이다

해석 오랫동안 최악의 범법자였던 브라질은 2009년에 밀림 개간의 속도가 과거의 3분의1까지 떨어지는 급속한 하강을 겪고 있다. 이는 부분적으로 경기 침체 때문인데, 물가 하락으로 인해 농장의 개간 사업 이윤이 그다지 크지 않기 때문이다.

분석 분수 표현

② 분수를 표현할 때 분자는 기수(one, two, three, four 등)로, 분모는 서수(first, second, third 등)로 표현한다. 의미상 세 번째가 아니라 3분의 1의 속도까지 떨어지는 것이므로 분수 표현인 one[a] third로 고쳐야 한다. one 대신에 같은 뜻을 갖는 부정관사(a)를 써도 좋다.

① long은 형용사와 부사를 둘 다 가지고 있는 단어이다. 문법 문제에서 형용사와 부사의 선택을 묻는 것이 가장 큰 주제인데 형용사, 부사로 둘 다 쓰일 수 있다면 정답으로 묻지 못한다.

③ 「be due to + N」는 '~ 때문이다'의 뜻을 가진 표현이다.

④ 「make + O + O.C(형용사)」 5형식 동사의 어형으로 목적보어 자리에 형용사는 적절하다.

22

(Over the course of his career) he designed (over)
                                        S   V   ~ 이상
_____ for homes, offices and hotels.
       O

① one thousand furnitures

② one thousand furniture

③ one thousand pieces of furnitures

④ one thousand pieces of furniture

정답 ④

해석 현역 시절, 그는 가정, 사무실, 호텔에서 쓰일 가구를 천
점이 넘게 디자인했다.

분석 절대 불가산명사(집합적 물질명사) furniture / 조수사(단
위 표현)

④ 절대 불가산명사(집합적 물질명사)는 a/an 혹은 -(e)s
가 붙을 수 없다. 따라서 ②, ④로 좁혀지고, 불가산명
사를 세어 줄 때는 조수사(단위 표현)를 이용하여 표현
한다. (ex. a cup of beer, two cups of beer, a
piece of information, two pieces of information)

23

(① As job hunts became tough after the financial crisis,)
  부사절   S   V   C
② an anecdotal evidence suggested [that ③ more
     S   V   명사절(O)
young people ④ considered public service.]
   S   V   O

정답 ② (an anecdotal evidence → anecdotal evidence)

해석 일화성 근거에 따르면 재정 위기 이후 구직이 어려워짐에
따라 공직을 고려하는 젊은이들이 더 많아졌다.

분석 절대 불가산명사(집합적 물질명사) evidence

② 절대 불가산명사(집합적 물질명사)는 a/an 혹은 -(e)s
가 붙을 수 없다. anecdotal evidence로 고쳐야 한다.

① 부사절 접속사(as)로 쓰여 「주어 + 동사」를 받아 적절
하다.

③ that절의 주어의 역할로 명사는 적절하다.

④ 「S(사람) + suggest + that + S + (should) + R ~」,
「S(사물) + suggest + that + S + Vs / Ved ~」와 같이
suggest는 주어의 종류에 따라 should가 생략되어
동사원형을 써야 할 수도 있고 should가 없어 수 일
치와 시제를 표현해야 하는 2가지 용법으로 나뉜다.

24

Air Force One was (① due to land in Washington) (②in
              S   V   C   on
Tuesday morning) (after an overnight flight) (from the
island of Oahu.) The president is returning (from
                              S   V
                   (at)
vacation) (③ the same day) (Republican presidential
                         (when)   S
candidates square off in the Iowa caucuses, the first
            V   O   =
④ nominating contest of the 2012 campaign.)

정답 ② in Tuesday morning → on Tuesday morning

해석 미국 대통령 전용기는 오아후섬에서 밤샘 비행 후 화요일
아침에 워싱턴에 착륙할 예정이었다. 대통령은 공화당 대
통령 후보가 2012년 대선의 첫 번째 경선인, 아이오와 코
커스에 대비하는 바로 그날 휴가에서 돌아올 것이다.

분석 요일을 나타내는 전치사 on

② 요일과 함께 쓰이는 전치사는 in이 아니라 on을 써야
한다. on Tuesday morning으로 고쳐야 한다.

① 「be due to R ~」는 '~할 예정이다'의 표현이다.

③ 시간명사 앞에는 전치사가 생략이 가능하여 명사만 나
온 형태이다.

④ 분사가 아니라 nominating은 '선임'의 뜻의 명사로
nominating contest은 '선임 대회(경선)'라는 뜻의
복합명사이다.

25

These four major corporations ① have tasked their
           S   V
troops (② to employ all ③ means) (necessary to explore
  O   R₁
④ moon for rubium deposits, ⑤ then establish and
  the   (to) R₂   (to)
secure rubium refineries.)
   R₃

정답 ④ (moon → the moon)

해석 이 네 주요 기업들은 그들이 선발한 무리가 매장된 루비
움을 위해 달을 탐사하는 데 필요한 모든 수단을 사용하
도록 지시했으며, 루비움 정제소를 건설하여 확보했다.

분석 태양과 달 앞에 정관사 the

④ 태양(the sun)과 달(the moon) 앞에는 반드시 정관사
the와 함께 써야 한다. the moon으로 고쳐야 한다.

① 주어(These four major corporations)와 동사(have)
의 수 일치가 적절하다.

② to R의 부사적 용법으로 결과의 뜻을 나타내는 표현이다.

③ means(수단)는 -s가 붙어야 명사로 쓰일 수 있다. mean은 동사와 형용사의 역할로만 쓰인다.

⑤ 수식어인 부사로 문장의 의미를 돕기 위해 나와 적절하다.

12강 대명사

Practice

01	④	02	③	03	④	04	③	05	③
06	④	07	②	08	③	09	②	10	③
11	③	12	①	13	④	14	①	15	④
16	②	17	②	18	⑤	19	①	20	②
21	③	22	④	23	③	24	①	25	③

01
[2014 가천대]

The duties (of the priest) (①towards the secrecy) (of the ②confessional) seemed so grave (to me) that I wondered [③how anybody had ever found (in himself) the courage to undertake ④it.]

정답 ④ (it → them)

해석 고해 성사의 내용을 숨겨야 하는 사제의 의무가 내겐 너무 무거워 보여서, 누군가는 어떻게 그 의무를 받아들일 용기가 있었는지 궁금했다.

분석 대명사(대신 받는 명사)의 수 일치
- ④ 해석상 it을 대신 받는 명사는 성직자의 비밀 유지에 대한 의무(the duties)이다. 복수명사를 대신 받는 대명사 them으로 고쳐야 한다.
- ① 명사와 명사의 충돌을 피해 주기 위해 전치사는 적절하다.
- ② confessional은 '고해 성사실'이라는 뜻의 명사이다.
- ③ how는 절 이하의 성분(명사)이 완전하여 항상 명사절을 이끌기 때문에 타동사 wondered의 목적어로 쓰여 적절하다.

02
[2017 단국대]

Martin Luther King Jr.'s assassination ironically ①resulted (in a series of violent ②riots) (across nearly every major city in America,) (though ③it always ④advocated the use of nonviolent protest.) (= Martin Luther King Jr.)

정답 ③ (it → he)

해석 마틴 루터 킹(Martin Luther King Jr.)은 늘 비폭력 시위를 지지해 왔지만, 아이러니하게도 그의 암살은 미국의 거의 모든 주요 도시에서 폭력 시위를 이끌었다.

분석 대명사(대신 받는 명사)의 수 일치
- ③ 해석상 it을 대신 받는 명사는 마틴 루터 킹(Martin Luther King Jr.)이다. 사람을 대신 받는 대명사 he로 고쳐야 한다.
- ① result는 자동사이고 수동태 절대 불가능 동사이므로 능동태로 쓰여 적절하다.
- ② 전치사의 목적어로 명사는 적절하다.
- ④ 마틴 루터 킹이 옹호하는 주체이고, 뒤에 목적어도 있어 능동태는 적절하다.

03
[2010 한국외대]

Researchers (at the university) ①are investigating a series of ②indicators (that ③could help ④themselves ⑤predict earthquakes.)

정답 ④ (themselves → them)

해석 그 대학의 연구원들이 지진을 예측하도록 도와줄 수 있는 일련의 지표들을 조사하고 있다.

분석 대명사(대신 받는 명사)의 선택
- ④ 재귀대명사(themselves)는 주어와 목적어가 같을 때 쓰는 대명사이다. could help의 주어는 선행사인 지표들(a series of indicators)인데, 지표들이 지표들에게 도움을 주는 것이 아니기에 연구원들(researchers)을 대신 받는 대명사 them으로 고쳐야 한다.
- ① 주어(Researchers)와 동사(are)의 수 일치가 적절하고 뒤에 목적어도 있어 능동태 역시 적절하다.
- ② 전치사의 목적어로 명사는 적절하다.
- ③ 뒤에 동사원형을 보아 조동사는 적절하다.
- ⑤ 「help + O + (to) R ~」 5형식 동사의 어형으로 쓰여 적절하다. 이 경우 목적보어 자리에 to는 써도 되고 생략해도 좋다.

04
[2010 경기대]

Government authorities will focus their attention (①on the expansion of the nation's railway facilities,) (②as ③it is emerging ④as the most environmentally-friendly method of transportation.)

정답 ③ (it is → they are)

해석 정부 관계자들은 국가의 철도 시설 확장에 집중할 것이다. 그 이유는 가장 환경 친화적인 수송 수단으로 발달하고 있기 때문이다.

분석 대명사(대신 받는 명사)의 수 일치

③ 해석상 it을 대신 받는 명사는 철도 시설(railway facilities)이다. 복수명사를 대신 받는 대명사 they are로 고쳐야 한다.

① focus A on B: focus는 전치사와 함께 쓸 때 항상 on을 쓰는 동사이다.

② 부사절 접속사(as)로 쓰여 문장을 받아 적절하다.

④ 자격의 전치사(as)로 쓰여 명사를 받아 적절하다.

---

05   [2013 세종대]

(For the last two weeks) I ① have had to ② stay up
                   S   V
③ the most of the night (to observe star configurations
④ for a project for my astronomy class.)

정답 ③ (the most of → most of)

해석 지난 2주 동안 나는 천문학 수업 과제에 필요한 별의 배열을 관측하기 위해 밤을 새웠다.

분석 부정대명사 most

③ most는 여러 가지 역할(대명사, 형용사, 부사, 최상급)을 가지고 있다. 단, 「most of + N/Ns」의 형태처럼 most와 of가 붙어 나오면 대명사로 쓰인 것이다. 대명사 앞에는 정관사 the를 쓰지 못한다.

① 「for + the last + 기간 N」 현재완료 시점부사와 동사의 시제가 일치되어 적절하다.

② must의 대용어구 have[had] to는 뒤에 반드시 동사원형이 나와야 한다.

④ 명사와 명사의 충돌을 피해 주기 위해 전명구는 적절하다.

---

06   [2010 명지대]

I should like to see children ① taught [that they should
S   (that) V   O.C   명사절(D.O)
not say they like things] (② which they do not like)
V   형용사절
(③ merely because certain other people say they like
                         S   V(that)
④ it.)
them

정답 ④ (it → them)

해석 단순히 타인들이 그것들을 좋아한다고 해서 자신이 좋아

하지 않는 것을 선호한다고 말하면 안 된다는 것을 아이들이 꼭 배웠으면 좋겠다.

분석 대명사(대신 받는 명사)의 수 일치

④ 해석상 it을 대신 받는 명사는 things다. 복수명사를 대신 받는 대명사 them으로 고쳐야 한다.

① see의 목적보어 자리이다. 아이들이 가르치는 주체가 아니라 가르침을 받는 대상이므로 수동의 관계인 과거분사(taught)는 적절하다.

② 선행사가 사물(things)이고 절 이하 성분(명사)이 불완전하여 관계대명사 which는 적절하다.

③ 뒤에 「주어 + 동사」가 있기 때문에 접속사 because는 적절하다.

---

07   [2010 세종대]

_____ the writers (who have produced important
                     S   형용사절
work since our last edition) have been updated.
                         V

① The most of   ② Almost all

③ The almost   ④ Almost some

정답 ②

해석 우리의 지난 호가 발간된 이후, 중대한 작품을 써 온 거의 모든 작가의 정보가 최신화되어 있다.

분석 부사 almost

② 부사(almost)는 명사를 꾸밀 수 없다. almost는 all과 함께 나올 경우만 명사를 받을 수 있다. 「most = almost all」 이렇게 생각하면 된다. (most people (O), almost all people (O), almost people (X))

① most와 of가 붙는 경우 대명사로 쓰인 것이다. 대명사 앞에는 the를 쓸 수 없다.

③ almost는 명사를 꾸밀 수 없어 부적절하다.

④ almost는 some과 해석상 어울릴 수 없는 단어이다. (ex. 거의 몇몇 (X))

---

08   [2014 아주대]

The conflict (over the past decade) ① has cost (more
S   =   V   ~ 이상
than) 100,000 lives (in Groznyy,) the capital of
Chechnya. ② Much (of the city) ③ remain in ruins and
                                 remains
④ Chechen-led terrorists are spreading the conflict (to
                  S   V   O
⑤ neighboring republics.)

정답 ③ (remain → remains)

해석 지난 10년간의 갈등은 Chechnya의 수도 Groznyy 거주자 10만 명 이상의 목숨을 앗아갔다. 도시의 많은 부분은 폐허로 남아 있고 체첸 반군의 지휘하에 있는 테러리스트들은 인접 국가들로 분쟁을 키우고 있다.

분석 대명사 much와 동사의 수 일치

③ 「much of N(불가산명사) + is(단수동사)」, 「many of Ns(복수명사) + are(복수동사)」 형태로 수 일치를 해야 한다. 지금과 같은 경우 much와 remain에 둘 다 밑줄이 있어 of the city를 단서로 잡으면 much는 적절하다. 그러므로 단수동사 remains로 고쳐야 한다.

① 주어(The conflict)와 동사(has)의 수 일치가 적절하고, has cost는 현재완료로 쓰인 것이다. (cost−cost−cost)

② 「much of + N(불가산명사)」로 쓰여 적절하다.

⑤ 형용사(neighboring)가 명사(republics)를 수식하여 적절하다.

09

[2015 가천대]

Science has obviously multiplied the power (of the warmakers.) The weapons (of the moment) can kill more people more secretly and more unpleasantly than _____ (of the past.)

① these   ② those

③ that   ④ this

정답 ②

해석 과학은 전쟁을 일으키는 사람들의 힘을 분명히 배가시켰다. 현재의 무기들은 과거의 것(무기)들에 비해 더 많은 사람들을 더 비밀스럽고 불쾌한 방식으로 죽일 수 있다.

분석 대명사 that과 those의 구분

② 영어에서 후치 수식(뒤에서 앞으로 꾸며 주는)을 받는 대명사는 that과 those만 가능하다. 빈칸 뒤 전명구를 보고 ①, ④는 탈락되고, that(단수)과 those(복수)의 차이는 대신 받는 명사의 수 일치. 해석상 대신 받는 명사는 무기들(The weapons)이므로 복수명사를 대신 받는 those가 적절하다.

10

[2013 경기대]

Two ①bus-crashes (in separate locations in Morocco) ②have claimed 27 lives, (including ③that[those] of a German and a ④Dutch tourist.)

정답 ③ (that → those)

해석 모로코의 여러 장소들에서의 두 건의 버스 충돌 사고는 독일과 네덜란드 여행객을 포함해 27명의 사망자를 낳았다.

분석 대명사 that과 those의 구분

③ 대명사 that(단수)과 those(복수)의 차이는 대신 받는 명사의 수 일치. 해석상 대신 받는 명사는 목숨들(lives)이기 때문에 those로 고쳐야 한다.

① 두 번(two)의 사고이기 때문에 복수명사로 쓰여 적절하다.

② 주어(Two bus-crashes)와 동사(have claimed)의 수 일치가 적절하다.

④ 형용사(Dutch)가 명사(tourist)를 수식하여 적절하다.

11

[2016 숭실대]

(Every year,) ①hundreds of people leave important jobs (in the government) (to take more lucrative positions in private industry.) ②Some go to work (as lobbyists,) ③another[others] (as consultants) (to business,) ④still others (as key executives) (in corporations, foundations and universities.)

정답 ③ (another → others)

해석 매년 수백 명에 달하는 사람들이 높은 수입을 얻을 수 있는 사기업 직책을 얻기 위해 정부의 주요 직책을 떠나고 있다. 일부는 로비스트로 활동하기 위해, 다른 일부는 기업의 컨설턴트로, 또 다른 나머지는 기업, 재단 그리고 대학 등에서 핵심 임원으로 일하기 위해 떠난다.

분석 one, another, the other / some, others, the others

③ 불특정 대상을 대신 받는 대명사(one, another, the other / some, others, the others)는 단수는 단수끼리, 복수는 복수끼리 비교한다. 물론 some에도 밑줄이 있지만 복수동사(go)가 고정되어 있어 some은 맞는 형태이다. some은 others와 비교하는 대명사이기 때문에 another을 others로 고쳐야 한다.

① 수단위 명사(score, hundred, thousand, million 등)는 단수와 복수의 형태를 묻는다. 뒤에 of가 있으면 복수형(thousands of books)으로 쓰고, of가 없다면 단수형(two thousand books)으로 써야 하므로 적절하다.

② 뒤에 others를 보아 some과의 비교는 적절하다.

④ some과 비교하는 대명사는 others이다.

12 [2016 아주대]

①A̶l̶m̶o̶s̶t̶ orders ship (within 3 to 5 business days of
   Most   S   V
purchase.) Shipping times may ② vary (due to
           S   V
availability of merchandise.) ③Should you change or
                     =If you should
cancel your order,) please contact us immediately.
                         명령문(R)
④Once the parcel was sent to the post office,) we will
   부사절   S
be unable to make ⑤any changes.
  V   O

정답 ① (Almost → Most)

해석 주문하신 대다수의 상품들은 영업일 기준 3일에서 5일 정도 내에 배송됩니다. 배송 시간은 재고의 유무에 따라 달라질 수 있습니다. 주문 내용을 변경하거나 취소하고자 하는 경우에는 즉시 저희에게 연락해 주세요. 소포가 우체국으로 보내지고 나면, 어떠한 변경도 불가합니다.

분석 부사 almost

① 부사(Almost)는 명사를 꾸밀 수 없기 때문에 형용사(Most)로 고쳐야 한다. 「most=almost all」 형태로 기억하면 된다. (most people (O), almost all people (O), almost people (X))

② vary는 자동사로 쓰여 적절하다.

③ 「If + S + should + R ~ = Should + S + R ~」의 형태처럼 if를 생략시켜 도치된 형태이다.

④ Once는 부사와 접속사의 역할로 쓰인다. 뒤에 주어, 동사가 있으므로 접속사로 쓰여 적절하다.

⑤ any는 대명사와 형용사의 역할을 둘 다 가지고 있으므로 명사를 수식하고 있다.

13 [2013 서울여대]

Some former White House residents have remained
              S   V
(①in the public eye ②for life,) (while ③t̶h̶e̶ others have
                                 부사절   S   V
slipped ④into obscurity.)

정답 ③ (the others → others)

해석 이전의 백악관 거주자 중 몇몇은 평생 동안 대중들의 관심을 받지만, 그 외 다른 이들은 차츰 세상에서 잊히고 있다.

분석 one, another, the other / some, others, the others

③ some은 보통 others와 함께 비교해 쓰인다. '몇몇(some)은 하얀색을 좋아하고 다른 이들(others)은 파란색을 좋아한다.' 다만 some을 the others와 비교하는 경우는 '10명 중 4명은(some) 하얀색을 좋아하고 나머지 6명(the others)은 파란색을 좋아한다.' 이와 같이 나머지 전부(the others)라는 배경이 필요하다. 문제에서 나머지 전부의 배경이 주어지지 않았기 때문에 others로 고쳐야 한다.

① remain은 자동사로 쓰여 전명구를 받아 적절하다.

② 명사와 명사의 충돌을 피해 주기 위해 전명구는 적절하다.

④ slip은 자동사로 쓰여 전명구를 받아 적절하다.

14 [2016 서강대]

         the
①Most of critics agrees [that the gothic has been ②an
 S   V   명사절(O₁)┌S   V
important presence in America beginning with Charles
     C
Brockden Brown] and [that ③it continues to influence
                   명사절(O₂) S   V   O₁
the nation's culture and to ④permeate the nation's
             and   O₂
literature at every level.]

정답 ① (Most of critics agrees → Most of the critics agree / Most critics agree)

해석 대다수의 비평가들은, 고딕 양식이 찰스 브록던 브라운과 더불어 시작되어 지금까지 중대한 역할을 해왔고, 미국 문화에 지속적인 영향을 미치고 있으며 미국 문학에 전반적으로 스며들어 있다는 사실에 대해 동의하고 있다.

분석 부정대명사 most, all, some

① all, some, most의 공통점은 역할이 많다는 것이다. 다만 이 단어들이 뒤에 of와 붙어 나오면 반드시 부정대명사 역할로 쓰인다. 「most of + the/소유격 + N(s)」처럼 반드시 of 뒤에는 한정사(the, 소유격 등)가 있어야 한다. Most of the critics agree로 고치거나 아예 형용사의 역할로 써서 Most critics agree로 고쳐야 한다.

② be동사의 보어로 명사는 적절하다.

③ 해석상 it은 고딕 양식(the gothic)을 받고 있어 수 일치가 적절하다.

④ to influence and to permeate로 병치된 형태이다.

15 [2016 성균관대]

(In science) one experiment, (①whether it ②succeeds or fails,) is ③logically followed (by ④other in a ⑤theoretically infinite progression.)

정답 ④ (other → another)

해석 과학에서, 하나의 실험은, 성공하든 실패하든 상관없이, 이론적으로 무한한 진보 속에서 또 다른 실험에 의해서 논리적으로 이어진다.

분석 one, another, the other / some, others, the others

④ 영어에서 other은 형용사로만 쓰인다. 대명사 another 로 고쳐야 한다.

① 주절이 있기 때문에 whether은 부사절로 쓰여 적절 하다.

② succeed는 자동사로 쓰여 적절하다.

③ be p.p.(수동태) 사이에 형용사는 절대 쓰지 못하고 부 사는 가능하다.

⑤ 부사가 형용사를 수식하여 적절하다.

16 [2016 한국외대]

(Although sleep disorder is ①associated (with heart disease in both men and women,) ②they may negatively ③affect the heart rates (of women) more than ④those of men.

정답 ② (they → it)

해석 비록 수면 장애가 남자와 여자 모두에게 발생하는 심장병 과 연관이 있지만, 남성보다는 여성의 심장 박동 수에 더 악영향을 미친다.

분석 대명사(대신 받는 명사)의 수 일치

② 해석상 they가 대신 받는 명사는 수면 장애(sleep disorder)이다. 단수명사를 대신 받는 대명사 it으로 고쳐야 한다.

① 수면 장애가 심장병과 연관되는 대상이므로 수동태는 적절하다.

③ 조동사 뒤에 동사원형이 적절하다.

④ 심장병 발병률(the heart rates)을 대신 받는 대명사 로 수 일치가 적절하다.

17 [2017 경기대]

(In ①the La Sierra region) you'll find the temperate weather ②patterns (that give Ecuador ③it's status ④as the Land of Eternal Spring.)

정답 ③ (it's → its)

해석 라 시에라(La Sierra) 지역에 가면, 에콰도르에게 영원한 봄의 나라라는 지위를 부여하는 온화한 기후 패턴을 당신 은 보게 될 것이다.

분석 문의구성

③ it's를 풀어쓰면 it is 혹은 it has이다. 하지만 that절 속에 동사 give가 있기 때문에 동사가 또 나올 수 없 으므로 소유격 its로 고쳐야 한다.

① 명사 앞에 정관사 the는 적절하다.

② weather patterns는 복합명사로 쓰여 적절하다.

④ 자격의 전치사 as로 쓰여 적절하다.

18 [2017 아주대]

Acute stress is ①the most common form (of stress.) It ②comes (from demands and pressures of ③the recent past and ④anticipated demands and pressures of the near future.) Acute stress is thrilling and exciting in small doses, but ⑤too many is exhausting.

정답 ⑤ (too many → too much)

해석 급성 스트레스는 가장 일반적인 형태의 스트레스이다. 급 성 스트레스는 최근에 있었던 여러 가지 부담과 압박, 그 리고 곧 있을 것으로 예상되는 여러 부담과 압박으로부터 발생한다. 약간의 급성 스트레스는 짜릿하고 흥분되지만, 너무 심하면 심신을 지치게 한다.

분석 대명사 many와 much의 구분

⑤ many와 much는 대명사로 쓰여 얼마든지 주어 자리 에 나올 수 있다. 하지만 many는 복수 취급을, much 는 불가산 취급을 해주는 대명사이기 때문에 단수동사 (is)를 보고 too much로 고쳐야 한다.

① 최상급 앞에는 정관사 the를 써야 한다.

② 자동사로 쓰여 전명구를 받아 적절하다.

③ 전치사의 목적어로 명사는 적절하다.

④ 요구와 압박이 예상되는 대상이므로 수동의 관계인 과 거분사(anticipated)는 적절하다.

19

Artificial intelligence (AI) is part (of our global culture,)
and ①their impact (on our everyday lives) ②is growing.
[Searching for news ③about AI] presents a deluge of
information. Why not ④use a little AI of our own ⑤to
better handle the task?

정답 ① (their → its)

해석 인공 지능(AI)은 글로벌 문화의 일부이며, 그것이 우리들
의 일상생활에 미치는 영향력이 늘어나고 있다. 인공 지
능에 관한 뉴스를 검색하면 엄청난 양의 정보를 맞닥뜨린
다. 일의 능률을 높이기 위해 우리 자신의 작은 인공 지능
을 사용해 보는 것은 어떨까?

분석 대명사(대신 받는 명사)의 수 일치

① 해석상 their을 대신 받는 명사는 인공 지능(Artificial
intelligence)이다. 단수명사를 대신 받는 대명사의 소
유격 its로 고쳐야 한다.

② 주어(its impact)와 동사(is)의 수 일치가 적절하다.

③ 명사와 명사의 충돌을 피해 주기 위해 전치사는 적절
하다.

④ Why not + R ~?: '~하는 게 어때?'의 표현으로 쓰여
적절하다.

⑤ 「use + O + to R ~」 to R의 부사적 용법으로 쓰여 적
절하다.

20

(①By the time Ralph Rogers completes his testimony,)
every major executive (of our company) (but Mark
Jamieson ②and I) ③will have been accused (of
complicity in the stock swindle.) ④No error

정답 ② (and I → and me)

해석 랄프 로저스(Ralph Rogers)가 그의 증언을 마칠 즈음,
마크 재미슨(Mark Jamieson)과 나를 제외한 우리 회사
의 중역 모두가 주가 조작의 공범으로 고발될 것이다.

분석 전치사 뒤 대명사의 목적격

② 전체(every)를 뜻하는 단어와 함께 나오는 but은 전치
사(~을 제외하고)의 역할로 쓰인다. 전치사 뒤에 대명
사는 목적격을 써야 하기 때문에 and me로 고쳐야
한다.

①, ③ 「by the time + S + Vs(현재) ~, S + will have
p.p. ...」 형태로 시점부사와 동사의 시제 일치가 적절
하게 쓰였다.

④는 ①, ②, ③ 중에 오류가 없는 경우 선택한다.

21

①Most of the water (at the bottom of the North Pacific
Ocean) ②has not been exposed (to sunlight in at least
800 years) and ③some of them has been down there
④for two millennia.

정답 ③ (some of them → some of it)

해석 북태평양 심해수의 많은 부분은 800년 동안 햇빛에 노출
되지 않았고, 심해수 중 일부는 2000년 동안 그 장소에만
있었다.

분석 대명사(대신 받는 명사)의 수 일치

③ 해석상 them이 대신 받는 명사는 the water이다.
some of them을 some of it으로 고쳐야 한다. 동사
역시 단수(has)인 것으로 보아 some of 뒤에 단수명
사가 나와야 한다.

① Most of 뒤에는 반드시 한정사(the, 소유격 등)가 나
와야 하므로 적절하다.

② 부정대명사(Most of + the N/Ns)가 주어로 나오면
of 뒤에 명사와 수 일치를 해야 한다.

④ 문장이 끝난 뒤 수식어구(전명구)로 쓰여 적절하다.

22

Those (who distrust science ①as a guide to conduct,)
(②whether individual or social,) ③seem to overlook
④their pragmatic nature, or perhaps they scorn it for
that very reason.

정답 ④ (their → its)

해석 개인적인 것이든 사회적인 것이든 상관없이, 행동하기 위
한 지침으로 과학을 불신하는 사람들은 과학의 실용적인
특성을 간과하는 듯 보이거나 아마도 바로 그런 이유로
인해서 과학을 혐오한다.

122 _에듀윌 편입 솔루션 문법 Basic

분석 대명사(대신 받는 명사)의 수 일치

④ 해석상 대명사 their이 대신 받는 명사는 과학(science)
이다. 단수명사를 대신 받는 대명사의 소유격 its로 고
쳐야 한다.

① 「distrust + O + as + O.C」 5형식 동사의 어형으로
쓰여 적절하다.

② 주절이 있기 때문에 부사절로 쓰여 적절하다.

③ 주어(Those)와 동사(seem)의 수 일치가 적절하다.

분석 부정대명사 none / 부정형용사 no

① none은 대명사이고 no는 형용사이다. 명사와 명사의
충돌을 피해 주기 위해 형용사 no로 고쳐야 한다.

② be동사의 보어로 명사는 적절하다.

③ 조동사 뒤에 동사원형은 적절하다.

④ 어떠한 것(something)이 결정짓는 주체가 아니라 결
정지어지는 대상이므로 수동태는 적절하다.

⑤ 단수명사(survey) 앞에 부정관사(a)는 적절하다.

23
[2011 세종대]

① [Spending money on tablet computers] may ② seem
        S   the
an extravagance, but some ③ of educators say [they
    C   S   V
are more than ④ just a cool toy.]
                    (that)
                    명사절(O)

정답 ③ (of educators → of the educators 또는 educators)

해석 태블릿 컴퓨터에 돈을 쓰는 것이 사치처럼 보일 수도 있
지만, 일부 교육자들은 이 컴퓨터가 단지 흥미로운 장난
감 그 이상이라고 말한다.

분석 부정대명사 most, all, some

③ all, some, most의 공통점은 역할이 많다는 것이다.
다만 이 단어들이 뒤에 of와 붙어 나오면 반드시 부정
대명사 역할로 쓰인다. 「some of + the/소유격 + N(s)」처
럼 반드시 of 뒤에는 한정사(the, 소유격 등)가 있어야
한다. some of the educators로 고치거나 아예 형용
사의 역할로 써서 some educators로 고쳐야 한다.

① 동명사구(Spending ~ computers)가 주어의 역할로
쓰여 적절하다.

② 2형식 동사 seem은 명사 혹은 형용사를 보어로 받을
수 있다.

④ 단수명사(toy) 앞에 부정관사(a)는 적절하다.

25
[2012 경기대]

(In this movie,) a young woman (working as a sales
                 S
associate at a department store) takes a mannequin
                                  V₁   O
(that resembles _____ to the rooftop of the
형용사절
building) and drops it (to the ground,) (morbidly curious
          V₂   O   ∅
to know what it feels like to jump off there.)
         N

① him   ② himself

③ her   ④ herself

정답 ③

해석 이 영화에서 백화점 영업 사원으로 일하는 젊은 여자는
옥상에서 뛰어내린다면 어떤 기분일지에 대해 병적인 호
기심을 갖고, 자신을 닮은 마네킹을 가지고 옥상으로 올
라가서 마네킹을 땅에 떨어뜨렸다.

분석 명사를 대신 받는 대명사의 선택

③ 동사(resemble)의 주어는 마네킹(a mannequin)이
다. 주어와 목적어가 같을 때 써 주는 것이 재귀대명사
인데 해석상 마네킹이 마네킹을 닮은 것이 아니기에
②, ④는 탈락된다. 마네킹이 닮은 것은 젊은 여성(a
young woman)이므로 여성을 받는 대명사 her이 정
답으로 적절하다.

24
[2011 아주대]

[Why a person has ① none friendship] is ② something
                       no
      S   S   V   C
(that cannot ③ be adequately ④ determined by ⑤ a
형용사절
                          V
survey.)

정답 ① (none → no)

해석 어떤 사람에게 우정이 부족한 이유는 단지 조사에 의해서
단정될 수 없다.

13강 형용사

Practice

01	②	02	③	03	④	04	①	05	③
06	②	07	④	08	①	09	①	10	④
11	④	12	②	13	①	14	①	15	①
16	②	17	④	18	④	19	③	20	③
21	②	22	④	23	④	24	④	25	④

01
[2010 단국대]

① Those (who pass their lives in foreign travel) find [they contract ②much ties (of hospitality,) but ③form no ④friendships.]

정답 ② (much → many)

해석 해외여행을 하며 인생을 보내는 사람들은 많은 유대 관계를 맺을 수 있지만 우정을 느끼지는 못한다.

분석 수량형용사 many와 much의 구분
- ② much는 불가산명사(N)를 수식하고, many는 가산명사(a/an N, Ns)를 수식한다. 한국어의 해석상 셀 수 있냐, 없냐를 따지는 것이 아니라 명사를 보고 판단하면 된다. 뒤에 ties(가산명사)가 있으니 many로 고쳐야 한다.
- ① 선행사가 사람들(Those)이고 절 속에 주어 자리가 불완전하여 주격 관계대명사 who는 적절하다.
- ③ contract but form으로 동사가 병치된 형태이다.
- ④ form의 목적어로 쓰여 적절하다.

02
[2010 성균관대]

The prime minister ①held to his long-standing goal (②of a balanced budget) and, (③alike his predecessor,) ④called for considerable ⑤increase (in public expenditure.)

정답 ③ (alike → like)

해석 수상은 오랫동안 목표로 삼아 온 수지 균형을 고수하였으며, 전임자와 마찬가지로 공공 지출에서의 상당한 증액을 요구하였다.

분석 후치 수식의 형용사
- ③ alike, alive, alone, asleep, afraid는 항상 뒤에서 앞에 있는 명사를 수식해야 하는 형용사이다. 이 단어들은 문제로 물을 때 항상 뒤에 명사를 주고 묻는다. 이 단어들 뒤에 명사가 있으면 무조건 틀리고, 없으면 무조건 맞는 보기이다. alike를 like로 고쳐야 한다.
- ① 「hold to N」는 '~을 고수하다'라는 뜻으로, 「stick to N」와 동의어로 쓰이는 표현이다.
- ② 명사와 명사의 충돌을 피해 주기 위해 전치사는 적절하다.
- ④ held and called로 동사가 병치된 형태이다.
- ⑤ 전치사의 목적어로 명사는 적절하다.

03
[2013 경기대]

The fertility rate (of women) (with ①higher incomes) ②is higher (while women (who ③pursue careers) tend to have ④less babies.)

정답 ④ (less → fewer)

해석 전문직을 원하는 여성들이 아이를 덜 가지는 경향이 있는 반면에, 고소득층 여성들의 출산율이 더 높다.

분석 수량형용사 few와 little의 구분
- ④ little은 불가산명사(N)를 수식하고, few는 가산명사(Ns)를 수식한다. 한국어의 해석상 셀 수 있냐, 없냐를 따지는 것이 아니라 명사를 보고 판단하면 된다. 뒤에 가산명사(babies)가 있는데 less는 little의 비교급이므로 few의 비교급 fewer로 고쳐야 한다.
- ① 앞에 비교급이 있다고 항상 뒤에 than이 있어야 하는 것은 아니다. '더 ~한'이라는 의미를 더해 주고 싶다면 얼마든지 비교급(-er/more ~)을 써도 좋다.
- ② 주어(The fertility rate)와 동사(is)의 수 일치가 적절하다.
- ③ 주격 관계대명사절 속에 동사(pursue)는 선행사(women)와 수 일치가 되어 적절하다.

04
[2014 상명대]

(When I mailed ①the 200-pages manuscript ②to my editor,) I didn't ③realize [that the pages were ④completely ⑤out of order.]

정답 ① (the-200-pages → the-200-page)

해석 내가 200페이지의 원고를 편집자에게 전송했을 때 나는 페이지들이 완전히 엉망인 것을 알지 못했다.

분석 숫자-(하이픈) 연결명사

① 숫자가 2 이상 몇이 나오든 숫자와 하이픈(-)으로 연결되는 명사는 반드시 단수명사로 연결해야 한다. the 200-page로 고쳐야 한다.

② 명사와 명사의 충돌을 피해 주기 위해 전명구는 적절하다.

③ 목적어로 that절을 받고 있어 능동태는 적절하다.

④ 부사(completely)가 형용사(out of order)를 수식하여 적절하다.

⑤ be동사(were)의 보어로 형용사는 적절하다.

05 [2014 아주대]

The number (of work permits) (①issued to Hong Kong
S   (which were)
② nationals) (during the ③twelve-months period)
④was ⑤eight hundred.
V   C

정답 ③ (twelve-months → twelve-month)

해석 12개월 동안 홍콩 국민들에게 발급된 근로 허가서의 수는 800장이었다.

분석 숫자-(하이픈) 연결명사

③ 숫자가 2 이상 몇이 나오든 숫자와 하이픈(-)으로 연결되는 명사는 반드시 단수명사로 연결해야 한다. twelve-month로 고쳐야 한다.

① 근로 허가서가 발급하는 주체가 아니라 발급되는 대상이므로 수동의 관계인 과거분사(issued)는 적절하다.

② Hong Kong nationals는 '홍콩 국민들'이라는 뜻의 명사로 쓰여 적절하다.

④ 「The number of + Ns」는 the number에 수 일치를 맞춰 단수동사를 써야 한다.

⑤ be동사의 보어로 명사는 적절하다.

06 [2015 홍익대]

A distinction (①between 'fact' and 'fiction') seems
S unlikely   V
②unlike to get us very far, (not least because ③the
        C   부사절
distinction itself ④is often a questionable one.)
S   └ = ┘   V   C

정답 ② (unlike → unlikely)

해석 '사실'과 '허구'의 구분은 우리를 그다지 먼 곳으로 데려가는 것 같지는 않다. 특히 그 이유는 그러한 구분 자체가 의심스럽기 때문이다.

분석 unlike와 unlikely의 구문

② unlike는 전치사(~와 달리)와 형용사(서로 다른)의 역할을 가지고 있는데 여기서는 seem의 보어 자리이므로 형용사로 봐야 한다. 하지만 그렇게 보면 해석이 부적절하다. unlikely는 to R와 함께 나와 '~할 것 같지 않는'의 의미로 쓰이는 표현이다. unlike를 unlikely로 고쳐야 한다. 「be (un)likely to + R ~」는 '~할 가능성이 있다(없다)'의 뜻이다.

① 「between A and B」의 표현으로 쓰여 적절하다.

③ 명사 앞에 정관사 the는 적절하다.

④ 주어(the distinction)와 동사(is)의 수 일치가 적절하다.

07 [2017 국민대]

(Although the unique circumstances (of every life)
부사절   S
①result in ② (each of us) having an individual way ③of
V   P   의미상 주어   동명사구(N)
speaking,) we generally tend [to ④sound alike others]
S   S   V   O like
(who share similar educational backgrounds with us.)
형용사절

정답 ④ (sound alike → sound like)

해석 삶에서 겪는 특별한 상황들로 인해 개개인은 자신만의 말투를 갖고 있지만, 우리와 유사한 교육 배경을 공유하는 다른 사람들과 유사하게 들리는 경향이 있다.

분석 후치 수식의 형용사

④ alike, alive, alone, asleep, afraid는 항상 뒤에서 앞에 있는 명사를 수식해야 하는 형용사이다. 이 단어들은 문제로 물을 때 항상 뒤에 명사를 주고 묻는다. 이 단어들 뒤에 명사가 있으면 무조건 틀리고, 없으면 무조건 맞는 보기이다. alike를 like로 고쳐야 한다.

① result는 전치사 in 혹은 from을 받는 자동사이다.

② 동명사의 의미상 주어의 역할로 적절하다.

③ way(방법)는 동격을 표현할 때 to R와 「of + R-ing」를 둘 다 쓸 수 있다.

08

[2017 국민대]

It was July 10, 2012, and I was an ordinary ① 17-years-old girl, (who'd been ② feeling unwell.) ③ With my mother by my side,) I now sat (in Dr. Mahbob's office) and ④ awaited my diagnosis.

정답 ① (17-years-old girl → 17-year-old girl)

해석 2012년 7월 10일, 나는 건강이 좋지 않은 평범한 17살의 소녀였다. 나는 그때 마봅(Mahbob) 박사의 병원에서 어머니와 나란히 앉아 나의 진단을 기다리고 있었다.

분석 숫자-(하이픈) 연결명사

① 숫자가 2 이상 몇이 나오든 숫자와 하이픈(-)으로 연결되는 명사는 반드시 단수명사로 연결해야 한다. 17-year-old girl로 고쳐야 한다.

② 형용사(unwell)를 보어로 받는 오감동사 feel로 쓰여 적절하다.

③ 뒤에 문장이 완전하게 있어 수식어구(전명구)는 적절하다.

④ await은 타동사로 쓰여 목적어를 전치사 없이 받아야 한다.

09

[2017 상명대]

① Many evidence ② indicates [that ③ the number (of gorillas ④ in the wild) is decreasing ⑤ drastically.]

정답 ① (Many evidence → Much evidence)

해석 많은 증거가 야생 고릴라의 수가 급격히 줄어들고 있다는 것을 보여 주고 있다.

분석 수량형용사 many와 much의 구분

① much는 불가산명사(N)를 수식하고, many는 가산명사(a/an N, Ns)를 수식한다. 한국어의 해석상 셀 수 있냐, 없냐를 따지는 것이 아니라 명사를 보고 판단하면 된다. 뒤에 evidence(불가산명사)가 있으니 much로 고쳐야 한다.

② 주어(Much evidence)와 동사(indicates)의 수 일치가 적절하다.

③ 「a number of + Ns + are(복수동사)」, 「the number of + Ns + is(단수동사)」의 형태로 수 일치하기 때문에 적절하다.

④ 명사와 명사의 충돌을 피해 주기 위해 전치사는 적절하다.

⑤ 자동사 뒤에 부사는 적절하다.

10

[2017 한국외대]

Today's young people have very adult worries (about the uncertainty of the future and the lack of jobs in particular,) (far _____.)

① different to what their parents' generation

② from different their parents' generation

③ different what their parents' generation

④ different from their parents' generation

정답 ④

해석 오늘날의 젊은이들은, 그들의 부모 세대와 매우 달리, 미래의 불확실성과 특히 일자리 부족에 대해 매우 성숙한 걱정을 한다.

분석 형용사와 연결되는 전치사 / 문의구성

④ 「different from + N」는 '~와 다른'의 표현으로 어순과 전치사가 적절한 것은 ④가 유일하다.

①, ③ what이라는 접속사 뒤에 동사도 없어 부적절하다.

11

[2017 한국항공대]

(When a fluid is ① in motion,) its flow can be characterized (in one of two ways.) The flow ② is said (to be streamline, or laminar,) (if every particle (that ③ passes a particular point) moves along exactly ④ smooth the same path (followed by previous particles passing that point.))

정답 ④ (smooth the same → the same smooth)

해석 유동체가 움직일 때 그 흐름은 두 가지 중 하나의 방식으로 특징지어질 수 있다. 만약 특정한 지점을 지나는 모든 입자들이 그 지점을 지난 이전 입자들이 따라간 것과 정확히 똑같은 부드러운 경로를 따라 이동한다면, 그 흐름은 유선형 또는 층류를 판단된다고 말해진다.

분석 형용사의 위치

④ 형용사는 관사(a/an, the) 뒤에 위치해야 하기 때문에 the same smooth로 고쳐야 한다.

① be in motion은 '움직이다'의 표현으로 쓰인다.

② 흐름이 말하는 주체가 아니라 말해지는 대상이므로 수동태는 적절하다.

③ 주격 관계대명사절 속에 동사(passes)는 선행사(every particle)와 수 일치되어 적절하다.

12

The World Conference Against Racism is supposed to
put (① on the table) such sensitive issues (② that
reparation for slavery and the question of [③ whether
Zionism is racism ④ or not.])

* such A as B: B와 같은 A

정답 ② (that → as)

해석 세계 인종 차별 철폐 회의(The World Conference
Against Racism)는 노예 제도의 배상 문제와 시오니즘
이 인종 차별인지 아닌지에 대한 문제와 같은 민감한 문
제들을 현 사안으로 다룰 것이다.

분석 「such A as B」

② 「such A as B(명사)」의 형태로 쓰인다. 뒤에 명사
(reparation)만 있기 때문에 전치사 as로 고쳐야 한다.

① 「put + O + on N」 형태로, 이때 목적어가 길면 전명구
(on N) 뒤로 빼주어도 괜찮다. 지금과 같은 문장이 그
런 형태이다.

③ 전치사의 목적어로 명사절(whether절)은 적절하다.

④ whether은 or not이 나와도 좋고, 나오지 않아도 좋다.

13

① None direct flights are ② currently scheduled (from
New York to Seoul,) ③ but an airline agent can
recommend ④ an alternative travel route.

정답 ① (None → No)

해석 현재 어떤 직항 노선도 뉴욕에서 서울까지 예정되어 있지
않지만, 항공사는 다른 대안의 이동 경로를 추천할 수는
있다.

분석 부정대명사 none / 부정형용사 no

① none은 대명사이고 no는 형용사이다. 명사와 명사의
충돌을 피해 주기 위해 형용사 No로 고쳐야 한다.

② be p.p(수동태) 사이에 형용사는 절대 쓰지 못하고 부
사는 가능하다.

③ 문장과 문장을 이어 주는 접속사로 쓰여 적절하다.

④ 단수명사 앞에 부정관사(a/an)는 적절하고, 형용사는
명사를 수식하고 있다.

14

The Olympic Games, (which take place once every four
① year,) are ② considered the most competitive ③ of
athletic ④ competitions.

정답 ① (year → years)

해석 올림픽은 4년마다 개최되며, 운동 경기 중 경쟁이 가장
심하다고 여겨진다.

분석 「every + 기수 + Ns(복수)」 / 「every + 서수 + N(단수)」

① '~당, ~마다'의 표현은 「every + 기수(two, three,
four 등) + 복수명사(Ns)」, 「every + 서수(second,
third, fourth 등) + 단수명사(N)」 이 두 가지 형태로
표현한다. every 뒤에 기수(four)가 있으므로 years로
고쳐야 한다.

② 올림픽 경기가 여기는 주체가 아니라 경쟁이 치열하다
고 여겨지는 대상이므로 수동태는 적절하다.

③ 최상급(the -est/most ~) 뒤에 셋 이상의 배경(of Ns)
이 쓰여 적절하다.

④ 최상급(the -est/most ~) 뒤에 셋 이상의 배경(of Ns)
이 쓰여 적절하다.

15

Recent presidents have made ① a great deal of
pledges (they didn't keep.) You may not like everything
(I tell you tonight,) but you ② deserve [to hear the truth.]
(On the economy) we've made ③ a little progress, but
we still have ④ a great deal of work to do.

정답 ① (a great deal of pledges → a great number of
pledges)

해석 최근 몇 명의 대통령들은 지키지도 못하는 약속을 많이
했다. 당신들은 내가 오늘밤 당신들에게 들려줄 모든 것
을 선호하지 않을 수 있지만 진실을 들을 자격이 있다. 경
제에 대해서는 우리는 약간의 성과가 있었지만, 여전히
해야 할 일들이 많다.

분석 「much = a great deal of」 / 「many = a number of」

① 「a great deal of = much」이므로 불가산명사(N)만을
수식할 수 있으므로 pledges를 수식할 수 없다. a
great number of로 고쳐야 한다.

② deserve는 to R를 목적어로 받는 타동사이다.

③ a little은 불가산명사(N)를 수식하여 적절하다.

④ a great deal of는 불가산명사(N)를 수식하여 적절하다.

16

[2011 서경대]

(If you want ①to be happy,) here are ②a little tips (③for overcoming six common ④barriers to happiness.)

부사절 / V / S (a few)

정답 ② (a little → a few)

해석 만약 당신이 행복하고자 하면, 행복을 가로막는 여섯 가지 장애물을 극복하는 방법이 있다.

분석 수량형용사 a few와 a little의 구분

② a little은 불가산명사(N)를 수식하고, a few는 가산명사(Ns)를 수식한다. 한국어의 해석상 셀 수 있냐, 없냐를 따지는 것이 아니라 명사를 보고 판단하면 된다. 뒤에 가산명사(tips)가 있으므로 a few로 고쳐야 한다.

① want는 to R를 목적어로 받는 타동사이다.

③ 전치사의 목적어로 동명사는 적절하다.

④ overcoming의 목적어로 쓰였고 명사와 명사의 충돌을 피해 주기 위해 전치사는 적절하다.

17

[2011 서경대]

Nearly ①two-thirds of Americans ②choose higher payroll taxes (for Medicare and Social Security) (over ③reduced benefits in either ④programs.)

S / V / O

정답 ④ (programs → program)

해석 미국인의 거의 3분의 2는 의료 보험과 사회 보장 제도의 감소된 혜택보다 높은 소득세를 선택한다.

분석 형용사 (n)either의 용법

④ (n)either이 형용사의 역할로 명사를 수식할 경우 반드시 단수명사(N)를 수식해야 하기 때문에 program으로 고쳐야 한다.

① 분수 표현이다. 분자는 기수로, 분모는 서수로 쓰고, 분자가 2이상이면 분모에 -s를 붙인다.

② 분수 표현이 주어로 나오면 항상 of 뒤에 명사(Americans)와 동사(choose)의 수 일치를 한다.

③ 혜택이 줄이는 주체가 아니라 줄어드는 대상이므로 수동의 관계인 과거분사(reduced)는 적절하다.

18

[2011 성신여대]

CPRSS, the ①official news organization of China, ②disseminates information (③to domestic ④and internationally newspapers.)

S / V / O / (p) / (a) / (a)

정답 ④ (and internationally → and international)

해석 중국의 새로운 공식 보도 기관, CPRSS가 자국과 국제 신문사에 정보를 퍼트리고 있다.

분석 형용사와 부사의 구분

④ 형용사는 명사를 수식하는 단어이고, 부사는 명사 외에 모든 품사(형용사, 부사, 동사)를 수식하는 단어이다. 부사가 명사(newspapers)를 수식할 수 없기에 형용사 international로 고쳐야 한다.

① CPRSS와 동격을 나타내는 명사로 쓰여 적절하다.

② 주어(CPRSS)와 동사(disseminates)의 수 일치가 적절하다.

③ 명사와 명사의 충돌을 피해 주기 위한 전치사로 쓰였고, domestic and international로 병치되어 적절하다.

19

[2011 세종대]

The company is _____, (flying to 80 destinations in 55 countries.)

S / V / C

① a world second profitable airline

② the world secondly profitable airline

③ the world's second most profitable airline

④ a world's secondly most profitable airline

정답 ③

해석 그 회사는 55개국의 80개 도시로 출항하는 세계에서 2번째로 수익이 많은 항공사이다.

분석 최상급의 어순

③ 「the + 서수 + 최상급 + 명사」의 어순으로 적절하다.

① 서수(second) 앞에는 부정관사(a/an)가 아닌 정관사(the)를 써야 한다.

② secondly는 부사로 명사를 수식할 수 없다.

④ secondly는 부사로 명사를 수식할 수 없고, '세계'는 the world로 표현한다.

20

(During the past decade) _____ have
　　　　　　　　　　　　　　　　　　S
cobwebbed (across the continent,) (putting cheap
 V　　　　　　　　　　　　　　　　　　분사구문
flights within the reach of every vocationer or

jobseeker.)

① the score of new routes

② scores of new route

③ scores of new routes

④ the score of new route

정답　③

해석　지난 10년간 수많은 새로운 항로들이 대륙 전역에 우후
　　　죽순 생겨나, 모든 근로자와 구직자에 한해서 저렴한 항
　　　공을 제공하였다.

분석　수단위 명사의 단수형과 복수형

　　　③ 수단위 명사(score, hundred, thousand, million 등)
　　　　의 단수와 복수의 형태를 묻는다. 뒤에 of가 있으면 복
　　　　수형(hundreds of eggs)으로 쓰고, of가 없다면 단수
　　　　형(two thousand eggs)으로 써야 한다. 이 조건을
　　　　성립하는 것은 ③이다.

　　　② scores of 뒤에도 복수명사(Ns)가 나와야 한다.

21

Credit insurance (against default) (on corporate bonds)
　　　　　S
costs _____ default insurance (for the
 V　　　　　　　　　　　　　　　　O
government debt.)

① nine time as many as

② nine times as much as

③ nine times as many as

④ nine time as much as

정답　②

해석　기업 채권의 채무 불이행에 대비하는 신용 보험이 정부
　　　부채의 채무 불이행 보험보다 9배나 많은 비용을 발생시
　　　킨다.

분석　수량형용사 many와 much의 구분

　　　② much는 불가산명사(N)를 수식하고, many는 가산명
　　　　사(a/an N, Ns)를 수식한다. 한국어로 해석상 셀 수
　　　　있냐, 없냐를 따지는 것이 아니라 명사를 보고 판단하
　　　　면 된다. 빈칸 뒤에 insurance(불가산명사)가 있으니

much를 써야 하고, nine은 2 이상의 숫자이기 때문
에 복수명사(times)가 나와야 한다.

22

_____ here is [that these situations tend
　　　　　　　　　　　 C　　 V　명사절(S)　　S　　　 V
to repeat themselves and things seem to roughly
　　　O　　　　　　　　　　 S　　　 V
continue the same.]
　　　　C

① What interesting

② What an interesting

③ Being interested

④ Of interest = interesting

⑤ Having been interested

정답　④

해석　이러한 상황들이 반복되는 경향이 있으며 거의 동일한 형
　　　태를 유지한다는 사실이 흥미로운 점이다.

분석　「of + 추상명사 = 형용사」

　　　④ 「동사(is) + 주어(that ~ the same)」의 형태로 도치된
　　　　문장이다. 위 문장처럼 주어가 너무 길면 동사 뒤로 빼
　　　　주고, 동사 뒤에 있던 보어를 앞으로 끌고 나올 수 있
　　　　다. 「of + 추상명사 = 형용사」로 쓰이기 때문에 be동
　　　　사의 보어로 「of interest = interesting」이 적절하다.

23

Government economists are taking a _____
　　　　　S　　　　　　　 V　　　　　　 O
view (of the country's IT market this year,) (citing a

recent pattern of slowing growth.)

① conserved　　　　　　② conserving

③ conservation　　　　　④ conservative

정답　④

해석　정부 경제학자들은 최근 느린 성장 패턴을 인용하며, 올
　　　해 국가 IT 분야에 대해서 보수적인 견해를 취하고 있다.

분석　유사 형태 형용사의 의미 구분

　　　④ view를 수식하는 형용사가 필요한 자리이다. 명사인
　　　　③은 탈락되고, 보수적인 관점(견해)의 의미로 쓰인 형
　　　　용사 conservative가 적절하다.

24

Robinson ①desired a happy marriage and hoped ②to
be a great man (③in politics ;) he achieved ④neither
goals.

정답 ④ (neither goals → neither goal)

해석 로빈슨은 행복한 결혼을 꿈꿨고 정계에서 거물이 되길 바
랐다. 하지만 그는 둘 중 어떤 목표도 이루지 못했다.

분석 형용사 (n)either의 용법

④ (n)either이 형용사의 역할로 명사를 수식할 경우 반드
시 단수명사(N)를 수식해야 하기 때문에 neither goal
로 고쳐야 한다.

① 뒤에 목적어가 있어 능동태 동사는 적절하다.

② hope는 to R를 목적어로 받는 타동사이다.

③ 명사와 명사의 충돌을 피해 주기 위해 전명구는 적절
하다.

25

United Nations ①is accusing the militia (②of blocking
emergency food supplies) (to ③tens of ④~~thousand~~ of
thousands
people) (in the suburban area.)

정답 ④ (thousand of → thousands of)

해석 유엔은 교외 지역에 있는 수만 명의 사람들에게 긴급 구
호 식량을 전하지 못하게 한 이유로 그 군대를 비난하고
있다.

분석 수단위 명사의 단수형과 복수형

④ 수단위 명사(score, hundred, thousand, million 등)
의 단수와 복수의 형태를 묻는다. 뒤에 of가 있으면 복
수형(hundreds of pencils)으로 쓰고, of가 없다면
단수형(two thousand pencils)으로 써야 한다.
thousands of로 고쳐야 한다.

① 유엔이 비난하는 주체이고, 목적어도 있기 때문에 능
동태는 적절하다.

② 「accuse A of B」의 어형으로 적절하다.

③ ④의 설명과 동일하다.

14강 부사

Practice

01	②	02	③	03	④	04	④	05	④
06	④	07	①	08	④	09	①	10	③
11	②	12	②	13	④	14	①	15	④
16	①	17	①	18	①	19	②	20	④
21	④	22	③	23	②	24	④	25	⑤

01

[2010 명지대]

The son (① of Italian immigrants) grows up ② <s>poorly</s> (poor) (in San Francisco) and becomes the greatest baseball player (③ of his day,) marries an American goddess and never (④ in word or deed) befouls his legend and greatness.

정답 ② (poorly in San Francisco → poor in San Francisco)

해석 이탈리아 이민자의 아들이 샌프란시스코에서 가난하게 자라, 당대 최고 야구 선수가 되고, 미국의 여신과 결혼하고 언행 어느 면에서도 그의 전설과 같은 위대함을 결코 더럽히지 않았다.

분석 형용사와 부사의 구분

② 형용사는 명사를 수식하는 단어이고, 부사는 명사 외에 모든 품사(형용사, 부사, 동사)를 수식하는 단어이다. 언뜻 보면 poorly가 '가난하게 성장하다'처럼 동사(grows up)를 수식하는 것처럼 보이지만 정확히 따져 보면 '가난한 이민자의 아들이 성장한다'의 의미가 적절하다. 수식하는 것은 명사(이민자의 아들)이므로 형용사 poor로 고쳐야 한다.

① 명사와 명사의 충돌을 피해 주기 위해 전명구는 적절하다.

③ 명사와 명사의 충돌을 피해 주기 위해 전명구는 적절하다.

④ in word or deed: '말이나 행동 면에서'의 뜻으로 쓰이는 표현이다.

02

[2010 한국외대]

① At issue is [whether Treasury Inflation-Protected Securities, (commonly ② known as TIPS,) (which is) are ③ too a good deal for investors:] Opponents say [the government ④ has been losing money on them (while defenders question ⑤ the accounting.)]

정답 ③ (too a good deal → too good a deal)

해석 TIPS라고 널리 알려진 재무국 인플레 보호 증권들이 투자자들에게 과연 괜찮은 거래 조건인가 하는 것이 논란 중에 있다. 반대하는 사람들은 정부가 그곳에 돈을 잃어 버리고 있다고 주장하고 (TIPS의) 옹호하는 사람들은 그 회계가 잘못된 것이 아닌가 하는 의심을 하고 있다.

분석 「too + 형용사 + a/an + 명사」의 어순

③ 부사 too는 「too + a/an + 형용사 + 명사」의 어순이 아니라, 「too + 형용사 + a/an + 명사」의 어순으로 써야 한다. too good a deal로 고쳐야 한다.

① 동사(is)와 주어(whether절)가 도치된 문장으로 be동사의 보어로 전명구가 형용사의 역할로 쓰인 형태이다.

② 수식받는 명사가 TIPS라고 알려지는 대상이므로 수동의 관계인 과거분사(known)는 적절하다.

④ 목적어(money)를 받고 있어 능동태는 적절하다.

⑤ 동사(question)의 목적어로 쓰여 적절하다.

03

[2010 세종대]

(It) would ① thus be futile [to argue [that industrialization destroyed the great ② extended family of ③ the past,] (since such a family type ④ <s>rare</s> (rarely) existed.)]

정답 ④ (rare → rarely)

해석 따라서 산업화가 과거의 대가족 제도를 없앴다고 주장하는 것은 무익하다. 그 이유는 그러한 가족의 형태가 (그 당시에) 거의 없었기 때문이다.

분석 형용사와 부사의 구분

④ 형용사는 명사를 수식하고, 부사는 명사 외에 모든 품사(형용사, 부사, 동사)를 수식한다. 해석상 동사(existed)를 수식하고 있으므로 부사 rarely로 고쳐야 한다.

① thus는 부사로 수식어의 역할이다.

② extended family는 '대가족'이라는 표현으로 절대 extending을 쓰지 않는다.

③ 전치사의 목적어로 명사는 적절하다.

04

① Most people think ② of deserts as dry, flat areas (with little vegetation and little ③ or no rainfall,) but this is ④ hard true.
~~hard~~ hardly

정답 ④ (hard → hardly)

해석 대부분의 사람들은 사막을 식물도 없고 비도 거의 오지 않는 건조하고 평평한 땅으로 생각하지만, 이는 거의 사실이 아니다.

분석 형용사와 부사의 구분

④ 형용사는 명사를 수식하고, 부사는 명사 외에 모든 품사(형용사, 부사, 동사)를 수식한다. 해석상 동사구(is true)를 수식하고 있어 부정부사 hardly로 고쳐야 한다.

① 형용사(Most)가 명사(people)를 수식하여 적절하다.

② 「think of + O + as + O.C」 5형식 동사의 어형으로 쓰여 적절하다.

③ 형용사와 형용사를 접속사(or)로 연결하여 적절하다.

05

(① Although mankind has ② undergone no general improvement in intelligence or ③ morality,) it has made ④ ~~extraordinarily~~ progress (in the accumulation of extraordinary knowledge.)

정답 ④ (extraordinarily → extraordinary)

해석 인류가 지능 혹은 도덕성에서는 보편적인 발전을 이루지 못했지만, 지식 축적이라는 면에서는 엄청난 발전을 했다.

분석 형용사와 부사의 구분

④ 형용사는 명사를 수식하고, 부사는 명사 외에 모든 품사(형용사, 부사, 동사)를 수식한다. 뒤에 명사(progress)를 수식하고 있으므로 형용사 extraordinary로 고쳐야 한다.

① 보기 뒤에 「주어 + 동사」가 있는 것으로 보아 접속사(Although)는 적절하다.

06

Photoperiodism is the ① functional or behavioral ② response (of an organism) (to ③ changes) (in duration) (of daily, ④ ~~seasonally,~~ or yearly periods) (of light and seasonal darkness.)

정답 ④ (seasonally → seasonal)

해석 광주기(Photoperiodism) 현상은 빛과 어둠의 일간, 계절간, 또는 연간 주기의 지속 시간 변화에 대한 생물의 기능적 혹은 행동적인 반응을 의미한다.

분석 형용사와 부사의 구분

④ 형용사는 명사를 수식하고, 부사는 명사 외에 모든 품사(형용사, 부사, 동사)를 수식한다. 「A, B, and/or C」의 형태로 병치가 되고 있는데 A(daily)와 C(yearly)가 명사 periods를 수식하는 형용사이므로 seasonal로 고쳐야 한다.

① 「형용사(functional) or 형용사(behavioral)」가 병치된 형태이다.

② 정관사 the 뒤에 명사가 나와 적절하다.

③ 전치사의 목적어로 명사는 적절하다.

07

She has ① so a ② good memory ③ that she can
such
remember ④ a person's exact words (⑤ even a week later.)

정답 ① (so → such)

해석 그녀는 너무 기억력이 좋아서 누군가의 말을 심지어 일주일이 지난 후에도 완벽하게 기억할 수 있다.

분석 「so + 형용사 + a/an + 명사」 / 「such + a/an + 형용사 + 명사」의 어순

① 「such + a/an + 형용사 + 명사」의 어순을 묻고 있다. so를 such로 고쳐야 한다.

② 형용사가 명사를 수식하여 적절하다.

③ 결과의 「such ~ that ...」으로 쓰여 적절하다.

④ 명사와 명사의 충돌을 피해 주기 위해 소유격은 적절하다.

⑤ 전치초점부사(수식어)로 쓰여 적절하다.

08 [2014 서울여대]

A scandal (last month) (at the University of Virginia,)
S
(where 122 students are ① being investigated for
형용사절
② possible plagiarism of term papers,) ③ revealed
V
[④ how easily cheating has become.]
명사절(O) easy   S   V   C

정답 ④ (how easily → how easy)

해석 지난달 버지니아 대학(the University of Virginia)에서 122명의 학생들이 학기말 과제를 표절했다는 것이 밝혀진 사건은 얼마나 손쉽게 부정행위를 할 수 있는지를 단적으로 보여 주고 있다.

분석 how 뒤 형용사/부사의 구분

④ how 바로 뒤에 형용사/부사에 밑줄이 있다면 반드시 그 선택을 묻게 된다. 이때 형용사와 부사의 선택은 형용사/부사 뒤를 잘라 구조를 살펴보면 된다. 동사 뒤에 형용사 자리가 불완전하다면 형용사를, 완전하다면 부사를 써야 한다. 동사 become 뒤에 형용사 자리가 불완전하므로 how easy로 고쳐야 한다.

① 122명의 학생들이 조사를 받은 대상이므로 수동태는 적절하다.

② 형용사(possible)가 명사(plagiarism)를 수식하여 적절하다.

③ 목적어(how절)를 받고 있어 능동태 동사는 적절하다.

09 [2015 상명대]

Tomatoes, ① actual a fruit (that is used as ② a
S   actually   형용사절 S
vegetable,) began [③ gaining wide acceptance] (as ④ a
V
food plant in the United States) (⑤ between 1820 and
1850.)

정답 ① (actual → actually)

해석 사실상 야채로 간주되는 과일인 토마토는 1820년에서 1850년 사이에 미국에서 식용 식물로 널리 인정받기 시작했다.

분석 형용사와 부사의 구분

① 형용사는 명사를 수식하고, 부사는 명사 외에 모든 품사(형용사, 부사, 동사)를 수식한다. actual을 명사(fruit)를 수식하는 형용사로 봤다면 위치가 틀렸다. 형용사는 관사(a/an, the) 뒤에 위치해야 한다. 문장 전

체의 의미를 돕기 위해 단독 부사 actually로 고쳐야 한다.

② 전치사의 목적어로 명사는 적절하다.

③ begin은 to R와 R-ing를 둘 다 목적어로 받을 수 있다.

④ 전치사의 목적어로 명사는 적절하다.

⑤ 「between A and B」의 형태로 쓰여 적절하다.

10 [2015 서울여대]

① A jet stream is a flat and narrow tube (② of air) (that
S   V   C   형용사절
moves more ③ rapid than the ④ surrounding air.)
rapidly

정답 ③ (rapid → rapidly)

해석 제트 기류는 주변에 있는 공기의 흐름보다 훨씬 더 빠르게 이동하는 평평하고 비좁은 공기의 터널이다.

분석 「more ~ than」 사이에서 형용사/부사의 구분

③ 「more ~ than」 사이에 형용사/부사에 밑줄이 있다면 반드시 그 선택을 묻게 된다. 이때 형용사와 부사의 선택은 more 앞을 잘라 구조를 보고, 동사 뒤에 형용사 자리가 불완전하다면 형용사를, 완전하다면 부사를 써야 한다. move는 자동사로 쓰여 형용사를 받지 못하므로 부사 rapidly로 고쳐야 한다.

① 주어의 역할로 명사는 적절하다.

② 명사와 명사의 충돌을 피해 주기 위해 전명구는 적절하다.

④ surrounding air: '주변 공기'라는 뜻의 복합명사로 쓰이는 표현이다.

11 [2016 상명대]

(When I spoke English,) people nodded ① at me, smiled
부사절   S   V₁   V₂
② sweet, said encouraging words. (③ Even) the people
sweetly V₃   S
(in my culture) ④ would say [that I'd do well in ⑤ life.]
V   명사절(O)

정답 ② (sweet → sweetly)

해석 내가 영어로 말했을 때, 사람들은 나에게 고개를 끄덕여 줬고, 밝게 웃어 주었으며, 격려하는 말도 해주었다. 심지어 나와 같은 문화권의 사람들조차도 내가 잘할 것이라고 격려해 줬다.

분석 형용사와 부사의 구분

② 형용사는 명사를 수식하고, 부사는 명사 외에 모든 품

사(형용사, 부사, 동사)를 수식한다. 해석상 동사
smiled를 수식하기 때문에 부사 sweetly로 고쳐야
한다.
① nod는 자동사로 쓰이기 때문에 전치사와 함께 명사가
나와야 한다.
③ 의미를 세게 전달하기 위한 단어 앞에 위치하는 전치
초점부사이므로 적절하다.
④ 보기 뒤에 동사원형을 보아 조동사는 적절하다.

분석 형용사와 부사의 구분
④ 자동사(depends)와 전치사(on) 사이에서는 항상 동사
를 꾸미는 것만 가능하다. 부사 heavily로 고쳐야 한다.
① in spite of = despite: 전치사의 목적어로 명사는 적
절하다.
② 형용사(electronic)가 명사(gadgetry)를 수식하여 적
절하다.
③ 주어 자리에 명사는 적절하다.

12
[2016 서울여대]

Bone is one (of ① the hardest materials in the body)
$\underset{S}{\text{}}$ $\underset{V}{\text{}}$ $\underset{C}{\text{}}$ (it is)
and, (although ② ~~relative~~ light in weight,) it has a
분사구문   relatively   S V
remarkable ability (③ to resist tension and other forces)
O
(④ acting on it.)

정답 ② (relative → relatively)
해석 뼈는 신체에서 가장 단단한 것 중 하나이다. 그 무게가 상
대적으로 가볍기는 하지만, 뼈는 그 위에 작용하는 장력
과 다른 힘들을 견딜 수 있는 엄청난 능력을 가지고 있다.
분석 형용사와 부사의 구분
② 형용사는 명사를 수식하고, 부사는 명사 외에 모든 품
사(형용사, 부사, 동사)를 수식한다. 해석상 형용사
(light)를 수식하고 있기 때문에 relatively로 고쳐야
한다.
① 최상급 앞에는 정관사(the)를 써야 한다.
③ ability는 to R로 동격을 표현하는 명사이다. (ex.
ability to R ~)
④ 다른 힘(other forces)이 뼈에 작용하는 주체이므로
능동의 관계인 현재분사(acting)는 적절하다.

14
[2017 상명대]

① ~~Environmental conscious~~ and ② socially minded
 Environmentally   ⓐ₁   ⓐ₂
travelers ③ should try [to determine ④ [how much of an
S   V   명사절 = great
opportunity they will have (to ⑤ make a contribution at
O   S   V   ∅
their destinations.)]]

정답 ① (Environmental conscious → Environmentally
conscious)
해석 환경에 대해 관심이 있고 사회적 인식을 가진 여행자들은
그들의 여행 목적지에서 공헌할 기회를 얼마나 얻을 수
있을지를 알아보도록 노력해야 한다.
분석 형용사와 부사의 구분
① 형용사는 명사를 수식하고, 부사는 명사 외에 모든 품
사(형용사, 부사, 동사)를 수식한다. 해석상 형용사
(conscious)를 수식하기 때문에 부사 Environmentally
로 고쳐야 한다.
② 부사(socially)가 형용사(minded)를 수식하여 적절하다.
③ try는 to R와 R-ing를 둘 다 목적어로 받을 수 있다.
④ 「much of a/an = great」의 숙어 표현이다. (much of
an opportunity = great opportunity)
⑤ have to 뒤에 동사원형을 써야 한다.

13
[2016 한국외대]

(① In spite of a tremendous amount of ② electronic
gadgetry,) ③ air traffic control still depends ④ ~~heavy~~ on
S   V   heavily ⓟ
people.
ⓝ
정답 ④ (heavy → heavily)
해석 엄청난 양의 전자 기계에도 불구하고, 항공관제 시스템은
여전히 사람에게 많이 의존한다.

15
[2017 상명대]

① Humans leave their ② nuclear families (when they
S   V   O   부사절
③ get married.) (④ ~~Similar,~~) chimpanzees often join a
Similarly   S   V
new group (to ⑤ mate and reproduce.)
O
정답 ④ (Similar → Similarly)
해석 인간은 결혼을 하게 되면 자신의 핵가족을 떠난다. 이와

유사하게, 침팬지는 종종 짝짓기와 번식을 하기 위해 새로운 무리에 합류한다.

분석 형용사와 부사의 구분

④ 형용사는 명사를 수식하고, 부사는 명사 외에 모든 품사(형용사, 부사, 동사)를 수식한다. 형용사 Similar가 수식할 수 있는 명사가 없다. 문장 전체에 의미를 더해 주기 위해 부사 Similarly로 고쳐야 한다.

① 주어 역할로 명사는 적절하다.

② nuclear families는 '핵가족'이라는 뜻의 복합명사로 쓰여 적절하다.

③ be p.p.와 마찬가지로 get p.p.도 수동을 나타내어 적절하다.

⑤ to R의 부사적 용법(목적)으로 쓰여 적절하다.

16
[2017 서울여대]

The terrain (of Antarctica,) (①near one and a half
S   nearly
②times as big ③as the United States,) ④is amazingly
                                              V
varied.
C

정답 ① (near → nearly)

해석 미국의 거의 1.5배 정도 크기인 남극 대륙의 지형은 놀라울 정도로 다양하다.

분석 -ly가 붙어 뜻이 달라지는 부사

① near는 '가까운, 가까이', nearly는 '거의'의 뜻으로 쓰이는 부사이다. 해석상 '거의 1.5배'의 의미가 자연스럽기 때문에 nearly로 고쳐야 한다.

② 배수사를 표현할 때 항상 times를 복수로 쓴다. (three times, four times 등)

③ 「as ~ as ...」 원급 비교 형태로 쓰여 적절하다.

④ 주어(The terrain)와 동사(is)의 수 일치가 적절하다.

17
[2011 한국외대]

We think and talk (_____) (to have
S   V₁   V₂
conscious awareness of and control over everything)
(that)   Ø   (to)
(we think and say.)

① at too fast a rate

② in too fast a rate

③ at a too fast rate

④ in a too fast rate

정답 ①

해석 우리는 너무 빠른 속도로 생각하고 말해서 우리가 생각하며 말하는 모든 것을 의식하지 못하고 통제할 수 없게 된다.

분석 「too + 형용사 + a/an + 명사」의 어순 / 전치사의 선택

① 부사 too는 「too + a/an + 형용사 + 명사」의 어순이 아니라, 「too + 형용사 + a/an + 명사」의 어순으로 써야 하기 때문에 ③, ④는 탈락되고, rate는 항상 전치사 at과 함께 쓰는 명사이다.

18
[2011 서경대]

(Due to our ①overwhelmingly growth of nearly 1,000%
            P   overwhelming   N
②over the last three years,) we have an immediate
                              S   V₁   O
need and ③are willing to train even ④non-experienced
                    V₂   O
individuals (in local markets.)

정답 ① (overwhelmingly growth → overwhelming growth)

해석 지난 3년간 거의 1,000%라는 압도적인 성장 덕분에 우리는 국내 시장에서 경력이 없는 사람들조차 훈련시킬 필요와 의지가 있다.

분석 형용사와 부사의 구분

① 형용사는 명사를 수식하고, 부사는 명사 외에 모든 품사(형용사, 부사, 동사)를 수식한다. 명사(growth)를 수식하고 있기 때문에 형용사 overwhelming으로 고쳐야 한다.

② 명사와 명사의 충돌을 피해 주기 위해 전명구는 적절하다.

③ 「be willing to R ~」는 '기꺼이 ~하다'의 뜻으로 쓰이는 표현이다.

④ to train의 목적어로 쓰여 적절하다.

19
[2011 성신여대]

①The actual causes (for international conflicts) may
        S
differ ②substantial ③from the reasons (④provided in
V   substantially   P   N   (which are)
public statements.)

정답 ② (substantial → substantially)

해석 국제 갈등의 실질적인 원인은 공식 성명에서 발표한 이유와는 상당히 다를지도 모른다.

분석 형용사와 부사의 구분

　　② 자동사(differ)와 전치사(from) 사이에서는 항상 동사를 꾸미는 것만 가능하다. 부사 substantially로 고쳐야 한다.

　　① 형용사(actual)가 명사(causes)를 수식하여 적절하다.

　　③ 자동사 differ는 명사를 받을 때 전치사 from을 써야 한다.

　　④ 이유(the reasons)가 제공하는 것이 아니라 제공되는 것이므로 수동의 관계인 과거분사(provided)는 적절하다.

20 　　　　　　　　　　　　　　　　　　[2011 아주대]

① The question (of [② whether computers can have ③ minds]) is ④ rapid becoming ⑤ a significant issue.
　　S　　　　　P　　　명사절
　　　　　rapidly　　　V　　　　C

정답 ④ (rapid → rapidly)

해석 컴퓨터가 생각을 할 수 있는지에 대한 문제가 빠르게 중요한 논쟁점이 되고 있다.

분석 형용사와 부사의 구분

　　④ be R-ing(진행), be p.p.(수동), have p.p.(완료) 사이에서는 항상 동사만을 수식하기 때문에 형용사는 절대 쓸 수 없다. 부사 rapidly로 고쳐야 한다.

　　① 명사 앞에 정관사 the는 적절하다.

　　② 전치사의 목적어로 명사절(whether절)은 적절하다.

　　③ 동사의 목적어로 쓰여 명사는 적절하다.

　　⑤ 단수가산명사 앞에 a/an은 적절하다.

21 　　　　　　　　　　　　　　　　　　[2012 서울여대]
분사구문
(With electronic health records ① seen ② widely as a
　　　　　　　　　　　N　　　　　p.p.
way (to make medical care better,)) it is ③ disturbing
　　　　　　　　　　　　　　　　　가S　　　　　ⓐ
[④ how slow they are being adopted by doctors.]
진S slowly　S　　　　V

정답 ④ (how slow → how slowly)

해석 전자 건강 기록이 의료 서비스를 개선하기 위한 방법으로 널리 인식되고 있는데, 의사들에 의해서 이토록 느리게 채택되고 있다는 것이 어처구니없는 일이다.

분석 how 뒤 형용사/부사의 구분

　　④ how 바로 뒤에 형용사/부사에 밑줄이 있다면 반드시 그 선택을 묻게 된다. 이때 형용사와 부사의 선택은 형용사/부사 뒤를 잘라 구조를 살펴보면 된다. 동사 뒤에 형용사 자리가 불완전하다면 형용사를, 완전하다면 부사를 써야 한다. 주어(they), 동사(are being adopted)가 완전한 것으로 보아 how slowly로 고쳐야 한다.

　　① 「with + 분사구문」이다. 전자 건강 기록이 인식되는 대상이므로 수동태 분사구문(seen)은 적절하다.

　　② 형용사 역할을 하는 분사(seen)를 수식하여 부사는 적절하다.

　　③ disturbing은 '혼란스러운'이라는 뜻의 형용사로 쓰여 적절하다.

22 　　　　　　　　　　　　　　　　　　[2012 인천대]

The internet now plays ＿＿＿＿＿＿＿ (in many
　　　　S　　　　V
people's lives) that it is essential for us [to try to decide
　　　　　　　　가S　　　　　　　　　진S
whether it is good or bad.]

① such important a part

② such a part important

③ so important a part
　　O

④ a part so important

정답 ③

해석 인터넷이 이제는 많은 사람들의 삶에 있어 너무나 중요한 역할을 하기 때문에 인터넷이 좋은 것인지 나쁜 것인지 판단해 보는 것은 필수적이다.

분석 「so + 형용사 + a/an + 명사」 / 「such + a/an + 형용사 + 명사」의 어순

　　③ 어순을 올바르게 쓴 것은 ③이 유일하다.

23 　　　　　　　　　　　　　　　　　　[2012 한국외대]

　　　　　　　　　　　　V
Barbara McLintock was a creative thinker (among
　　　　　　　　　　=　　　C
scientists,) one (for whom intuition played ＿＿＿＿＿＿
　　　　　　　　형용사절　　　S　　　V
formal experimentation and analysis.)

① as an important role as

② as important a role as
　　　　　O

③ as a role important

④ as important as a role

정답 ②

해석 바바라 맥린톡(Barbara McLintock)은 과학자들 사이에서도 창조적 사고를 하는 사람이었다. 그에게는 공식적인 실험과 분석보다 직관이 더 중요한 역할을 했다.

분석 「as + 형용사 + a/an + 명사 + as」의 어순

② 원급 비교 「as ~ as ...」 사이에서는 「as + 형용사 + a/an + 명사 + as」의 어순으로 쓰인다. 어순이 올바르게 쓰인 ②가 적절하다. 이 경우 전치사(as) 혹은 접속사(as)가 아니고 반드시 「as ~ as ...」 사이에서 어순이 「형용사 + a/an + 명사」로 쓰인다.

24
[2012 홍익대]

(While [① being big] is still an advantage) — (size offers ② a better survival cushion (if food ③ proves hard to find)) — there are other factors (that limit [④ how easy that trait is passed down].])

정답 ④ (how easy → how easily)

해석 음식을 찾는 것이 어렵다면, 크기는 더 나은 생존책을 제공해 주기 때문에, 크다는 것이 장점이긴 하지만, 얼마나 쉽게 그 특징이 전수될 수 있을지를 제한하는 다른 요소들이 있다.

분석 how 뒤 형용사/부사의 구분

④ how 바로 뒤에 형용사/부사에 밑줄이 있다면 반드시 그 선택을 묻게 된다. 이때 형용사와 부사의 선택은 형용사/부사 뒤를 잘라 구조를 살펴보면 된다. 동사 뒤에 형용사 자리가 불완전하다면 형용사를, 완전하다면 부사를 써야 한다. 주어(that trait), 동사(is passed down)가 완전한 것으로 보아 how easily로 고쳐야 한다.

① 동명사(being big)가 주어의 역할로 쓰여 적절하다.

② 동사(offers)의 목적어로 쓰여 적절하다.

③ 「prove + (to be) + 명사/형용사」의 형태로 쓰여 적절하다.

25
[2014 상명대]

(After the Grimm Brothers ① had ② collected "housewives' tales" ③ from around the country,) they ④ edited them (into stories) (⑤ appropriately for children.)

정답 ⑤ (appropriately → appropriate)

해석 그림(Grimm) 형제들은 전국 각지에 있는 '주부들의 이야기들'을 모아, 아이들에게 적합한 이야기로 편집했다.

분석 형용사와 부사의 구분

⑤ 형용사는 명사를 수식하고, 부사는 명사 외에 모든 품사(형용사, 부사, 동사)를 수식한다. 해석상 명사(stories)를 수식하고 있기 때문에 형용사 appropriate으로 고쳐야 한다.

①, ② 주절이 과거(edited)이기에 종속절에 과거완료(had collected)는 적절하다.

③ 명사와 명사의 충돌을 피해 주기 위해 전명구는 적절하다.

④ 뒤에 목적어가 있어 능동태 동사는 적절하다.

15강 비교

Practice

01	③	02	①	03	③	04	②	05	①
06	②	07	④	08	③	09	④	10	③
11	④	12	①	13	②	14	④	15	④
16	②	17	②	18	④	19	②	20	④
21	②	22	③	23	②	24	④	25	①

01

[2010 단국대]

(In a study of local brain activity) (in people) (① performing a language task,) people (with ② stroke-related aphasia) showed ③ high activity levels (in the right half of the brain) than ④ people who did not have aphasia.

정답 ③ (high → higher)

해석 언어 과제를 수행하는 사람들의 국부적인 뇌 활동 연구에서, 뇌졸중과 관련된 실어증을 겪은 사람들이 실어증을 겪지 않은 사람들보다 우뇌에서 더 높은 활동 수준을 보였다.

분석 than과 상관관계를 이루는 「-er/more ~」

③ 앞에 비교급(-er/more ~)이 있다고 하여 반드시 뒤에 than을 써야 하는 것은 아니다. 비교 대상이 있다면 than을 쓰는 것이고, 없다면 안 쓰면 그만이다. 하지만 만약 문장에 than이 있다면 반드시 앞에 비교급(-er/more ~)이 있어야 하기 때문에 high를 higher로 고쳐야 한다.

① 사람들이 언어 과제를 수행하는 주체이므로 능동의 관계인 현재분사(performing)는 적절하다.

② 실어증(aphasia)이 연관시키는 주체가 아니라 뇌졸중과 연관되는 대상이므로 수동의 관계인 과거분사(related)는 적절하다.

④ 선행사가 사람(people)이고 절 속에 주어 자리가 불완전하여 주격 관계대명사 who는 적절하다.

02

[2010 서울여대]

The students (whose parents let them see R-rated movies sometimes or all the time) were _____ have tried smoking during the study period as those (who never saw the movies.)

① almost five times as likely to

② almost as five times likely to

③ as almost five times likely to

④ almost five times more likely to

정답 ①

해석 연구 기간 동안 부모들이 가끔 혹은 항상 R등급(19금)의 영화를 볼 수 있도록 허락한 학생들은 그런 영화를 보지 않은 학생들에 비해 시험 삼아 담배를 피워 보는 비율이 거의 5배 정도 더 많았다.

분석 배수 비교의 형태와 어순

① 배수사(three times, four times 등)는 「as ~ as ...」, 「-er/more ~ than」, 「the N」의 형태와 함께 나온다. 이때 배수사는 반드시 「as ~ as ...」, 「-er/more ~ than」, 「the N」보다 앞에 위치해야 한다. 어순으로 ②, ③은 탈락되고, 빈칸 뒤 as those가 있는 것으로 보아 「as ~ as ...」 형태인 ①이 적절하다.

03

[2010 세종대]

The more I learned (about the current trend in intellectual property law,) _____ [that novel forms of cultural copyright come with substantial risks.]

① the more became it obvious

② it became the more obvious

③ the more obvious it became

④ the more it obvious became

정답 ③

해석 내가 지적 재산권의 최신 트렌드를 더 많이 공부할수록, 새로운 형태의 문화 저작권이 상당한 위기에 맞닿아 있다는 것이 분명해졌다.

분석 「the -er/more 형용사 + 부사 + S + V ~, the -er/more 형용사 + 부사 + S + V ...」

③ 원칙적으로 비교급 앞에는 the를 쓰지 못한다. 그 예외적 경우 중 한 가지는 바로 점진 비교를 나타내는

138 _에듀윌 편입 솔루션 문법 Basic

「the -er/more 형용사/부사 S + V ~, the -er/more 형용사/부사 + S + V ...」 구문이다. 문두에 The more 을 보고 빈칸 역시 the more로 시작하는 ①, ③, ④로 좁혀지고, 「the -er/more 형용사/부사 + S + V~, the -er/more 형용사/부사 + S + V ...」 구문은 동사 뒤에 있는 형용사/부사를 끌고 나온 뒤에 「주어 + 동사」의 어순으로 써야 한다.

04
[2013 가천대]

(Of several word processors) (that are ① being used these days,) most of Americans and Europeans think [that MS Word is ② ~~the better~~ since it is ③ easier to learn than other ④ ones.)]

정답 ② (the better → the best)

해석 요즈음 사용되는 몇몇 워드 프로세서들 중에서 대부분의 미국인들과 유럽인들은 다른 프로세서들보다 배우기 쉽다고 생각하기 때문에 MS Word를 가장 선호한다.

분석 최상급 표현 「the -est/most ~」
  ② 비교 표현은 몇 가지 예외를 제외하고 원칙적으로 정관사 the를 쓰지 않는다. 반대로 최상급 표현은 「the -est/most ~」의 형태로 정관사 the와 함께 써야 한다. the better을 the best로 고쳐야 한다.
  ① are being used는 현재진행 수동을 표현한 것이다. 진행 불가능 동사가 아니라면 진행은 얼마든지 써도 좋다.
  ③ 뒤에 than이 있기 때문에 앞에 비교급(-er/more ~)이 있어야 한다.
  ④ word processors를 대신 받는 대명사로 수 일치가 적절하다.

05
[2016 홍익대]

She finally became even ① ~~very~~ violent (in her disposition) than her husband himself. She was not satisfied (② with simply doing ③ as well as he had commanded;) she seemed anxious (④ to do better.)

정답 ① (very → more)

해석 결국 그녀는 남편보다 성질이 더 난폭해졌다. 그녀는 남편이 명령한 대로 단순히 잘하는 것에 만족하지 않았다. 그녀는 더 잘하기를 갈망하는 것처럼 보였다.

분석 than과 상관관계를 이루는 「-er/more ~」
  ① 앞에 비교급(-er/more ~)이 있다고 하여 반드시 뒤에 than을 써야 하는 것은 아니다. 비교 대상이 있다면 than을 쓰는 것이고, 없다면 안 쓰면 그만이다. 하지만 만약 문장에 than이 있다면 반드시 앞에 비교급(-er/more ~)이 있어야 하기 때문에 very를 more로 고쳐야 한다.
  ② be satisfied with: '~에 만족하다'의 표현으로 동사와 전치사가 어울려 적절하다.
  ③ 「as ~ as ...」 원급 비교의 형태이다. 이 경우 뒤에 나온 as는 접속사의 역할로 얼마든지 「주어 + 동사」가 나와도 좋다.
  ④ anxious to + R: '~하기를 갈망하는'의 표현으로 적절하다.

06
[2013 상명대]

① Hurricane Charley is one (of ② most destructive hurricanes) (③ ever to hit ④ the United States.) (More than) 20 people died (⑤ because of Charley's effects.)

정답 ② (most destructive hurricanes → the most destructive hurricanes)

해석 허리케인 찰리(Charley)는 이전에 미국을 강타했던 가장 파괴적인 허리케인 중 하나이다. 찰리의 영향 때문에 20명 이상의 사람들이 사망했다.

분석 최상급 표현 「the -est/most ~」
  ② 최상급 표현은 「the -est/most ~」의 형태로 정관사 the와 함께 써야 한다. most 앞에 정관사 the를 추가해야 한다.
  ① Charley는 허리케인의 이름으로 동격 표현이다.
  ③ ever는 부사의 역할로 to R를 수식하여 적절하다.
  ④ 미국 앞에는 반드시 정관사 the와 함께 써야 한다.
  ⑤ because of는 전치사로 쓰여 명사가 나와 적절하다.

07
[2013 아주대]

(① Although ② most of the wild horses (in the western range) have already been ③ rounded up,) the more remote the area, ④ ~~the greatest~~ the possibility [that ⑤ they can still be found].

정답 ④ (the greatest → the greater)

해석 서부권에 있는 대부분의 야생마들은 이미 모여 있지만, 지역이 멀면 멀수록 그 말들이 발견될 가능성이 여전히 더 크다.

분석 「the -er/more 형용사/부사＋S＋V ~, the -er/more 형용사/부사＋S＋V ...」

④ 원칙적으로 비교급 앞에는 the를 쓰지 못한다. 그 예외적 경우 중 한 가지는 바로 점진 비교를 나타내는 「the -er/more 형용사/부사＋S＋V ~, the -er/more 형용사/부사＋S＋V ...」 구문이다. 앞에 the more remote the area가 있는 것으로 보아 the greatest를 the greater로 고쳐야 한다.

① Although는 접속사로 쓰여 「주어＋동사」가 나와 적절하다.

② most와 of가 붙으면 대명사로 쓰인 것이다. 주어 역할로 대명사는 적절하다.

③ 야생마들이 모으는 주체가 아니라 모이는 대상이므로 수동태는 적절하다.

⑤ the wild horses를 대신 받는 대명사로 쓰여 수 일치가 적절하다.

② a[one] third는 '3분의 1'이라는 분수 표현이다.

④ 「help＋O＋(to) R ~」 5형식 동사의 어형으로 쓰여 적절하다. help는 to를 써도 되고 생략해도 무방하다.

---

09 [2015 가톨릭대]

I can tell you [that the new director (of our department)
　S　V　I.O　　명사절(D.O)　　　　　　S
is ＿＿＿＿＿＿ man (I have ever met.)]
V　　　　C　　　　　(that)　　　　Ø

① the most quite stupid

② most the quite stupid

③ the quite most stupid

④ (quite) the most stupid

정답 ④

해석 나는 우리 부서의 새로 온 부서장이 내가 여태 만난 사람들 가운데 가장 멍청한 사람이라고 너에게 말할 수 있다.

분석 최상급 강조부사 quite의 어순

④ quite은 최상급을 강조하는 부사로 쓰일 수 있다. 이 경우 quite의 위치는 최상급 「the -est/most ~」보다 앞에 위치해야 하기 때문에 ④가 적절하다.

---

08 [2014 경기대]

Mortgage ① approvals (in Britain) were (more than)
　　　　　　　　S　　　　　　　　V　　　~ 이상
② a third higher (in November) ③ as (a year earlier) (as
　　　　C　　　　　　　　　　　　　than　　　　　　　　　부사절
government subsidies for homebuyers helped the
　　　　　　　　S　　　　　　　　　　　　V
property recovery ④ gather pace.)
　　　O　　　　(to) O.C

정답 ③ (as → than)

해석 주택 구매자들을 위한 정부의 보조금이 부동산 회복을 가속화하도록 도와줌에 따라, 영국에서 대출 승인 건수가 1년 전보다 3분의 1 이상 증가하였다.

분석 우등 비교 「-er/more ~ than ...」

③ 앞에 비교급 higher가 있고 in November와 a year earlier의 시점을 비교하는 형태이다. as를 than으로 고쳐야 한다. 뒤에 as가 있기 때문에 원급 비교 「as ~ as ...」라고 착각할 수 있지만 뒤에 나온 as는 단순히 부사절 접속사 '~함에 따라'의 의미로 쓰인 것이다.

① 동사(were)의 주어(Mortgage approvals) 역할로 수 일치가 적절하다.

---

10 [2015 서울여대]

Young adults (who live with their parents) are ① nearly
　　S　　　　　형용사절(that)　　　　　　V
as ② likely to say [they are satisfied (with their housing
　　V　　　　　명사절(O) S　　S　V
situation) ③ like those (who live ④ on their own.)]
　　　　　　　as　　　　　형용사절

정답 ③ (like → as)

해석 부모와 함께 사는 젊은이들이 혼자 살아가는 젊은이만큼이나 자신들의 주거 상황에 만족한다고 말할 가능성이 있다.

분석 원급 비교 「as ~ as ...」

③ 앞에 as가 있는 것으로 보아 Young adults와 those를 원급 비교로 표현하고 있다는 것을 알 수 있다. like를 as로 고쳐야 한다.

① nearly는 '거의'라는 뜻의 부사로 쓰여 적절하다.

② 「be likely to R ~」의 표현으로 쓰여 적절하다.

④ on one's own: '혼자서, 단독으로'의 표현으로 쓰여 적절하다.

11

[2017 경기대]

(In some countries,) ①higher levels (of enrollment) (for
                      S

young adult women) ②are linked (to improved access
                V

③to education,) but they can also imply a later
                S   V

insertion (into the labor market) ④then (for men.)
O   than

정답 ④ (then → than)

해석 일부 나라에서, 젊은 성인 여생들의 높은 입학 수준이 교
육으로의 향상된 접근성과 연결된다. 하지만 그것은 또한
남성들의 경우에서보다 여성들의 경우에서 노동 시장으
로의 진입이 더 늦어진다는 것을 암시할 수도 있다.

분석 우등 비교 「-er/more ~ than」

    ④ 앞에 later이라는 비교급이 있고 for young adult
       women과 for men을 비교하고 있기 때문에 then을
       than으로 고쳐야 한다.

    ① 앞에 비교급(-er/more ~)이 있다고 하여 반드시 뒤에
       than을 써야 하는 것은 아니다. '더 ~한'이라는 의미
       가 필요하다면 얼마든지 비교급(-er/more ~)을 써도
       좋다.

    ② 주어(higher levels)와 동사(are)의 수 일치가 적절
       하다.

    ③ 「access to ~」는 '~에 대한 접근'이라는 의미로,
       access는 항상 전치사 to와 어울리는 단어이다.

12

[2017 단국대]

New York City commuters spend ①little time
               S   V   less O

(②annually delayed by traffic congestion) ③than the
(which is)

average (④for very large cities.)

정답 ① (little → less)

해석 뉴욕에서 출퇴근하는 사람들은 해마다 교통 혼잡으로 지
체되는 시간이 대도시 평균보다 적은 편이다.

분석 than과 상관관계를 이루는 「-er/ more ~」

    ① 앞에 비교급(-er/more ~)이 있다고 하여 반드시 뒤에
       than을 써야 하는 것은 아니다. 비교 대상이 있다면
       than을 쓰는 것이고, 없다면 안 쓰면 그만이다. 하지만
       만약 문장에 than이 있다면 반드시 앞에 비교급(-er/
       more ~)이 있어야 하기 때문에 little을 less로 고쳐야
       한다.

    ② 부사(annually)가 형용사(delayed)를 수식하여 적절
       하다.

③ 앞에 비교급(-er/more ~)이 있고 뒤에 비교 대상을 쓸
    때 than으로 받아 준다.

④ 명사와 명사의 충돌을 피해 주기 위해 전치사는 적절
    하다.

13

[2011 상명대]

(①Of the three main forms of fossil fuels) — (coal,

petroleum, and natural gas) — petroleum is ②the more
                           S   V   most

common, (providing approximately 40 percent of ③the
C

world's energy,) (④with coal and natural gas (each)
                    분사구문   Ⓝ   =

providing nearly 25 percent.)
R-ing

정답 ② (the more common → the most common)

해석 3개의 주요 화석 연료 형태인 석탄, 석유, 천연가스 중에
서 석유가 가장 흔하다. 석유가 세계 에너지의 대략 40%
를 공급하는데, 이에 비해 석탄과 천연가스 각각은 대략
25%를 공급한다.

분석 최상급 표현 「the -est/most ~」

    ② 비교 표현은 몇 가지 예외를 제외하고 원칙적으로 정
       관사 the를 쓰지 않는다. 반대로 최상급 표현은 「the
       -est/most ~」의 형태로 정관사 the와 함께 써야 한다.
       the more common을 the most common으로 고
       쳐야 한다.

    ① 최상급은 숫자 셋 이상의 범위를 가진 표현으로 '3개
       의 주요 화석 연료 형태'는 최상급의 범위 표현으로 나
       온 것이다.

    ③ 전치사의 목적어로 명사는 적절하다.

    ④ 「with + N + R-ing ~」 형태의 분사구문이다. 석탄과
       천연가스가 25%를 공급하는 주체이고, 뒤에 목적어
       (25 percent)도 있기 때문에 능동태 분사구문(providing)
       은 적절하다.

14

[2011 서경대]

                  명사절(O)

①Many believe [that people (in Asian countries) ②tend
     S   V   S   V

[to be ③more reserved] than ④the western countries.]
  O   those in

정답 ④ (the western countries → those in the western
       countries)

해석 대다수의 사람들은 아시아 국가 사람들이 서양 사람들보
다 더 내성적인 경향이 있다고 믿고 있다.

분석 비교 대상의 일치 「-er/more ~ than ...」

④ 영어는 비교 대상의 일치를 중요시한다. (ex. 내 키가 그녀보다 크다. (X) / 내 키가 그녀의 키보다 크다. (O)) 지금 비교하는 대상은 아시아 나라들과 서양 나라들이 아니라 아시아의 사람들(people)과 서양의 사람들이다. those in the western countries로 고쳐야 한다. 이때 those는 people을 대신 받는 대명사이다.

① Many는 대명사로 쓰여 believe의 주어 역할이다.

② 주어(people)와 동사(tend)의 수 일치가 적절하다.

③ 문장에 than이 있으면 앞에 비교급(-er/more ~ than ...)이 있어야 한다.

15 [2011 서울여대]

Researchers have found (①in a review of studies) [that the density (of billboards) (advertising tobacco products) ②is ③(more than) twice as high in black neighborhoods ④~~than~~ in white.]

정답 ④ (than → as)

해석 연구원들은 보고서에서 담배를 광고하는 옥외 광고 게시판의 밀집도가 백인 지역보다 흑인 지역에서 두 배 더 높다는 사실을 밝혀냈다.

분석 2배의 배수사 「twice as ~ as ...」

④ 2배의 뜻을 가진 twice는 반드시 뒤에서 「as ~ as ...」 혹은 「the + N」의 형태로 비교하며, 절대 「-er/more ~ than ...」을 쓰지 않는다. twice 뒤에 이미 as도 있기 때문에 than을 as로 고쳐야 한다.

① 문장의 구성이 완전하기 때문에 수식어구(전명구)는 적절하다.

② 주어(the density)와 동사(is)의 수 일치가 적절하다.

③ 숫자 앞에 more than은 '숫자 이상'의 뜻을 가진 수식어일뿐 비교급이 아니다. (ex. more than three people: 세 명 이상의 사람들)

16 [2011 서울여대]

Babies' intelligence, (①the research shows,) is very ②different (from adults) and (③from the kind of intelligence) (we usually ④cultivate in school.)

정답 ② (different from adults → different from that of adults)

해석 그 조사에 따르면, 아이의 지능이 성인의 지능 그리고 우리가 보통 학교에서 계발하는 그런 종류의 지능과는 매우 다르다는 것을 보여 준다.

분석 비교 대상의 일치 「be different from」

② 영어는 비교 대상의 일치를 중요시한다. (ex. 내 성격이 그녀와 다르다. (X) / 내 성격이 그녀의 성격과 다르다. (O)) 지금 비교하는 대상은 아이들과 성인들이 아니라 아이들의 지능과 성인들의 지능을 비교하고 있다. different from that of adults로 고쳐야 한다. 이때 that은 intelligence를 대신 받는 대명사이다.

① 삽입절로 쓰인 형태이다.

③ 「from N and from N」의 형태로 병치되어 적절하다.

④ we 앞에 목적격 관계대명사 that이 생략되어 cultivate의 목적어가 불완전하다.

17 [2011 아주대]

The longer the treatment (for snakebite) is delayed, _____.

① one risks losing a limb is greater
② the greater one risks [losing a limb]
③ the greatest one risks losing a limb
④ the greater one risks to lose a limb
⑤ one risks to lose a limn is greater

정답 ②

해석 뱀한테 물린 부위의 치료가 더 지연될수록, 손발을 잃게 될 위험성이 더 커진다.

분석 「the -er/more 형용사/부사 + S + V ~, the -er/more 형용사/부사 + S + V ...」 / 「risk + R-ing」

② 원칙적으로 비교급 앞에는 the를 쓰지 못한다. 그 예외적 경우 중 한 가지는 바로 점진 비교를 나타내는 「the -er/more 형용사/부사 + S + V ~, the -er/more 형용사/부사 + S + V ...」 구문이다. 문두에 the longer이 있는 것으로 보아 빈칸 역시 「the -er/more ~」로 시작해야 하므로 ②, ④로 좁혀진다. 또한 risk는 동명사(R-ing)를 목적어로 받는 동사이므로 ②가 적절하다.

18 [2011 홍익대]

(My) [①going to such a place] was part (of my mother's not so secret plan) (②to change my character,) (which (she worried) ③was becoming too much like ④her.)

정답 ④ (her → hers)

해석 내가 그러한 곳에 가는 것은 엄마의 비밀스럽지 않은 계획의 일부였다. 그 계획은 엄마가 걱정할 정도로 자신의 성격과 닮아가는 내 성격을 바꾸려는 것이었다.

분석 비교 대상의 일치 「be like」

④ 영어는 비교 대상의 일치를 중요시한다. (ex. 서울의 날씨가 대전과 비슷하다. (X) / 서울의 날씨와 대전의 날씨가 비슷하다. (O)) 「be(come) like(~와 비슷하다)」의 주어는 선행사인 my character이다. 내 성격이 엄마와 비슷한 것이 아니라 엄마의 성격과 비슷한 것이므로 her을 hers(= her character)로 고쳐야 한다.

① 동명사구(going ~ a place)가 주어 역할로 적절하다.

② 「plan + to R」 형태로 plan은 동격을 나타낼 때 to R로 표현한다.

③ 진행형 절대 불가능 동사가 아니라면 진행형은 얼마든지 가능하다.

19 [2011 홍익대]

We are as much delighted (①by benevolence) ②than we are gratified by the scent ③of perfume ④or nauseated by a foul stench.

정답 ② (than → as)

해석 우리는 향기에 기쁘거나 악취에 의해 메스꺼웠던 것만큼 자비로움에 행복했다.

분석 원급 비교 「as ~ as ...」

② 앞에 as가 있는 것으로 보아 than을 as로 고쳐야 한다. 또한 문장에 than이 있으면 앞에 비교급(-er/more ~)이 있어야 하는데 그것도 없는 것으로 보아 ②가 틀렸다는 것을 알 수 있다.

① 수동태 뒤에 「by + N」 형태는 적절하다.

③ 명사와 명사의 충돌을 피해 주기 위해 전치사는 적절하다.

④ gratified or nauseated를 연결하는 접속사로 쓰여 적절하다.

20 [2012 경기대]

①One big advantage (writing ②offers over speaking) is [that we can refine our message, (making ③it as ④succinctly as possible.)]

정답 ④ (succinctly → succinct)

해석 말보다 글이 제공하는 하나의 커다란 장점은 우리가 메시지를 순화하고, 그것을 가능한 한 간결하게 만들 수 있다는 것이다.

분석 「as + 형용사/부사 + as」 형용사와 부사의 구분

④ 「as ~ as」 사이에 형용사/부사에 밑줄이 있다면 그 선택을 묻는다. 이때 앞에 있는 as 앞을 잘라 형용사 자리가 불완전하면 형용사를, 완전하게 나오면 부사를 써야 한다. 「make + O + O.C(형용사)」 5형식의 어형으로 목적어(it) 뒤에 목적보어(형용사) 자리가 불완전하다. succinctly를 succinct로 고쳐야 한다.

① 뒤에 단수명사가 나와 One은 적절하다.

② 목적격 관계대명사 that이 생략되어 offers의 목적어가 불완전하다.

③ our message를 대신 받는 대명사로 쓰여 수 일치가 적절하다.

21 [2012 경기대]

The institutions (of science) mean [①that the theories and ideas (that scientists have developed) are far superior ②than the ③ones (that we human ④beings had) (before the growth of modern science.)]

정답 ② (than → to)

해석 과학 제도는 과학자들이 발전시킨 이론과 생각들이 근대 과학의 성장 이전부터 우리 인간들이 가졌던 것들보다 훨씬 우월하다는 것을 의미한다.

분석 라틴계 비교급 「-ior to」

② -ior로 끝나는 형용사(senior, junior, superior, inferior, prior)는 뒤에서 전치사 to로 비교한다. -ior than이 나오면 무조건 틀린 형태이므로 than을 to로 고쳐야 한다.

① mean의 목적어로 명사절(that절)이 나와 적절하다.

③ theories and ideas를 대신 받는 대명사로 수 일치가 적절하다.

④ human beings는 '인간'이라는 뜻의 명사이고 「we = human beings」는 동격으로 쓰였다.

22

[2012 홍익대]

We really ①(do) perceive the sun ②as ③~~close~~ to us
S   강조 V   O   closer O.C
④than it actually is.

정답 ③ (close → closer)

해석 우리는 태양을 실제로 가까이 있는 것보다 더 가까이 있
다고 인식한다.

분석 than과 상관관계를 이루는 「-er/ more ~」

③ 앞에 비교급(-er/more ~)이 있다고 하여 반드시 뒤에
than을 써야 하는 것은 아니다. 비교 대상이 있다면
than을 쓰는 것이고, 없다면 안 쓰면 그만이다. 하지만
만약 문장에 than이 있다면 반드시 앞에 비교급(-er/
more ~)이 있어야 하기 때문에 close를 closer로 고
쳐야 한다.

① 긍정문에서 do는 강조의 용법으로 쓰인다.

② 여기 as 때문에 ④를 고쳐야 하나 고민을 할 수 있다.
하지만 여기서 as는 「perceive/regard + O + as +
O.C」형태의 5형식 동사의 어형으로 쓰여 적절하다.

④ 비교급(-er/more ~)과 어울리는 접속사 than은 적절
하다.

23

[2011 이화여대]

The problem (of school education) (that John ①is
S   ∅   형용사절
experiencing) is similar (to ②you) ③in that they (both)
V   C   yours   부사절   S└=┘
④stem from the lack of interaction between students
V   Ⓟ   Ⓝ
and teachers.)

정답 ② (you → yours)

해석 존이 경험한 학교 교육의 문제점은 학생과 선생님 사이에
상호 작용의 부족에서 생긴 것이라는 점에서 당신이 경험
한 문제점과 유사하다.

분석 비교 대상의 일치 「be similar to」

② 영어는 비교 대상의 일치를 중요시한다. (ex. 톰의 키
가 존과 비슷하다. (X) / 톰의 키가 존의 키와 비슷하
다. (O)) 존이 경험한 문제와 당신이 비슷한 것이 아니
라 존이 경험한 문제와 당신이 경험한 문제가 비슷한
것이기 때문에 you를 yours(=your problem)로 고쳐
야 한다.

① 목적격 관계대명사 that이 있기 때문에 목적어가 불완
전하다.

③ 「in that + S + V ~」는 '~하기 때문에, ~한다는 점에
서'의 표현으로 유일하게 전치사 뒤에 that절이 나올
수 있는 형태이다.

④ stem은 자동사로 쓰여 명사를 받을 때 전치사 from
과 함께 온다.

24

[2010 상명대]

The placement (of ①the sun at the center of the
S
universe by Galileo) was ②certainly more important
V₁   C
than ③the principle of buoyancy and may be more
V₂
important than ④any scientific discovery in the history
C   other
of the world.

정답 ④ (any scientific discovery in the history → any
other scientific discovery in the history)

해석 갈릴레오의 우주의 중심에 태양이 있다는 주장은 부력의
원칙보다 더 중요했고 아마 지구의 역사에 있어 어떤 과
학적 발견보다도 더욱 중요할 것이다.

분석 비교급(-er/more) than any other N(단수명사)

④ 비교급을 이용한 최상급의 의미를 표현하는 방법이다.
any 뒤에 other을 추가해야 한다.

① 명사와 명사의 충돌을 피해 주기 위해 전명구는 적절
하다.

② be동사의 보어로 형용사는 적절하고, 「more ~ than
...」의 상관관계 역시 적절하다.

③ 태양이 우주의 중심에 있다고 주장하는 원리와 부력의
원리를 비교하고 있다.

25

[2011 국민대]

She makes ①much ~~high~~ grades than her sisters;
S   V   higher O
(however,) ②they are a great deal ③more sociable than
S   V   C
④she is.

정답 ① (much high → much higher)

해석 그녀는 자매들보다 훨씬 더 높은 성적을 받는다. 하지만
자매들이 그녀보다 훨씬 더 사교적이다.

분석 than과 상관관계를 이루는 「-er/ more ~」

① 앞에 비교급(-er/more ~)이 있다고 하여 반드시 뒤에
than을 써야 하는 것은 아니다. 비교 대상이 있다면
than을 쓰는 것이고, 없다면 안 쓰면 그만이다. 하지만

만약 문장에 than이 있다면 반드시 앞에 비교급(-er/more ~)이 있어야 하기 때문에 much high를 much higher로 고쳐야 한다.

② her sisters를 대신 받는 대명사로 수 일치가 적절하다.

③ be동사의 보어로 형용사는 적절하고, 「more ~ than ...」의 상관관계 역시 적절하다.

④ 원급 비교의 「as ~ as ...」 / 우등 비교의 「-er/more ~ than ...」에서 뒤에 있는 as와 than은 접속사이다. 하지만 이때 as와 than 뒤에 항상 문장만 나오는 것은 아니다. 그 이유는 앞과 뒤의 같은 성분은 생략이 가능하기 때문이다. she is (sociable)의 형태로 쓰여 적절하다.

16강 일치와 도치

Practice 01

01	④	02	④	03	②	04	③	05	①
06	②	07	④	08	⑤	09	③	10	④
11	②	12	④	13	②	14	①	15	①
16	④	17	③	18	④	19	⑤	20	④
21	①	22	①	23	③	24	③	25	④

01
[2010 단국대]

A computerized map (of the freeways) (using information) (gathered by sensors) (embedded in the pavement) (which is) (which is) _____ on a local cable channel during rush hours.

① to air
② airing
③ air
④ airs

정답 ④

해석 포장도로에 내장된 센서에 의해 수집된 정보를 이용하는 전산화된 고속 도로 지도는 출퇴근 시간 동안 지역 케이블 채널에서 방송된다.

분석 문의구성 / 주어와 동사의 수 일치
④ 빈칸은 주어(A computerized map)에 대한 동사가 필요한 자리이므로 단수동사(airs)와 수 일치해야 한다.
①, ② 동사가 필요한 자리이다.
③ 수 일치가 되지 않아 부적절하다.

02
[2010 서울여대]

Beijing's decision (to require [that all new personal computers (①sold in China) ②contain software] (that ③bars access to certain Internet content)) ④seem self-destructive and foolish.

정답 ④ (seem → seems)

해석 중국 내에서 판매되는 모든 신형 개인 컴퓨터에 특정 인터넷 콘텐츠의 접속을 금지하는 소프트웨어를 설치해야만 한다는 중국의 결정은 자멸적이고 어리석어 보인다.

분석 주어와 동사의 수 일치
④ 주어(Beijing's decision)와 동사(seem)의 수 일치가 맞지 않아 seems로 고쳐야 한다.
① 컴퓨터가 팔리는 대상이므로 수동의 관계인 과거분사(sold)는 적절하다.
② 「require + that + S + (should) + R ~」의 형태로 쓰여 동사원형(contain)은 적절하다.
③ 주격 관계대명사절 속의 동사(bars)와 선행사(software)의 수 일치가 적절하다.

03
[2010 성균관대]

One study found [①that those (who consistently felt impatient and pressed for time) ②was (more than) twice as likely ③as laid-back types ④to develop high blood pressure over ⑤a 13-year period.]

* be likely to R: ~할 가능성이 있다

정답 ② (was → were)

해석 한 연구는 지속적으로 참지 못하고 시간의 압력을 받는 사람들이 13년의 기간 동안 고혈압이 생길 가능성이 느긋한 사람들의 2배 이상 높다고 밝혀냈다.

분석 주어와 동사의 수 일치
② 주어(those)와 동사(was)의 수 일치가 맞지 않아 were로 고쳐야 한다.
① 명사절(that)절이 found의 목적어로 쓰여 적절하다.
③ 배수사 twice는 뒤에서 「as ~ as ...」로 비교하여 적절하다.
④ 「be likely to R ~」의 형태이다.
⑤ 단수명사 앞에 부정관사(a)는 적절하다.

04
[2010 한국외대]

Writers (①intent on informing their readers often,) (②without realizing it,) ③includes a word or phrase (that ④expresses their ⑤personal point of view.)

정답 ③ (includes → include)

해석 독자들에게 정보를 주려고 열중하고 있는 작가들은 자신
도 모르게 개인적인 관점을 표현하는 단어나 구를 포함시
킨다.

분석 주어와 동사의 수 일치

③ 주어(Writers)와 동사(includes)의 수 일치가 맞지 않
아 include로 고쳐야 한다.

① 형용사가 전명구와 결합되어 앞에 있는 명사를 수식하
여 적절하다.

② 전치사의 목적어로 동명사는 적절하다.

④ 주격 관계대명사절 속의 동사(expresses)와 선행사(a
word or phrase)의 수 일치는 적절하다.

⑤ 형용사가 명사를 수식하여 적절하다.

05 [2010 삼육대]

①Seldom we have (do we have) these types of arguments, but (if
we're ②concerned about our friendship,) we need [to
③talk about it more] and try [to ④cooperate with each
other.]

정답 ① (Seldom we have → Seldom do we have)

해석 우리는 이런 종류의 논쟁을 거의 한 적이 없다. 만약 우리
가 우정을 우려하는 것이 있다면 그것에 관하여 더욱 논
의를 하고 서로 협조하도록 노력해야 한다.

분석 부정부사 문두 강조 도치

① 부정부사(seldom, rarely, barely, no sooner,
hardly, scarcely, nowhere)가 문두에 위치하여 강
조되는 경우 반드시 주어, 동사는 도치가 되어야 한다.
Seldom do we have로 고쳐야 한다.

② 「be concerned about ~」은 '~에 대해 걱정하다'의
표현으로 적절하다.

③ need는 to R를 목적어로 받는 동사이고, talk는 자동
사로 전치사 of/about과 함께 쓴다.

④ try는 to R와 R-ing를 둘 다 목적어로 받을 수 있고,
cooperate은 자동사로 명사를 받을 때 전치사가 나
와야 한다.

06 [2009 한양대]

(①Since the end of World War II,) the dynamic growth
(of communication systems of all types) ②have (has)
provided a unique opportunity (for the development of
new methods) (③to influence public opinion ④on a
wide range of activities and behaviors.)

정답 ② (have provided → has provided)

해석 2차 세계 대전 종식 이래, 모든 종류의 통신 체계의 역동
적인 성장이 다양한 범위의 활동과 행동에서 여론에 영향
을 미칠 새로운 방법을 위한 특별한 기회를 제공했다.

분석 주어와 동사의 수 일치

② 주어(the dynamic growth)와 동사(have)의 수 일치
가 맞지 않아 has provided로 고쳐야 한다.

① 「Since + 과거 N」는 현재완료 시점부사이다.

③ to R의 형용사적 용법으로 명사(new methods)를 수
식하여 적절하다.

④ 명사와 명사의 충돌을 피해 주기 위해 전명구는 적절
하다.

07 [2013 서강대]

The series ① of natural phenomena ② could be
described (in ③their entirety) (without mentioning the
value of things,) and our scale (of valuation) remains
meaningful, (whether or not one (of its objects) ④appear (appears)
frequently or at all in reality.)

정답 ④ (appear → appears)

해석 자연의 대상 중 하나가 현실에서 자주 등장하느냐 그렇지
않냐와는 상관없이, 일련의 자연 현상이 그 물건들의 가
치를 거론하지 않고서도 완전히 묘사될 수 있고, 그러면
서도 우리의 가치 체계는 의미 있게 남아 있을 수 있다.

분석 주어와 동사의 수 일치

④ 주어(one)와 동사(appear)의 수 일치가 맞지 않아
appears로 고쳐야 한다.

① 명사와 명사의 충돌을 피해 주기 위해 전명구는 적절
하다.

② 조동사 뒤에 동사원형은 적절하다.

③ natural phenomena(복수명사)를 대신 받는 대명사
로 수 일치가 적절하다.

08

(Throughout the ① developed world,) we are at a point
(② in our evolution) (③ at which famine, (④ which
essentially governed the rise and fall of civilizations
throughout history,) ⑤ are no longer an acute threat.)

정답 ⑤ (are → is)

해석 선진국에서는, 원초적으로 역사적 문명의 등장과 몰락을
결정지었던 기근이 더 이상 심각한 위협이 아닌 우리가
발전하는 시기에 있다.

분석 주어와 동사의 수 일치

⑤ 주어(famine)와 동사(are)의 수 일치가 맞지 않아 is로
고쳐야 한다.

① developed world는 '선진국,' developing world는
'개발 도상국'이라는 뜻으로 두 가지의 의미 구분을 묻
지 않는다.

② 명사와 명사의 충돌을 피해 주기 위해 전치사는 적절
하다.

③ 「전치사 + 관계대명사」는 절 이하의 성분(명사)이 완전
하게 나와 적절하다.

④ 선행사가 사물(famine)이고 절 이하에 주어 자리가 불
완전하여 관계대명사 which는 적절하다.

09

[Paying for union services] (① only when you need
② them) ③ are like [paying taxes for police and fire
services] (only if you use ④ them.)

정답 ③ (are → is)

해석 노조의 도움이 필요할 때만 돈을 내는 것은 경찰과 소방
서비스를 사용할 때만 세금을 내는 것과 마찬가지이다.

분석 주어와 동사의 수 일치

③ 주어(Paying ~ service)와 동사(are)의 수 일치가 맞
지 않아 is로 고쳐야 한다. 동명사(R-ing) 혹은 부정사
(to R)가 주어 자리에 오면 동사는 단수 취급을 한다.

① 부사절로 쓰여 적절하다.

② union services를 대신 받는 대명사로 수 일치가 적
절하다.

④ police and fire services를 대신 받는 대명사로 수
일치가 적절하다.

10

Only occasionally _____ reading Tom's
newspaper, (over his shoulder,) (as she sat in the
station waiting room.)

① found she herself
② she finds herself
③ did herself she find
④ did she find herself

정답 ④

해석 그녀가 대합실에 앉아 있을 때, 어깨너머로 Tom의 신문
을 아주 가끔 읽고 있음을 알게 되었다.

분석 「only 부사」 강조 도치

④ 「only 부사, only 전명구, only 부사절」이 문두에 위치
하여 강조되는 경우 반드시 주어, 동사는 도치가 되어
야 한다. 일반동사의 도치는 「do/did/does + S + R
~」의 형태로 해야 하기 때문에 ③, ④로 좁혀지고,
herself는 find의 목적어이므로 ④가 적절하다.

11

The takeover (of the New York Stock Exchange's
owner) illustrates ① starkly [how trading (in commodities
and derivatives) ② have become ③ much more lucrative
than ④ trading in corporate shares.]

정답 ② (have become → has become)

해석 뉴욕 증권 거래소 소유주의 경영권 인수는 어떻게 상품과
파생 상품 거래가 기업의 주식을 거래하는 것보다 훨씬
더 수익성이 좋은지를 명확하게 보여 주고 있다.

분석 주어와 동사의 수 일치

② 주어(trading)와 동사(have)의 수 일치가 맞지 않아
has become으로 고쳐야 한다.

① 부사(starkly)가 동사(illustrates)를 수식하여 적절하다.

③ become의 보어로 형용사는 적절하고, 「more ~ than
...」의 상관관계 역시 적절하다. much는 비교급 강조
부사이다.

④ trading in commodities and derivatives와 trading
in corporate shares를 비교하여 적절하다.

148 _에듀윌 편입 솔루션 문법 Basic

12

[2013 단국대]

_____ scholars) (who regularly publish their professional works) has doubled since 2002.

① As many as
② As most of
③ The quantity of
④ The number (of

정답 ④

해석 정기적으로 전문적인 연구들을 발표하는 학자들의 수가 2002년 이래 두 배나 되었다.

분석 주어와 동사의 수 일치

④ 뒤에 동사(has doubled)가 단수로 고정되어 있기 때문에 빈칸에 단수 형태의 주어가 나와야 하므로 ③, ④로 좁혀진다. ③은 학자들의 양이 두 배가 된다는 뜻으로 부적절하고, ④의 학자들의 수(the number)가 두 배가 되는 것이 적절하다.

13

[2015 아주대]

Those (who favor the new administrative law) say [that the present law does not set spending limits on lobbyists' gifts to politicians,] _____ statewide funds.

① nor it limits
② nor does it limit
③ nor they limit
④ nor do they limit
⑤ nor they are limited

정답 ②

해석 새로운 행정법을 찬성하는 사람들은 현행법이 로비스트가 정치인에게 주는 선물에 대한 지출 제한선을 정해 놓지 않고 있으며, 주 전체의 기금에도 정해 놓지 않는다고 말하고 있다.

분석 「nor + V + S (O)」 / 「nor + S + V」 (X) / 대명사의 수 일치

② nor 뒤에 문장이 나오는 경우 반드시 「동사 + 주어」의 어순으로 도치를 시켜야 하기 때문에 ②, ④로 좁혀진다. ②와 ④의 차이는 대명사 it과 they의 선택을 묻고 있다. 해석상 현행법(the present law)을 받고 있기 때문에 대명사 it이 나온 ②가 적절하다.

14

[2013 서울여대]

The religion (of the Hopi Indians) ① include ② several different ceremonies (③ intended to influence or ④ pay respect to nature.)

정답 ① (include → includes)

해석 호피족 원주민의 종교는 자연에 영향을 미치거나 경의를 표하기 위해 의도된 다양한 의식을 포함하고 있다.

분석 주어와 동사의 수 일치

① 주어(The religion)와 동사(include)의 수 일치가 맞지 않아 includes로 고쳐야 한다.
② 동사의 목적어 역할로 명사는 적절하다.
③ 다양한 의식이 의도하는 주체가 아니라 의도되는 대상이므로 수동의 관계인 과거분사(intended)는 적절하다.
④ to influence or (to) pay로 병치된 형태이다. to R ~ 를 병치할 때 to는 생략해도 되고 써도 된다.

15

[2013 서울여대]

Every non-Western society is searching (for a path to modernity) (that (it can feel) _____ (in some way) local, authentic and, (in that sense,) non-Western.)

① is
② are
③ being
④ be

정답 ①

해석 모든 비서구 사회는 그 사회가 생각하기에 어떤 면에서 지역적이고 정확하며, 또한 그런 의미에서 비서구적인 근대성에 도달하는 길을 모색하고 있다.

분석 주격 관계대명사절 속에 동사의 수 일치

① 구조 분석에서 알 수 있듯이 it can feel은 주격 관계대명사 that절 안에서 삽입절로 쓰인 형태이다. 결국 빈칸은 modernity를 수식하는 주격 관계대명사절 속의 동사가 필요한 자리이므로 ③은 탈락되고, 선행사(modernity)가 단수명사이므로 단수동사(is)와 수 일치가 되어야 한다.

16 [2017 단국대]

(From that act of civil disobedience) _____
spawned the New Power Party, (which allied with the
DDP and won five legislative seats of its own.)

① had   ② were
③ has   ④ was

정답 ④

해석 그 시민 불복종 행위에서, 민주 진보당(DDP)과 연합하여
5개의 의석을 차지한 시대 역량당(New Power Party)이
생겼다.

분석 주어와 동사의 수 일치 / 능동태와 수동태의 구분

④ 전명구(From ~ disobedience)를 문두로 이동시켜
강조했기 때문에 도치가 된 형태이다. 주어(the New
Power Party)가 단수이므로 ①, ③, ④로 좁혀지고,
정당이 만드는 주체가 아니라 만들어지는 대상이므로
수동태(was spawned)를 써야 하기 때문에 ④가 적절
하다.

17 [2013 세종대]

It is true [that ① much of the Korean Art (as it
② developed through the early years) ③ were influenced
(by ④ the Chinese.)]

정답 ③ (were → was)

해석 한국 예술이 발달하던 초기에 대부분이 중국 예술에 영향
을 받았다는 것은 사실이다.

분석 「much of + N + is(단수동사)」/「many of + Ns + are
(복수동사)」

③「much of + N(불가산명사) + is(단수동사) / many
of + Ns(복수명사) + are(복수동사)」형태로 수 일치를
해야 한다. 지금과 같은 경우 much와 were에 둘 다
밑줄이 있어 much를 many로 고치려는 학생도 있겠
지만 그렇다면 of the Korean Art와 어울릴 수 없다.
of the Korean Art를 단서로 잡고 much가 고정이
되면 단수동사 was로 고쳐야 한다.

① of the Korean Art(불가산명사)가 있어 much는 적절
하다.

② 부사절(as)에서 developed는 자동사로 쓰여 적절하다.

④ 뒤에 Art가 생략된 형태이다.

18 [2014 가천대]

(Just as the early 20th century had the great master
Pablo Casals,) ① the latter part (of the last century) had
Rostropovich. (Despite ② being regarded as the best in
his era,) he was modest and humble. [③ That he
recorded the entire Bach Cello Suites] (when he was
over 60) ④ prove his modesty.

정답 ④ (prove → proves)

해석 20세기 전반부에 위대한 명인 Pablo Casals가 있었듯
이 20세기 후반부에는 Rostropovich가 있었다. 그는 그
시대 최고의 인물로 간주되었지만, 겸손한 사람이었다. 그
가 60세가 넘어서 바흐의 첼로 스위트 전곡을 녹음했다
는 사실이 그의 겸손함을 입증해 준다.

분석 주어와 동사의 수 일치

④ 주어가 명사절(That ~ Bach Cello Suites)이다. 명사
절이 주어로 나올 경우 동사는 단수로 수 일치하기 때
문에 proves로 고쳐야 한다.

① 형용사(latter)가 명사(part)를 수식하여 적절하다.

② 전치사 뒤에 동명사로 쓰였고, 「as + 목적보어」가 붙어
나왔기 때문에 수동태 동명사(being regarded) 역시
적절하다.

③ that절 이하의 성분(명사)이 완전하게 나와 명사절 접
속사 that은 주어의 역할로 적절하다.

19 [2015 성균관대]

(① Like baseball parks and basketball-hockey arenas,)
football stadiums have (② for decades) ③ been evolving
(into places) (④ where an increasing amount of the real
estate ⑤ are devoted to premium-priced seating.)

정답 ⑤ (are → is)

해석 야구 경기장, 농구 경기장 그리고 하키 경기장처럼, 미식
축구 경기장은 지난 수십 년 동안 부지의 많은 부분을 최
고의 값을 지불하도록 할애한 장소로 진화해 왔다.

분석 주어와 동사의 수 일치

⑤ 주어(the real estate)와 동사(are)의 수 일치가 맞지
않아 is로 고쳐야 한다. an amount of는 much의 대
용어구이다.

① 문장의 구성이 완전하게 나와 수식어구인 전명구는 적절하다.

② 「for + 기간 N」는 시점부사로 쓰여 적절하다.

③ 현재완료(have p.p.)는 have 뒤에 p.p.를 써야 한다.

④ where은 장소명사를 수식하는 관계부사이므로 적절하다.

20
[2015 한국외대]

(Each year) the number (of students) (who ① are unable to find ② a dorm room for the semester and forced to live ③ off campus without meal plans) ④ are soaring.

정답 ④ (are soaring → is soaring)

해석 매년, 학기 중에 쓸 수 있는 기숙사를 잡지 못해 식단 계획 없이 어쩔 수 없이 캠퍼스 밖에 살아야 하는 학생들의 수가 급격히 늘고 있다.

분석 「the number of + Ns」 수 일치

④ 「the number of + Ns」 형태가 주어로 나오면 복수명사들의 수(the number)가 주어이기 때문에 단수동사와 수 일치해야 한다. are soaring을 is soaring으로 고쳐야 한다.

① 주격 관계대명사절 속의 동사의 수 일치를 하기 위해 선행사를 따질 때는 해석을 해야 한다. The number(수)가 기숙사 방을 찾는 것이 아니라 학생들(students)이 기숙사 방을 찾는 것이기에 수 일치는 적절하다.

② find의 목적어 역할로 명사는 적절하다.

③ 「live off + N」는 '~ 외부에서 살다'라는 뜻의 표현이다.

21
[2017 한국외대]

_____ that everyone left the auditorium.

① So monotonously did he speak
② He so did speak monotonously
③ Monotonously did he speak so
④ So did he monotonously speak

정답 ①

해석 그가 너무 단조롭게 말해서, 모든 사람들이 강당을 빠져나갔다.

분석 결과의 「so ~ that ...」 강조 표현

① 「S + V + so + 형용사 / 부사 + that + S + V ~」 형태의 결과의 「so ~ that ...」 구문에서 「so + 형용사 / 부사」가 문두에 위치하여 강조되는 경우 반드시 주어, 동사는 도치가 되어야 한다. 이 형태를 만족시키는 보기는 ①이 적절하다. 「so + 형용사 / 부사」를 강조할 때는 so와 함께 문두로 이동을 해야 하기 때문에 ③, ④는 부적절하다.

22
[2015 단국대]

Wages and the cost (of living) _____ (in virtually equal proportions) (through the generations.)

① have grown
② having grown
③ growing
④ grows

정답 ①

해석 임금과 생활비는 여러 세대에 걸쳐 사실상 같은 비율로 증가했다.

분석 문의구성 / 주어와 동사의 수 일치

① 빈칸은 동사가 필요한 자리이므로 ①, ④로 좁혀진다. 주어(Wages and the cost)가 복수이기에 복수동사(have)와 수 일치가 되어야 한다.

23
[2016 성균관대]

It ① is often remarked [that the advent (of the movies) and the ② ever faster pace (of modern life) ③ has conspired (to make description a ④ less essential part of prose narrative in our ⑤ own times.)]

정답 ③ (has conspired → have conspired)

해석 영화의 도래와 현대적인 삶의 더욱 빨라진 속도는 우리 시대의 산문 이야기 속에서 묘사를 보다 덜 필수적인 부분으로 만드는 데에 일조해 왔다.

분석 주어와 동사의 수 일치

③ 주어(the advent and the ever faster pace)와 동사(has)의 수 일치가 맞지 않아 have conspired로 고쳐야 한다.

① 「It(가주어) ~ that절(진주어) ...」 문장이다. that절의 내용이 언급되는 대상이므로 수동태는 적절하다.

② 부사(ever)가 형용사(faster)를 수식하여 적절하다.

④ 열등 비교(덜 ~한)의 의미가 필요하여 less를 활용한 형태이다.

⑤ own은 소유격 강조 표현으로 쓰여 적절하다.

24

People (in a growth mindset) do not just seek challenge,
S   V   O
they ① thrive on it. The bigger the challenge, ② the
S   V   P   N   S can it (is)
more they stretch. And (nowhere) ③ it can be seen
S   V   강조   V   S
more clearly than in the world of sport. You can just
S   S   V -
watch people ④ stretch and grow.
       O   O.C

정답 ③ (it can be → can it be)

해석 성장 마인드가 장착된 사람들은 도전을 찾는 데서 그치지 않는다. 그들은 그것을 통해 성장한다. 도전이 크면 클수록 그들은 더 많이 성장한다. 그리고 운동 경기에서 보다 더 그것이 잘 보여지는 곳은 없다. 당신은 사람들이 경쟁하고 성장하는 것을 볼 수 있다.

분석 부정부사 문두 강조 도치

③ 부정부사(seldom, rarely, barely, no sooner, hardly, scarcely, nowhere)가 문두에 위치하여 강조되는 경우 반드시 주어, 동사는 도치가 되어야 한다. can it be로 고쳐야 한다.

① thrive on은 '~을 잘 해내다'라는 뜻의 자동사로 쓰여 적절하다.

② 「the -er/more 형용사/부사 + S + V ~, the -er/more 형용사/부사 + S + V ...」 형태의 점진 비교 구문이다.

④ 「watch + O + O.C(R/R-ing)」 5형식 지각동사의 어형으로 목적보어 자리에 동사원형은 적절하다.

25

Good parents wouldn't jump (to conclusions,)
S   V
_____ assume that every problem was a
            R
catastrophe they needed to fix.

① never they would

② or would they

③ neither they would

④ nôr would they
    V   S

정답 ④

해석 훌륭한 부모는 속단하지 않고 모든 문제가 그들이 교정할 필요가 있었던 불행이었다고 생각하지도 않는다.

분석 「nor(= and neither) + V + S」의 도치 구문

④ 앞 문장이 끝나고 나서 nor 뒤에 문장이 나오면 반드시 도치가 되어야 한다.

① 접속사 없이 문장이 두 개가 나와 부적절하다.

② or은 도치를 시키는 접속사가 아니다.

③ 「nor = and neither」 neither은 부사이기 때문에 문장 두 개를 연결하는 접속사로 쓰일 수 없다. 또한 and neither이 나와도 주어, 동사는 도치를 시켜야 한다.

152 _에듀윌 편입 솔루션 문법 Basic

Practice 02

01	③	02	③	03	①	04	②	05	④
06	⑤	07	②	08	②	09	②	10	②
11	②	12	③	13	②	14	④	15	②
16	③	17	①	18	①	19	④	20	③
21	②	22	②	23	④	24	④	25	④

01
[2017 가천대]

Companies (①taking a longer term view of profit) (with
the idea of being ②socially responsible through
sustainable development) ③is being rewarded (both
with government support and by consumers) (④as
they make their purchases.)

정답 ③ (is → are)

해석 지속 가능한 개발을 통해 사회적 책임을 다한다는 생각을
가지고 이윤을 장기적으로 바라보는 회사들은 정부의 지
원과 물건을 구매하는 소비자들에게 보상을 받고 있다.

분석 주어와 동사의 수 일치
　③ 주어(Companies)와 동사(is)의 수 일치가 맞지 않아
　　 are로 고쳐야 한다.
　① 회사들이 장기적인 견해를 취하는 주체이고, 뒤에 목
　　 적어도 있기 때문에 능동의 관계인 현재분사(taking)
　　 는 적절하다.
　② 부사(socially)가 형용사(responsible)를 수식하여 적
　　 절하다.
　④ 부사절 접속사(as)로 쓰여 「주어 + 동사」를 받아 적
　　 절하다.

02
[2017 국민대]

The danger (of eating ①too much pepper,) (②not to
speak of drinking only soft drinks and beers,) ③do not
seem [to worry ④either Susan or John.]

정답 ③ (do → does)

해석 청량음료와 맥주를 마시는 것은 말할 것도 없고 후추를
너무 많이 먹는 위험성도 수잔(Susan)과 존(John)을 걱
정시키지 않는 것 같다.

분석 주어와 동사의 수 일치
　③ 주어(The danger)와 동사(do)의 수 일치가 맞지 않아
　　 does로 고쳐야 한다.
　① 부사(too)가 형용사(much)를 수식하고, 형용사
　　 (much)가 명사(pepper)를 수식하여 적절하다.
　② not to speak of는 '～은 말할 것도 없이'의 표현으로
　　 쓰여 적절하다.
　④ 등위상관접속사 「either A or B」의 상관관계가 적절하
　　 게 쓰여 있다.

03
[2013 서울여대]

(Somewhere) (between the business newsletter, the
consumer magazine, and a hobby) _____
zines (pronounced "zeens").
① are periodicals called
② are called periodicals
③ periodicals are called
④ called periodicals are

정답 ①

해석 경제 뉴스, 대중 잡지, 그리고 취미 잡지 사이 그 어딘가
에 zines('zeens'로 발음되는)라고 불리는 정기 간행물이
있다.

분석 부사구(전명구) 강조 도치
　① 전명구(between ~ a hobby)가 문두에 위치하여 강
　　 조되는 경우 반드시 주어, 동사는 도치가 되어야 한다.
　　 「주어 + be동사 ～」의 도치는 「be동사 + 주어 ～」형태
　　 로 도치해야 하기 때문에 ①이 적절하다.
　② 주어와 be동사의 위치를 바꿔 「be동사 + 주어」 형태
　　 로 도치해야 한다.
　③ 도치가 되지 않아 부적절하다.
　④ 도치의 형태가 부적절하다.

04
[2017 단국대]

Some scientists propose [that thumb ①sucking (in
children) ②are a habit (which is ③developed at
random,)] but recent theory suggests [that is
neurologically and genetically ④based.]

정답　② (are → is)

해석　일부 과학자들은 아이들이 엄지손가락을 빠는 행위가 무작위로 발달되는 습관이라고 목소리를 내고 있지만, 최근의 이론은 이 버릇이 신경학적이고 유전적인 것을 기반으로 발달된 것임을 보여 주고 있다.

분석　주어와 동사의 수 일치

　　② 주어(thumb sucking)와 동사(are)의 수 일치가 맞지 않아 is로 고쳐야 한다.

　　① thumb sucking은 '엄지손가락 빨기'라는 뜻의 복합명사로 쓰여 적절하다.

　　③ 습관이 발달시키는 주체가 아니라 발달되는 대상이므로 수동태는 적절하다.

　　④ that은 thumb sucking을 받는 대명사이다. 습관이 기반으로 만들어지는 대상이므로 수동태는 적절하다.

05
[2011 성균관대]

The truth is [that ① the commonest response (to
S　　V　명사절(C₁)　　　　　　　　S
violence) is ② one of repugnance,] and [③ that a
　　　　　V　　C　　　　　　　　　　명사절(C₂)
significant number of people (everywhere) ④ tries [to
　　　　　　　　　　　　S　　　　　　　　try
oppose it] ⑤ (in whatever ways they can.)]
　= many
oppose it]　　　　　　　　　　　　　　　V
　　　　　　　　　　　　　　　　　　　O

정답　④ (tries → try)

해석　사실은 폭력에 대한 가장 흔한 반응은 반감이며, 상당히 많은 사람들이 할 수 있는 모든 방법을 동원해서 폭력에 대항하려고 전국 각지에서 노력하고 있다.

분석　「a number of + Ns」의 수 일치

　　④ 「a number of + Ns」에서 a number of는 many의 대용어구이기 때문에 복수명사(Ns)를 수식하는 형용사에 불과하고 결국 주어는 복수명사(Ns)이다. people에 수 일치하여 try로 고쳐야 한다.

　　① the -est/most ~: 최상급 앞에는 정관사 the를 써야 한다.

　　② one은 response를 대신 받는 대명사로 수 일치가 적절하다.

　　③ be동사의 보어로 「that절 and that절」로 병치되어 적절하다.

　　⑤ 복합관계형용사 「whatever N + S + V ~」는 명사절과 부사절로 쓰일 수 있어 전치사의 목적어로 적절하다.

06
[2011 성균관대]

The point (① at which physical decline (② with age)
S　　　　　형용사절　　　　　　　S
③ begins adversely to affect ④ a driver's capability)
V　　　　　　　　　　　　　　　O
has not
⑤ have not yet been studied.
　　　　　　　V

정답　⑤ (have not → has not)

해석　연령에 의한 신체적 능력의 감소가 운전자의 능력에 악영향을 미치는 시점은 아직 연구된 바 없다.

분석　주어와 동사의 수 일치

　　⑤ 주어(The point)와 동사(have)의 수 일치가 맞지 않아 has not으로 고쳐야 한다.

　　① 「전치사 + 관계대명사」는 절 이하의 성분(명사)이 완전해야 하므로 적절하다.

　　② 명사와 명사의 충돌을 피해 주기 위해 전명구는 적절하다.

　　③ 주어(physical decline)와 동사(begins)의 수 일치가 적절하다.

　　④ 명사와 명사의 충돌을 피해 주기 위해 소유격은 적절하다.

07
[2011 성균관대]

　　　　　　　　　　　　　　　　　　　(that)
The lowest stockpiles (in ① decades) mean [there ② are
　　　　　　　　　　S　　　　　　　　V　　is
less grain (to buffer the impact of drought, ③ floods,
S　　　　　　　　　　　　　　　　　P　　N₁
and crop failures,)] (④ making prices ⑤ more volatile.)
　　N₃　　　　　　　　분사구문　　O　　　O.C
　　N₂

정답　② (are → is)

해석　수십 년 만에 가장 낮은 식량 비축량은 가뭄과 홍수, 흉작의 충격을 완화시켜 줄 곡물이 별로 없다는 것을 의미한다. 이러한 사실이 곡물 가격을 변동하도록 만들고 있다.

분석　주어와 동사의 수 일치

　　② there/here로 시작하는 문장의 주어는 동사 뒤에 있는 첫 번째 명사이다. 주어(grain)와 동사(are)의 수 일치가 맞지 않아 is로 고쳐야 한다.

　　① a decade: 10년 / decades: 수십 년

　　③ 전치사의 목적어로 「A, B, and C」의 형태로 명사가 병치되어 적절하다.

　　④ 뒤에 목적어와 목적보어가 있기 때문에 능동태 분사구문(making)은 적절하다.

　　⑤ '더 ~한'이라는 의미의 비교급(-er/more ~)으로 쓰여 적절하다.

08

(①As is usual in such cases,) she was the apple (of his
부사절   S   V was C
father's eye.) (Among his courtiers) ②were young man
강조   V   S
(of that fineness of blood and lowness of station)
(common to the heroes of romance) (who love royal
형용사절
maidens.) This royal maiden was well content (with her
O   S   V   C
lover,) (③for he was handsome and brave (to a degree)
부사절 S V   C₁   C₂
(④unsurpassed in all this kingdom.))
    ⓐ

정답 ② (were → was)

해석 그러한 경우에 흔히 있는 일이지만, 그녀는 아버지의 눈
에 넣어도 아프지 않은 딸이었다. 그의 신하들 가운데는
고귀한 혈통과 비천한 신분을 가진 젊은이가 있었는데,
이런 유형의 젊은이는 왕가의 여자를 사랑하는 영웅이 나
오는 연애 소설에서 흔히 볼 수 있다. 젊은이는 왕국에서
유례없을 정도로 잘 생겼고 용감했기 때문에 왕가의 여인
은 자신의 애인에게 매우 만족했다.

분석 주어와 동사의 수 일치

② 도치가 된 형태에서 주어와 동사의 수 일치를 묻고 있
다. Among his courtiers를 강조하여 문두로 이동시
켜 도치가 되었기 때문에 동사 뒤에 있는 주어와 수 일
치를 해야 한다. 동사(were)와 주어(young man)의
수 일치가 맞지 않아 was로 고쳐야 한다.

① as is usual은 '늘 ~ 그렇듯이'의 표현으로 쓰여 적절
하다. 같은 뜻의 표현으로 as is often the case, as
always 등이 있다.

③ 이유의 접속사(for)로 쓰여 「주어 + 동사」를 받아 적절
하다.

④ unsurpassed는 '유례없는, 탁월한, 그 누구[무엇]에
게도 뒤지지 않는'이라는 뜻을 가진 형용사이다.

09

①Neither the Bronte sisters nor their brother Branwell
S   A   B
②are remembered (③as healthy or happy.) ④No error
is   V   분사구문

정답 ② (are → is)

해석 브론테 가문의 자매들과 그들의 남동생인 브랜웰도 건강
했거나 행복했던 것으로 기억되지 않는다.

분석 등위상관접속사의 수 일치

② 등위상관접속사 「neither A nor B」가 주어로 나오면

반드시 B에 수 일치한다. 주어(their brother Branwell)
와 동사(are)의 수 일치가 맞지 않아 is로 고쳐야 한다.

① 등위상관접속사의 상관관계가 적절하다.

③ 분사구문에서 접속사가 남은 형태이다.

④는 ①, ②, ③ 중에 오류가 없는 경우 선택한다.

10

①Neither (of my parents,) (②who was born in Eastern
S   S were
형용사절
Europe,) ③understands the full implications (of ④a
V   O
democratic electoral system.)

정답 ② (who was born → who were born)

해석 동유럽에서 태어나신 내 부모님 중 어느 누구도 민주주의
선거 제도의 의미를 완벽히 이해하시지 못한다.

분석 주격 관계대명사절 속에 동사의 수 일치

② 주격 관계대명사절 속에 동사(was)와 선행사(my
parents)의 수 일치가 맞지 않아 who were born으
로 고쳐야 한다.

① 「(n)either of + Ns」 형태로 나오면 (n)either은 대명
사로 쓰인 것이다.

③ 주어가 대명사 (n)either라면 동사는 단수동사와 수 일
치하여 적절하다.

④ 전치사의 목적어로 명사는 적절하다.

11

The number (of countries) (①capable of developing
S   has
nuclear weapons) ②have increased (to more ③than 20
V
④in recent years.)

정답 ② (have increased → has increased)

해석 핵무기를 개발할 수 있는 나라들의 수가 최근 몇 년간 20
개국 이상으로 늘었다.

분석 「the number of + Ns」의 수 일치

② 「the number of + Ns」 형태가 주어로 나오면 복수명
사들의 수(the number)가 주어이기 때문에 단수동사
와 수 일치해야 한다. has increases로 고쳐야 한다.

① 형용사와 전명구가 결합되어 앞에 명사를 수식하는 것
은 적절하다.

③ 숫자 앞에 more than은 숫자 '이상'의 표현이다.

④ 명사와 명사의 충돌을 피해 주기 위해 전명구는 적절
하다.

12

(In April,) Steve Jobs launched his iPad. And it was
good. The iPad was not the first eReader or Tablet (on
the market,) nor _____ as multi-functional as
the iPhone. You can't make phone calls with an iPad.

① it was not   ② it was

③ was it   ④ it was so

정답 ③

해석 4월에 스티브 잡스가 iPad를 출시했고 그것은 훌륭했다.
iPad는 시장에 출시된 최초의 전자책도 아니었고 태블릿
PC도 아니었고, 또한 iPhone처럼 다양한 기능도 없었
다. 당신은 iPad로 전화도 걸 수 없다.

분석 「nor + V + S (O)」 / 「nor + S + V (X)」

  ③ nor 뒤에 문장이 나오는 경우, 반드시 「동사 + 주어」의
    어순으로 도치를 해야 한다. 이에 해당되는 것은 ③이
    유일하다.

13

(Only ① with recent advances in genetic science) ② has
physicians been able to begin ③ [curing genetic
diseases.] Doctors can now treat ④ a number of
genetic diseases (that individuals may inherit from their
parents.)

정답 ② (has → have)

해석 최근 유전학의 발전 덕분에 의사들은 유전병을 치료할 수
있게 되었다. 이제 의사들은 사람들이 부모로부터 물려받
는 많은 유전병을 치료할 수 있다.

분석 도치된 문장에서 주어와 동사의 수 일치

  ② 「only 부사, only 전명구, only 부사절」이 문두에 위치
    하여 강조되는 경우 반드시 주어, 동사는 도치가 되어
    야 한다. 동사(has)와 주어(physicians)의 수 일치가
    맞지 않아 have로 고쳐야 한다.

  ① Only ~ science는 강조 표현으로 도치가 되어 적절
    하다.

  ③ begin은 to R와 R-ing를 둘 다 목적어로 받을 수 있
    는 동사이다.

  ④ a number of = many

14

Research (in ① learning) ② suggests [that ③ [getting
good grades] ④ depend more on effective study skills
than on a high IQ.]

정답 ④ (depend → depends)

해석 학습에 대한 연구가 좋은 성적을 얻는 것은 높은 지능보
다 효율적인 학습 기술에 달려 있다는 것을 보여 준다.

분석 주어와 동사의 수 일치

  ④ 주어(getting good grades)와 동사의 수 일치가 맞
    지 않아 depends로 고쳐야 한다. 동명사(R-ing)가 주
    어일 때는 단수 취급한다. 또한 suggest의 주어로 사
    물이 나오는 경우 that절 속에 조동사 should는 생략
    되지 않는다.

  ① 전치사의 목적어로 명사는 적절하다. learning은 '학
    습'이라는 뜻이다.

  ② 주어(Research)와 동사(suggests)의 수 일치가 적절
    하다.

  ③ that절의 주어로 동명사가 쓰여 적절하다.

15

I say (① with confidence) [that neither (of my children)
② have (③ ever before) bothered to read ④ a single
word of this book.]

정답 ② (have → has)

해석 나는 우리 아이들 중 어느 누구도 이 책의 단어를 읽도록
애쓴 적이 없다고 자신 있게 말할 수 있다.

분석 대명사 「(n)either of + Ns」의 수 일치

  ② 대명사 「(n)either of + Ns」가 주어 자리에 나오면 반
    드시 단수동사와 수 일치해야 한다. have를 has로 고
    쳐야 한다.

  ① 동사를 수식하는 부사(전명구)로 쓰여 적절하다.

  ③ 단독 부사의 역할로 동사를 수식하여 적절하다.

  ④ 단수명사 앞에 부정관사(a/an)는 적절하다.

16

[That the committee members could not agree (with
each other) (about solving those problems)]
_____ caused more serious problems.

① is   ② was

③ **has**   ④ have

정답   ③

해석   위원회의 구성원들이 문제들을 해결하는 데 있어 서로에게 동의하지 않는다는 사실이 더욱 심각한 문제들을 발생시켰다.

분석   주어와 동사의 수 일치 / 능동태와 수동태의 구분

③ 주어(That ~ problems)는 명사절(that절)이다. 명사절이 주어일 경우 동사는 단수동사와 수 일치해야 하므로 ④는 탈락된다. ①과 ②는 수동태, ③은 능동태로 쓰여 태를 묻고 있는데, 빈칸 뒤에 목적어가 있기 때문에 능동태를 써야 하므로 ③이 적절하다.

17   [2012 명지대]

The prominence (of names like Rockefeller, Carnegie, Hill and Armour) ① indicate [that business ② was still thought of as a field (of personal competition,) (③ of heroic endeavor,) and (④ not of corporate manipulation.)]

정답   ① (indicate → indicates)

해석   록펠러(Rockefeller), 카네기(Carnegie), 힐(Hill)과 아머(Armour)와 같은 이름들의 명망이 경제가 기업의 조작이 아니라 여전히 개인적인 경쟁, 영웅적인 노력으로 여겨진다는 사실을 보여 주고 있다.

분석   주어와 동사의 수 일치

① 주어(The prominence)와 동사(indicate)의 수 일치가 맞지 않아 indicates로 고쳐야 한다.

② 「think of + O + as + O.C」 5형식 동사의 어형을 수동태로 쓴 형태이다.

③ 「A, B, and C」 형태로 전명구가 병치된 형태이다.

④ 「A, B, and C」 형태로 전명구가 병치된 형태이다.

18   [2017 아주대]

(Only when the skill is repeated with consistently correct outcomes) _____ .

① **has it truly been learned**

② has been it truly learned

③ it has truly been learned

④ has it truly been learning

⑤ it has been truly learning

정답   ①

해석   기술이 일관되게 올바른 결과를 낳으면서 되풀이될 때, 비로소 그 기술은 진정으로 습득된다.

분석   「only 부사절」의 강조 도치 / 능동태와 수동태의 구분

① 「only 부사, only 전명구, only 부사절」이 문두에 위치하여 강조되는 경우 반드시 주어, 동사는 도치가 되어야 한다. 원래 문장 it has truly been learned에서 도치가 되면 has it truly been learned가 되어 ①이 적절하다.

② 완료를 나타내는 have p.p.는 도치할 때 「have + S + p.p. ~」로 도치한다.

③, ⑤ 도치가 되지 않아 부적절하다.

④ it은 기술(the skill)을 대신 받는 대명사인데 기술이 학습되는 대상이므로 수동태를 써야 한다.

19   [2012 성균관대]

(① At least) part of their great secret ② is [that ③ they (both) live in the same country.] White and black have shared that secret (for a long time now,) and ④ has done an efficient job (of keeping ⑤ it from each other.)

정답   ④ (has done → have done)

해석   적어도 엄청난 비밀 중 하나는 그들 둘 다 같은 나라에 살고 있다는 것이다. 흑인과 백인은 이제까지 오랫동안 그 비밀을 공유해 왔고, 그 비밀을 서로가 눈치채지 못하도록 하는 일을 효율적으로 수행해 왔다.

분석   주어와 동사의 수 일치

④ 주어(White and black)와 동사(has)의 수 일치가 맞지 않아 have done으로 고쳐야 한다. 또한 have shared and have done으로 병치된 형태이다. and (white and black)처럼 주어가 같아 생략된 형태이다.

① at least는 '적어도'라는 뜻의 수식어구(전명구)로 쓰여 적절하다.

② 부분명사 「part of + N/Ns」가 주어 자리에 나오면 of 뒤에 나온 명사(secret)에 수 일치해야 하므로 is는 적절하다.

③ they와 both는 동격을 나타내고 있다. (they both: 그들 둘 다 / they all: 그들 모두)

⑤ that secret(그 비밀)을 대신 받는 대명사로 수 일치는 적절하다.

20

The ① varied classes (of organic compounds) (with
their basically common pattern) as well as ② with their
peculiarities and reactions) ③ serves (as groundwork
for this course.) ④ No error

정답 ③ (serves → serve)

해석 독특한 성질과 화학적 반응뿐 아니라 기본적으로 공통된
패턴을 지닌 다양한 종류의 유기 화합물들은 이 과정의
토대가 된다.

분석 주어와 동사의 수 일치
  ③ 주어(The varied classes)와 동사(serves)의 수 일치
  가 맞지 않아 serve로 고쳐야 한다.
  ① varied = various: '다양한'의 의미를 가진 형용사이다.
  ② 등위상관접속사 「A as well as B」의 형태로 A와 B는
  같은 품사로 연결하기 때문에 전명구가 연결되어 적절
  하다.
  ④는 ①, ②, ③ 중에 오류가 없는 경우 선택한다.

21

(Beneath the epidermal cells) _____ the body-
wall muscle, (which is relatively thick in some species
under certain circumstances.)

① exist   ② exists
③ exist where   ④ where it existed
⑤ where exist

정답 ②

해석 표피 세포 밑에 체벽 근육이 존재한다. 이 체벽 근육은 특
정 환경에서 어떤 종들에게 상대적으로 더 두껍다.

분석 부사구(전명구) 강조 도치 / 주어와 동사의 수 일치
  ② 전명구(Beneath ~ cells)가 문두에 위치하여 강조되
  는 경우 주어, 동사는 도치가 되어야 한다. 빈칸은 동
  사가 필요한 자리이기 때문에 ①, ②로 좁혀지고, 주어
  가 빈칸 뒤의 the body-wall muscle이기 때문에 단
  수동사(exists)와 일치해야 한다.

22

Avery's most recent works, (① in addition to television
shows,) ② has been several popular movies and cable
broadcast comedy programs. He also frequently
③ donates his time (to charity events) ④ to help raise
money for children in need.)

정답 ② (has been several popular movies → have been
several popular movies)

해석 TV show와 더불어 에이버리(Avery)의 최근작들은 인기
있는 몇몇 영화와 케이블 방송 코미디 프로그램들이다.
그는 또한 시간을 내서 가난한 아이들을 위해 모금하는
자선 행사를 자주 연다.

분석 주어와 동사의 수 일치
  ② 주어(Avery's most recent works)와 동사(has)의 수
  일치가 맞지 않아 has를 have로 고쳐야 한다.
  ① in addition to: '~와 더불어'라는 뜻의 전치사로 쓰
  여 명사를 받아 적절하다.
  ③ 주어와 동사의 수 일치도 적절하고, 목적어도 있기 때
  문에 능동태도 적절하다.
  ④ to R의 형용사적 용법으로 앞에 명사(charity events)
  를 수식하여 적절하다. 「help + (to) R ~」에서 help
  는 to R를 목적어로 받을 때 to는 써도 되고 생략해도
  된다.

23

The grand, ① leading principle, (② toward which every
③ argument (unfolded in these pages) directly
converges,) ④ are the absolute and essential
importance (of human development in its richest
diversity.)

정답 ④ (are → is)

해석 이 책에 펼쳐지는 모든 주장이 직접 수렴되는 그 원대하
고 중요한 원칙은 다양성 안에서 이뤄지는 절대적이며 필
수적으로 중요한 인간의 개발이다.

분석 주어와 동사의 수 일치
  ④ 주어(The grand, leading principle)와 동사(are)의
  수 일치가 맞지 않아 is로 고쳐야 한다.
  ① grand, leading은 형용사로 쓰여 명사(principle)을
  수식하여 적절하다. 명사 앞 형용사는 접속사 없이 여

러 개가 나와도 괜찮다. leading은 '주요한, 뛰어난, 선도하는'의 뜻이다.

② 「전치사＋관계대명사」는 절 이하의 성분(명사)이 완전하게 나와 적절하다.

③ every는 해석만 '모든'이라고 할 뿐, 항상 단수명사(N)만을 수식한다.

24

[2010 경기대]

But [①<u>what</u> genuinely recommends the service] is the public playlist facility, (allowing individual users ②to curate and publish groupings of songs (③based on whatever criteria ④takes their fancy.))

정답 ④ (takes → take)

해석 하지만 그 서비스를 진심으로 추천하게 된 것은 대중들이 주도하는 재생 목록 시설 때문이다. 이것은 개개인의 사용자들이 그들이 좋아하는 그 어떤 기준에 맞춰 여러 노래 묶음을 관리하고 발표할 수 있도록 허용한다.

분석 주어와 동사의 수 일치

④ criteria는 criterion(기준)의 복수 형태이다. 동사를 take로 고쳐야 한다.

① what절은 절 이하의 성분(명사)이 불완전하여 통째로 하나의 명사로 쓰이므로 문장의 주어 역할로 적절하다.

② 「allow＋O＋to R~」 5형식 동사의 어형으로 쓰여 적절하다.

③ 노래 묶음이 기반으로 만드는 주체가 아니라 만들어지는 대상이고, 뒤에 목적어도 없기 때문에 수동의 관계인 과거분사(based)는 적절하다.

25

[2012 고려대]

Mistinguett was not highly talented as a dancer, _____ a good voice, but she had vitality and conviction, and even in old age she was able to play young parts.

① neither had she

② nor she have

③ neither did she have

④ nor did she have

정답 ④

해석 미스팅게트(Mistinguett)는 댄서로서 매우 재능이 있지도 않았고, 마찬가지로 좋은 목소리를 가지지도 않았다. 하지만 그녀는 활력과 강한 신념을 갖고 있어서, 심지어 나이 들어서도 젊은 사람의 역할을 할 수 있었다.

분석 「nor(= and neither)＋V＋S」의 도치 구문

④ 앞 문장이 끝나고 나서 nor 뒤에 문장이 나오면 반드시 도치가 되어야 하기 때문에 ④가 적절하다.

①, ③ neither은 접속사가 아니기 때문에 문장과 문장을 연결할 수 없다. 「nor = and neither」이기 때문에 and 없이 neither만으로 문장을 연결할 수 없다.

② 「nor＋S＋V (X)」 / 「nor＋V＋S (O)」

17강 문의구성

Practice

01	②	02	②	03	④	04	①	05	③
06	①	07	①	08	②	09	③	10	②
11	①	12	②	13	②	14	④	15	④
16	④	17	②	18	④	19	④	20	④
21	④	22	③	23	⑤	24	①	25	②

01
[2010 강남대]

There ①is inscribed (on the walls) the ②follow(following) proverb: "Do unto others ③as you would have ④them unto you."

정답 ② (follow → following)

해석 벽에 다음의 속담이 새겨져 있다. '다른 사람들이 당신에게 해주길 바라는 대로 다른 사람에게 하라.'

분석 문의구성

② 정관사(the) 뒤에 명사(proverb)가 나왔는데 그 사이에 동사는 쓸 수 없다. 형용사의 역할인 현재분사(following)로 고쳐야 한다.

① there/here로 시작하는 문장은 동사 뒤 첫 번째 명사가 주어이다. 주어(the following proverb)와 동사(is)의 수 일치가 적절하다.

③ 부사절 접속사(as)로 쓰여 「주어 + 동사」를 받아 적절하다.

④ others를 대신 받는 대명사로 쓰여 수 일치가 적절하다.

02
[2010 강남대]

He cannot find a suitable job (despite _____.)

① has been trained thoroughly in repairing and maintaining computers

② his thorough training (in the repair and maintenance of computers)

③ being trained thoroughly in how to repair and maintaining computers

④ the fact of receiving a thorough computer training in their repair and their maintenance

정답 ②

해석 그는 컴퓨터 수리와 유지 관리의 철저한 훈련에도 불구하고 적당한 일자리를 찾을 수 없다.

분석 전치사 despite

② 전치사의 목적어로 명사(his thorough training)가 적절하다.

① 전치사 뒤에 동사는 나올 수 없다.

③ to repair and maintaining의 병치가 부적절하다.

④ their이라는 대명사가 받을 수 있는 대상이 없어 부적절하다.

03
[2010 국민대]

Controversial matters (①involving the whole sections) (which were) ②were discussed; (nevertheless,) ③most of the representatives ④remaining calm. (remained)

정답 ④ (remaining calm → remained calm)

해석 전반적인 부분을 포함한 논쟁의 여지가 있는 문제들이 토론되었다. 그럼에도 불구하고 대부분의 대표들은 침착함을 유지했다.

분석 문의구성

④ 앞에 접속사의 역할을 대신할 수 있는 세미콜론(;)이 있다. 주어(most of the representatives)까지 나왔으므로 동사 remained calm으로 고쳐야 한다.

① 뒤에 목적어도 있으므로 능동의 관계인 현재분사(involving)는 적절하다.

② 주어(Controversial matters)와 동사(were)의 수 일치가 적절하다.

③ most와 of가 붙으면 대명사로 쓰인 형태이다.

04
[2010 단국대]

Our appetite (for food,) (_____ many modern humans,) is a natural drive for survival.

① a problem for

② is a problem for

③ being a problem

④ its problem is

정답 ①

해석 많은 현대인들의 문제, 즉 음식에 대한 우리의 식욕은 생존을 위한 자연스런 욕구이다.

분석 동격의 명사

① 이미 주어(Our appetite)와 동사(is)가 있다. 빈칸은 수식어구가 나와야 하는데 「명사 + 콤마(,) + 명사」 형태가 동격으로 쓰일 수 있기 때문에 ①이 적절하다.

②, ④ 접속사 없이 동사가 또 나올 수 없다.

③ 명사(a problem)와 명사(many modern humans)가 충돌되어 부적절하다.

05
[2010 상명대]

(When ①the final story has been written (for that final newspaper) ②sometime in the future,) you can be sure [(③that it's substance will be some ④violent act (that has occurred.)]

정답 ③ (that it's substance → that its substance)

해석 미래의 언젠가 마지막 신문의 결말이 쓰였을 때, 그 결말의 내용이 이미 일어나고 있는 몇몇 폭력 행위가 될 것이라는 것을 당신은 확신할 수 있다.

분석 문의구성

③ that절 안에 이미 동사(will be)가 있기 때문에 동사가 또 나올 수 없다. that its substance로 고쳐야 한다.

① When은 부사절 접속사로 쓰여 주어, 동사가 나와 적절하다.

② 명사와 명사의 충돌을 피해 주기 위해 전명구는 적절하다.

④ 관계대명사 that절이 선행사(violent act)를 수식하여 적절하다.

06
[2010 서울여대]

Socrates was _____ searches for the truth and the meaning of life.)

① a philosopher, a person (who
② a philosopher, a person
③ a philosopher and a person who
④ a philosopher and person

정답 ①

해석 소크라테스는 철학자였다. 그는 삶의 의미와 진리를 추구한 사람이었다.

분석 동격의 콤마(,)

① 「명사 + 콤마(,) + 명사」 형태로 동격을 나타낼 수 있다. a philosopher, a person은 동격으로 쓰였고 주격 관계대명사 who절이 선행사(a person)를 수식하여 적절하다.

② 접속사 없이 두 개의 문장이 나올 수 없다.

③ 「A and B」의 형태로 쓰면 두 명을 나타낸다. 소크라테스는 한 명이기 때문에 부적절하다. 또한 주격 관계대명사절 속에 단수동사(searches)가 있어 선행사가 두 명일 수 없다.

④ '소크라테스는 철학자이고 사람이 탐구한다'의 의미가 어색하여 부적절하다.

07
[2010 홍익대]

(_____부사절_____ small specimen (of the embryonic fluid) is removed from a fetus,) (it will be possible [to determine whether the baby will be born with birth defects.]

① If a
② That a
③ A
④ After it is a

정답 ①

해석 만약 태아에게서 배아 체액의 작은 표본을 채취한다면 그 아기가 선천적인 장애를 가지고 태어날 것인지 아닌지를 알아보는 것이 가능할 것이다.

분석 문의구성

① 콤마(,) 뒤에 주절(it will be ~ defects)이 완전하게 나왔기 때문에, 빈칸부터 a fetus까지는 수식절이어야 한다. 「If + 주어(a small specimen) + 동사(is removed)」를 부사절로 보아 수식절로 적절하다.

② that절 이하의 성분(명사)이 완전할 경우 명사절이기 때문에 부적절하다.

③ 접속사 없이 두 개의 문장이 나와 부적절하다.

④ after절 속에 동사가 두 개(is, is)가 나와 부적절하다.

08

Now mobile chatting is a widely accepted phenomenon,
S   V   C
but _____ a novelty (in the telecommunications
C
industry.)

① once it being

② it was (once)
   S   V

③ once there being

④ there was once

정답 ②

해석 지금 모바일 채팅은 널리 받아들여지는 현상이지만, 한때
그것은 통신업계에서 새로운 것이었다.

분석 문의구성

② 등위접속사(but)가 있기 때문에 빈칸에는 주어, 동사가
나와야 한다. it은 mobile chatting을 대신 받는 대명
사로 '모바일 채팅이 한때는 신선한 것이었다'라는 의
미가 되어 적절하다.

①, ③ 동사가 없어 부적절하다.

④ '하지만 한때 통신업계에 신선한 것이 있었다'라는 의
미가 어색하여 부적절하다.

09

[2013 상명대]

(In November 1989,) (① amid the tide of revolt) (that
                                                   S
was sweeping Eastern Europe,) ② (protesters') [seizing
                                 의미상 주어   S₁
the moment] and ③ demand new elections] ④ led (to
            demanding   S₂   V
the resignation of the communist leadership) and (⑤ to
the end of communism in Czechoslovakia.)

정답 ③ (demand new elections → demanding new
elections)

해석 1989년 11월, 동유럽을 휩쓸었던 반란 중에 시위자들이
그 당시의 상황을 장악하고 새로운 선거를 요구함으로써
체코슬로바키아(Czechoslovakia)에서 공산주의 지도자
가 물러나고 공산주의 체제가 종식되었다.

분석 등위접속사 and의 병치

③ and는 앞과 뒤를 대등하게 연결하는 접속사이다. and
앞에 어디를 봐도 동사가 없기 때문에 demand라는
동사가 또 나올 수 없다. seizing and demanding으
로 동명사의 병치를 이루도록 고쳐야 한다.

① amid는 전치사의 역할로 명사를 받아 적절하다.

② 동명사(seizing the moment and demanding new
elections)가 동사(led)의 주어 역할로 나오고,
protesters'(소유격)는 동명사의 의미상 주어이다.

④ 「lead to + N」는 자동사의 용법으로 쓰여 적절하다.

⑤ 「to + N」 and 「to + N」으로 병치된 형태이다.

10

[2013 서울여대]

Chloroplasts evolved (① about 1.6 billion years ago)
             when S   V
(② then one cell, (incapable of using the ③ sun's
                                  S (which was)
energy,) engulfed ④ another cell (that could.)
         V   O

정답 ② (then → when)

해석 태양 에너지를 사용할 수 없었던 하나의 세포가 그 에너
지를 사용할 수 있는 또 다른 세포를 흡수했던 대략 16억
년 전에 엽록체가 진화했다.

분석 문의구성

② 두 개의 문장(Chloroplasts evolved / one cell engulfed)
이 있는데 접속사가 없다. then을 접속사의 역할인 관
계부사(when)로 고쳐야 한다.

① 숫자 앞에 about은 '대략'이라는 뜻의 수식어이다.

③ 정관사(the) 뒤에 명사로 쓰여 적절하다.

④ another은 단수명사(N)를 수식하기 때문에 적절하다.

11

[2013 세종대]

           강조   various
So profuse and ① vary is our use (of these words) that
        ⓐ   V   S
② it is not easy [to define just ③ what we mean ④ by
   가S   진S
them.]

정답 ① (vary → various)

해석 이러한 단어들을 사용하는 경우가 너무나 많고 다양해서
그 단어들을 통해 우리가 무엇을 말하는지 정의하기란 쉽
지 않다.

분석 등위접속사 and의 병치

① and는 앞과 뒤를 대등하게 연결시킨다. 만약 and 뒤
에 동사가 있으려면 and 앞에도 동사가 있어야 한다.
형용사(profuse)를 and로 연결하는 형태이므로 동사
(vary)를 형용사(various)로 고쳐야 한다.

② 「가주어(it) ~ 진주어(to define ~)」 구문으로 쓰여 적
절하다.

③ what은 절 이하의 성분(명사)이 불완전하고 명사절을
이끌기 때문에 define의 목적어로 적절하다.

④ what절에서 mean의 목적어가 불완전해야 하기 때문
에 수식어구(전명구)는 적절하다.

③ 「want + O + to R」 5형식 동사의 어형으로 쓰여 적절
하다.

④ 장소의 명사를 수식하는 관계부사(where)는 적절하다.

⑤ everyone은 단수 취급하는 명사이므로 수 일치가 적
절하다.

12

[2013 아주대]

Trucks routinely need [fuel, oil, and _____ (to
remove road grime from the chassis and windows.)

① thorough washed
② a thorough washing
③ thoroughly washed
④ a thoroughly washing
⑤ are thoroughly washed

정답 ②

해석 트럭은 보통 연료, 석유, 그리고 차대와 창문에 묻은 길가
의 먼지를 제거하는 철저한 세척을 필요로 한다.

분석 「A, B, and/or C」 병치 / 형용사와 부사의 구분

② 「A, B, and/or C」로 병치된 형태이다. 이때 A, B, C
의 품사는 항상 일치되어야 한다. A(fuel), B(oil), and
C(명사)가 나와야 하기 때문에 ②, ④로 좁혀진다. 명
사를 수식하는 것은 형용사(thorough)이므로 ②가 적
절하다.

①, ③, ⑤ 명사가 나오지 않아 부적절하다.

④ 부사는 명사를 수식할 수 없다.

13

[2014 상명대]

Frederick Law Olmsted, (who ①designed Manhattan's
Central Park,) ②wanting the park ③to be a "democratic
playground" (④where everyone ⑤was equal.)

정답 ② (wanting → wanted)

해석 맨해튼의 Central Park를 설계한 Frederick Law
Olmsted는 이 공원이 모든 사람이 평등한 '민주적 놀이
터'가 되기를 원했다.

분석 문의구성

② 문장의 주어(Frederick Law Olmsted)는 있는데 동
사가 없다. wanting을 동사 wanted로 고쳐야 한다.

① 목적어가 있기 때문에 능동태는 적절하다.

14

[2014 상명대]

Our teacher ①expects us to be on time, ②to do ③all
our homework, and ④sitting quietly ⑤in class.

정답 ④ (sitting → to sit)

해석 우리 선생님은 우리가 시간을 잘 지키고, 모든 숙제를 하
고, 수업 시간에 조용히 앉아 있기를 기대한다.

분석 「A, B, and/or C」 병치

④ 「A(to be), B(to do), and/or C(sitting)」의 형태로 병
치가 된 형태이다. 이때 같은 품사로 일관되게 연결해
야 하기 때문에 sitting을 to sit으로 고쳐야 한다.

① 「expect + O + to R」 5형식 동사의 어형으로 쓰여 적
절하다.

② 목적보어 to R가 병치되어 적절하다.

③ all은 전치 한정사로 한정사(the, 소유격)보다 앞에 위
치해야 한다.

⑤ 명사와 명사의 충돌을 피해 주기 위해 전명구는 적절
하다.

15

[2014 아주대]

(①Undoubtedly,) Cathy was taking ②a social science
class (when her father went to ③the school to see her.)
Anyone (④has taken the course) was not ⑤allowed to
use a mobile phone.

정답 ④ (has taken → taking)

해석 의심할 여지 없이, Cathy의 아버지가 그녀를 보러 학교
에 갔을 때, Cathy는 사회 과학을 듣고 있었다. 이 강좌를
듣는 어느 누구도 휴대 전화를 쓰지 못하게 되어 있었다.

분석 문의구성

④ 주어(Anyone)와 동사(was)가 있기 때문에 동사가 또
나올 수 없다. Anyone을 수식할 수 있도록 현재분사
인 taking으로 고쳐야 한다.

① 단독 부사로 쓰여 문장 전체에 의미를 도와주는 부사
이다.
② 단수명사 앞에 부정관사(a)는 적절하다.
③ 명사 앞에 정관사(the)는 적절하다.
⑤ 「allow + O + to R ~」 5형식 동사의 어형이 수동태로
쓰여 적절하다.

16
[2015 성균관대]

Detroit was the birthplace (of ①both the industrial age
and the ②nation's middle class,) and the ③city's rise
and fall ④being a window (into the challenges) ⑤facing
all of modern America.)

정답 ④ (being → is)

해석 디트로이트는 산업 시대와 미국 중산층의 발생지이며, 이
도시의 흥망성쇠는 현대 미국이 직면하고 있는 도전 과제
들이 투영된 창이라고 볼 수 있다.

분석 문의구성

④ 문장과 문장이 and로 병치된 형태이다. and 이하에
주어(the city's rise and fall)가 있는데 동사가 없기
때문에 being을 동사 is로 고쳐야 한다.

① 등위상관접속사 「both A and B」의 상관관계가 적절
하게 쓰여 있다.

② 명사와 명사의 충돌을 피해 주기 위해 소유격은 적절
하다.

③ 명사와 명사의 충돌을 피해 주기 위해 소유격은 적절
하다.

⑤ 뒤에 목적어가 있기 때문에 능동의 관계인 현재분사
(facing)는 적절하다.

17
[2015 서울여대]

Multinational companies _____ ①it increasingly
important [to employ internationally acceptable brand
names.]

① finding   ② are finding
③ they are finding   ④ that find

정답 ②

해석 다국적 기업들은 국제적으로 받아들여지는 상표명을 활
용하는 것이 점점 중요하다는 사실을 발견하고 있다.

분석 문의구성

② 문장에 주어(Multinational companies)만 있고 동사
가 없기 때문에 빈칸에는 동사가 필요하다. 동사가 나
온 ②가 적절하다.

18
[2015 홍익대]

The notes are ①by Robert, (who is a Dante scholar
and a professor (emeritus ②at Princeton,)) ③where he
taught the Divine Comedy ④during forty-two years.)

정답 ④ (during → for)

해석 그 원고는 Dante를 연구하는 학자이자 Princeton 대학
의 명예 교수로서 Princeton 대학에서 42년 동안 신곡을
가르친 Robert가 쓴 것이다.

분석 「during + 특정 기간 명사」 / 「for + 불특정 기간 명사」

④ 특정 기간과 불특정 기간의 구분하는 기준은 언제인지
알 수 있으면 특정 기간(ex. the summer vacation)
이고, 언제인지 알 수 없으면 불특정기간(ex. five
years)이다. 언제인지 알 수 없는 42년이기 때문에 불
특정 기간을 받는 전치사 for로 고쳐야 한다.

① be동사의 보어로 전명구는 가능하다. (ex. She is in
the class.)

② 명사와 명사의 충돌을 피해 주기 위해 전치사는 적절
하다.

③ 장소의 명사를 수식하는 관계부사(where)는 적절하다.

19
[2016 광운대]

(When he ①was a little boy,) Mark Twain ②would walk
(along the piers,) ③watch the river boats, ④swimming
and fish in the Mississippi, (⑤much like his famous
character, Tom Sawyer.)

정답 ④ (swimming → swim)

해석 그가 어린아이였을 때, 마크 트웨인(Mark Twain)은 소설
속의 유명한 등장인물 톰 소여(Tom Sawyer)처럼 부두를
따라 걷고, 강에 떠 있는 배를 바라보고, 미시시피강에서
수영과 낚시를 하곤 했다.

분석 「A, B, C, and D」 병치

④ 「A(walk), B(watch), C(swimming) and D(fish)」의 형태로 병치가 된 형태이다. 이때 같은 품사로 일관되게 연결해야 하기 때문에 swimming을 swim으로 고쳐야 한다.

① 과거(would)를 나타내고 있어 when절 속에 과거동사도 적절하다.

② 조동사 뒤 동사원형은 적절하다.

③ 「A, B, C, and D」의 형태로 동사가 병치되어 적절하다.

⑤ 문장이 끝나고 수식어구(전명구)는 적절하다.

20 [2016 서울여대]

Classroom routines are ①<u>an important factor</u> (in keeping children ②<u>constructively busy</u>,) (in ③<u>encouraging</u> self-discipline,) and above all, ④<u>to facilitate</u> learning.)

정답 ④ (to facilitate → in facilitating)

해석 교실에서 일어나는 일상적인 일들은 아이들을 건설적으로 바쁘게 만들고, 자제력을 장려하며, 무엇보다도 학습을 용이하게 해주는 중요한 요소이다.

분석 「A, B, and/or C」 병치

④ 「A(in keeping), B(in encouraging), and C(to facilitate)」의 형태로 병치가 된 형태이다. 이때 같은 품사로 일관되게 연결해야 하기 때문에 to facilitate를 in facilitating으로 고쳐야 한다.

① 형용사(important)가 명사(factor)를 수식하여 적절하다.

② 「keep + O + O.C(형용사)」 5형식 동사의 어형으로 목적보어 자리에 형용사(busy)는 적절하다.

③ 「A, B, and C」의 형태로 병치된 형태로 적절하다.

21 [2017 국민대]

Rory, a ranger (in an African National Park,) ①<u>believes</u> [that people should ②<u>do their bit</u> to stop poaching,] ("whether it's putting some coins ③<u>in a tin</u>, writing an article, or ④<u>just spread the word</u>.")

정답 ④ (just spread the word → just spreading the word)

해석 아프리카 국립 공원의 순찰대원 로리(Rory)는 '깡통에 동전을 모으는 것, 기사를 쓰는 것, 단순히 말을 퍼뜨리는 것이든 상관없이' 사람들은 밀렵을 막기 위해 자신의 의무를 다해야 한다고 믿는다.

분석 「A, B, and/or C」 병치

④ 「A(putting), B(writing), or C(spread)」의 형태로 병치가 된 형태이다. 이때 같은 품사로 일관되게 연결해야 하기 때문에 spread를 spreading으로 고쳐야 한다.

① 주어(Rory)와 동사(believes)의 수 일치가 적절하다.

② 조동사 뒤에 동사원형이 쓰였고, people을 대신 받는 대명사(their)의 수 일치도 적절하다.

③ 명사와 명사의 충돌을 피해 주기 위해 전명구는 적절하다.

22 [2011 서울여대]

(Only now) are questions (such as [how a material was produced,] [how much energy will be used to take care of it,] and [what happens to it at the end of its life]) _____ to echo through the industry.

① begin   ② begins

③ beginning   ④ has begun

정답 ③

해석 이제야 어떻게 한 물질이 만들어지고, 그 물질을 유지하는 데 얼마나 많은 에너지가 사용되며, 그 물질이 사라질 때 무슨 일들이 생기는지와 같은 문제들이 비로소 산업 전반에 걸쳐 메아리치고 있다.

분석 문의구성

③ 「only 부사」가 문두에 위치하여 강조되어 도치된 형태이다. 동사(are)와 주어(questions)가 있고 such ~ life까지 전부 수식어구이다. 이미 동사(are)가 있기 때문에 동사가 또 나올 수 없어 ①, ②, ④는 탈락되고, 동사가 아닌 ③이 적절하다. 원래 문장 Questions are beginning의 현재진행에서 도치가 된 형태이다.

23

Emerson ①himself, (however,) (writing at the dawn of
②the industrial ③age,) (observing ④with interest) the
proliferation of railways, ware houses, canals and
factories,) ⑤wishing [to make room for the possibility
of alternative forms of beauty.]

정답 ⑤ (wishing → wished)

해석 하지만 철도, 창고, 운하, 공장의 급증을 흥미롭게 바라보
며, 산업화 시대의 초기에 글을 썼던 에머슨 자신은 산업
화 시대가 아름다움을 대신하는 형식의 가능성에 여지를
만들기를 원했다.

분석 문의구성

⑤ 문장에 주어(Emerson)는 있는데 동사가 없다.
wishing을 동사 wished로 고쳐야 한다.

① 명사 뒤에 재귀대명사가 붙어 나오면 동격을 나타낸다.

② 명사 앞에 정관사(the)는 적절하다.

③ 전치사의 목적어로 명사는 적절하다.

④ with interest=interestingly : 부사로 쓰여 수식어구
로 쓰였다.

24

(More than) two-thirds of about 20,680 Olympic athletes
(_____ for a recent report) had caffeine in their
urine.

① studied   ② study

③ to study   ④ studying

정답 ①

해석 최근 검사받은 대략 20,680명의 올림픽 선수 중 3분의 2
이상의 선수들이 소변에서 카페인이 검출되었다.

분석 문의구성

① 주어(two-thirds ~ athletes), 동사(had), 목적어
(caffeine)가 전부 있기 때문에 빈칸은 수식어구가 필
요한 자리이다. 선수들이 조사를 받은 대상이므로 수
동의 관계인 과거분사(studied)가 적절하다.

② study는 명사 혹은 동사인데 둘 모두 빈칸에 나올 수
없다.

③, ④ 선수들이 직접 조사한 주체가 아니기 때문에 능동
의 관계를 나타내는 준동사는 부적절하다.

25

① Talks (with North Korea) ②which may create a
situation (favorable ③to the emergence) (of ④a middle
class) (that will push for ⑤democratization.)

정답 ② (which → 삭제)

해석 북한과의 회담은 민주화를 부추길 중산층의 출현에 유리
한 상황을 만들어 낼 수 있다.

분석 문의구성

② 주어(Talks)만 있고 동사가 없는 형태이다. 문장에 동사
는 반드시 있어야 하기 때문에 which를 삭제하여 may
create을 주어(Talks)의 동사로 만들어 줘야 한다.

① 주어 자리에 명사는 적절하다.

③ 형용사가 전명구와 결합되어 앞 명사를 수식하여 적절
하다.

④ 단수명사 앞에 부정관사(a/an)는 적절하다.

⑤ 전치사의 목적어로 명사는 적절하다.

Review Test 정답 한눈에 보기

1강 동사

Practice 01

01	②	02	①	03	③	04	③	05	②
06	①	07	①	08	④	09	③	10	②
11	②	12	④	13	②	14	②	15	⑤
16	⑤	17	③	18	②	19	②	20	②
21	⑤	22	②	23	④	24	④	25	③

Practice 02

01	②	02	④	03	②	04	③	05	②
06	④	07	③	08	②	09	④	10	④
11	③	12	②	13	④	14	④	15	③
16	④	17	②	18	⑤	19	②	20	②
21	④	22	③	23	①	24	③	25	③

2강 시제

Practice

01	④	02	②	03	④	04	②	05	③
06	①	07	①	08	③	09	①	10	①
11	④	12	④	13	④	14	②	15	①
16	②	17	②	18	②	19	④	20	②
21	①	22	③	23	④	24	④	25	②

3강 수동태

Practice 01

01	③	02	②	03	②	04	②	05	③
06	①	07	③	08	②	09	①	10	④
11	③	12	②	13	③	14	①	15	①
16	②	17	③	18	②	19	③	20	①
21	①	22	②	23	②	24	④	25	③

Practice 02

01	①	02	②	03	②	04	④	05	①
06	③	07	③	08	③	09	④	10	②
11	③	12	③	13	③	14	①	15	②
16	①	17	①	18	①	19	①	20	④
21	①	22	②	23	②	24	③	25	⑤

4강 조동사

Practice

01	②	02	④	03	②	04	②	05	④
06	③	07	②	08	③	09	②	10	④
11	④	12	③	13	③	14	③	15	③
16	②	17	④	18	③	19	②	20	③
21	④	22	③	23	②	24	③	25	①

5강 가정법

Practice

01	②	02	②	03	①	04	②	05	②
06	②	07	③	08	④	09	④	10	③
11	④	12	④	13	④	14	④	15	③
16	③	17	④	18	①	19	①	20	①
21	①	22	①	23	④	24	③	25	⑤

6강 부정사

Practice

01	②	02	④	03	④	04	④	05	④
06	②	07	④	08	②	09	④	10	④
11	②	12	③	13	③	14	④	15	①
16	②	17	③	18	④	19	④	20	④
21	④	22	④	23	③	24	②	25	②

7강 동명사

Practice

01	①	02	③	03	③	04	③	05	③
06	②	07	④	08	④	09	④	10	③
11	③	12	①	13	①	14	④	15	③
16	①	17	④	18	①	19	③	20	②
21	③	22	①	23	②	24	③	25	①

8강 분사

Practice 01

01	①	02	④	03	①	04	③	05	④
06	④	07	①	08	②	09	③	10	③
11	①	12	④	13	①	14	③	15	②
16	③	17	②	18	④	19	③	20	③
21	③	22	①	23	①	24	③	25	④

Practice 02

01	②	02	②	03	②	04	①	05	④
06	②	07	③	08	①	09	④	10	②
11	④	12	③	13	②	14	②	15	③
16	③	17	④	18	②	19	②	20	②
21	④	22	④	23	②	24	③	25	④

9강 접속사

Practice 01

01	④	02	③	03	②	04	③	05	③
06	②	07	②	08	①	09	④	10	③
11	①	12	①	13	④	14	②	15	②
16	③	17	④	18	④	19	④	20	①
21	①	22	③	23	①	24	③	25	②

Practice 02

01	④	02	①	03	①	04	①	05	③
06	②	07	③	08	③	09	③	10	④
11	③	12	①	13	③	14	④	15	④
16	②	17	①	18	③	19	③	20	①
21	③	22	③	23	①	24	③	25	②

11강 명사와 관사

Practice

01	②	02	②	03	③	04	③	05	③
06	④	07	③	08	②	09	③	10	②
11	①	12	②	13	④	14	④	15	①
16	①	17	③	18	①	19	②	20	④
21	②	22	④	23	②	24	②	25	④

10강 관계사

Practice 01

01	①	02	③	03	④	04	③	05	④
06	①	07	②	08	①	09	④	10	②
11	③	12	④	13	④	14	①	15	④
16	④	17	④	18	②	19	④	20	①
21	①	22	①	23	⑤	24	②	25	③

12강 대명사

Practice

01	④	02	③	03	④	04	③	05	③
06	④	07	②	08	③	09	②	10	③
11	③	12	①	13	③	14	①	15	④
16	②	17	③	18	⑤	19	①	20	②
21	③	22	④	23	③	24	①	25	③

13강 형용사

Practice

01	②	02	③	03	④	04	①	05	③
06	②	07	④	08	①	09	①	10	④
11	④	12	②	13	①	14	①	15	①
16	②	17	④	18	④	19	③	20	③
21	②	22	④	23	④	24	④	25	④

Practice 02

01	③	02	④	03	④	04	③	05	②
06	④	07	③	08	③	09	①	10	⑤
11	③	12	④	13	③	14	①	15	②
16	②	17	①	18	②	19	①	20	③
21	①	22	②	23	②	24	⑤	25	③

14강 부사

Practice

01	②	02	③	03	④	04	④	05	④
06	④	07	①	08	④	09	①	10	③
11	②	12	②	13	④	14	①	15	④
16	①	17	①	18	①	19	②	20	④
21	④	22	③	23	②	24	④	25	⑤

15강 비교

Practice

01	③	02	①	03	③	04	②	05	①
06	②	07	④	08	③	09	④	10	③
11	④	12	①	13	②	14	④	15	④
16	②	17	②	18	④	19	②	20	④
21	②	22	②	23	②	24	④	25	①

16강 일치와 도치

Practice 01

01	④	02	④	03	②	04	③	05	①
06	②	07	④	08	⑤	09	③	10	④
11	②	12	④	13	②	14	①	15	①
16	④	17	③	18	④	19	⑤	20	④
21	①	22	①	23	③	24	③	25	④

Practice 02

01	③	02	③	03	①	04	②	05	④
06	⑤	07	②	08	②	09	②	10	②
11	②	12	③	13	②	14	④	15	②
16	③	17	①	18	①	19	④	20	③
21	②	22	②	23	④	24	④	25	④

17강 문의구성

Practice

01	②	02	②	03	④	04	①	05	③
06	①	07	①	08	②	09	③	10	②
11	①	12	②	13	②	14	④	15	④
16	④	17	②	18	④	19	④	20	④
21	④	22	③	23	⑤	24	①	25	②

에듀윌 편입 솔루션 문법 Basic

발 행 일	2023년 7월 12일 초판
편 저 자	에듀윌 편입 LAB
펴 낸 이	김재환
펴 낸 곳	(주)에듀윌
등록번호	제25100–2002–000052호
주 소	08378 서울특별시 구로구 디지털로34길 55
	코오롱싸이언스밸리 2차 3층

www.eduwill.net

대표전화 1600-6700

여러분의 작은 소리
에듀윌은 크게 듣겠습니다.

본 교재에 대한 여러분의 목소리를 들려주세요.
공부하시면서 어려웠던 점, 궁금한 점,
칭찬하고 싶은 점, 개선할 점, 어떤 것이라도 좋습니다.

에듀윌은 여러분께서 나누어 주신 의견을
통해 끊임없이 발전하고 있습니다.

에듀윌 도서몰 book.eduwill.net
• 부가학습자료 및 정오표: 에듀윌 도서몰 → 도서자료실
• 교재 문의: 에듀윌 도서몰 → 문의하기 → 교재(내용, 출간) / 주문 및 배송

문법
BASIC

eduwill
에듀윌은 합격이다!

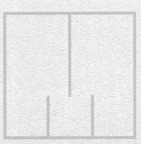

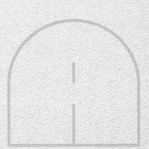

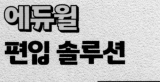

에듀윌
편입 솔루션

문법 BASIC 정답과 해설

펴낸곳 (주)에듀윌 **펴낸이** 김재환 **출판총괄** 오용철
개발책임 김진우, 김기임, 윤대권 **개발** 허은지 **디자인** 디자인본부
주소 서울시 구로구 디지털로34길 55 코오롱싸이언스밸리 2차 3층
대표번호 1600-6700 **등록번호** 제25100-2002-000052호
협의 없는 무단 복제는 법으로 금지되어 있습니다.

에듀윌 도서몰 book.eduwill.net
• 부가학습자료 및 정오표: 에듀윌 도서몰 → 도서자료실
• 교재 문의: 에듀윌 도서몰 → 문의하기 → 교재(내용, 출간) / 주문 및 배송

1위 에듀윌만의
체계적인 합격 커리큘럼

원하는 시간과 장소에서, 1:1 관리까지 한번에
온라인 강의

① 최대 500% 환급! 강력한 동기부여 시스템
② 서성한 100% 합격 1타 교수진 강의 무제한 수강
③ 합격 메이커 군단의 1:1 밀착 관리

노베이스도 9관왕 합격! 쌩기초 풀패키지 무료 신청

기존 편입학원에서는 찾아볼 수 없는 관리 스케일
직영 학원

① 소수정예 맞춤 관리
② 교수+담임선생님 더블 담임제 시행
③ 정규 수업 외 1:1 맞춤 상담
④ 개별 성적을 통한 학습 관리

당일 등록 회원
시크릿 추가 혜택

방문상담 당일 등록 시크릿 추가 혜택 제공

* 2023 대한민국 브랜드만족도 편입 교육 1위 (한경비즈니스)